Essential
Biological Psychology

SAGE has been part of the global academic community since 1965, supporting high quality research and learning that transforms society and our understanding of individuals, groups and cultures. SAGE is the independent, innovative, natural home for authors, editors and societies who share our commitment and passion for the social sciences.

Find out more at: **www.sagepublications.com**

Essential
Biological Psychology
Jim Barnes

Los Angeles | London | New Delhi
Singapore | Washington DC

Los Angeles | London | New Delhi
Singapore | Washington DC

SAGE Publications Ltd
1 Oliver's Yard
55 City Road
London EC1Y 1SP

SAGE Publications Inc.
2455 Teller Road
Thousand Oaks, California 91320

SAGE Publications India Pvt Ltd
B 1/I 1 Mohan Cooperative Industrial Area
Mathura Road
New Delhi 110 044

SAGE Publications Asia-Pacific Pte Ltd
3 Church Street
#10-04 Samsung Hub
Singapore 049483

Library of Congress Control Number: 2011937056

British Library Cataloguing in Publication data

A catalogue record for this book is available from
the British Library

Editor: Michael Carmichael
Editorial assistant: Alana Clogan
Production editor: Vanessa Harwood
Marketing manager: Alison Borg
Cover design: Jennifer Crisp
Typeset by: C&M Digitals (P) Ltd, Chennai, India
Printed in India at Replika Press Pvt Ltd

ISBN 978-1-84787-540-2
ISBN 978-1-84787-541-9 (pbk)

To Laura, Oscar and Zoe

SUMMARY OF CONTENTS

CONTENTS

ABOUT THE AUTHOR

Jim Barnes is a Reader in Psychology at Oxford Brookes University. He read Psychology and Neuroscience at the University of London and studied for his PhD in Neuropsychology at King's College London. He has publications across the full range of topics that comprise social cognition and neuroscience – from studies into face perception and dominance, to the role of the occipital lobe in the occurrence of visual hallucinations. His research has been funded by grants from the Medical Research Council and the British Academy, and his work with Parkinson's UK has contributed to the understanding of the visual disturbances associated with the disorder.

PREFACE

There are many incredible biological psychology textbooks out there, which explain all the intricacies of the subject and discuss the current developments of human brain science. So, you may ask, why should you buy this book? The simple answer is that most of the current textbooks are enormous and require you to plough through the chapters and examples to find the information you really need for your studies. These huge books are designed to be read when you want to study the subject matter in more detail and have more time to devote to the topic. In addition to this, the explosion of information about brain and behaviour has created a need for an easily digestible textbook of biological psychology. This essential guide will give you a general introduction to and overview of the structure and processes of the nervous system and their role in determining behaviour. It contains the necessary and essential information required for biological psychology as prescribed by the British Psychological Society and gives you accessible information in an enjoyable fashion so you can pass your biological psychology exams.

What you get with this book is short, easily digestible chapters, which take you on a journey around the nervous system. Each chapter gives you the information you need for your exams and is aimed at the undergraduate student who is new to the subject. All the essential information is provided about the nervous system as well as details of classic and recent studies in the field, along with interesting real-life applications to theory and research. I have tried to be informative without overloading you with all the information about a particular topic. To achieve this I have used the following key features:

⚙ Summaries at the end of every chapter will consolidate your learning.

⚙ The many illustrations correspond to key concepts introduced in the text.

⚙ Text boxes provide in-depth information on new and classic studies in biological psychology.

⚙ Essential key terms and definitions are provided throughout the text.

⚙ Suggested reading and memory maps are given for each chapter, which enable you to organise your knowledge ready for the exams.

A companion website is also available for students, which provides multiple choice test questions. Memory maps can also be downloaded from this website. There is also a password protected section for lecturers that includes PowerPoint slides for each chapter and a test bank of multiple choice questions for exam use.

I hope you become eager to learn the material covered in this textbook and you find it useful in your study of psychology. Finally, please remember that the biological approach to studying behaviour is not the only way to explain why humans behave the way they do, and although we know a lot about biology and action there is still a great deal we don't yet know. However, it is still the most stimulating and dynamic field in psychology, which still excites me every time I encounter it. I hope after reading this book you will want to explore the subject further and maybe one day help fill the gaps in our current knowledge. I wish you every success in your study of this fascinating subject.

COMPANION WEBSITE

Be sure to visit the companion website (www.sagepub.co.uk/barnes) to find additional teaching and learning material for both lecturers and students.

For lecturers:
- PowerPoint slides: Slides are provided for each chapter and can be edited as required for use in lectures and seminars.
- Multiple Choice Questions: Test students' knowledge with a downloadable MCQ Testbank organized by chapter.

For students:
- Multiple Choice Questions: Check your understanding of each chapter or test yourself before exams.

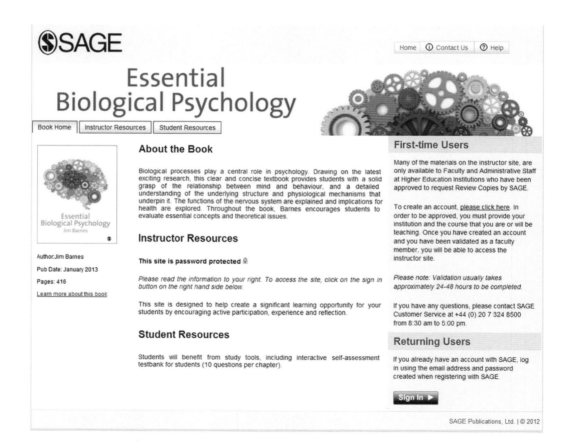

ACKNOWLEDGEMENTS

Chapter 1

Figure 1.2   http://chsweb.lr.k12.nj.us/mstanley/outlines/nervous/nervous.htm
Figure 1.3   Modified from the Wiley Online Library. http://onlinelibrary.wiley.com
Figure 1.8   The American Heritage® Science Dictionary Copyright © 2010 by Houghton Mifflin Harcourt Publishing Company.
Figure 1.9   http://www.wpclipart.com/medical/anatomy/glands/endocrine_system.jpg.html
Box 1.2, Figures 1 and 2 Martinez, D., Orlowska, D., Narendran, R., Slifstein, M., Liu, F., Kumar, D., et al. (2010). Dopamine type 2/3 receptor availability in the striatum and social status in human volunteers. *Biological Psychiatry*, 67(3), 275–278.

Chapter 2

Figure 2.1   http://www.clker.com/clipart-anatomical-directions-of-brain.html
Figure 2.2   http://en.wikipedia.org/wiki/File:Gray726-Brodman.png
Figure 2.3   http://faculty.washington.edu/chudler/slice.html
Figure 2.4   from *Biological Psychology* by Klein and Thorne. Copyright © 2007 by Worth Publishers. Used with permission.
Figure 2.5   Adapted from http://www.bnog.org.uk/Glioma_Astrocytoma.aspx
Figure 2.6   © 2012 Wolters Kluwer Health|Lippincott Williams & Wilkins.
Figure 2.7   Based on Dr Jennifer Tobin's illustration for the Accelerated Cure Project at http://www.acceleratedcure.org/msresources/neuroanatomy/
Figure 2.8   http://en.wikipedia.org/wiki/File:Brain_human_normal_inferior_view_with_labels_en-2.svg Based on drawing by Patrick J. Lynch, medical illustrator.
Figure 2.9   John W Kimball, Kimball's Biology Pages http://users.rcn.com/jkimball.ma.ultranet/BiologyPages/P/PNS.html
Figure 2.11   O'Neill, Michael J. and Clemens, James A. Rodent models of focal cerebral ischemia, *Current Protocols in Neuroscience*, John Wiley and Sons
Figure 2.12   http://en.wikipedia.org/wiki/File:Schematic_illustration_of_a_microdialysis_probe.png

Chapter 3

Figure 3.2   http://en.wikipedia.org/wiki/File:DNA_replication_en.svg
Figure 3.3   http://www.biology.iupui.edu/biocourses/N100/2k4ch8mitosisnotes.html
Figure 3.4   http://en.wikipedia.org/wiki/Meiosis
Figure 3.5   http://www.biology.iupui.edu/biocourses/N100/2k4ch9meiosisnotes.html
Figure 3.6   http://www.biology.iupui.edu/biocourses/N100/2k4ch9meiosisnotes.html
Figure 3.7   http://en.wikipedia.org/wiki/File:Simple_transcription_initiation1.svg

Figure 3.8	http://en.wikipedia.org/wiki/File:Simple_transcription_elongation1.svg
Figure 3.9	http://en.wikipedia.org/wiki/File:Simple_transcription_termination1.svg
Figure 3.11	http://biobook.nerinxhs.org/srbio/outlines/srbio_ol_genes_and_chromosomes.htm
Figure 3.12	from Peter Sandiford (1913) *The Mental and Physical Life of School Children*, Longmans, Green and Company.

Chapter 4

Figure 4.2	National Institute of Health (NIH), 9000 Rockville Pike, Bethseda, Maryland 20892
Figure 4.4	http://en.wikipedia.org/wiki/File:Embryonic_spinal_cord.jpg
Figure 4.5	from Breedlove, Rosenzweig and Watson, *Biological Psychology: An Introduction to Behavioral, Cognitive, and Clinical Neuroscience*, fifth edition. Sinauer Associates.
Figure 4.6	from Breedlove, Rosenzweig and Watson. Sinauer Associates.

Box 4.2, Figure 1 from Sadato, N., Okada, T., Honda, M., & Yonekura, Y. (2002). Critical period for cross-modal plasticity in blind humans: a functional MRI study. *Neuroimage, 16,* 389–400. Elsevier.

Chapter 5

Figure 5.1	National Eye Institute, National Institutes of Health http://www.nei.nih.gov/health/eyediagram/index.asp

Box 5.1, Figure 1 from Kanwisher, N., McDermott, J., & Chun, M.M. (1997). The fusiform face area: a module in human extrastriate. *The Journal of Neuroscience*, June 1, 17(11):4302– 4311.

Figure 5.2	Netter illustration from www.netterimages.com. © Elsevier Inc. All rights reserved.
Figure 5.4	http://en.wikipedia.org/wiki/File:Receptive_field.png
Figure 5.5	from Michael S. Gazzaniga, Richard B. Ivry, & George R. Mangun, Cognitive *Neuroscience: The Biology of the Mind*, second edition. Copyright © 2002 by W.W. Norton & Company, Inc. Used by permission of W. W. Norton & Company Inc.

Box 5.1, Figure 1 from Kanwisher, N., McDermott, J., & Chun, M.M. (1997). The fusiform face area: a module in human extrastriate. *The Journal of Neuroscience*, June 1, 17(11):4302– 4311.

Box 5.2, Figure 1 from Goldstein, E. B. (1996) *Sensation and Perception*. New York: Brooks/Cole. Page 66, fig. 2.33.

Box 5.2, Figure 2 from Blake, R. and Sekuler, R. *Perception.* MacGraw Hill. Figure 4.8.

Figure 5.6	http://dericbownds.net/bom99/Ch08/Ch08.html
Figure 5.7	based on Dicklyon's PNG version, itself based on data from Stockman, MacLeod & Johnson (1993) *Journal of the Optical Society of America A, 10,* 2491-2521d.
Figure 5.8	http://www.msapper17.blogspot.co.uk/

Chapter 6

Figure 6.2	http://www.proprofs.com/flashcards/upload/a888326.gif
Figure 6.3	from A. B. Vallbo & R. S. Johansson (1984), Properties of cutaneous mecha-noreceptors in the human hand related to touch sensation, *Human*

Neurobiology, 3: 3–14. With kind permission from Springer Science+Business Media B.V.

Figure 6.5	from The Encyclopedia of Science, David Darling, http://www.daviddarling.info/encyclopedia/S/spinal_cord.html
Figure 6.6	Ralf Stefan http://www.ark.in-berlin.de
Figures 6.8, 6.9, 6.11	from Pinel, John P.J., *Biopsychology*, eighth edition © 2011. Reprinted by permission of Pearson Education,Inc., Upper Saddle River, NJ.
Figure 6.10	http://www.frca.co.uk/article.aspx?articleid=100119
Figure 6.13	Image courtesy of http://www.nasa.gov
Figure 6.14	The Encyclopedia of Science, David Darling http://www.daviddarling.info/encyclopedia/S/spinal_cord.html
Figure 6.15	from Brownell, W. E. (1997). How the Ear Works: Nature's Solutions for Listening. *Volta Rev* 99:9-28.
Figure 6.16	http://firstyears.org/anatomy/ear.htm
Figure 6.17	Adapted from Daniel Williamson: Processing Sounds http://cnx.org/content/m22651/1.3/
Figure 6.18	http://michaeldmann.net/mann9.html
Figure 6.20	http://upload.wikimedia.org/wikipedia/commons/0/0e/Taste_bud.svg
Figure 6.21	http://library.thinkquest.org/3750/taste/taste.html
Figure 6.22	http://antranik.org/chemical-sense-taste-gustation/
Figure 6.23	from *Biological Psychology* by Klein and Thorne. Copyright © 2007, Worth Publishers. Used with permission.

Chapter 7

Figure 7.3	http://www.bioedonline.org/slides/slide01.cfm?q=muscle+type&st=
Figure 7.4	Reprinted and redrawn with permission from Encyclopædia Britannica © 2006. By Encyclopædia Britannica, Inc.
Figure 7.6	Based on Dr Jennifer Tobin's illustration for the Accelerated Cure Project at http://www.acceleratedcure.org/msresources/neuroanatomy/
Figure 7.7	Image courtesy of http://anatomycorner.com/
Figure 7.8	from Purves, D., Augustine, G.J., Fitzpatrick, D., et al., (eds.) (2001) *Neuroscience*, second edition. Sunderland, MA: Sinauer Associates.
Figure 7.9	from Purves, D., Augustine, G.J., Fitzpatrick, D., et al., (eds.) (2001) *Neuroscience*, second edition. Sunderland, MA: Sinauer Associates.
Figure 7.10	from Marieb, Elaine N., Human Anatomy and Physiology, sixth edition © 2004. Adapted by permission of Pearson Education, Inc., Upper Saddle River, NJ.
Figure 7.11	Pinel, John P.J., *Biopsychology*, eighth edition © 2011. Reprinted by permission of Pearson Education,Inc., Upper Saddle River, NJ.
Figure 7.14	http://www.ipernity.com/doc/sculpix/4213963
Figure 7.12	Pinel, John P.J., *Biopsychology*, eighth edition © 2011. Reprinted by permission of Pearson Education,Inc., Upper Saddle River, NJ.
Figure 7.17	from Purves, D., Augustine, G.J., Fitzpatrick, D., et al., (eds.) (2001) *Neuroscience*, second edition. Sunderland, MA: Sinauer Associates.
Figuer 7.14	Carlson *Physiology of Behaviour*. Allyn & Bacon.
Figure 7.16	from Klein and Thorne *Biological Psychology* by. Copyright © 2007 by Worth Publishers. Used with permission.
Figure 7.17	from Klein (2000). *Biological Psychology*. Prentice-Hall.

Chapter 9

Figure 9.1   National Institute of General Medical Sciences http://www.nigms.nih.gov/ Education/Factsheet_CircadianRhythms.htm

Figrue 9.4   from Pinel, John P.J., *Biopsychology*, eighth edition © 2011. Reprinted by permission of Pearson Education,Inc., Upper Saddle River, NJ.

Chapter 11

Figure 11.8   http://www.futurity.org/health-medicine/hippocampus-minds-the-memory-gap/

Box 11.2, Figure 1   http://www.ratbehavior.org/RatsAndMazes.htm

Box 11.2, Figure 2   http://www.ratbehavior.org/RatsAndMazes.htm

Box 11.2, Figure 3   http://www.ratbehavior.org/RatsAndMazes.htm

Box 11.2, Figure 4   http://www.ratbehavior.org/RatsAndMazes.htm

Box 11.2, Figure 5   http://www.ratbehavior.org/RatsAndMazes.htm

Box 11.2, Figure 6   http://www.ratbehavior.org/RatsAndMazes.htm

Figure 11.9   from Purves, D., Augustine, G.J., Fitzpatrick, D., et al., (eds.) (2008) *Neuroscience*, fourth edition. Sunderland, MA: Sinauer Associates.

Figure 11.10   from Purves, D., Augustine, G.J., Fitzpatrick, D., et al., (eds.) (2008) *Neuroscience*, fourth edition. Sunderland, MA: Sinauer Associates.

Chapter 12

Figure 12.2   from Purves, D., Augustine, G.J., Fitzpatrick, D., et al., (eds.) (2008) *Neuroscience*, fourth edition. Sunderland, MA: Sinauer Associates.

Figure 12.5   http://www.nidcd.nih.gov/health/voice/pages/aphasia.aspx

Figure 12.6   http://en.wikipedia.org/wiki/File:Wernickeges2.gif

1

NEURONS, NEUROTRANSMISSION AND COMMUNICATION

The purpose of biological psychology is to elucidate the biological mechanisms involved in behaviour and mental activity. Biological psychologists (sometimes referred to as neuropsychologists) attempt to understand how the neural circuits and connections are formed and put together during the development of the brain, allowing the individual to perceive and interact with the world around them. We cannot answer all of the questions that we would like to, nor do we believe that we have access to the best possible tools for studying the brain, but the questions do stir up curiosity and a better understanding of the biological processes that play a role in behaviour. It can be hard to remember the complicated names of **nerve cells** and brain areas. However, to develop theories of behaviour regarding the brain, a psychologist must know something about brain structure. This chapter will focus on the **nervous system**: its organisation, its cell composition, and the type of chemical signals that make it possible for us to process an incredible amount of information on a daily basis.

HOW THE NERVOUS SYSTEM IS ORGANISED

In **vertebrates,** the nervous system has two divisions: the peripheral nervous system and the central nervous system (Figure 1.1). The central nervous system (CNS), which consists of the brain and spinal cord, is surrounded by another nervous system called the peripheral nervous system (PNS). The PNS gathers information from our surroundings and environment and relays it to the CNS; it then acts on the signals or decisions that the CNS

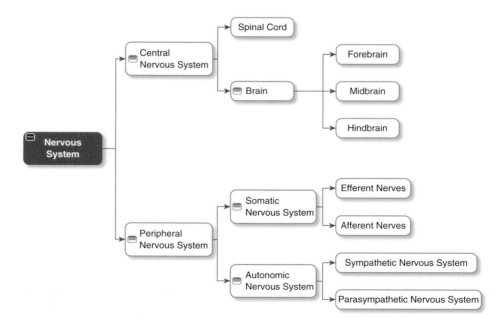

Figure 1.1   *Components of the nervous system*

returns. The peripheral nervous system itself consists of two parts: the somatic nervous system and the **autonomic nervous system**. The autonomic nervous system is divided into two subsystems: the **parasympathetic nervous system** and the **sympathetic nervous system**. The parasympathetic system is responsible for slowing the heart rate, increasing the intestinal and gland activity and undertaking actions when the body is at rest. Its action can be described as opposite to the sympathetic nervous system, which is responsible for controlling actions associated with the fight-or-flight response. The somatic system contains the sensory **receptors** and motor **nerves** which activate the skeletal muscles, and it is concerned with detecting and responding to environmental stimuli.

CELLS OF THE NERVOUS SYSTEM

THE NEURON

Neurons are the basic information processing structures in the CNS. They are electrically **excitable** cells that process and transmit information around the nervous system. Neurons transmit information either by electrical or by chemical signalling, which as you will see later occurs via **synapses**. Neurons are the core apparatus of the nervous system, and a number of specialised types exist. Neurons are very much like other body cells, possessing common features like the following:

- Neurons are encased in a cell membrane (also known as a plasma membrane).
- The nucleus of a neuron contains **chromosomes** and genetic information.
- Neurons consist of cytoplasm (fluid found within the cell), mitochondria and other organelles.
- Basic cellular processes occur in a neuron. **Ribosomes** are where **proteins** are produced, and mitochondria are responsible for metabolic activities that energise the cell.
- Neurons contain a Golgi complex – a network of vesicles that get **hormones** and other products ready to be secreted.

However, neurons or nerve cells are different from other body cells in that:

- Extensions emanate from the central body of the neuron. We refer to these as **dendrites** and **axons**. Dendrites carry information to the cell body while axons transmit information away from the cell body.
- Neurons transmit and receive information via an electrochemical mechanism.
- Neurons have some distinct and specialised structures like the synapse (the junction between one neuron and the next).
- Neurons synthesise chemicals that serve as neurotransmitters and neuromodulators.

Neuron structure

A typical neuron possesses a cell body (the **soma**), dendrites and an axon. Dendrites are filaments that emanate from the cell body, branch numerous times and give rise to a complex *dendritic tree* (Figure 1.2). An axon is like the wire in an electrical cable. It starts at the cell body at a site called the **axon hillock** and travels to the site in the nervous system where it connects with another nerve cell or different type of cell, such as muscle. The cell body of a neuron frequently gives rise to multiple dendrites, but never to more than one

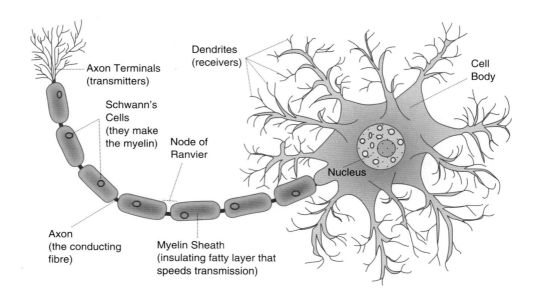

Figure 1.2   *Neuron structure*

Table 1.1   *Differences between axons and dendrites*

Axons	Dendrites
Take information away from the cell body	Bring information to the cell body
Large axons have a distinct swelling called the axon hillock	No hillock
Usually have few or no ribosomes	Usually have ribosomes
Smooth surface	May have rough surface: spiny as in pyramidal cells or non-spiny as in interneurons
Often covered with myelin	Seldom covered with myelin
Generally only one axon or none per cell	Usually many dendrites per cell, each with many branches
May be any length: 1 metre or longer	Usually shorter than axons
Branch further from the cell body	Branch near the cell body

axon. A layer of fatty cells called the myelin sheath segmentally encases the fibres of many neurons that greatly increase the transmission speed of neutral impulses. Table 1.1 summarises the differences between axons and dendrites.

Inside the neuron

The inside of a neuron is much like the other cells of the body in many ways, as a neuron has many of the same organelles, including a nucleus and mitochondria. Figure 1.3 shows the following components of a typical animal cell:

- *Nucleus*: contains genetic material within the chromosomes comprising information for development and maintenance of the cells as well as the production of proteins. The nucleus is covered by a membrane.

- *Nucleolus*: produces ribosomes, which are essential for translating genetic information into proteins.

- *Lysosomes*: contain enzymes that reduce chemicals to their individual components.

- *Centrosome*: this microtubule regulates the cells and the cell cycle.

- *Cytoplasm*: this is a partially transparent, gelatinous substance that fills the cell.

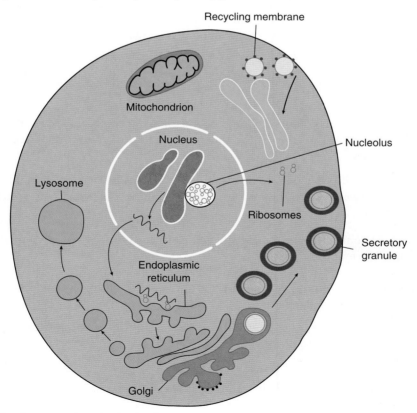

Figure 1.3   *Cross-section of animal cell*

⊛   *Vacuole*: these are compartments bound by membranes that carry out various functions including storage and secretion of neurotransmitters.

⊛   *Endoplasmic reticulum* (ER): a network of tubes that are used to move materials around the cytoplasm. Endoplasmic reticula which are made from ribosomes are called rough ER, whereas those which have no ribosomes are called smooth ER. ER including ribosomes are vital for protein synthesis.

⊛   *Golgi body or Golgi apparatus*: a membrane-bound structure that is critical to the process of encasing peptides and proteins into vesicles.

⊛   *Microfilaments or neurotubules*: the system that moves materials within a neuron. These elements can also be used for structural help.

Neuron classification

The study of the microscopic anatomy of cells and tissues is termed histology (see Box 1.1). As with many things in the nervous system, neurons may be classified in a variety of ways, according to their function (sensor, motor, interneuron), their location (cortical, subcortical), the identity of the neurotransmitter they synthesise and release (**cholinergic**, glutamatergic) and their shape (pyramidal, granule, etc.). One easy way to categorise them is by how their axons and dendrite leave their cell body or soma. This gives three main types of neurons:

⊛   *Bipolar*: similar to retinal cells, two processes extend from the body of bipolar neurons.

⊛   *Unipolar*: there are two **dorsal** root ganglion axons for each unipolar cell. One axon stretches out in the direction of the spinal cord and the other in the direction of the skin or muscles.

⊛   *Multipolar*: multipolar neurons contain many processes that branch out from the cell body. However, here the neurons each only have one axon (e.g. spinal motor neurons).

Another very basic method for the classification of neurons is by identifying which way they transmit information:

⊛   *Efferent neurons (motor neurons)*: these direct information away from the brain towards muscles and glands.

⊛   *Afferent neurons (sensory neurons)*: these transmit information to the central nervous system from sensory receptors.

⊛   *Interneurons*: found in the central nervous system, these pass information between motor neurons and sensory neurons.

BOX 1.1   Examination of brain tissue: histology

Histology is in fact the microscopic study of tissue, not just brain tissue. In the field of biological psychology the mapping and visualisation of the cellular composition of the brain or its cytoarchitecture are an important complement to the studies of function and gross anatomy. Histology generally refers to the techniques used to prepare tissue for microscopic study. This includes staining brain tissue for light and electron microscopy and also advanced techniques for tracing fibre tracts or classifying receptor types present in a given brain region. There is a wide variety of staining techniques. In neuroscience, perhaps the most familiar is Golgi staining; this method was discovered by Italian physician and scientist Camillo Golgi (1843–1926) in 1873. It stains only a few cell bodies in their entirety, and in so doing allows a detailed visualisation of individual neurons. Other techniques available include myelin stains for visualising fibre bundles and several techniques for cell body staining. Nissl staining is a method which stains the cell body and in particular the endoplasmic reticulum. The Nissl substance, which consists of the rough or granular endoplasmic reticulum, appears dark blue when a dye such as cresyl violet is used.

NEUROGLIAL CELLS

The glial cells are simply the so-called glue (as the name implies) by which the nervous system is held together. Neuroglial cells are the other major cell type in neural tissue; they provide structural integrity and nutrition to the nervous system and maintain **homoeo stasis** (Finch, 2002). While some glial cells physically support other cells, others control the internal environment surrounding neurons or nerve cells and provide them with nutrients. Glial cells are also involved in cortical development, the guidance of neurons and the growth of axons and dendrites, and are crucial in the development of the nervous system (Hidalgo, 2003; Howard, Zhicheng, Filipovic, Moore, Antic, & Zecevic, 2008). Because glial cells do not form synapses it was thought that they were merely the housekeepers of the nervous system, required for the maintenance of neurons but not involved in processing information. However, in recent years there have been some changes to this assumption with the discovery that one type of glial cell, the oligodendrocyte precursor cell, is involved in synaptic signalling in the hippocampus (Lin & Bergles, 2004).

Types of glial cell

A number of different types of glial cell exist. Some can be found in the central nervous system and others are essential to the functioning of the peripheral nervous system.

Astrocytes (CNS)

Astrocytes are responsible for maintaining the external chemical environment around nerve cells (Malhotra, Shnitka, & Elbrink, 1990). They do so by disposing of surplus **ions**, particularly potassium and chloride, and reprocessing and recycling neurotransmitters that were released during synaptic transmission. An additional feature of astrocytes is the formation of end feet; these are small swellings that surround and support the endothelial cells of the blood–brain barrier (BBB). This is a membranic structure of capillary endothelial cells which protects the brain from any harmful substances circulating in the blood while still allowing metabolic function to occur normally (Holash, Noden, & Stewart, 1993).

The brain contains two different kinds of astrocytes: protoplasmic astrocytes and fibrous astrocytes (Miller & Raff, 1984). The grey matter contains the protoplasmic astrocytes, while the white matter of the spinal cord and brain contains fibrous astrocytes. Astrocytes are typically small cells and, even though these cells are the most prevalent glial cells, numbers are found in different areas of the brain.

Oligodendrocytes (CNS)

Oligodendrocytes surround axons in the CNS forming a myelin sheath that insulates the axon and makes it possible for electrical signals to be generated and propagated more effectively (Yamazaki, Hozumi, Kaneko, Fujii, Goto, & Kato, 2010). One oligodendrocyte is capable of coating as many as 50 axons. Myelin, which is white in colour, increases the speed at which **action potentials** are sent along an axon. The sheaths of myelin that cover the axon have gaps between them, referred to as the *nodes of Ranvier*. It is at these gaps that ions can cross the membrane and an action potential occurs. Thus the action potential jumps from one node to the next, enabling action potential to travel along **myelinated** axons quicker than along their **unmyelinated** counterparts. Cognition and behaviour are affected by myelin loss within the CNS, as in the demyelinating disorder of multiple sclerosis (Zeis & Schaeren-Wiemers, 2008).

Schwann cells (PNS)

The cell in the PNS that is functionally equivalent to the oligodendrocytes in the CNS, the Schwann cell, only insulates one discrete axon. Schwann cells are specialised types of glial cell that provide myelin insulation to axons in the peripheral nervous system (Bruska & Wozniak, 1999). Non-myelinating Schwann cells have a role to play in maintaining axons and have a critical role for neuronal survival.

Microglia (CNS)

Microglia are glial cells that serve the CNS immune system and are also specialised **macrophages**. Microglia are important protectors of the central nervous system, and guard and support the neurons of the CNS. Using a process called **phagocytosis**, they actively cleanse the waste from the nervous system. Microglial cells are not derived from ectodermal tissue like other glial cells but instead derive embryologically from haematopoietic precursors, which are multipotent stem cells producing all types of blood cell. Microglia are found in all parts of the brain and spinal cord and they comprise approximately 15–17% of all the cells of the CNS. Microglia continually sample their surroundings and multiply in response to brain injury. Microglia are thought to be a factor in neurodegenerative disorders like multiple sclerosis, motor neurone disease and Alzheimer's disease. These cells are also responsible for creating the inflammatory response to brain trauma (Dheen, Kaur, & Ling, 2007) and they are the main target cells for the HIV-1 virus in the central nervous system (Erfle et al., 1991).

Radial glial cells (CNS)

Radial glial cells (RGCs) are a temporary cell population present only in the developing central nervous system. They function both as precursor cells and as a scaffolding framework to support neuron migration.

Glial cells and injury

As already suggested, the glial cells react to both central and peripheral nervous system damage, supporting neurons. The debris from injuries in the CNS, like a stroke, is engulfed by astrocytes and digested in the process of phagocytosis. Scar tissue is also formed as astrocytes fill the gaps that occur because of tissue death. Oligodendrocytes in the central nervous system provide support for the axons and create myelin. Schwann cells accomplish the same functions in the PNS.

Gliosis

While neurons cannot undergo cell division in adulthood, glial cells keep that capability. It seems that the mature nervous system cannot replace neurons that have been damaged as a result of a lesion or an injury. However, there is intense proliferation of glial cells, called gliosis, which congregate close to or at the site of the damage. Recently, studies have shown that the 'mature' glia, such as astrocytes, do not maintain the capacity for **mitosis**. It is believed that only oligodendrocyte precursor cells keep this capacity to multiply after the nervous system matures. There is some recent evidence that production of new neurons can occur in a few parts of the mature nervous system such as the subventricular zone and the dentate gyrus of the hippocampus (Seri, García-Verdugo, McEwen, & Alvarez-Buylla, 2001).

INFORMATION EXCHANGE IN THE NERVOUS SYSTEM

Neurons constantly relay information between each other, and also between themselves and their environment. Information is transmitted from cell to cell using the following forms:

- axon to dendrite – axodendritic exchange
- axon to cell body – axosomatic exchange
- axon to axon – axoaxonic exchange
- dendrite to dendrite – dendrodendritic exchange.

The cell membrane is sometimes at rest and not receiving information from other neurons; in this state, it is said to be at the **resting membrane potential**.

THE RESTING MEMBRANE POTENTIAL

The resting potential (or resting voltage) of the cell is the membrane potential that is maintained if there are no action potentials or synaptic potentials present. The intracellular fluid of a neuron at rest is more negatively charged than the extracellular fluid, and this polarity difference is termed the resting potential. The resting membrane potential of a neuron is about −70 millivolts (mV); this means that the inside of the neuron is 70 mV less than the outside. The disparity between voltages across the cell membrane is due to the fact that there is a higher concentration of positive ions outside the cell than inside the cell. There is approximately 10 times more sodium (Na$^+$) on the outside of the cell and approximately 20 times more potassium (K$^+$) on the inside. This is frequently called the cell's concentration gradient.

The properties of the membrane and the **sodium/potassium pump** are each partially responsible for the distribution of electrically charged ions. As the membrane is semi-permeable, molecules like water, oxygen, urea and carbon dioxide can cross the cell membrane whereas larger or electrically charged ions and molecules generally cannot. Certain ions, like potassium (K$^+$), chloride (Cl$^-$) and sodium (Na$^+$), pass through the membrane at gates formed by **channel** proteins which are located in the membrane and regulate how fast the ions can enter. Though drawn to the negative interior of the nerve cell, the Na$^+$ gates stay shut until the membrane is depolarised. As a result, there is an increased concentration of Na$^+$ ions outside the membrane. The greater concentration of K$^+$ ions on the inside of the membrane can cross the membrane at a regulated rate by passively diffusing out of the cell because they are drawn to a region of lesser concentration; they remain, however, held by the negative interior of the cell. K$^+$ ions are returned to the inside of the membrane via the sodium/potassium pump which uses an active transport system, with energy supplied by adenosine triphosphate (ATP) molecules. Other ions that have a negative charge, such as chloride, also cross the membrane at a controlled rate; these help in maintaining the negative interior. As a result the resting potential is sustained by Na$^+$ being held out of the cell, while K$^+$ diffuses out, only to be brought back into the cell. Three Na$^+$ ions are actively removed from the cell by the sodium/potassium pump for every two K$^+$ ions that are allowed to enter.

THE ACTION POTENTIAL AND NERVE IMPULSE

The membrane resting potential is present when a neuron is at rest. However, when our nervous system transmits information, an action potential or a nerve impulse occurs. An action potential is a short-term event in which the electrical **membrane potential** of a cell rapidly increases and falls. Positive ions flowing into the cell will reduce the negative charge and thus reduce the charge across the entire membrane; we refer to this as **depolarisation**. When depolarisation gets to around −55 mV (the tipping point) a neuron will give off an action potential. No action potential will fire if the neuron does not reach the **threshold** level. Once the threshold value is reached, an action potential of a fixed size will always fire; and for any given neuron, the size of the action potential is always the same. Often this is referred to as the **all-or-nothing principle**.

The exchange of ions across the neuron membrane causes nerve impulses or action potentials to take place. A stimulus, for example at the touch receptors, first causes Na^+ channels to open, and because there are many more Na^+ ions on the outside, and the inside of the neuron is negative relative to the outside, Na^+ enters the neuron. Thus, the neuron becomes both more positive and depolarised. Then K^+ channels open (they take a bit more time than Na^+ channels) and K^+ rushes out of the cell, reversing the depolarisation. When Na^+ enters, the membrane potential increases, and when K^+ exits, it drops sharply back down, giving rise to the alternative name for this potential: the spike potential. Na^+ channels then start to go back to their normal closed state, which causes the action potential to revert towards −70 mV (a **repolarisation**). However, the membrane potential actually moves past −70 mV to nearly −80 mV (a **hyperpolarisation**) due to the K^+ channels remaining open just a bit too long. Ion concentrations will steadily return to the resting membrane, and the cell will return to −70 mV.

For a short period in the middle of the action potential, the neuron is totally resistant to additional stimulation. This is known as the **absolute refractory period,** where the neuron cannot make another action potential. The absolute refractory period precedes another brief period, known as the **relative refractory period,** during which the neuron can generate another action potential but the stimulus must be of greater intensity than normal (Figure 1.4).

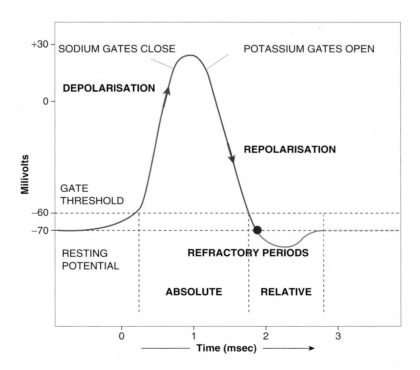

Figure 1.4   *The action potential*

One anatomical part of a neuron that connects the cell body to the axon is termed the axon hillock, and it is here that **inhibitory postsynaptic potentials** (IPSPs) and **excitatory postsynaptic potentials** (EPSPs) from various synaptic inputs on the dendrites or cell body accumulate. From the axon hillock an action potential moves along the axon in the form of a nerve impulse. The acceleration of transmission is different in all axons and is separate from stimulus intensity. Actually, the propagation speed is dependent on three things: the measurement of the axon's diameter, whether or not the axon is coated in myelin, and how many synapses there are. If everything else is the same, action potentials are quicker in axons that are larger in diameter, usually travelling at a speed ranging between 10 and 100 m/s. Myelinated axons send information faster than unmyelinated axons, and the number of synapses *en route* will also affect propagation rates: the more synapses, the slower the propagation rate. When an action potential happens, sodium ions travel along the inside of the cell membrane, depolarising the segment of the membrane that lies just ahead. The thicker the axon is, the faster the sodium ions move along the membrane, similar to the way in which water flows faster through a large bore pipe.

Earlier, we discussed how several axons in the nervous system have a myelin coating, which was formed by a specific type of glial cell. The myelinated segments together are better known as the myelin sheath, and the segments are divided by small spaces known as the nodes of Ranvier. These node gaps are the only locations where the cell membrane has any exposure to the extracellular fluid. In addition they also contain **ion channels** where ions can move into and out of the cell and respond to the depolarising stimulus, causing the action potential to jump from node to node. This process of the action potential appearing to jump along the length of an axon while at the same time speeding up the propagation of a nerve impulse is referred to as **saltatory conduction**. Myelinated axons transfer information at a much higher speed, 100 m/s, than unmyelinated axons which normally have an action potential of 1 m/s. Thus the process of saltatory conduction mitigates the necessity of an increase in axon diameters and enables a reduction in the size of the nervous system in organisms.

SUMMATION EFFECTS

Neurons receive multiple excitatory and inhibitory inputs on a continual basis. The determination of whether the axon will fire or not is based on the total effect of all excitations and inhibitions that take place. So, at what point is an action potential produced? The EPSPs and IPSPs received by the dendrites and cell bodies of the neurons are graded potentials. As discussed above, each EPSP results in a depolarisation and each IPSP results in a hyperpolarisation of the postsynaptic membrane. These various EPSP values at different times are added together and produce a combined level of depolarisation, while the IPSPs combine in the same manner to produce a combined level of hyperpolarisation. The method of introducing both positive and negative influences on the cell membrane is called summation. **Spatial summation** occurs when excitatory potentials from lots of different presynaptic neurons cause the postsynaptic neuron to reach its threshold and fire. **Temporal summation** occurs when a single presynaptic neuron fires many times in succession, causing the postsynaptic neuron to reach its threshold and fire.

SYNAPTIC TRANSMISSION

The discovery that neurons do not physically merge began in the late 1900s when Ramón y Cajal observed a narrow gap separating one neuron from the next. In 1906, Sir Charles Scott Sherrington identified the **synaptic delay** (typically 0.3 to 0.5 ms) and concluded that a certain form of communication occurs at these gaps between nerve cells. He called this point of communication a synapse. Today, these junctions through which the neuronal cells signal to each other and to non-neuronal cells like those found in muscles or glands are still known as synapses. Synapses make it possible for nerve cells in the central nervous system to create interconnected neural circuits or networks. The synapse comprises a synaptic terminal, a nerve cell that transmits information (or the presynaptic ending), a nerve cell that receives the information (the postsynaptic ending), and the gap between them, which is known as the **synaptic cleft** (Figure 1.5).

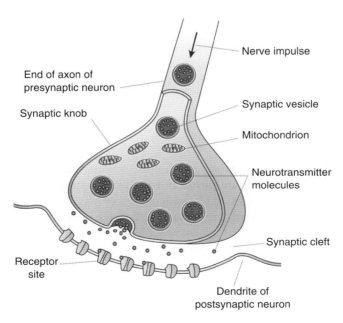

Figure 1.5   *The synapse*

Communications across the synapse are facilitated by neurotransmitters – chemicals that are synthesised by neurons and utilised to engage in communications with other cells. The presynaptic ending or synaptic terminal, also known as the **synaptic knob,** bouton or button, holds cell organelles like mitochondria and neurotransmitters. The neuron sending the impulse triggers the migration of vesicles which contain the neurotransmitter to the membrane of the synaptic terminal. The vesicle membrane then fuses with the presynaptic membrane, and neurotransmitter is released into the synaptic cleft (a gap of width approximately 20 nm); it then binds to receptors of the connecting cell and these excite or inhibit electrical impulses. The region of the synapse that releases neurotransmitters is called the active zone. Here, cell adhesion molecules keep the membranes of the pair of neighbouring cells close to one another. The postsynaptic cell may be a muscle cell or a gland, not just another neuron.

One of the most important features of the synapses is that they are the site of action for the majority of psychoactive drugs. Psychotropic medications and neurotoxins can alter neurotransmitter release and reuptake, and the accessibility of receptor binding sites. For example, lysergic acid diethylamide (LSD) interferes with serotoninergic synapses, while cocaine blocks reuptake of dopamine and therefore increases its effects. The poison strychnine blocks the inhibitory effects of the neurotransmitter glycine which results in uncontrollable muscle spasms and convulsions.

The synapses discussed so far communicate with other cells via chemical signalling molecules or neurotransmitters, and this is why they are sometimes termed 'chemical synapses'. Electrical and immunological synapses also exist inside the nervous system; however, unless otherwise designated, the word 'synapse' generally refers to a chemical synapse. **Electrical synapses** or gap junctions make it possible for ions to flow directly through protein channels from one nerve cell to another, allowing the fast transmission of information. Because of the rate of transmission, electrical synapses are mainly involved in behaviours and neural processes that require quick responses such as escape mechanisms (Bennett & Zukin, 2004).

THE SYNAPTIC VESICLE

When an action potential arrives at the presynaptic terminal, calcium channels open and Ca^+ ions enter the cell. This calcium influx causes the movement and fusion of secretory vesicles to the cell membrane (a process known as exocytosis). Within the presynaptic cell, vesicles holding neurotransmitters are placed or 'locked in' at the synaptic membrane. Proteins in the presynaptic terminal referred to as SNAREs control fusion of the vesicles. The arriving action potential leads to a defined amount (a quantum) of neurotransmitter to be released into the synaptic cleft. The neurotransmitter molecules then travel across the synaptic cleft by **diffusion** to particular receptor sites on the presynaptic membrane, opening ion channels in the postsynaptic cell membrane. This results in ions moving, which consequently modifies the cell's local transmembrane potential and leads to a change in the potential of the postsynaptic cell or a postsynaptic potential (PSP). Usually within the nervous system, the result is an excitatory reaction (EPSP) as a result of depolarisation or an inhibitory reaction (IPSP) as a result of hyperpolarisation. The response of a synapse, and whether it is excitatory or inhibitory, is dependent on the type of receptors and neurotransmitters at the synapse.

MODULATION OF SYNAPTIC TRANSMISSION

Various processes affect the amount of the neurotransmitter required for release. One process called **presynaptic inhibition** causes a decrease in the quantity of neurotransmitter released despite an action potential in the presynaptic neuron. This takes place when a neurotransmitter release from one neuron impacts on the release of another neuron through an axoaxonic synapse, resulting in the partial depolarisation of the presynaptic neuron (Wu & Saggau, 1997). Fewer calcium (Ca^+) ions enter the presynaptic membrane as the action potential arrives, which causes less neuron transmitter release. The opposite effect occurs if there is a hyperpolarising release of the neurotransmitter at the axoaxonic synapse; there is an increased amount of neurotransmitter release or presynaptic facilitation.

It is also possible for a neurotransmitter to inhibit its own nerve cell. It sometimes happens that the neurotransmitter not only binds to postsynaptic receptors but also binds to presynaptic receptors, known as autoreceptors. These autoreceptors are located on presynaptic nerve cell membranes and serve as part of a feedback loop in signal transduction. It is possible to deactivate the influence of the neurotransmitter molecules on the postsynaptic membrane through enzymatic degradation, as in the case of **acetylcholinesterase** (AChE) or as with some other neurotransmitters via neurotransmitter reuptake.

NON-SYNAPTIC CHEMICAL COMMUNICATION

While neurotransmitters are released from the terminal buttons and have a local effect, neuromodulators – another communication substance released by neurons – travel greater distances and are dispersed more widely around the nervous system. Most neuromodulators are peptides, which are chains of **amino acids** linked together by peptide bonds. Neuromodulators affect general behavioural states such as vigilance and fearfulness.

Hormones also play a role in the communication of information around our bodies. Hormones are chemical substances that are secreted by cells of the endocrine glands or cells in other organs such as the stomach and kidneys. Most hormones fall into three categories: amino acid derivatives, peptides and proteins, and steroids.

The endocrine system is shown in Figure 1.6. Hormones are released by the endocrine gland into the extracellular fluid and are then distributed through the bloodstream. Specialised receptors for these hormones are located either on the surface of cells or deep within their nuclei. Cells that have these receptors for a particular hormone are called target cells. Many

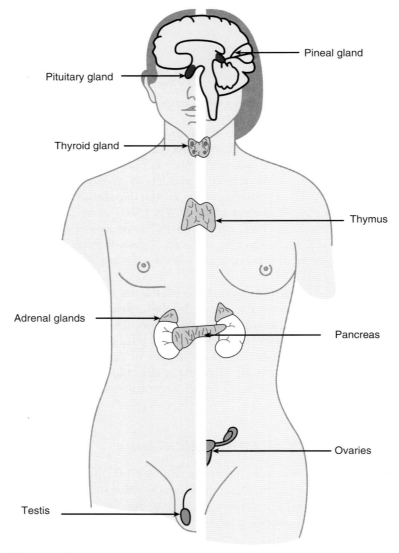

Figure 1.6   *The endocrine system*

neurons contain hormone receptors, so our behaviour is regularly affected by these substances. **Testosterone**, which is a sex hormone for instance, increases the aggressiveness of male animals. The following is a summary of the various glands of the endocrine system:

- *Adrenal glands*: secrete hormones which play a role in the body's reaction to stressful events.

- *Hypothalamus*: controls automatic functions such as regulating sleep; it also plays a major role in hunger and appetite.

- *Ovaries* and *testicles*: influence female and male characteristics.

- *Pancreas*: secretes **insulin,** a hormone that regulates the levels of glucose present in the body.

- *Parathyroid glands*: maintain calcium levels in the body by secreting a regulatory hormone.

- *Pineal body*: involved with sleep cycles and the daily biological cycles.

- *Pituitary gland*: plays a role in regulating other endocrine glands.

- *Thymus gland*: important in maintaining the body's immune system.

- *Thyroid gland*: plays a role in the metabolism of the body, including bone growth and heat production.

POSTSYNAPTIC RECEPTORS AND RECEPTOR TYPES

The effects of neurotransmitters is seen on the postsynaptic membrane, where the release of neurotransmitters results in a rapid opening of ion channels, involving a kind of receptor called **ionotropic** receptors or channel-linked receptors. Within this sort of receptor, the ion channel opens directly and the neurotransmitter alone is involved in the information transfer. Metabotropic receptors or G-protein-linked receptors are another type of receptor, and in these the ion channels open indirectly. When the neurotransmitter binds to a metabotropic receptor, another protein that is connected to the inside of the cell membrane becomes activated. This is referred to as a G protein. The G proteins trigger the production of another chemical known as a **second messenger**. This second messenger triggers the opening of the ion channels in the postsynaptic membrane. One of these second messengers is cyclic adenosine monophosphate (**cyclic AMP**), which is synthesised by adenosine triphosphate (ATP). Cyclic AMP is essential to the memory formation process (Jackson & Ramaswami, 2003) and may also play a role in the sedative effects of ethanol (Misra & Pandey, 2003).

The features of ionotropic receptors are:

- They are sometimes called ligand-gated ion channels.

- Action is instant and short.

- The channels in the excitatory receptors are for positively charged ions, otherwise known as cations.

- Depolarisation is achieved mostly by Na^+.

- Hyperpolarisation is achieved by Cl^- influx or K^+ efflux permitting inhibitory action.

Metabotropic receptors are not direct, and can have widespread actions which are often prolonged. An example is muscarinic ACh receptors.

NEUROTRANSMITTERS

We can categorise neurotransmitters into two broad groupings: the 'classical' small molecule neurotransmitters, and the larger neuropeptide neurotransmitters (Figure 1.7). Among neurotransmitters in the category of small molecule neurotransmitters there is a group termed the monoamines; these include dopamine, noradrenaline and serotonin, which are often looked upon as a unique group due to their correlation in terms of their chemical makeup.

The criteria for classifying a biochemical substance as a neurotransmitter are:

⚙ The substance has to be packaged into synaptic vesicles and be present in the presynaptic nerve terminal.

⚙ On depolarisation or on arrival of an action potential at the presynaptic membrane, the substance must be released from the nerve terminal.

⚙ Specific receptors for the substance must be available on the postsynaptic membrane.

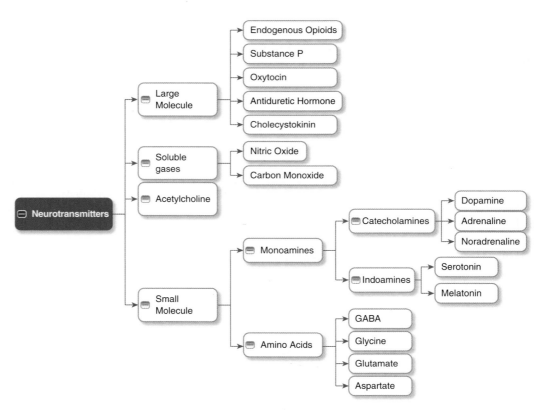

Figure 1.7   *Neurotransmitters*

Neurotransmitters act in two ways: direct and indirect. In *direct action*, the neurotransmitter opens ion channels by binding to a channel-linked receptor; this causes very fast responses. Examples are amino acids and AChE. In *indirect action*, the action takes place via a G-protein-linked receptor, and when the neurotransmitter binds it causes a cascade of intracellular second messenger systems; this generally has long-lasting effects. Examples are soluble gases such as NO, and neuropeptides.

The major types of neurotransmitter are described in the following sections.

THE AMINO ACIDS

GABA

GABA is the main inhibitory neurotransmitter in the CNS, occurring in 30–40% of all synapses. GABA is located in high concentrations in the substantia nigra and globus pallidus nuclei of the basal ganglia, the hypothalamus, the periaqueductal grey matter and the hippocampus. The concentration of GABA within the brain is 200–1000 times greater than that of the monoamines or **acetylcholine**. Gamma-aminobutyric acid is created from glutamate via the enzyme glutamate decarboxylase. Synapses using GABA are referred to as GABAergic synapses. GABA's activity ends with reuptake, just as with any other amino acid neurotransmitter. GABA A and GABA B are the most analysed of the five types of GABA receptors (Enz, 2001). Several disorders have been connected to GABA receptors; dysfunction with this inhibitory neurotransmitter can cause seizures (Pearl, 2004) and anxiety disorders (see Froestl, 2010 for a review of treatment).

Glycine

Another inhibitory neurotransmitter, found mainly in the spinal cord, **brain stem** and retina, is glycine. This neurotransmitter is only present in vertebrates (Hernandes & Troncone, 2009). It is a simple amino acid in both structure and function. It is formed of an amino group and a carboxyl (acidic) group attached to a carbon atom; when released into a synaptic cleft it binds to receptors, making the postsynaptic membrane more penetrable to Cl⁻ ions. This movement hyperpolarises the membrane, creating less chance for depolarisation. Thus glycine is an inhibitory neurotransmitter. One glycine **antagonist** is strychnine, which can stick to the glycine receptor and prevent the opening of the chloride ion channel, thus stopping inhibition. This disinhibition and consequent spinal hyperexcitability are the very things that make strychnine poisonous (by suffocating or exhausting its victims).

Glutamate (glutamic acid)

Glutamate is the most commonly found excitatory neurotransmitter. The excitatory action of glutamate is stopped by a chloride-independent membrane transport system that reabsorbs glutamate and aspartate into the presynaptic membrane. The **N-methyl-D-aspartate** (NMDA) glutamate receptor is one of the subtypes of the glutamate receptors and is the only receptor known to be regulated by a ligand (i.e. glutamate) and by voltage. NMDA receptors have a role to play in the process known as long-term potentiation or LTP. LTP takes place in the hippocampus where an activity-dependent increase in synaptic efficiency occurs, making the process key to some forms of learning and memory (see Chapter 11).

The amygdala and basal ganglia also contain high concentrations of NMDA receptors. Too much of the excitatory neurotransmitter released brings on glutamic acid excitotoxicity. Once glutamate is released into the cleft of a synapse, it is either reabsorbed into nerve cells by way of the ion-exchange transport system or changed by astrocytes into glutamine, which is not involved in excitotoxicity and therefore can be safely returned to the nerve cells to be converted back into glutamate.

Aspartate

Aspartate behaves as an excitatory neurotransmitter, stimulating NMDA receptors (Grem, King, O'Dwyer, & Leyland-Jones, 1988). Aspartate, along with glycine, opens ion channels and is primarily in the **ventral** spinal cord; it is inactivated when reabsorbed into the presynaptic membrane.

MONOAMINES

Serotonin

Serotonin is also referred to as 5-hydroxytryptamine (5-HT). Serotonin is synthesised from the amino acid tryptophan. Serotonin is believed to play an important role in the central nervous system in regulating anger, aggression, mood, sleep, body temperature, sexuality, vomiting and appetite (Folk & Long, 1988). The main source of 5-HT in the brain is the cells in the raphe nuclei which are a cluster of nuclei found in the brain stem. Serotonergic pathways travel widely all over the brain stem, the cerebral cortex and the spinal cord. The serotonin receptors are called 5-HT receptors. The 5-HT3 receptor is a ligand-gated ion channel; additional 5-HT receptors are G-protein-coupled receptors that depend on intracellular second messenger configuration, as previous explained. Serotonergic action is stopped mainly by the uptake of 5-HT from the synaptic cleft. This action takes place via the 5-HT reuptake transporter on the presynaptic neuron. Selective serotonin reuptake inhibitors (SSRIs) and **tricyclic antidepressants** (TCAs) are used for treating depression. Amphetamine, cocaine and 3,4-Methylenedioxymethamphetamine or MDMA (ecstasy) can all inhibit the reuptake of 5-HT.

Melatonin

Melatonin is derived from serotonin within the pineal gland and the retina. The pineal parenchymal cells secrete melatonin into the blood and cerebrospinal fluid. Melatonin plays a role in the sleep/wake cycle; its synthesis and secretion rise during the dark hours and are maintained at a low level during daylight hours (see Chapter 9). Melatonin also functions as an inhibitor of the synthesis and secretion of other neurotransmitters such as dopamine and GABA.

Noradrenaline

Noradrenergic neurons can be found in the locus coeruleus, the pons and the reticular formation in the brain, and project to the cerebral cortex, midbrain and hippocampus.

Noradrenaline is an excitatory neurotransmitter, and noradrenergic pathways are thought to play a key role in behaviours like attention and arousal. Noradrenergic activity may trigger modifications in several functions including heart rate, blood pressure and digestive processes (Lambert, 2001).

Dopamine

Dopamine also falls under the classification of monoamine neurotransmitters. In the central nervous system, dopamine acts on the five types of dopamine receptors – D1, D2, D3, D4 and D5 – and their variants. Dopaminergic neurons can be found in four dopamine pathways in the brain: the nigrostriatal, the mesocorticolimbic, the mesocortical and the tuberoinfundibular pathways. Dopamine is seen as the reward neurotransmitter, and recent work has shown larger receptor numbers in individuals with a higher social status, suggesting these individuals may experience more pleasure from their experiences. More details can be found in Box 1.2. Dopamine also acts as a hormone and restricts the release of prolactin from the **anterior** lobe of the pituitary.

A shortage of cells that produce dopamine in the substantia nigra contributes to the development of **Parkinson's disease**, while excessive dopamine may be involved in the development of schizophrenia (Stone, Morrison, & Pilowsky, 2007). When used medically, dopamine works on the sympathetic nervous system, resulting in increased heart rate and blood pressure. However, because dopamine cannot permeate the blood–brain barrier, it cannot have a direct effect on the CNS. To increase the level of dopamine in the brains of Parkinsonian patients, **L-DOPA** (levodopa), the precursor of dopamine, is administered because it can pass across the blood–brain barrier and enter into the CNS (Tedroff, 1997).

BOX 1.2   Dopamine receptor density and social status

Background

Previous positron emission tomography (PET) imaging studies in non-human primates had shown that striatal dopamine type 2/3 (D2/3) receptors are associated with social hierarchy in monkeys, and that the more dominant animals exhibit higher levels of D2/3 receptor binding. This study (Martinez et al., 2010) looked at the phenomenon in human participants.

Methods

Healthy volunteers ($N = 14$) were scanned using PET technology to measure D2/3 receptor binding potential (BP). The Barratt Simplified Measure of Social Status (BSMSS) was used to assess social status. Individuals were also assessed on their level of social support using the Multidimensional Scale of Perceived Social Support (MSPSS).

(Continued)

(Continued)

Results

A correlation was seen between social status and dopamine D2/3 receptors, as measured by striatal binding of the PET ligand [11C]raclopride (Figure 1). A similar correlation was seen with perceived social support, where higher [11C]raclopride BP correlated with higher scores on the MSPSS (Figure 2).

Interpreting the findings

The results of this study supported the idea that social status and social support are correlated with D2/3 receptor binding, and suggest that individuals who attain greater social status would be expected to have more rewarding and stimulating experiences in life as they have more receptors for dopamine to act upon within the striatum. This finding may also shed light on the risk for alcoholism among vulnerable individuals, as it suggests that individuals with low D2/3 receptors may be vulnerable to lower social status and other disadvantageous social factors which have previously been found to be associated with alcohol and substance use.

Reference

Martinez, D., Orlowska, D., Narendran, R., Slifstein, M., Liu, F., Kumar, D., et al. (2010). Dopamine type 2/3 receptor availability in the striatum and social status in human volunteers. *Biological Psychiatry*, *67*(3), 275–278.

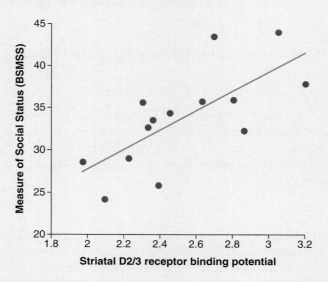

Figure 1 *Correlation between [11C]raclopride BP (x-axis) and social status as measured with the Barratt Simplified Measure of Social Status (BSMSS)*

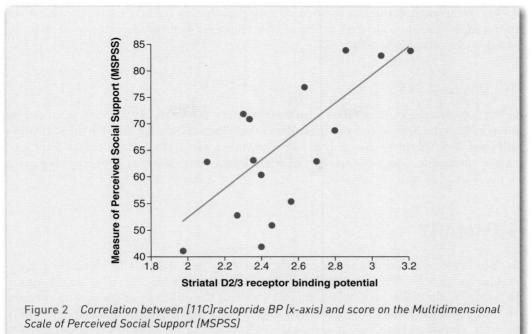

Figure 2   *Correlation between [11C]raclopride BP (x-axis) and score on the Multidimensional Scale of Perceived Social Support (MSPSS)*

ACETYLCHOLINE

Acetylcholine (ACh) was the first neurotransmitter to be identified. We find ACh in both the PNS and the CNS. The common consensus is that cholinergic pathways play a role in cognitive functions, memory in particular. ACh is also a major neurotransmitter of the parasympathetic nervous system, and anticholinergic drugs will modify body functions associated with this part of the nervous system. We see this with some antidepressant medications, where blocking cholinergic receptors and other anticholinergic activity result in side effects like dry mouth. ACh is also associated with Alzheimer's disease, in which patients have a noticeable acetylcholine deficiency (Perry, 1988) (see Chapter 13).

There are two primary kinds of acetylcholine receptors: nicotinic acetylcholine receptors (nAChR) and muscarinic acetylcholine receptors (mAChR). Nicotine, found in cigarettes, stimulates nicotinic receptors, while muscarine, a poison found in mushrooms, activates muscarinic receptors. Almost every receptor in the CNS is muscarinic, while the main centres of nicotinic receptors are located on muscle **motor end-plates** and autonomic ganglia.

NEUROPEPTIDES AND NEUROMODULATORS

Neuropeptides are constructed of short amino acid chains and belong to a class of protein-like molecules which act as neurotransmitters (Yew, Chan, Luo, Zheng, & Yu,

1999). Neuromodulators, as their name suggests, do not directly excite or inhibit the postsynaptic cell, but increase or reduce the release of neurotransmitter or modify the reaction of postsynaptic cells.

SOLUBLE GASES

Certain soluble gases also act as neurotransmitters. Nitric oxide (NO) is produced by many cells in the body such as the vascular endothelium cells; it is central in the regulation of blood flow and may also play a role in memory and learning. Another soluble gas, carbon monoxide, does not appear to be released in a directed manner but may play a role in the relaxation of blood vessels.

SUMMARY

In this chapter we have discovered that the nervous system has two divisions: the peripheral nervous system (PNS) and the central nervous system (CNS). We have also discussed the various cells of the nervous system and seen that the cell body of the neuron contains all the components that allow the cell to function. Neurons may be classified in a variety of ways, according to their shape, function or location, or the neurotransmitter they synthesise and release. Neurons have an input side called dendrites, which look like the bare branches of a tree, and an output side emerging from the cell called an axon. The thickening of a neuron at its far or distal end is called the terminal bouton; it houses the synaptic vesicles that contain neurotransmitter which is used for communication between the neuron and whatever it connects to via a synapse. The synapse comprises the presynaptic region, the synaptic cleft and the postsynaptic region. We also discussed the concept of non-synaptic chemical communication and detailed the endocrine system. The endocrine system is a collection of glands that produce hormones that regulate your body's growth, metabolism and sexual development and function. The hormones are released into the bloodstream and transported to target cells and organs throughout the body. We have also found that not all the cells in the nervous system are neurons, which represent approximately 50% of the volume of the CNS; the remainder consists of various supporting cells called glial cells which maintain homoeostasis in addition to providing support and nutrition. We also discussed the cellular membrane and the presence of a voltage across the membrane when the neuron is at rest. This is called the resting potential and is typically −70 mV. We have also seen how the movement of ions across the membrane produces an action potential which is generated at the axon hillock and conducted along the axon by progressive depolarisation. Finally, we examined the various neurotransmitters in the nervous system which are released from the end of the terminal bouton when the conditions are right. There are different types of neurotransmitter substance and they facilitate the communication between neuron and target cell.

FURTHER READING

Gazzaniga, M.S., Ivry, R.B., & Mangun, G.R. (2008). *Cognitive neuroscience: the biology of the mind* (3rd edn). New York: Norton.

Roger, B., & Barasi, S. (2008). *Neuroscience at a glance*. Chichester: Wiley-Blackwell.

 KEY QUESTIONS

1 Describe the organisational structure of the nervous system.

2 How is information transmitted around the nervous system?

3 What are the different types of neurotransmitter?

NEUROANATOMY AND BRAIN MAPPING

In this chapter we will outline the gross anatomy of the nervous system, that is the components visible with the unaided eye. As previously mentioned from this viewpoint, there are two parts of the nervous system: a central nervous system (CNS) that includes the brain and spinal cord, and a peripheral nervous system (PNS) that refers to the components of the nervous system that lie outside the skull and spinal cord. This chapter will first deal with the central nervous system, detailing aspects of the brain and spinal cord. It will then turn to the autonomic nervous system which regulates the self-governing aspects of the body such as **cardiac muscle** and glands.

ANATOMICAL TERMS OF LOCATION

Prior to learning about the CNS structures, it is a good idea to know some basic directional terms for finding your way through the brain. Relative direction terminology terms are: dorsal, ventral, **medial**, **lateral**, anterior and **posterior**. In addition to these terms, three basic orientations or planes are used to illustrate internal regions of the brain: coronal, horizontal and sagittal (Figure 2.1). It will be very helpful to be familiar with these terms, especially when reading literature regarding brain imaging.

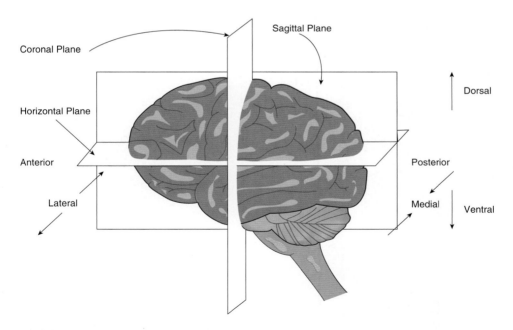

Figure 2.1 *Anatomical terms of location*

BRODMANN AREAS

Brodmann areas were originally identified by Korbinian Brodmann (Figure 2.2). They referred to areas of the cortex based on its cytoarchitecture, which is the organisation of the cortex by cell type (Strotzer, 2009). Certain staining compounds, which are useful in identifying specific types of nerve cells, are applied to the tissue prior to making this observation. Brodmann areas range in number from 1 to 52, and some are even further subdivided (for example, in the cingulated cortex they are labelled 23a and 23b).

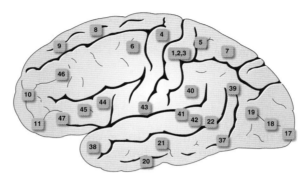

Figure 2.2 *Brodmann areas*

PLANES OF SECTION

As mentioned earlier and shown in Figure 2.1, three basic planes or orientations are typically used to examine internal structures of the brain: coronal, horizontal and sagittal. These are shown individually in Figure 2.3.

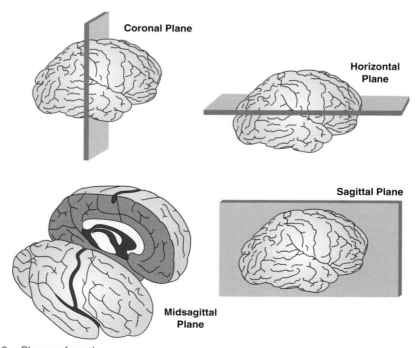

Figure 2.3 *Planes of section*

THE CENTRAL NERVOUS SYSTEM

BASIC BRAIN STRUCTURE

For anyone who does not already know, the brain can be found in the head, is covered by the skull, and is the organ that is responsible for organising behaviour. Not surprisingly, the human brain is quite complex, containing over 100 billion neurons that are each linked to as many as 10,000 other neurons. The hindbrain, the midbrain and the forebrain are the three main parts of the brain (Figure 2.4).

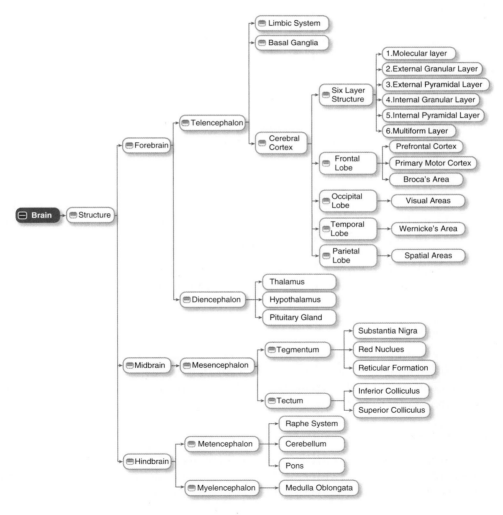

Figure 2.4 *Brain structure*

THE HINDBRAIN

The hindbrain can be found directly adjacent to the spinal cord and contains two huge divisions: the myelencephalon and the metencephalon. Located in the myelencephalon, the medulla oblongata controls basic functions such as heart rate, breathing and reflexive responses like coughing, sneezing and salivating.

The raphe system, cerebellum and pons are contained in the metencephalon. The pons obtains information from body movements and the visual system for controlled eye movements, and is located above the medulla. It also has a role in affecting sleep and arousal. The pons also transmits information to the cerebellum to regulate the coordination of muscular movements and to maintain equilibrium. The raphe system, which is vital to the body clock, consists of a collection of nuclei situated between the midbrain and the medulla.

The cerebellum, a walnut-shaped structure, can be found at the base of the brain. It regulates motor coordination, posture and equilibrium and is involved in motor, emotional and cognitive associative learning (Timmann et al., 2010). The pons, medulla oblongata and midbrain are commonly considered to be part of the brain stem.

THE MIDBRAIN

In front of the pons, the midbrain or mesencephalon consists of two parts: the tegmentum and the tectum. The tegmentum is home to four major structures: the first two are structures of the motor system known as the substantia nigra and the red nucleus; the third is the reticular formation which is involved in arousal. The fourth is the periaqueductal grey matter (PAG), which plays a role in the descending modulation of pain and in defensive behaviour. The substantia nigra helps to integrate voluntary movement; dopaminergic cell loss in this region results in the development of Parkinson's disease (Clarke, 2007). The red nucleus plays a role in the regulation of basic body movements. It controls posture modifications and the swinging of your arms when you walk. The tectum represents itself in the form of two structures: the **inferior** and the superior colliculi. The superior colliculus plays a role in sight and regulating eye movements, and the inferior colliculus plays a role in hearing.

THE FOREBRAIN

The largest region of the brain, the forebrain, has two parts: the diencephalon and the telencephalon. Within the diencephalon are the thalamus, the hypothalamus and the pituitary gland. The telencephalon comprises the **limbic system**, the basal ganglia and the cerebral cortex (neocortex).

The diencephalon

The thalamus is located in the middle of the forebrain. Its main nuclei gather information from the sensory systems, like **vision**, and then transmit this information to certain parts of the cortex. This location is often called the relay area for sensory information. Sensory receptors transmit information through the lateral geniculate nucleus (LGN) while auditory information is sent through the medial geniculate nucleus (MGN).

The hypothalamus, located ventral to the thalamus, is a small area with widespread connections to the rest of the forebrain and midbrain. Nuclei are found in this region, containing sensors that are able to sense internal body conditions. Harm to these nuclei leads to abnormalities in motivational behaviours like feeding, drinking, sexual behaviour and temperature regulation.

The pituitary gland, an endocrine gland (gland that produces hormones), is located at the bottom of the hypothalamus and is approximately the size of a pea. The structure comprises two primary regions, the anterior lobe and the posterior lobe. The anterior lobe releases hormones that regulate other endocrine glands in humans; the hormones include somatotrophin and thyrotrophin. The posterior lobe releases oxytocin, which maintains uterine contractions while women are in labour and prostrate contractions in males. It also releases antidiuretic hormone or vasopressin; this prompts the kidneys to reabsorb water, thereby conserving bodily fluids, i.e. it concentrates the urine (see Chapter 8).

The telencephalon

The limbic system is a group of interconnected brain structures, mainly the hippocampus, the cingulate gyrus and amygdala, that support numerous different functions such as emotion, behaviour and memory. The hippocampus has an essential role in memory (Squire, 1992) and any injury to the hippocampus can result in an inability to store and recall memory (Clark, Zola, & Squire, 2000). The amygdala is involved in how we experience feelings of fear and anger (Davis, 1992), while the cingulate gyrus plays a key part in emotional processing and has been linked to the experience of pain (Gao, Ren, Zhang, & Zhao, 2004).

The basal ganglia consist of three principal nuclei: the caudate nucleus, the putamen (which together make up the striatum) and the globus pallidus. Other sources will have many additional structures also, like the substantia nigra and the nucleus accumbens. The structure is an integral part of the cerebral cortex, thalamus and brain stem, and is related to several functions such as learning, motor control and emotional aspects. In patients with Parkinson's disease, it is the loss of pigmented dopamine-secreting cells in the pars compacta area of the substantia nigra that causes the disorder's most prominent symptoms of impaired movement (see Chapter 13).

CEREBRAL CORTEX OR NEOCORTEX

The forebrain comprises two cerebral hemispheres which are delineated by the body's median plane. Therefore it is separated into left and right cerebral hemispheres, divided by the longitudinal fissure. The human cerebral cortex is convoluted, consisting of sulci (small grooves), fissures (large grooves) and gyri (bulges between adjacent sulci). The two hemispheres each have a cerebral cortex – an outer layer consisting of grey matter that is supported by an inner layer made up of white matter. The cortex is approximately 2–4 mm thick with a total surface area of roughly 2360 cm^2 (2.5 ft^2). Several groups of axons – the large corpus callosum, the smaller anterior commissure, the posterior commissure and the hippocampal commissure – are responsible for communicating between the two hemispheres.

In most mammals, including humans, the cerebral cortex consists of six distinct layers of cell bodies running parallel to the surface. Fibres running to and from the cell bodies separate each layer. In each region of the cortex, the thickness of each layer is different because of the function of the various regions of the cortex. Details of the layers, from outside to inside, are as follows:

❋ molecular layer

❋ external granular layer

❋ external pyramidal layer

❋ internal granular layer

❋ internal pyramidal layer

❋ multiform layer.

Millions of axons are located underneath the cerebral cortex and join the neurons to the cortex. These axons have an opaque white appearance owing to the great amount of myelin layering them; hence the phrase 'white matter'.

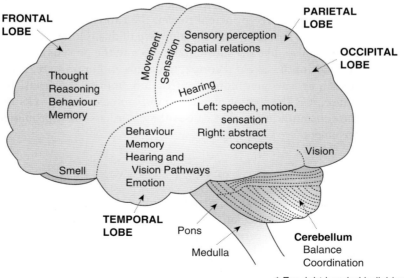

Figure 2.5   *Lobes of the brain*

For the most part, the cerebral hemispheres are given information from the opposite side of the body. For instance, the right side of the brain controls the activity on the body's left side, which is called **contralateral** control. The hemispheres are each separated into four different lobes: occipital, parietal, temporal and frontal (Figure 2.5).

Occipital lobe

The occipital lobe is the region where visual stimuli are processed. Information transmitted by the visual receptors enters the primary visual cortex, which is more commonly known as V1 (visual area 1), by way of pathways from the LGN in the thalamus. A large stripe of myelin is an identifier for V1, which is also knows as striate cortex. Cortical blindness results when V1 is destroyed (Zeng, Zhang, Xin, & Zou, 2010). Visual areas outside V1 are referred to as extrastriate cortex. These extrastriate areas are distinct for different visual tasks, such as visuospatial processing, colour processing (V4) (Heywood, Gadotti, & Cowey, 1992) and motion perception (V5) (Watson et al., 1993). These will be explained in Chapter 5.

Parietal lobe

The parietal lobe is located between the occipital lobe and the central sulcus. The area integrates sensory information from various modalities, especially spatial awareness and navigation. The front of the lobe, just behind the central sulcus, is referred to as the somatosensory cortex, which is where touch sensations are processed. In addition, the posterior part of the parietal lobes obtains information from the occipital lobe and is involved in visuospatial processing.

When the parietal lobe suffers injury, most especially on the right side, the individual can experience hemispatial neglect, also known as unilateral neglect. When this occurs on one side of the brain, the individual experiences a deficit in attention to the opposite side of space (Halligan, Marshall, & Wade, 1989).

Temporal lobe

The temporal lobes are found in the cerebral cortex; they are located laterally on each hemisphere under the lateral or Sylvian fissure. The primary auditory cortex is located here and is where auditory processing takes place. High-level auditory processing takes place in regions of the temporal lobes, with the left temporal lobe seemingly specialised for human speech. **Wernicke's area** is situated between the temporal and parietal lobes and is integral for language comprehension. Lesions to this area give rise to Wernicke's **aphasia** or receptive aphasia (Anzaki & Izumi, 2001). A tumour in the temporal region can lead to visual as well as auditory hallucinations. Research has found that psychiatric patients who report hallucinations have abnormal activity in this region (Hugdahl, Loberg, Specht, Steen, van Wageningen, & Jorgensen, 2007). The temporal lobe also plays a part in emotional and motivational behaviour; it contains the hippocampus and therefore plays a role in memory formation.

Frontal lobe

Found anterior to the parietal lobe and dorsal to the temporal lobe is the frontal lobe. The frontal lobe is the biggest of the four lobes that form the structure of the brain. The primary **motor cortex** is located in the frontal lobe and is responsible for the control of the voluntary movements of specified body parts. Also located in the left frontal lobe is **Broca's area**, which is believed to play a role in the programming and sequencing of the movements that make it possible to speak. Injury to this region will result in speech production problems (Broca's aphasia). The **prefrontal** cortex is part of the frontal lobe and is in charge of complex processes including planning, coordinating, controlling and carrying out behaviour; these processes are also known as the executive functions of the frontal lobes. Hence, individuals who have damage to this area have issues with these parts of cognitive function, being hindered in their capability to plan and execute complex sequences of actions (Jurado & Rosselli, 2007). In addition, the prefrontal cortex plays a role in attentional and emotional processing (Faw, 2003). The prefrontal cortex has also been associated with the cognitive deficits that are seen in schizophrenia. A medical treatment for mental illness, which was popular in the early twentieth century, involved inflicting damage to the connections between the frontal lobe and the limbic system. This was referred to as a frontal lobotomy (or a frontal leucotomy); it was reportedly very successful in decreasing a person's level of distress, but it frequently resulted in modifications to emotional processing and personality.

VENTRICULAR SYSTEM

The ventricular system comprises hollow structures in the brain that are connected to the central canal of the spinal cord. The ventricular system has four ventricles: the right and left

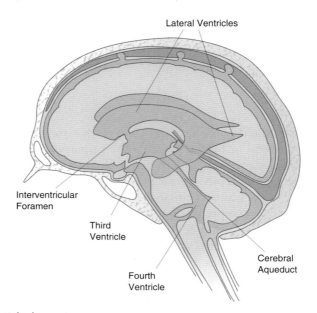

Figure 2.6   *The ventricular system*

lateral ventricles, the third ventricle and the fourth ventricle. The ventricles contain the choroid plexus, which produces the cerebrospinal fluid (CSF) that protects and bathes the brain and spinal cord. CSF is absorbed into the blood so that it does not accumulate excessively in the brain. The interventricular foramen joins the two lateral ventricles to the third ventricle and the cerebral aqueduct joins the third ventricle to the fourth ventricle (Figure 2.6).

SPINAL CORD

The spinal cord can be thought of as a continuation of the hindbrain, specifically the medulla oblongata. It starts its journey at the foramen magnum of the occipital bone and travels down the vertebral column, terminating at the lower boundary of the first lumbar vertebra. The spinal cord is around 45 centimetres in an adult male and about 42 centimetres in an adult female. The spinal cord houses the **nerve fibres** which travel to and from the brain, and it is responsible for reflex actions (see Chapter 7). The spinal cord has grooves on its anterior and posterior surfaces which divide it into left and right halves (Figure 2.7).

There are 31 pairs of nerves called spinal nerves which are attached to the sides of the spinal cord. Each spinal nerve has a ventral root (towards the front of the body) and a dorsal root (towards the back of the body); the latter has a bulb-like structure called dorsal root ganglion.

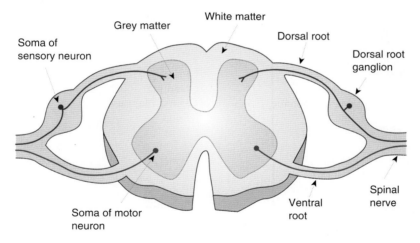

Figure 2.7   *Spinal cord*

THE PERIPHERAL NERVOUS SYSTEM

SPINAL NERVES

When someone says 'spinal nerves' they are generally referring to a combination of nerves which carry motor, sensory and autonomic signals and connect the spinal cord with the rest of the body. As mentioned above, humans have 31 pairs of spinal nerves, which correspond to a segment of the vertebral column. They are generally labelled as eight cervical spinal nerve pairs (C1–C8), 12 thoracic pairs (T1–T12), five lumbar pairs (L1–L5), five sacral pairs (S1–S5) and one coccygeal pair.

Spinal nerves are created by the grouping of nerve fibres from the dorsal and ventral roots of the spinal cord. The ventral roots carry efferent motor axons, while the dorsal roots carry afferent sensory axons (see Chapters 6 and 7).

CRANIAL NERVES

In contrast to spinal nerves, which emerge from segments of the spinal cord, cranial nerves emerge directly from the brain. In humans there are traditionally 12 pairs of cranial nerves (Table 2.1). Only the first and the second pair emerge from the **cerebrum**; the remaining 10 pairs emerge from the brain stem (Figure 2.8). We shall be talking about these nerves in later chapters.

Table 2.1   *Cranial nerves*

Cranial nerve	Nucleus name	Nucleus location	Function
Olfactory (CNI)	Anterior olfactory	Olfactory tract	Smell
Optic (CNII)	Lateral geniculate nucleus	Thalamus	Vision
Oculomotor (CNIII)	Oculomotor	Midbrain	Eye movement (elevation, adduction)
	Edinger–Westphal	Midbrain	
Trochlear (CNIV)	Trochlear	Midbrain	Eye movement (depression of adducted eye)
Trigeminal (CNV)	Principal	Pons	Facial sensation
	Spinal	Medulla	Mastication
	Mesencephalic	Pons/midbrain	
	Motor	Pons	
Abducent (CNVI)	Abducent	Pons	Eye movement (abduction)
Facial (CNVII)	Motor	Pons	Facial expression
	Solitary	Pons	Taste
	Superior salivatory	Pons	Salivation, lacrimation
Vestibulocochlear (CN VIII)	Vestibular	Medulla	Balance
	Cochlear	Medulla	Hearing
Glossopharyngeal (CN IX)	Nucleus ambiguus	Medulla	Taste
	Inferior salivatory	Medulla	Salivation
	Solitary	Medulla	Innervation of pharynx
Vagus (X)	Nucleus ambiguus	Medulla	Swallowing and talking
	Dorsal motor vagal	Medulla	Cardiac, GI tract, respiration
	Solitary	Medulla	Taste
Cranial accessory (XI)	Nucleus ambiguus	Medulla	Pharynx/larynx muscles
	Spinal accessory	Cervical cord	Neck and shoulder movement
Hypoglossal (XII)	Hypoglossal	Medulla	Tongue movement

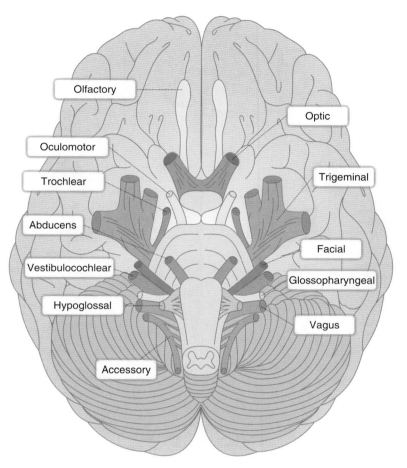

Figure 2.8 *Cranial nerves*

THE AUTONOMIC NERVOUS SYSTEM

The involuntary or autonomic nervous system is that division of the nervous system which controls the activity of the viscera. This system has two components: the sympathetic and the parasympathetic (Figure 2.9).

The actions of the autonomic nervous system are largely involuntary and use two groups of motor neurons to stimulate the effector. The first, the preganglionic neurons, which originate in the CNS, travel to a ganglion in the body. Here they make synactic connections with postganglionic neurons, which then travel to the effector organs; these include muscles and glands. The parasympathetic postganglionic fibres release acetylcholine, and are called cholinergic fibres. Most sympathetic postganglionic fibres release noradrenaline, and so are called adrenergic. Sympathetic postganglionic fibres attached to the sweat glands and blood vessels of skeletal muscles liberate acetylcholine, i.e. are cholinergic.

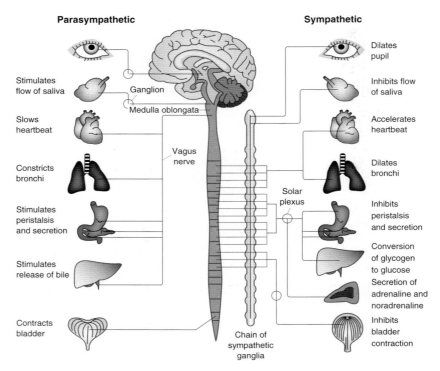

Figure 2.9   *Autonomic nervous system*

Sympathetic nervous system

This is the part of the autonomic nervous system which prepares the body for vigorous activity or emergencies (fight or flight) in response to urgent situations (fear, stress, haemorrhage, cold, etc.).

The preganglionic neuron has two main actions in the sympathetic ganglion, and it can do one of three things:

1   Synapse with postganglionic neurons, which then re-enter the spinal nerve and travel to the surface of the body to sweat glands and the walls of blood vessels.

2   Travel up or down the sympathetic chain (the paired bundle of nerve fibres that runs from the base of the skull to the coccyx) and then make synaptic connections with postganglionic neurons.

3   Exit the ganglion and travel to special ganglia like the solar plexus, where it can synapse with postganglionic sympathetic neurons travelling to the **smooth muscle** of the viscera. Alternatively, it can travel through this second ganglion and into the adrenal medulla, where it makes synaptic connections with the postganglionic cells that create the secretory part of the adrenal medulla, which releases noradrenaline.

Some of the actions of sympathetic stimulation are that it:

⚙ raises blood pressure

⚙ stimulates heart rate

⚙ dilates the pupils

⚙ stimulates the conversion in the liver of glycogen into glucose (glycogenolysis)

⚙ moves blood away from viscera and the skin to the skeletal muscles, brain and heart

⚙ inhibits the gastrointestinal tract action of peristalsis.

Parasympathetic nervous system

The tenth cranial nerves or the vagus nerves, which originate in the medulla oblongata, are the main nerves of the parasympathetic system. Other preganglionic parasympathetic neurons are also present from the brain and spinal cord and synapse with the postganglionic neurons, which are located near or in a muscle or a gland, i.e. the effector organ. The parasympathetic system returns the body functions to normal following the changes by stimulation of the sympathetic system. In hazardous conditions or when damage is present, the sympathetic system prepares the body for the fight-or-flight response. The parasympathetic system returns the body to its original state when the threat is over.

Some of the actions of parasympathetic stimulation are that it:

⚙ slows down heart rate

⚙ lowers blood pressure

⚙ constricts the pupils of the eyes

⚙ increases blood flow to the viscera and the skin.

Even though the autonomic nervous system is believed to be involuntary, it has been shown that some aspects of conscious control can be used to control some of its features, as has been demonstrated by practitioners of yoga and Zen Buddhism. Individuals who practise meditation seem to be able to modify a number of autonomic functions such as their oxygen consumption and heart rate.

BRAIN MAPPING TECHNIQUES

This section provides an overview of some of the different research techniques for studying the nervous system, and aims to shed some light on the behavioural function of our neural tissue (Figure 2.10).

There are several ways to study the brain, and they can be classified as follows:

- *ex vivo*: post-mortem (i.e. dead body)
- *ex vitro*: slices, cultures
- *in vivo*: whole animal, invasive and non-invasive techniques.

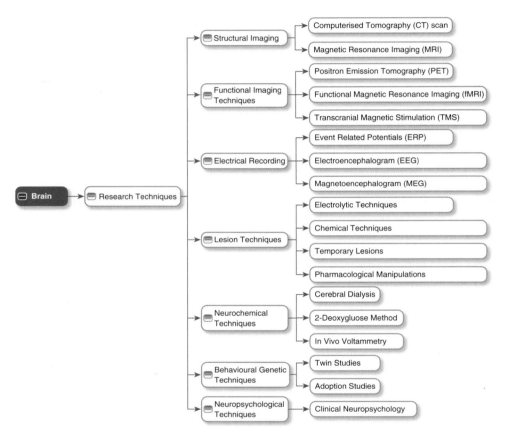

Figure 2.10   *Brain research techniques*

LESION TECHNIQUES

The distinguishing characteristic of lesion research in biological psychology testing is that the nervous system of the animal under study is permanently or temporarily modified and the subsequent behaviour of the animal is measured. Marie-Jean-Pierre Flourens (1794–1865) developed the lesion or ablation technique, which is considered a classic method employed in biological psychology, and is one of the oldest techniques in neuroscience. The method is performed on animals such as rodents and is carried out with the help of stereotaxic apparatus. The animal is anaesthetised and put into the stereotaxic device. The animal cannot move, allowing the researchers to make very precise subcortical lesions (Figure 2.11). The procedure involves first removing the bone covering the brain, and then excising the dura (outer brain covering). Utilising a number of methods, the cortical or subcortical tissue of the brain is then removed or lesioned.

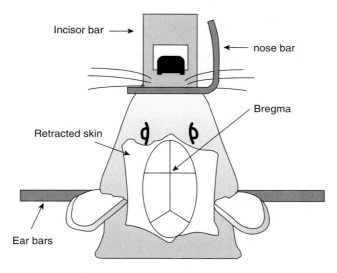

Figure 2.11   *Rodent in a stereotaxic device*

Brain lesions are created in several different ways, and the methods used are classified differently depending on the source. The most common methods are:

- *Electrolytic lesions*: the destruction of neural tissue by an electric current that passes through a platinum or stainless steel wire.

- *Chemical lesions*: destruction of neural tissue by injecting a chemical neurotoxin like kainic acid.

- *Temporary lesions*: temporarily disabling neural tissue by cooling it off or administering anaesthetics like tetrodotoxin.

- *Pharmacological manipulations*: a chemical receptor antagonist which alters neurotransmission.

The stereotaxic atlas is the guide to brain areas. The atlas reveals cross-sections of the brain along with grid coordinates of regions of the brain. This allows accurate identification of the brain region under investigation by the use of x, y, z coordinates. All references are relative to a single point on the animal skull referred to as the bregma; this is the junction of the sagittal and coronal sutures of the skull (Figure 2.11).

ELECTRICAL RECORDING

Electroencephalography (EEG)

Another way of shedding some light on brain activity involves amplifying and recording activity while the animal is completing a specific task. Two methods are available to record this. One is to use macroelectrodes – devices for the purpose of measuring activity from several neurons simultaneously. With this technology, electrodes are placed on the scalp and the activity in the cortices is recorded. Electroencephalography (EEG) is one common means of calculating the amount of electrical activity of the brain by recording from electrodes situated on the scalp. It has good temporal resolution but poor spatial resolution. The output electrical traces are referred to as an electroencephalogram (also EEG) and correspond to the combination of all the postsynaptic potentials from numerous neurons. Sleep researchers make extensive use of cortical EEG, and it is also used to monitor and diagnose some clinical conditions like **epilepsy** (Holmes, 2008). In addition to medical uses, it is possible for the EEG signal to be utilised in cognitive research to measure brain responses to particular stimuli or events. Event-related potentials (ERPs) are extracted from the recordings by taking the mean EEG signal from each of the trials within a certain condition. The resulting output provides both individual voltage waveforms and a scalp voltage map that relates to or reflects the electric activity of the brain through the skull and scalp to a discrete stimulus. Spatial resolution of an ERP study is not good. It is not easy to pinpoint exactly where within the brain the voltage originated or which neurons are responsible. It is possible to estimate using source localisation software (a procedure referred to as dipole modelling) but the results will only be estimates, as there are many unknowns in the calculation – the number, site and magnitudes of the electrical sources as well as the precise structure of the brain which the electrical signal passed through. This issue of source localisation from scalp voltage maps is called the inverse problem.

Magnetoencephalography (MEG)

Electrical activity inside the brain produces magnetic fields outside the head, which can be measured by a magnetoencephalogram (MEG). Usually MEG sensors are located in a helmet-like container (or Dewar) in which the subject places their head while measurements are taken. The magnetic fields produced in the brain are the same electrical sources that produce the classic EEG signal; that is, they are principally a product of postsynaptic currents present from pyramidal neurons. In contrast to the EEG, the conductivity of the tissues within the head has very little effect on the magnetic fields outside the head. Thus more accurate reconstructions of the neuronal activity that created the external magnetic fields can be produced as the inverse problem is decreased. The good spatial and temporal resolution of brain activity gives a very valuable insight into how neural networks communicate *in vivo*. This has important clinical applications. All electrical current including that from the brain produces a magnetic field that can be measured. In the case of the MEG, it is measured using extremely sensitive devices called superconducting quantum interference devices (SQUIDs).

STRUCTURAL IMAGING TECHNIQUES

Computerised tomography (CT)

A computerised tomography (CT) scanner is a fancy kind of X-ray machine. Ordinary X-rays use one X-ray beam, while a CT scan involves several beams sent at the same time from various angles. Only after the X-rays have passed through the brain are they recorded and their strength measured. How much X-ray absorption occurs has to do with tissue density: fluids with lower densities, like cerebral spinal fluid, absorb less and therefore appear black; denser materials, like the skull, absorb more and appear white. Clinically, CT scans of the head are very effective for identifying brain tumours, swelling, or bleeding of the arteries. They are also quite helpful in evaluating the brain after a stroke. It is important to know that a CT scan is unable to distinguish between white and grey brain matter and it also cannot be utilised to perform functional imaging; it is strictly used to obtain structural information. CT scans are also known as CAT scans.

From its inception in the 1970s, CT has become a key tool in medical imaging to supplement X-rays and medical ultrasonography. More recently, it has been employed for preventive medicine or screening for disease; for example, CT colonography for those with a high risk of colon cancer, or full-motion heart scans for those with a high risk of heart disease. Several institutions have made full body scans available to people. However, this practice is controversial due to the cost involved, the levels of radiation exposure, the lack of proven benefit, and the risk of discovering insignificant abnormalities that may lead to unnecessary investigations and procedures.

Magnetic resonance imaging (MRI)

Magnetic resonance imaging (MRI) utilises magnetic fields and radio waves to generate images of a person's brain structures without having to expose the patient to ionising radiation (X-rays). The MRI scanner consists of a large tube-shaped magnet which surrounds the head. Nuclei located within certain molecules in the brain will begin to rotate in a specific way as a result of the magnetic field encountered. A short radio wave is subsequently put through the brain which knocks the orientation of these nuclei by 90 degrees from their first orientation. These molecules spin around in their new state, resulting in a modified magnetic field which can be detected to produce an image. Once the molecule is back into its 'relaxed' state in the magnetic field, an additional short radio wave pulse is applied. Repetitions of the process are performed, cutting sequential brain sections to create an image. With a technique called echo planar imaging (EPI), a fast MRI technique, we can scan a brain in approximately 2–3 seconds depending on the thickness of the slice. MRIs are only able to image structural information of the brain while fMRI provides both structural and functional information.

The two basic MRI scans are as follows.

T1-weighted MRI: spin–lattice relaxation time

One of the more standard basic scans is the T1-weighted scan. These scans are capable of distinguishing fat from water (with water appearing darker than fat) by using a gradient echo (GRE) sequence, with short echo time *TE* (the time in milliseconds between the application of the 90° pulse and the peak of the echo signal in spin echo and inversion recovery pulse sequences) and short repetition time *TR* (the time between successive pulse sequences applied to the same slice). This method represents the fundamental kind of MR contrast, which is typically performed for clinical purposes. Enlargement of T1 weighting (better contrast) can be achieved by the use of an inversion pulse as in an MP-RAGE sequence. Because the repetition time *TR* is so brief, you can run this scan very quickly, making it possible to collect high-resolution 3D information sets. In the brain, T1-weighted scans produce a high degree of contrast between grey matter and white matter; to put it another way, T1-weighted images highlight fatty deposits.

T2-weighted MRI: spin–spin relaxation time

T2-weighted scans are another basic kind of MRI scan. Similar to the way the T1-weighted scan works, fat is distinguished from water; but here, fat is dark and water is light in appearance. On the brain scans, cerebral white matter, which is fatty, appears darker than grey matter. A spin echo (SE) is used in T2-weighted scans, with long *TE* and long *TR*.

FUNCTIONAL IMAGING TECHNIQUES

Positron emission tomography (PET)

Positron emission tomography (PET) imaging requires the individual to be injected with a radioactive tracer. This method takes measurements of the metabolic activity occurring in the nervous systems, and neural activity is used as an indirect measure of the radioactive tracer. Oxygen-15 is the most commonly used tracer and it is typically administered as water; its half-life is 2.25 min by the emission of positrons. The scanner calculates the positron emissions and a computer combines the signals into a visual reproduction of neural activity; thus there is an association between the strength of the tracer element's signal in a specific area and the blood flow in that same area. A good number of radiotracers or radioligands have been produced for PET; these attach to specific receptors in the nervous system (e.g. dopamine D2) and consequently allow us to see the receptor type *in situ*.

Radionuclides used in PET scanning are generally isotopes with short half-lives, for example carbon-11 (about 20 min), nitrogen-13 (about 10 min), oxygen-15 (about 2 min) and fluorine-18 (about 110 min). These radionuclides are combined either with compounds the body typically uses, like glucose (or analogues of glucose), water or ammonia, or with molecules that bind to receptors or other sites of drug action. We refer to compounds that are labelled this way as radiotracers. It is noteworthy that PET scans are able to trace the biologic pathway of compounds in the human body (as well as in other living things), as long as you can radiolabel them with a PET isotope.

Functional magnetic resonance imaging (fMRI)

Functional magnetic resonance imaging (fMRI) uses the paramagnetic properties of oxygenated and deoxygenated haemoglobin to create images of the blood flow in the brain for evaluation. In this method we associate blood flow with neural activity. The more active a neuron is, the more oxygenated blood it will use. Oxygenated haemoglobin is diamagnetic, but when deoxygenated it is paramagnetic. Deoxygenated haemoglobin distorts the local magnetic field, and this distortion is used to provide an indication of the concentration of deoxyhaemoglobin in the blood. Thus, the magnetic resonance (MR) signal of blood differs to some extent depending on the level of oxygenation. These different signals in the magnetic field can be detected using different pulse sequences, which show blood-oxygen-level-dependent (BOLD) contrast. The common consensus is that modifications in BOLD signals strongly correlate with changes in the flow of blood and, consequently, neural activity in a specific part of the brain. In recent years, a number of studies have found an association between blood flow and metabolic rate (Forster et al., 1998). Non-invasive neuro-imaging methods such as BOLD-fMRI have become acceptable approaches for ascertaining sensorimotor and mental process neural bases in neuroscience. fMRI has been used to investigate the functional specialisation for visual recognition and visual pathways involved with what/where information (Ungerleider & Pasternak, 2003) as well as language (Démonet, Thierry, & Cardebat, 2005). Many other higher-level aspects of the human brain have been studied via fMRI, demonstrating the neural processes involved in many psychological functions such as emotions and more challenging aspects of cognition such as hallucinations. A study which scanned the brain while people were hallucinating is detailed in Box 2.1. Functional imaging technology is being used even more extensively, branching into several areas, like the humanities and social sciences, which examine the neural foundations of human moral judgement in economic decision making, and the workings of the 'human mind' or 'self'. However, since starting to employ this technique, fMRI has been strongly criticised, both as a research technique and in the way the information has been interpreted (Aue, Lavelle, & Cacioppo, 2009).

The benefits of using fMRI are:

⚙ It produces a non-invasive recording of brain signals without exposing the patient to the radiation risks associated with other scanning technologies, like CT or PET scans.

⚙ Its spatial resolution is quite good: 2–3 mm is typical but it can be as good as 1 mm.

⚙ It can record signals from all areas of the brain, unlike EEG and MEG which are biased towards the cortical surface.

⊗ It is widely employed, and standard information analysis applications have been developed which allow researchers to compare results across labs.

⊗ It makes it possible to see superior visual images of brain 'activation'.

The downsides of using fMRI are:

⊗ Careful interpretation is required: correlation is not evidence of causality, as brain processes are complex and not always localised.

⊗ It is vital to use statistical techniques carefully since they may generate false positive readings.

⊗ Being just an indirect gauge of neural activity, the BOLD signal is easily affected by non-neural alterations in the body. This also presents problems when trying to understand positive and negative BOLD responses.

⊗ The temporal resolution of fMRI is not very good. The BOLD response reaches its height at around 5 seconds after the neurons in an area begin to work. The significance is that for events taking place within a brief time span, it is difficult to differentiate the various BOLD responses. Careful experimental design may help to minimise this issue. In addition, some researchers have tried to use fMRI signals that have relatively high spatial resolution in conjunction with signals recorded using other methods, like EEG or MEG, which have a greater temporal resolution.

⊗ There are several things that can influence the BOLD response: medications or illicit substances; age and brain pathology; local differences in neurovascular coupling; attention; and carbon dioxide concentration in the blood.

BOX 2.1   fMRI study of auditory hallucinations

Background

Perceptions of speech in the absence of an auditory stimulus – or auditory hallucinations – are a feature of schizophrenia and are listed under the first-rank symptoms (see Chapter 13). This study (Shergill, Brammer, Williams, Murray, & McGuire, 2000) used fMRI to measure neural activity during auditory hallucinations as a way of examining the network of cortical and subcortical areas associated with the phenomena.

Methods

Six patients with schizophrenia who were experiencing frequent auditory hallucinations took part in the study. A novel approach with fMRI was used to measure spontaneous neural activity without requiring participants to signal when hallucinations occurred.

Of the order of 50 scans were acquired at intervals in each individual while they were irregularly hallucinating. Immediately after each scan, participants reported whether they had been hallucinating. Neural activity when individuals were and were not experiencing hallucinations was compared in each subject and the group as a whole.

Results

Auditory hallucinations were associated with activation in the inferior frontal/insular, anterior cingulate and temporal cortex bilaterally. Activation was also present in the right thalamus and inferior colliculus, and in the left hippocampus and parahippocampal cortex.

Conclusions

This study highlighted that auditory hallucinations may be mediated by a distributed network of cortical and subcortical areas. This was consistent with the notion that auditory hallucinations occur through the disruption of normal cognitive processes, such as monitoring of self-generated verbal material.

Reference

Shergill, S.S., Brammer, M.J., Williams, S.C.R., Murray, R.M., & McGuire, P.K. (2000). Mapping auditory hallucinations in schizophrenia using functional magnetic resonance imaging. *Archives of General Psychiatry, 57*, 1033–1038.

Transcranial magnetic stimulation (TMS)

This is a non-invasive means of stimulating neurons in the brain. A coil produces magnetic field impulses, stimulating the underlying tissue and temporarily interrupting the firing of neurons at the site where the stimulation occurred. TMS has a very high level of spatial resolution. It also has excellent temporal resolution, with disruption from a single pulse lasting between 20 and 80 ms depending on which neurons are being stimulated. By disrupting the neurons' functioning it can be determined if the neurons are used in a particular cognitive function. Therefore, the rationale underlying the procedure is simple: if the part of the brain that is connected to a task is suppressed (i.e. 'lesioned') with TMS stimulation and an individual performs more poorly on a task, then we can say that the area plays a role in the performance of a task (Stewart, Ellison, Walsh, & Cowey, 2001).

More information is still being gathered about the ways in which TMS functions. Two types of effect can occur with TMS, and they depend on the stimulation and mode. Single- or paired-pulse TMS causes neurons within the neocortex to discharge an action potential and depolarise at the site of stimulation. If employed in the primary motor cortex, it produces muscle activity, called a motor **evoked potential** (MEP), which can be recorded on

electromyography. When it involves the occipital cortex, the subject may report seeing flashes of light known as phosphenes. In the cortex, the subject usually does not consciously feel any effect, but there may be some modification to his or her behaviour, e.g. slower reaction time on a cognitive task.

Repetitive TMS (rTMS) produces longer-lasting effects, which persist beyond the first period of stimulation. It is not obvious how these effects work at present, but it is widely thought that they reflect changes in synaptic efficacy similar to long-term potentiation (LTP) and long-term depression (LTD).

NEUROCHEMICAL TECHNIQUES

Neurochemical techniques can be employed to determine various substances in the brain. Another of their functions is to help locate specific receptors, and to research the psychological functions of specific neurotransmitters.

Cerebral dialysis

Cerebral dialysis is used to take measurements of the concentration of specific neurochemicals outside the cells in behaving animals (see Robinson and Justice, 1991). Cerebral dialysis involves implanting a fine microdialysis probe which consists of a metal tube with an artificial semi-permeable membrane at the bottom (dialysis section). Such a probe is illustrated in Figure 2.12. Another small tube leads away from the probe to collect the fluid after it has passed through the dialysis section. A dilute salt solution is gradually

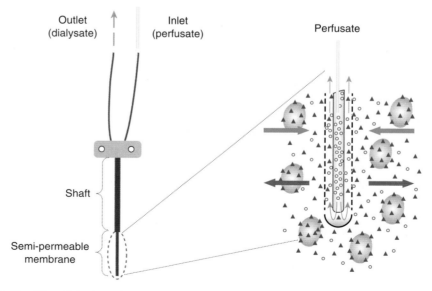

Figure 2.12 *Microdialysis probe*

added into the microdialysis tube, which then collects molecules from the brain's extracellular fluid, which has moved across the semi-permeable membrane via diffusion. This fluid is then collected and analysed by an automated chromatograph. The chromatograph separates the chemical components from the liquid, allowing detection of neurotransmitter substances and their breakdown products.

2-deoxyglucose method

An animal is injected with radioactive 2-deoxyglucose and then placed in a situation that will activate a particular behaviour. Because 2-DG is similar to glucose in its structure, the neurons that are active in a particular behaviour are able to absorb it to a greater degree. Slices of the brain are then examined at post-mortem under autoradiography. In this process, each tissue piece is put next to a small piece of X-ray film to gather information that the radioactivity emits. Autoradiography reveals which neural locations have absorbed the 2-DG and consequently are active for the behaviour under investigation.

In vivo voltammetry

In vivo voltammetry is a process by which the extracellular concentration of neurochemicals in behaving animals is measured (Blaha, Coury, Fibiger, & Phillips, 1990). In an indirect way, this method calculates changes in the concentration of the extracellular fluid by monitoring changes in the flow of current as the voltage across a carbon-based electrode rises. There are chemicals in the nervous system that are oxidised at different intensities and are identifiable. This process has been used extensively to study of the release of dopamine.

BEHAVIOURAL GENETIC TECHNIQUES

Examining how **genes** and our surroundings may or may not affect the behaviour of people can best be seen as trying to untangle a very complicated relationship between the environments that a person experiences and their genetic makeup.

Some have suggested that heredity and the environment each supply half of the makeup of an entire person, yet as you can imagine there has been much debate regarding specific percentages as well as the presence of higher percentages of one factor or the other in various age groups (Petrill et al., 2004). Adoption studies, twin studies and family studies have been carried out in the quest to find out how the various human characteristics are influenced by heredity and environment. While tentative conclusions may be drawn from these studies, far more research must take place, both in creating new research projects and in analysing methodologies and results that have been used previously, before this debate can find a satisfactory resolution.

Twin and adoption studies

Twin studies have played an essential role in unravelling the nature versus nurture debate. Monozygotic twins, more commonly known as identical twins, have identical **genotypes** and can provide information on what genes cause traits or characteristics in individuals. Fraternal twins, also known as dizygotic twins, have precisely 50% of the same genes in common. They do not provide the same foundation for determining genetic influence that identical twins provide, but they serve as a good comparison for twin studies as they are like first-degree relatives. If biology and genes are more important than environment, then identical twins should behave or have psychopathology similar to each other, more so than fraternal twins (Plomin, DeFries, McClearn, & Rutter, 1997). Whether a characteristic or trait is due to genes or environment is determined by what is called the heritability coefficient (Olson, Vernon, Harris, & Jang, 2001). It must be remembered however that identical twins, while they have the same genotype (genetic makeup), can display different **phenotypes** (external genetic expression); and although they are genetically identical, they have different experiences that help to form their personality, behaviour and psychopathology in ways that make them very different from one another (Hughes, Happé, Taylor, Jaffee, Caspi, & Moffitt, 2005). Another way to investigate the role of environmental and genetic influences on behaviour is to compare people who were adopted early in life with their biological and adopted parents. Box 2.2 details a classic study of separated twins carried out in 1966.

BOX 2.2 Adoption study of schizophrenia

Background

Some twin pairs are concordant for schizophrenia whereas others are not. This raises the possibility that there may be factors other than genes which must contribute to the development of schizophrenia. One way of studying heredity is through adoption studies. One of the first large adoption studies was that by Heston (1966).

Method

This study compared the psychosocial adjustment of 47 adults born to schizophrenic mothers with 50 control adults, where all participants had been separated from their natural mothers from the first few days of life. The comparison was based on a review of social information such as school and hospital records plus the Minnesota Multiphasic Personality Inventory (MMPI) which was administered to 72 subjects. Other information included was participants' IQ and social class. Three psychiatrists independently rated the participants.

Results

1 Schizophrenic and sociopathic personality disorders found in those individuals born to schizophrenic mothers were above chance levels. Five of 47 individuals born to schizophrenic mothers were schizophrenic, and no cases of schizophrenia were found in 50 control subjects.

2   Other comparisons with individuals having a psychiatric or behavioural issue demonstrated a significant amount of psychosocial disability in about one-half of the individuals born to schizophrenic mothers.

3   The remaining half of the individuals born to schizophrenic mothers were notably successful adults, with many possessing artistic talents and imaginative adaptations to life which were not as common as in the control group.

Interpreting the findings

The study highlighted that although none of the children were brought up by schizophrenic parents, the children who had schizophrenia in their biological families were more likely to develop the disorder.

Reference

Heston, L. (1966). Psychiatric disorders in foster home reared children of schizophrenic mothers. *The British Journal of Psychiatry, 112*, 819–825.

NEUROPSYCHOLOGICAL TECHNIQUES

Neuropsychological tests are examinations tailored for the purpose of measuring psychological functions that are believed to be attributed to a specific brain structure or pathway. Most of the time, the technique contains the systematic administration of precisely defined tests or stimuli in a controlled area.

Neuropsychological tests can be given to a person to evaluate cognitive process such as intelligence, language lateralisation, memory, visual perception and motor functioning (Chaytor & Schmitter-Edgecombe, 2003). Several current neuropsychological tests were developed based on psychometric theory. Within this framework, a comparison is made between the individual's raw score on a test or procedure and the scores of a larger population similar to the individual when one is available. These neuropsychological methods are also used in the field of clinical neuropsychology. Here neuropsychological techniques are used for the assessment, management and rehabilitation of people who have suffered illness or injury to the brain which has caused neuropsychological and cognitive problems.

SUMMARY

In this chapter an overview has been provided of the gross anatomy of the nervous system and anatomical terms of location; the mapping of the brain into Brodmann areas was discussed, and their relationship to the organisation of the cortex by cell type. We also discussed the various areas of the brain including the hindbrain, which we discovered was responsible for automatic functions like heart rate, breathing and reflexive responses like coughing, sneezing and salivating, and also contained the cerebellum, a walnut-shaped structure that regulates motor coordination and posture. The midbrain has two parts: the tegmentum and the tectum. The tegmentum regulates motor coordination and bodily movements, while the tectum comprises two structures: the inferior and the superior colliculi. The superior colliculus plays a role in vision and regulating eye movements and the inferior colliculus plays a role in hearing. The forebrain was also discussed, and it was discovered that it is the largest region of the brain and has two parts: the diencephalon and the telencephalon. The diencephalon contains the thalamus, the hypothalamus and the pituitary gland. The telencephalon consists of the limbic system, the basal ganglia and the cerebral cortex. The chapter went on to point out that the cerebral cortex comprises six separate and identifiable layers and again is divided into four separate lobes or areas: the occipital lobe, the parietal lobe, the temporal lobe and the frontal lobe. The occipital lobe is where visual stimuli are processed; the parietal lobe area integrates sensory information from various modalities, especially spatial awareness and navigation; and the temporal lobe contains the primary auditory cortex where auditory processing takes place. The largest lobe of them all is the frontal lobe, which amongst other things is in charge of complex processes including planning, coordinating, controlling and carrying out behaviour.

We also discussed brain imaging techniques and provided an overview of the techniques currently available to the researcher. Lesion techniques permanently or temporarily modify the nervous system of the animal under study and then the subsequent behaviour of the animal is measured. Electrical recording techniques such as EEG and MEG were reviewed and contrasted. Structural techniques of brain imaging were also discussed, including magnetic resonance imaging (MRI) which utilises magnetic fields to generate images of a person's brain structures without having to expose the patient to ionising radiation, and computerised tomography or a CT scan which is like a fancy X-ray of the brain. In addition, functional methods were examined and functional magnetic resonance imaging (fMRI) and positron emission tomography (PET) were discussed. The main advantage of fMRI is that it produces a non-invasive recording of brain signals without exposing the patient to the radiation risks associated with other scanning technologies, like CT or PET scans. Neurochemical techniques can be also be employed to determine the presence and distribution of various substances such as neurotransmitters in the brain. Cerebral dialysis is used to take measurements of the concentration of specific neurochemicals outside the cells in behaving animals, while in the 2-deoxyglucose method an animal is injected with radioactive 2-deoxyglucose which is absorbed by the active brain and examined at post-mortem. *In vivo* voltammetry is a process by which the extracellular concentration of neurochemicals in behaving animals is measured. Other methods include behavioural genetic techniques such as twin studies; such methods examine how genes and our surroundings may or may not affect the personalities, behaviours and psychopathologies of people. Finally we examined neuropsychological tests, where psychological functions are investigated utilising tasks which are believed to draw on a specific brain structure or pathway in both the normal population and clinical groups.

FURTHER READING

Aue, T., Lavelle, L.A., & Cacioppo, J.T. (2009). Great expectations: what can fMRI research tell us about psychological phenomena? *International Journal of Psychophysiology*, 73(1), 10–16.

Diamond, M.C., Scheibel, A.B., & Elson, L.M. (1985). *The human brain colouring book*. New York: HarperCollins.

KEY QUESTIONS

1 Describe the functions of each lobe of the brain.

2 Compare imaging and lesion techniques.

3 What are the advantages of the new imaging techniques for studying brain function?

3 GENES AND EVOLUTION

This chapter covers basic genetics and evolution and how our nervous system and our behaviour are affected by experiences. All of us inherit attributes from our parents, for instance our eye colour. However, some of the attributes we inherit are not visible. The mixture of the genes from your parents has established the characteristics of every cell in your body. These genetic sequences are found in the chromosomes of all cells, except the red blood cells, due to their lack of a nucleus.

DEOXYRIBONUCLEIC ACID (DNA)

DNA holds the information required to synthesise proteins. It controls the synthesis of enzyme proteins and structural proteins, thus having an impact on every facet of cell metabolism and growth. DNA holds the genetic information required to form cells and cellular components. The DNA carries this genetic information on structures called genes (Figure 3.1). The structure of DNA is based on two long polymers of components called **nucleotides**, which are composed of a five-carbon sugar (either ribose or 2-deoxyribose) and a phosphate group. DNA consists of four bases: adenine (A), cytosine (C), guanine (G) and thymine (T). Deoxyribose connects these four bases. Every base on one strand joins together with a corresponding base on the other strand; this is called complementary base pairing. A base pair is defined as a pair of nucleotides binding within the double helix.

A gene is a distinct portion of a cell's DNA, and genes are packaged in bundles called chromosomes. The location of a gene on a chromosome is referred to as its locus, and at any given locus a multitude of alternative forms of a gene can be exhibited; these are known as alleles. More information about gene mapping is given in Box 3.1. A dominant trait is the result of one allele dominating over another allele and expressing a particular trait, no matter what trait is carried by the other allele. An attribute influenced by a recessive allele will only be revealed in a person when there are two recessive alleles. When an allele pair is the same it is called **homozygous**, and a set of allele pairs that are different is called **heterozygous**.

BOX 3.1 How do we specify the location of a gene?

A review by Lander (2011) provides a brief overview of the way we locate a specific gene. Scientists will use a chromosome map to describe the location of a particular gene on a chromosome. One type of map uses the cytogenetic location to describe a gene's position. Cytogenetics is a branch of genetics that is concerned with the study of the structure and function of the cell. Cytogenetic locations are based on the distinct patterns of bands created when chromosomes are stained with particular agents or chemicals. Other types of map use molecular location, which is a precise description of the gene's position based on the sequence of DNA base pairs that make up the chromosome.

(Continued)

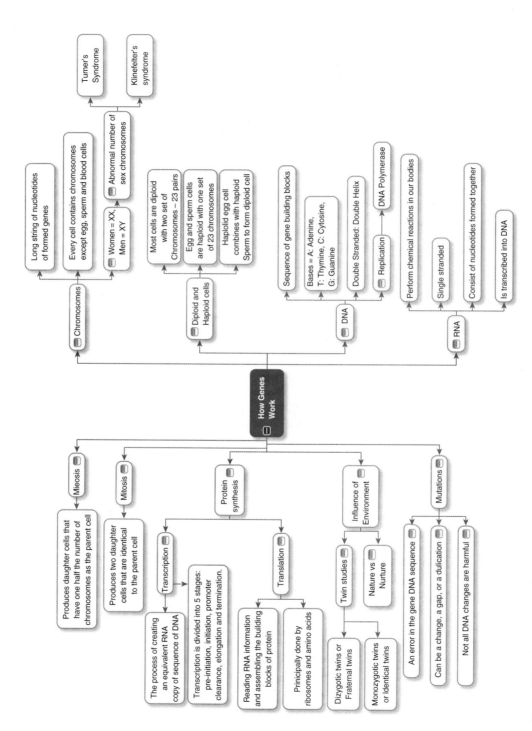

Figure 3.1 *How genes work*

(Continued)

Scientists who work on genes are called geneticists. They use a standard way of recording a gene's cytogenetic location. In this system the location describes the position of a particular band on a stained chromosome, such as 19q11. It can also be written as a range of bands if less is known about the exact location, e.g. 19q11–17. The arrangement of numbers and letters provides a gene's location or address on a chromosome. This location address is made up of several parts:

- The first number or letter represents the chromosome. Chromosomes 1 to 22 are designated by their chromosome number. The sex chromosomes are designated by X or Y.

- Chromosomes are divided into two sections by a centromere. The shorter arm is called p and the longer arm is called q. The chromosome arm is the second part of the gene's address.

- The final number in the address indicates the gene position on the chromosome, which increases with distance from the centromere. Thus 13q11 is closer to the centromere than 13q22.

In 2003 the Human Genome Project determined the sequence of base pairs for each human chromosome; this now allows a gene's molecular address to be specified and pinpoints the location of the gene in terms of base pairs. Lander (2011) provides an up-to-date impact report on the Human Genome Project.

Reference

Lander, E.S. (2011). Initial impact of the sequencing of the human genome. *Nature*, *10*(470), 187–197.

RIBONUCLEIC ACID (RNA)

Like DNA, ribonucleic acid or RNA is made up of a long chain of components called nucleotides. It is close in structure to DNA, with certain exceptions: RNA is usually single stranded, while DNA usually has two strands; in RNA nucleotides we find ribose, while in DNA we find deoxyribose (a type of ribose that is missing an oxygen atom); and RNA contains the base uracil and not thymine, which is found in DNA.

DNA enzymes (RNA polymerases) form RNA and are usually further processed by other enzymes. RNA is important for protein synthesis. In protein synthesis, a kind of RNA known as messenger RNA carries information from DNA to structures known as ribosomes. These ribosomes are created from a combination of proteins and ribosomal

RNAs, which unite to create a molecular machine that can interpret messenger RNAs and translate the information they contain into proteins. Modified versions of RNA are responsible for regulating gene expression.

DNA REPLICATION

Before cell division can take place, the DNA in the parent cell has to be duplicated so that after cell division the new cell contains the correct amount of DNA. This duplication process is sometimes referred to as DNA replication, and it ultimately produces new cells with one strand of original DNA and one strand of newly formed DNA. The process uses the original strand of DNA as a template to manufacture the new DNA. The process is very complicated and is as yet not fully understood; however, as we shall see there are many enzymes and proteins involved.

At a specific point along the DNA chain, the double helix of DNA unwinds, leaving each strand of DNA to serve as a template to guide the synthesis of its complementary strand of DNA. This initial unwinding of the DNA chain is aided by enzymes called topoisomerases; then DNA polymerases, another group of enzymes, assist in DNA replication. To begin synthesis, a short fragment of DNA or RNA called a primer is created and paired with the template DNA strand. DNA polymerase then synthesises a new strand of DNA by adding new nucleotides to the sugar (3') end matched to the template strand one at a time via the creation of phosphodiester bonds (Figure 3.2).

The next stage is that the DNA polymerase starts to move along the DNA strand in the sugar (3') to phosphate (5') direction. It does this by using the single-stranded DNA as a template. This newly synthesised strand is necessary for forming new nucleotides and reforming a double helix, and is often referred to as the leading strand because DNA synthesis can only occur in the 5' to 3' direction. As the double helix opens, a second DNA polymerase molecule is employed to attach to the other template strand. This molecule

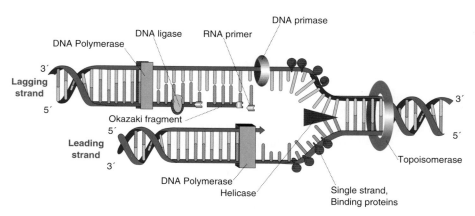

Figure 3.2   *DNA replication*

creates small segments of short DNA fragments called Okazaki fragments. DNA ligase, another enzyme, is responsible for stitching these fragments together into the lagging strand.

CELL DIVISION

Cell division is a process where two cells are formed from one. There are two types of division: mitosis, the process of making new cells in the body; and **meiosis**, the process of cell division that creates an ovum (egg cell) or sperm cell (Figure 3.1).

MITOSIS

Mitosis is a term used to describe cell division which results in the production of two daughter cells from a single parent cell. The daughter cells are identical to each other and to the original parent cell. This process is generally followed by another process called cytokinesis, which separates the nuclei, cytoplasm, organelles and cell membrane into two cells. The processes of mitosis and cytokinesis are termed the mitotic (M) phase of the cell cycle. Before a dividing cell enters the mitosis process, it undergoes a period of growth called interphase. Interphase is the preparation stage during which the cell replicates its genetic material and organelles in preparation for division.

The process of mitosis is divided into stages of prophase, prometaphase, metaphase, anaphase and telophase. Let's briefly look at some important events in each step in the process (Figure 3.3).

Prophase

During the prophase, the centrioles separate from each other, lengthening the microtubule bundle between them. In the nucleus, the chromosomes, which are organised into long entangled structures called chromatin, become more tightly coiled and condense into chromosomes. Each chromosome that has been duplicated is now seen as two identical sister chromatids joined at the centromere. At this stage of division, 46 chromosomes can be seen.

Prometaphase

During prometaphase the nuclear envelope begins to break down and the organelles decompose into vesicles. A structure called a kinetochore is formed as the spindle fibres from each centrosome link to one of the two sister chromatids. The centrosomes then start to journey to the opposite poles of the cell. When this process is taking place, the chromosomes are moved to the middle of the cell by the kinetochore microtubules.

Metaphase

The nuclear envelope breaks down in this phase and the metaphase plate is formed as all the chromosomes align at the centre of the cell. The metaphase plate forms a plane within the cell that is equally distant from the two spindle poles.

Anaphase

In anaphase the centromeres of each sister chromatid pair are pulled apart as the spindle fibres shorten. The process also sees the cell elongate.

Telophase

In this stage the chromosomes at each end of the cell are enclosed in a nuclear membrane. The chromosomes then form into chromatin, and the process of cytokinesis divides the nuclei, cytoplasm, organelles and cell membrane into two cells. Mitosis is then complete with the formation of two new cells.

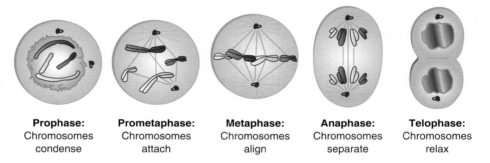

Prophase:
Chromosomes
condense

Prometaphase:
Chromosomes
attach

Metaphase:
Chromosomes
align

Anaphase:
Chromosomes
separate

Telophase:
Chromosomes
relax

Figure 3.3   *Mitosis*

MEIOSIS

Meiosis ensures that an organism has the same number of chromosomes in each generation. It is a two-step process, namely meiosis I and meiosis II, and it reduces the chromosome number by half, which in the case of humans is from 46 chromosomes to 23 chromosomes to form sperm and egg cells. When the sperm and egg cells unite at conception, each contributes 23 chromosomes, so the resulting embryo will have the usual 46 (see Figure 3.4).

Before entering the two stages of meiosis, the parent cell first goes through a preparatory phase known as interphase. In this phase, the cell mass is increased with the synthesis of more DNA and proteins, and the cell doubles its number of chromosomes. The cell then enters the first stage of meiosis.

In a similar way to mitosis, the process of meiosis is divided into four stages of prophase, metaphase, anaphase and telophase. Let's briefly look at some important events in each step in the process.

Meiosis I

Meiosis I is divided into four phases as follows (Figure 3.5).

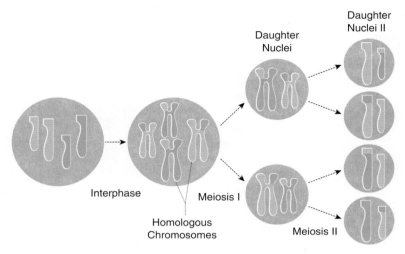

Figure 3.4   *Meiosis*

Prophase I

In this phase the chromosomes condense and attach themselves to the nuclear envelope. A process of synapsis occurs, in which homologous chromosomes line up together to form a tetrad of four chromatids. The exchange of genetic material between homologous chromosomes, or **crossing over,** can occur at this point. The chromosomes then thicken and detach from the nuclear envelope. The centrioles move away from one another and the nuclear envelope breaks down. The chromosomes then start to move to the metaphase plate.

Metaphase I

During this phase, pairs of homologous chromosomes take up positions along the centre line of the cell. The centromeres are located in the opposite poles.

Anaphase I

During this phase the chromosomes move to the opposite poles of the cell. The sister chromatids still remain together.

Telophase I

In telophase I the chromosomes maintain movement towards the poles which now have a haploid number of chromosomes. Cytokinesis takes place and the nuclear envelope begins to form. This results in the creation of two daughter cells with haploid chromosome numbers.

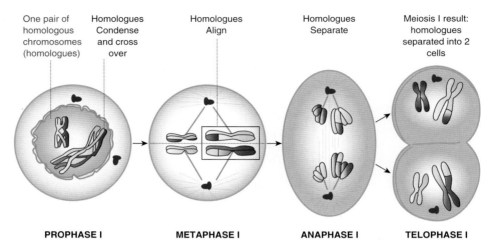

Figure 3.5   *Meiosis I*

Meiosis II

Meiosis II comprises the following four stages (Figure 3.6).

Prophase II
In prophase II the nuclei and nuclear membrane separate and the chromosomes begin their journey to the equatorial plane. The centromere still holds the two sister chromatids.

Metaphase II
In this phase the chromosomes align at the centre of the cell, or the equator, and the centromeres point in the direction of the opposite poles.

Anaphase II
The sister chromatids are separated by the spindle fibres.

Telophase II
Four nuclei are created, two in each daughter cell. The process of cytokinesis has also created four nuclei and nuclear envelopes, thus forming four daughter cells or **gametes**.

   The four gametes or daughter cells are haploid in nature, containing only half the number of chromosomes of a diploid cell. These two gamete cells, one from each parent, may be united by fertilisation, creating a cell or **zygote** with double the number of chromosomes. This process of meiosis and fertilisation of gametes creates the variation we see in organisms.

MEIOSIS II: Separate the Sister Chromatids (by mitosis)

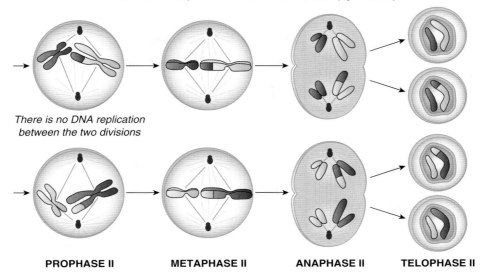

There is no DNA replication
between the two divisions

PROPHASE II   METAPHASE II   ANAPHASE II   TELOPHASE II

Figure 3.6   *Meiosis II*

PROTEIN SYNTHESIS

As already highlighted, the DNA that makes up the human genetic code can be broken down into small units of information called genes. Each gene is the blueprint for a distinctive protein that carries out specific functions in the cell. A two-step process of transcription and translation is used by each cell to read each gene and manufacture the sequence of amino acids that creates a protein.

Transcription is the means by which the genetic information accumulated in a strand of DNA is duplicated into a strand of RNA. RNA serves several purposes in the cell, a number of which have to do with translation, where the genetic code of messenger RNA facilitates the production of certain proteins in the ribosomes. **Transfer RNA** translates the nucleotide sequence into a sequence of amino acids. RNA molecules also have the ability to act as enzymes. They can work together with protein or they can work independently to assist the newly synthesised RNA molecules as they do their job.

PRE-INITIATION COMPLEX AND PROMOTERS

Transcription begins at sites on DNA known as promoters, which are usually 20 to 150 base pairs in length depending on the organism. RNA polymerase (RNAP), the enzyme that manufactures RNA, is able to identify the sequence of bases at a promoter.

The RNA polymerases in both viruses and bacteria can recognise specific promoter sequences without the aid of any other cellular proteins. But in organisms that have eukaryotic cells, other proteins known as initiation factors are able to recognise the promoter sequence and utilise RNA polymerase and other proteins to help the RNA polymerase to adhere to the DNA and manage the enzyme's actions. RNA polymerase is constructed on promoters in a specific arrangement.

This facilitates the production of RNA at a specific site and allows it to proceed in only one direction, 'downstream' towards the gene. The most common promoter in eukaryotes is a short DNA sequence called a TATA box; this is a DNA sequence that indicates where a genetic sequence can be read and decoded. It contains a promoter sequence, typically found 30 base pairs 'upstream' of the transcription start site, which specifies to other molecules where transcription begins. A transcription factor called the TATA binding protein (TBP) binds specifically to the TATA box. Another key substance, transcription factor IID (TFIID), binds directly to the promoters and proteins. Following this TFIID binding to the TATA box by way of the TBP, other transcription factors and RNA polymerases unite around the TATA box in a series of stages, thus forming a pre-initiation complex.

RNA SYNTHESIS

RNA, similarly to DNA, consists of a nucleotide containing sugar that is bound to a phosphate cluster and any of four bases. When RNA polymerase constructs the chain of nucleotides, it makes only one out of two adjacent strands of DNA. The first DNA strand serves as the template, and the other strand is referred to as the coding strand. The bases of the newly synthesised RNA complement the bases in the template DNA strand and fall into the same sequence as the bases in the coding strand, with the exception of the fact that RNA contains uracil (U) instead of the thymine (T) contained in the DNA.

Initiation

RNA synthesis begins with the initiation step (Figure 3.7). Initiation is the binding of the transcription mechanism to the DNA template; this process begins at sites selected by the promoter DNA sequence. When the growing RNA links obtain a length of around 10 nucleotides, the complex releases contact with the promoter and begins moving among the DNA. This is termed promoter 'clearance' or 'escape'. After the developing RNA chain reaches the critical length of approximately 10 nucleotides, the initiation stage is over and elongation starts. Just a tiny number of initiation events cause promoter clearance, and many attempts never achieve fruition. In these instances, RNA synthesis restarts. In some situations, a smaller RNA with fewer than 10 nucleotides separates from the polymerase, leading to a restart of the synthesis.

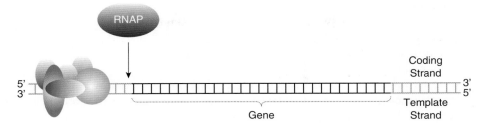

Figure 3.7   *Initiation*

Elongation

During the elongation phase of transcription, nucleotides are added to the developing RNA chain. As the RNA polymerase travels along the DNA template strand, it comes in contact with a number of genes that contain blocks of DNA called introns, which interrupt the coding information of the gene (Figure 3.8). Splicing removes these introns from the newly synthesised RNA.

Figure 3.8   *Elongation*

Termination

When the enzyme RNA polymerase arrives at a terminator, it separates the entire transcription molecule from the DNA that is being copied (Figure 3.9). The released RNA polymerase is then able to connect to a new initiation event.

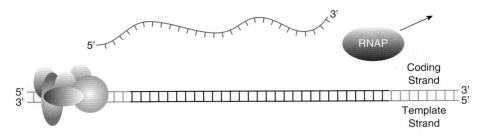

Figure 3.9   *Termination*

TRANSCRIPTION REGULATION

At any given moment, only a handful of an organism's genes are being expressed. Which genes are expressed relies on such things as the nutrition available, the cell's state of differentiation, and the age of the cell.

There are two major forms of transcription regulation. One is known as positive control, where transcription is an enhanced reaction to a specific set of circumstances. In opposition, so-called negative control suppresses transcription. Proteins that are activators allow positive control by sticking to the promoter to transport the RNA polymerase necessary for the beginning proteins. Repressor proteins are able to slow down the start of transcription by attaching themselves to the promoter and mitigating RNA polymerase.

TRANSLATION

Translation takes place in the cytoplasm within the cell, and is one of the phases of synthesising protein and of the general process of gene expression. The ribosome interprets the messenger RNA (mRNA) that was created by the process of transcription to synthesise a certain chain of amino acids that ultimately folds into an active protein.

GENETIC MUTATIONS

Gene mutations can be inherited from a parent or acquired during a person's lifetime. Hereditary mutations are passed from a parent, whereas the mutations picked up through a person's life are termed acquired mutations. Environmental factors such as ultraviolet radiation from the sun can cause these kinds of mutation.

The mutating of genes happens when the base order or number in a gene has been altered. Changes in nucleotide order, due to additions, subtractions, reversals or doubling, all impact the genetic code of the individual. The mutation of genes most often has little or no effect, but when it does, the effect may be fatal or disease inducing. Beneficial mutations will be selected for the evolutionary procedure and will continue to develop in the particular species until it becomes the norm.

SEX CELLS

The majority of human cells contain 46 chromosomes, but the sex cells (sperm and egg) only contain 23 chromosomes. Your mother and your father both pass one chromosome of each type to you. The somatic cells are called diploid, since they are two complete chromosome sets. The gametes, also known as the sex cells, i.e. the cells of the sperm and eggs, each contain 50% of the chromosomes in somatic cells (23 half pairs), and these are called haploid cells. During conception, the male sperm fuses with the female egg, resulting in a 46 chromosome embryo.

Gametogenesis is the process by which germ cells (gametocytes) are formed. The cells split via meiosis into gametes. Meiosis reduces the amount of chromosome sets from two to one; in other words, it changes diploid gametocytes into haploid gametes. **Gonads** are organs that produce gametes in animals. Genetic material recombines during meiosis through the crossing over of chromosomes. Crossing over makes it possible for genetic material to be transferred from one chromosome in the pair to the other, thereby combining the initial genes inherited from the mother and father, and increasing genetic differences between children (Figure 3.10). All chromosomes and their associated genes come in pairs, with the exception of **sex chromosomes**. The manipulations in the XY sex determination method give rise to girls, who have two identical sex chromosomes (XX), and boys, who have two different kinds of sex chromosomes (XY).

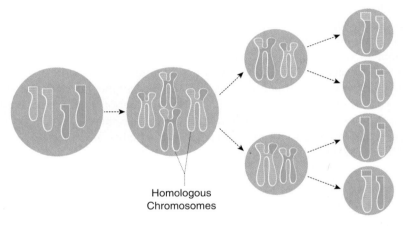

Homologous
Chromosomes

Figure 3.10   *Crossing over of chromosomes*

A number of disorders correlate to atypical quantities of sex chromosomes. Two of the most frequently occurring problems are Turner's syndrome and Klinefelter's syndrome.

Turner's syndrome

In Turner's syndrome, people only have a single sex chromosome, so males and females are either X or Y. This syndrome manifests as unnatural sexual development in females (Kyobe & Gitau, 1984). Affected people display characteristics like a low hairline, a strangely shaped chest, and nipples that are far apart. Individuals with this disorder tend to have abnormal cardiovascular and renal systems, and one in every 10 is also cognitively impaired. There is abnormal sexual development, as secondary sex traits are underdeveloped and ovarian dysgenesis (no ovaries) is frequently seen. It is not uncommon for this disorder to go undiagnosed until it is noted that the child has not begun puberty. Treatment typically consists of **oestrogen** hormones, allowing the child to begin puberty; however, individuals will remain sterile.

Klinefelter's syndrome

Most people with Klinefelter's syndrome exhibit one extra female sex chromosome, leading to an XXY pattern; hence they have 47 chromosomes instead of the usual 46 (Mandoki, Sumner, Hoffman, & Riconda, 1991). This happens in one out of 500 males and results in small **testes**, lack of sperm development, delayed puberty and diminished sexual traits; some people with the condition will have learning disabilities, with most of these having behavioural issues. Treating the patient with testosterone will result in a typical male appearance, but the person will remain sterile.

INFLUENCE OF THE ENVIRONMENT ON GENE EXPRESSION

When individuals discuss the topic of 'nature versus nurture', frequently there is a predisposition to talk about the proportion of a trait that is genetic as opposed to environmental. There are two major problems here. First, the proportionate contributions of genes and environment to a specific characteristic vary from individual to individual. Second, we are not able to reverse time and expose the same individual to different environments so that we can observe the influence of genetic and environmental factors in determining traits; thus we cannot fully be sure that a particular amount of someone's phenotype is the result of environment. So the old debate about whether there is more influence from heredity or environment doesn't mean much, since heredity and surroundings are both important (Ridley, 2003) (see Box 3.2).

BOX 3.2   Natural born killers?

Background

Although violent and criminal behaviour are probably related to a range of complex environmental and social circumstances, certain neurobiological factors have been implicated. One gene associated with impulsive aggression in animals and humans is the monoamine oxidase A (MAOA) gene. This study (Meyer-Lindenberg et al., 2006) investigated the impact of different variants of the MAOA gene on brain structure and function.

Methods

Three functional magnetic resonance paradigms were used to assess aspects of emotional and cognitive control in healthy volunteers. The participants were divided into groups according to variations of the MAOA gene and whether they had either the MAOA-L or the MAOA-H (low- or high-transcription variants). The tasks were associated with behaviours that were related to limbic circuitry and conceptually linked to impulse control.

Results

The study showed that when compared with the high-expression allele, the low-expression variant, which had previously been associated with increased risk of violent behaviour, showed limbic volume reductions and hyper-responsive amygdala during emotional arousal, with reduced activity of regulatory prefrontal regions. In males they found that the low-expression allele was associated with changes in orbitofrontal volume, amygdala and hippocampus hyper-reactivity during aversive recall, and impaired cingulate activation during cognitive inhibition.

Interpreting the finding

The differences in the activity of limbic regions which regulate emotion and cognitive control may be linked to the MAOA gene, previously believed to play a role in impulsive aggression and violence. This suggests that the neural systems for social adaptation and cognition could be partially under genetic control.

Reference

Meyer-Lindenberg, A., Buckholtz, J.W., Kolachana, B., Harari, R.A., Pezawas, L., Blasi, G., et al. (2006). Neural mechanisms of genetic risk for impulsivity and violence in humans. *Proceedings of the National Academy of Science USA, 103*(16), 6269–6274.

Inheritance and environment do not have equal input into each trait. For instance the iris pigmentation of the eye, otherwise known as eye colour, is influenced by hereditary factors, so individual variations in the colour of the eyes are usually due to genetic factors rather than environmental changes. However, one cannot draw the conclusion that other characteristics (like height, weight and intellect) are as minimally influenced by environment as is eye colour. Even though tall parents usually produce tall children (and short parents usually produce short children), which makes an argument for a hereditary influence on height, we also know that children with poor diets might not reach their potential height, which argues for an environmental influence as well. There is no method by which we can accurately determine the individual influences of genetics and environment on the height of a specific person, but we can draw inferences by using twin studies.

Monozygotic (identical) twins

Identical twins develop as a result of one egg being fertilised to form one zygote (monozygotic) that ultimately splits into two unique embryos. The two cells may grow in the uterus on their own and grow into an individual. The outcome of splitting at an early embryonic stage may be the development of a set of identical twins. Because identical twins develop out of the same egg, they carry exactly the same genetic material (even though their fingerprints differ).

Dizygotic (fraternal) twins

Sometimes two eggs are released by the ovaries concurrently, and it is possible for each egg to simultaneously be fertilised by separate sperm cells and implant themselves, resulting in the development of fraternal twins. Twins that develop in different eggs and have different sperm cells can be the same sex or opposites sexes; fraternal twins are genetically no closer in composition than siblings from different pregnancies. The only difference between them and other siblings is that they shared a womb and entered the world at approximately the same time.

What we can infer from twin studies

The twin studies performed today evolved from Sir Francis Galton's early use of twins to examine the influence of genetics and environment on human development and behaviour. Twin studies are often used in behavioural genetics to help identify the differences between environmental and genetic factors influencing behaviour. Researching twins is vital to separating the effects of nature and nurture because twins have the same genes and grow up in the same environment. Studying children in a family may demonstrate that these children are more alike than can be explained by chance. This may demonstrate shared environmental factors that all family members experience, like socioeconomic status, parenting styles, education, etc., but it also demonstrates genetic similarities inherited from the mother and father.

The twin design method makes a comparison between the similarities of identical twins (whose genetic information is 100% the same) and those of fraternal twins (whose genetic information is only 50% the same). By examining families of twins, researchers are able to investigate the role of genetic effects, and the effects of similar and disparate environments. Any characteristic that is objectively measurable among identical and fraternal twins may be evaluated for the specific mix of genetic and environmental factors that impinge upon it. Human intellect is an intricate characteristic and its genetics have been the centre of much controversy for many years (Deary, Johnson, & Houlihan, 2009). A good deal of the controversy is due to the fact that intelligence is ill defined, and the means of measuring intelligence is based on standardised IQ tests put together by psychologists, who generally did not build in control for cultural, environmental and schooling differences. Consequently, we describe intellect in terms of IQ scores, which are calculated by administering several different cognitive examinations. Some research has found that society influences IQ scores, but others have asserted that genetics may control IQ test scores by 60% to 80%. Intelligence has the greatest amount of assortative mating of any characteristic, which means that people tend to have relationships with people that have similar IQ (Mascie-Taylor & Boldsen, 1984). One should always be cautious in interpreting studies of twins dealing with psychological characteristics like IQ, because even identical twins can develop very different relationships with their parents and have disparate interests. This means that the environment and their interactions within it can be vastly different as well, thus making it very difficult to determine the relative contribution of genes and environments to specific attributes.

Twin studies can be used to evaluate how much of a role heredity plays in characteristics that are more black-and-white or qualitative. These investigators use case studies where at least one of the twins has the characteristic. For instance, in approximately 50% of all identical twin pairs where one of the two siblings demonstrates symptoms of schizophrenia, the other twin is concordant for the disorder, i.e. additionally reveals the signs of schizophrenia. Identical twins often share similar environments, so this information alone will not allow the effects of heredity and environment to be distinguished. In fraternal twins of the same gender that grow up together, the concordance of schizophrenia tends to be lower than 20%. It is apparent that schizophrenia develops far more readily in certain genotypes, suggesting a powerful genetic predisposition to developing the trait (Shastry, 2002).

THE EVOLUTION OF THE NERVOUS SYSTEM

The framework of evolution is founded upon the ideas that, similar to the evolution of our other organs and immune systems, our nervous system and the ability to process thought have a functional structure that is based in genetics and has evolved by natural selection; and that, similar to other aspects of evolution, this functional structure is common within a species (Darwin, 1859).

The mapping of these processes is sometimes illustrated as a **phylogenetic** tree, detailing the evolutionary relationships of a group of organisms that trace their roots back to the same ancestors. Evolution is defined as the process and ultimate change in the genetic coding of a group of organisms from one generation to the next. Even though the changes observed in a generation are minor, there is a cumulative effect as these slight changes occur during each generation and, in time, we can observe enormous changes in the organisms. We can follow the evolution of the nervous system from examining the most basic system to the most complex system (Figure 3.11).

DIFFUSE NERVOUS SYSTEMS

Most animals belong to the class of invertebrates – that is, lacking a backbone. Even though these creatures have a less complicated nervous system than vertebrates, they've effectively adapted to a broad and diverse environment. Studying invertebrates has been crucial to understanding the inner working of the nervous system, because although they have simpler nervous systems than vertebrates, it is far less complicated to isolate and evaluate neural functions in these animals.

The least complex nervous system is the diffuse nervous system. Nerve cells are found all through an organism that has a diffuse system. Neurons within these nervous systems combine to form ganglia. We see diffuse systems in cnidarians (like jellyfish, sea anemones and corals). The primitive nervous systems associated with these organisms will typically respond in the same way to stimuli regardless of where on the organism the contact occurs.

The majority of diffuse nervous systems seen in cnidarians have what is known as a nerve net – a mesh-like system of individual and separate neurons and fibres spread out throughout the organism. The nerve net permits an organism to exhibit a number of different behaviours, like eating and swimming.

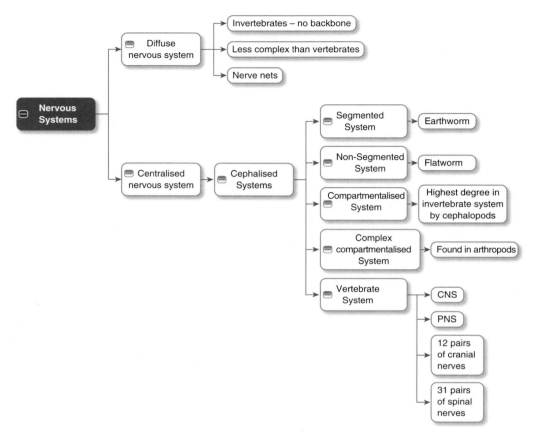

Figure 3.11   *Nervous systems*

A little more advanced is the 'brain' of a roundworm. These organisms seem to have a longitudinal nerve cord with an anterior gathering of nerve cells that we can consider to be a brain. There are sensory and other pathways in addition to coordinating interneurons. The complex nervous system that will develop later in the evolutionary process has its simple beginnings in ganglia concentrated at an organism's head. Through evolution, nerves have concentrated in the area of the head, a process known as cephalisation. As you move from complex invertebrates to vertebrates, you will observe an increase in cephalisation.

CENTRALISED NERVOUS SYSTEMS: CEPHALISED

One of the first organisms to develop a central nervous system governed by a brain was the flatworm (Figure 3.12a). When we observe the parts of a flatworm's nervous system, we see a brain, longitudinal nerve cords and peripheral nerve plexuses (enmeshed networks of peripheral nerves). Flatworms and roundworms have unsegmented nervous systems,

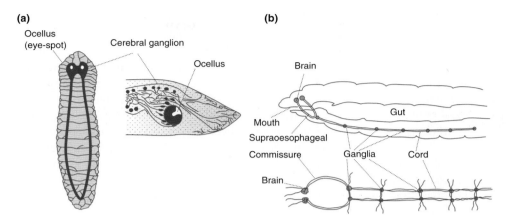

Figure 3.12 *(a) Flatworm nervous system: left, dorsal aspect of whole animal; right, section of anterior end, in plane parallel to midline. (b) Earthworm nervous system*

meaning they behave as one unit. In contrast, earthworms have nervous systems that are segmented (Figure 3.12b), and each segment is able to act entirely on its own. The cerebral region, or brain, is attached to the ventral nerve cord, which travels through the whole body. At every segment there is a branching off of segmental ganglia, which connect all of the segments to the worm's brain. The segments exchange information with one another using interneurons that connect to adjacent segments, allowing for the control of muscle contractions in each segment that facilitate locomotion.

CENTRALISED NERVOUS SYSTEMS: COMPARTMENTALISED

We see the greatest development of the invertebrate nervous system in cephalopods (squids, octopuses), molluscs and arthropods (insects and spiders). The basic plan of the nervous system might look like that of less complex organisms, but we observe more cephalisation, with nervous functions that are mainly concentrated in the head region of the animal and where ganglia are fused and located more towards the front. Also, the nervous system is broken down into sections, with certain behaviours, like locomotion and eating, being managed by certain parts of the nervous system.

The cephalopods' intricate nervous system correlates with the active motion and predatory behaviours exhibited by these organisms. Most of a mollusc's ganglia are grouped together or fused inside a brain that circles around the oesophagus. Some parts of the brain of a cephalopod can distinguish between different items using basic learning and memory skills. The squid is one example of a living being that has a well-developed giant fibre nervous system. These creatures have nerve fibres that have a larger diameter than is typical; the fibres are capable of rapid conduction, allowing for very quick motion.

The eyes of cephalopods are well evolved and are very much like the eyes of a vertebrate. The eye, located in a socket, is moved by external muscles on the perimeter. Overlaying the outside of the eye, a cornea is capable of focusing on distant and close objects. In addition, a pupil formed by an iris diaphragm controls how much light reaches the retina. The retina contains photoreceptors, or rod cells, that create the optic nerves which relay information to the visual areas of the brain.

The cephalopods' nervous system is much more advanced than those discussed earlier and, hence, the behavioural parts are much more complicated. Both visual and sensory receptors are used by these animals to detect food by looking for changes in the environment. These predators can differentiate between desirable and undesirable prey and can 'learn' to attack or not. They are able to alter their colour so that, if they need to, they can blend right into their environment (Barbato, Bernard, Borrelli, & Fiorito, 2007).

Basic learning and memory skills have been observed at a cellular level by evaluating the nervous system of the marine slug (*Aplysia californica*) (Bristol, Marinesco, & Carew, 2004). This basic mollusc will pull back its gill and siphon as a reaction to gentle touch. The neural path for this reflex is made up of a sensory component from the siphon that creates single-synapse connections with motor neurons that make the gill retract. After experiencing a stimulus, the sensory neurons produce large excitatory postsynaptic potentials (EPSPs) at both interneurons and motor neurons, resulting in the production of action potentials in the motor neurons that ultimately make the gill pull back. If the animal experiences the stimulus repeatedly, the postsynaptic potentials get smaller and you will observe a weaker reaction. If postsynaptic potentials become very small, action potentials will no longer be generated and the gill will not respond. We call this reduced behavioural reaction 'habituation'. It is possible that habituation is the result of calcium channels closing, thus reducing the amount of calcium flowing into the presynaptic terminals and, consequently, reducing the release of neurotransmitters. There is some evidence that indicates habituation is the result of a reduced number of nerve cells in the network being activated.

Sensitisation has also been observed in a behavioural paradigm with *Aplysia*. In sensitisation the reflex movement grows in strength with additional stimulation. The underlying function that results in this response is presynaptic facilitation, which we believe is the result of an increase in the second messenger cyclic adenosine monophosphate (cAMP) in the terminals of the sensory neurons (Hawkins, Cohen, Greene, & Kandel, 1998).

These two illustrations of habituation and sensitisation demonstrate that the major components of a more complicated nervous system can be observed in organisms at lower evolutionary stages. One such characteristic of the nervous system shown by the alterations in the strength of synaptic responses is plasticity of the nervous system. The flexibility of the nervous system that is seen in the changes of synaptic efficacy and the structural changes at synaptic connections that result may be what is behind certain mechanisms for short- and **long-term memory** capabilities in human beings (see Chapter 11).

CENTRALISED NERVOUS SYSTEMS: COMPLEX COMPARTMENTALISED

Arthropods (invertebrate organisms which have an external skeleton) are known for their complicated nervous systems with distinct functional regions. Arthropod brains are made up of three principal sections: the protocerebrum, the deutocerebrum and the tritocerebrum. The anterior protocerebrum, where the nerves of the eyes and other organs are located, contains neuropils, where the anterior sense organs become integrated, particularly the eyes, and where movement is controlled; they are also the centres for the start-up of complex behaviour. The association point for the first antennae is located in the deutocerebrum. The posterior tritocerebrum makes up the association neuropils for the second antennae and produces the nerves that stimulate the parts of the mouth and the anterior digestive canal.

The digestive canal is very similar to the vertebrate system in that nutritional intake is managed, then passed through the gut. Different arthropods demonstrate varied levels of union of the ganglia. The first ganglion in insects, which is known as the suboesophageal ganglion, develops out of a fusing together of three pairs of ganglia, sending nerves to the various parts of the mouth and to the salivary glands. The appendages, heart, sense organs and dorsal muscles are connected via nerves from the segmental ganglia located in the thorax and the abdomen. Insects may have as many as 10 abdominal ganglia and three pairs of thoracic ganglia.

The most common sensory receptors that we see in arthropods are the cuticular hairs. Some of these are mechanoreceptors, which are highly responsive to touch and vibration, while others are chemoreceptors, which detect scents or chemicals. Hairs that are in a place close to the joints are stimulated by movements and hence give proprioception of the joint or appendage while in locomotion or in the air. The antennae contain a plethora of organs and cells that receive and process sensory input.

Crustaceans and insects have two well-formed compound eyes, each of which has several visual units known as ommatidia, while spiders have a number of pairs of basic eyes that have retinas in the shape of a cup. Even though insects are so small, some of their nerve cells have larger diameters than human nerve cells. As the number of insect neurons is relatively low, each neuron has to be able to handle the greatest quantity of information. Without doubt, simple neural circuitry is needed for quick reactions; although some information may be lost, nothing interferes with escaping from danger. Many believe that speedy actions to evade predators have most likely had an affect on the development of the giant fibre systems of worms and squid, along with crustaceans and insects. Nerve impulses conducted through these large axons move faster than impulses conducted through smaller axons. Even though the information management capabilities of small axons working together is much larger than that of giant axons, the circumstances under which these creatures survive make it clear that different systems evolved in the invertebrate nervous system as a reaction to the different qualities of environmental stimuli to which the organism had to respond; one was responsible for staying alive and the other for information.

THE VERTEBRATE SYSTEM

As we have seen earlier, vertebrates have nervous systems that are divided into two parts: the central nervous system, which is made up of the brain and spinal cord, and the peripheral nervous system, which, in humans, consists of 12 pairs of cranial nerves and 31 pairs of spinal nerves.

Neurons of the vertebrae are grouped together in clumps. Ganglia are accumulated within the peripheral nervous system and nuclei accumulate in the central nervous system. Certain areas of the central nervous system (those where unmyelinated neurons and neuroglia are in the majority) are referred to as grey matter; where myelinated neurons are more dominant, the areas are referred to as white matter. Efferent or motor neurons are nerve fibres that transmit information away from the central nervous system; fibres that transmit information to the central nervous system are known as afferent or sensory neurons.

The nerve fibres in the central nervous system are divided into groups known as tracts. Ascending tracts transmit information through the spinal cord to the brain, and descending tracts transmit information away from the brain or from higher parts of the spinal cord to lower parts. The names of the tracts are usually derived from their start and end points: for instance, the corticospinal tract is made up of fibres that run from the cerebral cortex in the brain to the spinal cord.

THE PRIMITIVE STATE

Vertebrates are part of a group of animals known as **Chordates** (phylum Chordata) which contains a number of closely related invertebrates. During a stage in their life, all chordates develop a rod-like structure, known as notochord, along the length of the body. The lower chordates (like acorn worms, tunicates and amphioxus) do not have a vertebral column, demonstrating the most basic characteristics of the chordate nervous system. These animals have nerve cords that are like hollow dorsal tubes, much like the spinal cord of the vertebrates, which suggests that the spinal cord may be the most primitive part of the central nervous system.

Vertebrate brains are formed by the growth of nerve cells that gather together at the cephalic (head) end of the nerve cord. Initially, this group of nerve cells managed the reflex activity of spinal motor neurons, and it compares to the **reticular activating system** that is found in the brain stem of higher vertebrates. The oldest area of the human brain is the brain stem.

ENCEPHALISATION

Early on in the evolutionary process, the sensory system became associated with parts of the brain; the olfactory system with the forebrain, the eye with the midbrain, and the ears with the hindbrain. Progress in these regions led to the development of the parts of the brain we now see in humans.

The roof of the midbrain in fish and amphibians, or the tectum, is the core of the nervous system, and is the main influence on body activity. While this area is still important in other vertebrates, it is overshadowed in importance by the cerebrum or cerebral hemispheres. The majority of optical sensory information is passed to the cerebral cortex in the brain in mammalian animals. As the brain develops, the role of the cerebral cortex in behaviour is increased, and the significance of the thalamus diminishes as an association region and transforms into more of a sensory relay station of the brain.

DOMINANCE OF THE CEREBRUM

The cerebral hemispheres start out as outgrowths from the forebrain and form the olfactory centres. Then the forebrain splits into two segments: the olfactory bulb – the terminus of the olfactory nerve fibres – and the cerebral hemisphere. At this point the cerebral hemispheres, or palaeopallium, only serve the sense of smell.

Because the sense of smell is so crucial, the three sections of the amphibian brain – the palaeopallium or olfactory lobe, the archipallium and the basal nuclei – are all areas involved with **olfaction** in some way. In amphibians, the archipallium is the forerunner of the mammalian hippocampus, while the basal nuclei are the same as the corpus striatum, which acts as an association region to the thalamus. The neopallium, which is located between the palaeopallium and the archipallium, is found in reptiles as an association centre.

Birds have larger basal ganglia and lack neopallium, while mammals have an enlarged neopallium, which makes up the biggest part of the brain. In mammals, this area of the brain governs the ability of the higher kinds of activity in association as well as in learning. In time, the neopallium became bigger, enveloping other parts of the brain; the archipallium folded into a smaller area where it became the hippocampus. Additional development of the neopallium in primates and humans results in general folding of the cortex and an extremely convoluted brain surface.

SUMMARY

This chapter has given an overview of the structure of DNA, explaining that it comprises four bases – adenine (A), cytosine (C), guanine (G) and thymine (T) – and that a sugar known as deoxyribose connects these four bases. The chapter described the process of DNA replication and the cell division cycles of mitosis and meiosis. Mitosis produces two daughter cells that are identical to the parent cell, whereas meiosis produces daughter cells that have half the number of chromosomes as the parent cell. We then discovered that the DNA contains the information for protein synthesis and described the two stages that were necessary: transcription and translation. Transcription is the means by which the genetic data accumulated in a strand of DNA are duplicated into a strand of RNA. Translation takes place in the cytoplasm within the cell, and is one of the phases of synthesising protein and of the general process of gene expression. The sex cells or gametes were discussed, showing that girls have two identical sex chromosomes (XX) and boys have two different kinds of sex chromosomes (XY). Two disorders were highlighted which are caused by atypical quantities of sex chromosome: Turner's syndrome and Klinefelter's syndrome. The chapter then went on to discuss the environmental influences on gene expression and emphasised that inheritance and environment do not have equal input into each trait; at present there is no method by which we can accurately determine the individual influences of genetics and environment. We can however draw inferences from twin studies.

The second part of the chapter investigated the evolution of the nervous system and illustrated how the development can be mapped as a phylogenetic tree, detailing the evolutionary relationships of a group of organisms that trace their roots back to the same ancestors. The diffuse nervous system is the least complex nervous system and is present in cnidarians (like jellyfish, sea anemones and corals). Unsegmented cephalised nervous systems were detailed, and it is here we can observe some of the basic learning and memory skills at a cellular level by evaluating the nervous system of the marine snail (*Aplysia*). Compartmentalised cephalised nervous systems were the next step in the development of the nervous system, and these systems can be seen in cephalopods (squids, octopuses), molluscs and arthropods (insects and spiders). The cephalopods' nervous system is much more advanced than earlier systems, and hence the behaviours are more complicated. Next we have the centralised nervous systems, which are more complex and compartmentalised. One group of organisms with this type of nervous system is called arthropods. These are known for their intricate nervous systems with distinct functional regions, with their brains being made up of three principal sections: the protocerebrum, the deutocerebrum and the tritocerebrum. The most complex nervous systems are found in vertebrates which, as you will remember, have nervous systems that are divided into two parts: the central nervous system, which is made up of the brain and spinal cord, and the peripheral nervous system, which in humans consists of 12 pairs of cranial nerves and 31 pairs of spinal nerves. The final sections of the chapter explained how the cerebral hemispheres, which started out as outgrowths from the forebrain, resulted in the general folding of the cortex and the extremely convoluted brain surface we see in humans today.

FURTHER READING

Darwin, C.R. (1859). *On the origin of species by means of natural selection, or the preservation of favoured races in the struggle for life*. London: John Murray.

Ridley, M. (2003). *Genes, experience, and what makes us human*. New York: Harper Collins.

Shastry, B.S. (2002). Schizophrenia: a genetic perspective (review). *International Journal of Molecular Medicine*, 9(3), 207–212.

KEY QUESTIONS

1   Describe the evolution of the human brain.

2   Describe the processes of transcription and translation in protein synthesis.

3   What is the 'nature versus nurture' debate?

4

DEVELOPMENT AND PLASTICITY OF THE BRAIN

CHAPTER OUTLINE

In this chapter, we are going to look at how the nervous system is built into a functional collection of neurons and glial cells (sometimes called neuroglia or simply glia) and how developmental biological psychology is interested in examining how nerve cells and glia arise out of stem cells and assemble themselves into structures, making the correct synaptic connections with one another to form the central nervous system. As discussed in Chapter 3, the nature–nurture debate is still highly contested in this area of brain function and development. Many people think that the development of the nervous system mainly involves internal genetic signals, and some argue that the environment continually affects and forms the nervous system. The current view promotes the idea that events occurring very early on are largely governed by an internal programme, but several of the events that occur later rely upon interactions between cells or between nerve cells and the environment. It is the plasticity after birth which shapes brain development, and it is not predetermined by our genetic programme but depends on interaction with our environment.

THE EMERGENCE OF THE NERVOUS SYSTEM

The structural development of the human nervous system is concerned with neuronal events happening in sequence at a given time of gestation. During the first half of gestation, neural proliferation and migration are mostly occurring; while in the second half of gestation the functional areas of the brain develop, which culminates in glial cell production and the process of programmed cell death. Axons, together with their dendrites and synapses, form during the final trimester and continue to flourish during the first postnatal years. The process of myelination will also continue during this first year of life. Synapse elimination occurs throughout life, with the peak events happening during puberty and early adulthood, while neurotransmitter substances and systems are present early in gestation. You can see that these processes track the development of an individual from embryo to adult – otherwise termed a sequence of **ontogenetic** activities.

To aid in the understanding of the process, the development of the nervous system is separated into eight phases (Figure 4.1):

1 *induction* of the neural plate and formation of the neural tube

2 *proliferation* of precursor cells that will give rise to neurons and glial cells

3 *migration* of neurons and glial cells to the place where they will finally reside

4 *aggregation* of neurons into identifiable structures

5 *differentiation* into mature neurons

6 *synaptogenesis*, the formation of functional synapses with other neurons

7 *selective cell death* of many neurons or neuronal precursors

8 *functional validation* of the connections (begins before birth and continues throughout life).

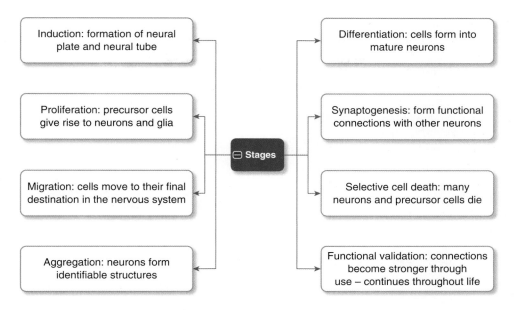

Figure 4.1 *Phases of development of the nervous system*

INDUCTION

The prenatal period of our life is split into three key stages: the germinal period between zero and two weeks, the embryonic stage between two and eight weeks, and the foetal period between week 9 and birth. All of this starts with fertilisation in the fallopian tube. After fertilisation, cell division occurs in the embryo and a ball of cells is formed called the morula, consisting of cells called blastomeres. A cavity then forms known as the blastocyst. There are two gastrula layers, the ectoderm (ecto = outside) and the endoderm (endo = inside), and later the mesoderm (meso = middle) forms a third layer between them. Cells inside the embryo are now noticeably different and these three layers give rise to different structures of the mature human. Eventually, the ectoderm becomes the skin and nervous system; the mesoderm will develop into the muscle, blood and bone of the mammal; and the endoderm creates the stomach and internal organs. The first stage of neurulation is the thickening of the ectoderm or outer layer forming the neural plate. The edges of the neural plate start to curl up from 'head' to 'tail' along the developing embryo, which results in the formation of the neural tube, called neural induction, which ultimately becomes the complete central nervous system (Figure 4.2). Neural tube defects like anencephaly or spina bifida occur when the neural folds in some embryos fail to close. In spina bifida, a disorder whose name is derived from the Latin for 'split spine', a baby is born with an incompletely developed spinal cord. In addition to this, the vertebrae surrounding the open area of the spinal cord do not totally form and remain unfused and open. Folic acid supplements taken every day

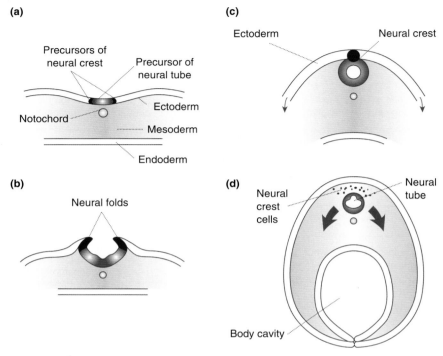

Figure 4.2   *Neural induction*

before conception can decrease the occurrence of spina bifida by as much as 70%. Anencephaly is a disorder where some of the neural tube that grows into the cerebrum fails to close. Infants with this ailment are typically stillborn, and those born alive die quickly following birth. The neural crest comprises separated, selected migratory cells that are located over the neural tube. The outward migration of the neural crest cells form several types of tissue that include both sensory and autonomic neurons, which are connected to the peripheral nervous system. The neural tube produces the central nervous system.

The developing brain

The rostral (anterior) area of the neural tube becomes the brain, while the caudal (posterior) region becomes the spinal cord. The developing brain first separates into three ventricles: the forebrain or prosencephalon; the midbrain or mesencephalon; and the hindbrain or rhombencephalon (Figure 4.3; see also Figure 2.4). Around the time the embryo reaches its fourth week of development, the forebrain and the hindbrain divide. The forebrain divides into the telencephalon and the diencephalon, and the hindbrain divides into the metencephalon and the myelencephalon (Table 4.1).

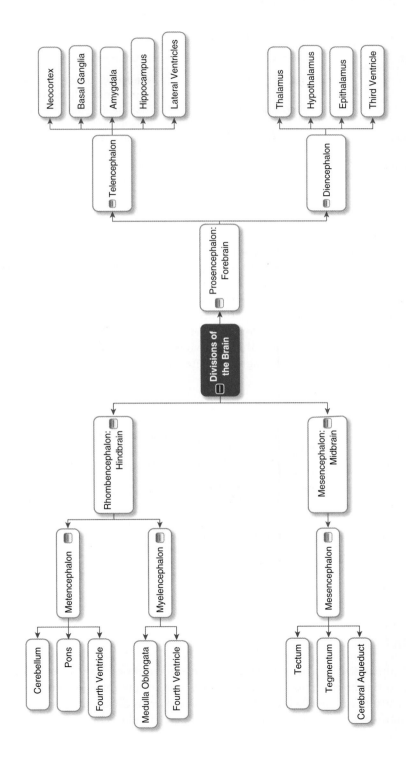

Figure 4.3 *Divisions of the brain*

Table 4.1 *Divisions of the brain: five-part structure*

Major division	Subdivision	Structures
Prosencephalon (forebrain)	Telencephalon	Neocortex; basal ganglia; amygdala; hippocampus; lateral ventricles
	Diencephalon	Thalamus; hypothalamus; third ventricle
Mesencephalon (midbrain)	Mesencephalon	Tectum; tegmentum; cerebral aqueduct
Rhombencephalon (hindbrain)	Metencephalon	Cerebellum; pons; fourth ventricle
	Myelencephalon	Medulla oblongata; fourth ventricle

Spinal cord development

During the development of the spinal cord, two major zones of cells form. A cross-section view of the mantle layer reveals that it forms grey matter in the shape of a butterfly and the lateral walls of the tube get thicker, leaving a shallow, longitudinal groove known as the sulcus limitans. The sulcus limitans separates the neural tube into a dorsal or alar plate and a ventral or basal plate. The alar plate becomes the sensory portion of the mature nervous system and the basal plate becomes the motor portion. The basal plate also gives rise to the sympathetic and parasympathetic nervous systems. The sulcus limitans extends the length of the spinal cord and through the mesencephalon of the brain (Figure 4.4).

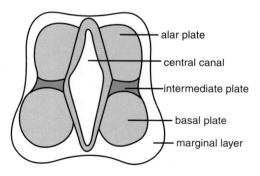

Figure 4.4 *Development of the spinal cord*

PROLIFERATION

As previously discussed, the nervous system develops from one layer of ectodermal cells that are located on the inner surface of the neural tube. New cells are produced as these cells divide or proliferate. Cells lining the ventricles start to divide early in their development. A few of these cells grow into stem cells and keep dividing, but other cells grow into glial cells and neurons then begin to move to their permanent place in the brain. Nearly all cell division in the neural tube happens in the ventricular zone, which is the area adjacent to the ventricle. At this point, groups of cells experience a process known as doubling, which can result in an exponential growth in cells; each generation of cells has twice as many cells as its predecessor.

MIGRATION

The early nerve cells that have developed in the proliferation stage move closer to the intermediate zone of the developing neural tube. The subventricular zone is formed of neurons that combine to form a layer between the intermediate and ventricular zones. Cells located in this subventricular zone will become glial cells or interneurons. When the ventricular area is complete, the remaining cells become ependymal cells, which form the protective cover of the central canal of the spinal cord and both brain ventricles. As new cells force their way through these layers, the cortical plate develops in the forebrain. Through further development, the forebrain becomes the cerebral cortex. The established cortex is composed of six layers; the newest cells comprise the deepest layers, so that cells that comprise the subsequent higher layers must pass through the deep layers. The daughter cells turn into nerve cells and move from the inside to the outside surface of the new nervous system; this is sometimes called the inside-out pattern of cortical development. Even though cells appear to travel along certain routes, we still do not know much about how cell migration occurs. However, it is known that cell migration has numerous steps that involve sequential alterations in the cytoskeleton, cell–substrate adhesion, and components of the extracellular matrix. Some cells move radially from the inside of the brain to the outside, while others move tangentially around the surface of the brain (Nadarajah & Parnavelas, 2002). Radial glial cells, which are radiated from the inside to the outside surface of the developing nervous system, direct the process of migration (Figure 4.5). Migrating neurons move around these radial glial cells to reach their final destination (Marin & Rubenstein, 2001). Along with receiving the structural help of the radial glial cells, the nerve cells are also guided along the route by glycoproteins. Glycoproteins are substances such as cell adhesion molecules and cadherins, which are located on the uppermost layers of both neurons and radial glial cells (Karagogeos, 2003). Cadherins (named for 'calcium-dependent adhesion') are a class of type 1 transmembrane proteins which, together with cell adhesion molecules, cause neurons to stick to other neurons and glial cells and thus assist the migration of neurons by providing a sticky substance for moving along. When there is a lack of these chemicals, the movement of nerve cells becomes impaired, resulting in a smaller brain and numerous cognitive difficulties.

AGGREGATION

Once the developing neurons have arrived at their final destination, they have to line up with other neurons in the same area to make up the new brain; this is called aggregation.

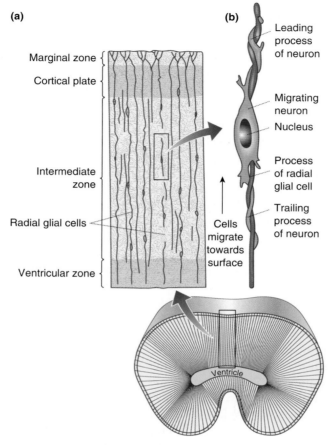

Figure 4.5 *The role of radial glial cells in development*

Neurons do not take on their final appearance until they attain their final destination in the developing nervous system, and this goal is achieved in two different ways:

⊛ *Cell-autonomous differentiation.* The nerve cell develops on its own, with no outside influences, ultimately attaining its final form by way of genetic programming. The Purkinje cell falls into this category, experiencing cell-autonomous differentiation and developing into a Purkinje cell even when cultured outside the body (Marino, Hoogervoorst, Brandner, & Berns, 2003).

⊛ *Induction.* Here nerve cells depend upon other nearby cells to dictate how they will ultimately appear. These nearby cells emit chemicals that cause the change of the nerve cell and, eventually, its ultimate form. For instance, the protein vitronectin has an impact on neurons to become spinal neurons (Pons & Marti, 2000).

Glial cells also develop in the ventricular area from cells identical to those that produce neurons, with the most prolific production happening after birth. No one knows why some cells grow into neurons and other cells turn into glial cells. One of the jobs performed by the glial cell is myelination of axons in the nervous system. This starts at approximately week 26 of gestation in the cranial and spinal nerves and then occurs in the spinal cord, hindbrain, midbrain and finally the forebrain.

This process of aggregation, similar to migration, is facilitated by a substance found on the nerve cell called a **neural cell adhesion molecule** (NCAM). Neural cell adhesion molecules combine with molecules that are located on different cells in the vicinity and bind with them, forming cell groups (Rutishauser, 1993).

DIFFERENTIATION AND AXON GROWTH

Once the neurons have reached their final destination, they establish connections with the nervous system to make a network of links. Axon growth is directed at the target cell, which can be another nerve cell or other structures like muscles or organs. The swollen ends of the developing axon, known as the growth cone, grow spiny cytoplasmic extensions referred to as filopodia (Figure 4.6), which stretch out from the growth cone, looking and reaching for their target. Upon reaching a target, they pull the growth cone which makes the growing axon longer.

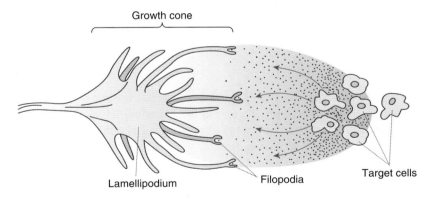

Figure 4.6 *Filopodia*

At present, researchers believe there are three ways growth cones find their intended goals: the chemoaffinity hypothesis, the blueprint hypothesis and the topographic gradient hypothesis.

Chemoaffinity theory

The chemoaffinity theory was originally formulated by Roger Sperry in the 1940s after he carried out a series of experiments on the growth of axons in the frog vision area. During one study, he cut the optic nerves of a frog and rotated each eyeball by 180° left to right. He then waited for the retinal ganglion cells of the visual system to repair themselves (Sperry, 1943). However, following the repair it was observed that the frog had inverted eyesight; for example, the frog moved its tongue in the wrong direction away from a food source stimulus. Sperry came to the conclusion that the regenerating fibres were restored to their original location in the optic tectum and resumed a topographical set of connections. In addition he postulated that each tectal neuron had chemical labels that uniquely identified their neuronal type and location so that optic fibres could utilise these chemical labels to selectively find their way to their corresponding target cell. This conclusion was constructed into a general theory as to how neurons form interconnections as they develop and regenerate, called the chemoaffinity hypothesis. The experiment is detailed in Box 4.1. Researchers think that the filopodia use the concentration gradient of the chemical which is released by the target cell in order to direct them. Additionally, target cells discharge **neurotrophins** to which filopodia are attracted, and lead the axon to its destination (Crone & Lee, 2002).

BOX 4.1   The chemoaffinity hypothesis

Background

The chemoaffinity hypothesis proposes that axons differentially distinguish chemical signals produced by target matching cells. In the early 1940s, Roger Sperry performed a series of experiments on the visual system of lower vertebrates that led him to draw two important conclusions about how the nervous system developed.

Method

Sperry (1943) designed a series of experiments in which the optic nerves were cut and the eyes rotated 180° left to right. The aim of the experiment was to see whether the animal's vision would return to normality after a period of adaptation or whether the animal would see the world as upside down.

Results

In all cases the results showed that the animal continued to act as if the world was upside down. When food was presented in the upper field, they looked down, and vice versa. These responses remained unchanged even after a period of training. When Sperry traced the regenerated optic nerves into the brain he found that the original pattern from eye to brain was maintained. The work was supported by further studies in amphibians and retinotectal regeneration in fish.

Interpreting the findings

Sperry's experimental results led him to theorise on the nature of this nerve guidance in the developing or regenerating nervous system. He suggested that each optic fibre and each tectal neuron had cytochemical labels that uniquely indicated their neuronal type and position. The optic fibre used these labels to selectively navigate to their targets. This idea was later formulated into what is known as the chemoaffinity hypothesis.

Reference

Sperry, R.W. (1943). Visuomotor coordination in the newt (*Triturus viridescens*) after regeneration of the optic nerve. *Journal of Comparative Neurology, 79,* 33–55.

Blueprint hypothesis

The chemoaffinity hypothesis can explain several facets of nerve cell development, but there are experiments where some target nerve cells have been transplanted into new locations in the nervous system and become incorrectly innervated (Whitelaw & Hollyday, 1983). One explanation, the blueprint hypothesis, suggests that the developing axons grow in the direction of their intended targets by following chemical or tactile cues. These chemicals or paths are thought to result from the work of the first growth cones to travel on a designated path. These first growth cones are called **pioneering** growth cones and follow the correct trail aided by neural cell adhesion molecules (Plachez & Richards, 2005). Other axons then travel along the routes laid down by the pioneering cells, and the bundling together of axons into tracts is called **fasciculation.**

The topographic gradient hypothesis

The topographic gradient theory suggests that axons growing from one topographic surface to another are guided to specific targets that are arranged on the target surface in the same way as the cell bodies of the axon are arranged on the original surface.

SYNAPTOGENESIS

After the axon arrives at the target cell, synaptogenesis (the development of a synapse) occurs. This stage continues throughout a person's lifespan, and while it does slow down as a person ages, it plays a key part in the plasticity of the brain in learning and rehabilitation following injury.

SELECTIVE CELL DEATH

In some parts of the nervous system, the majority of the nerve cells die while they are developing (Oppenheim, 1991) because of the competition of nerve cells for target cells. The nerve cells that make connections survive, while the ones that do not ultimately die. This is sometimes referred to as neural Darwinism. Nearly 50% more neurons are created than needed, and it is thought the cells that die do this because they compete for neurotrophins unsuccessfully. While cell death is occurring, the target's sympathetic nerve cells manufacture and release a protein called **nerve growth factor** (NGF), which is critical to the development, maintenance and sustenance of certain target nerve cells. If a neuron does not unite with its appropriate cell within a limited period, the neuron dies because of a mechanism called apoptosis (otherwise known as programmed cell death) (Wyllie, 2010). Nerve growth factor interferes with this process and it appears to deliver a message from the postsynaptic cell to the nerve cell telling it not to die. In addition, it works as a signalling molecule and helps to guide the axon to its target. Nerve growth factor developed in the brain works on specific nerve cells, promoting their survival and encouraging the development and differentiation of new nerve cells and synapses (Greenberg, Xu, Lu, & Hempstead, 2009). Neurotrophins increase the branching of an axon during life (van Ooyen, 2001), while a lack of these chemicals has been linked to neurodegenerative disorders (Jellinger, 2009).

Cell death in certain areas of the brain may signal that these parts have matured. Adolescents experience a great deal of cell loss in sections of the prefrontal cortex, at the same time experiencing a greater amount of neural activity in these regions, improving memory and executive function (Sowell, Thompson, Holmes, Jernigan, & Toga, 1999).

FUNCTIONAL VALIDATION

Nerves cells and axons adapt their structure and connections all through life (Purves & Hadley, 1985) and, although these changes slow down as we age, our experiences direct the amount and type of changes that occur (Gan, 2003). This tweaking of nerve cells is highly dependent on the environment: surviving in a rich and complex environment requires an elaborate nervous system with an elaborate composition, whereas surviving in an impoverished environment with little stimulation calls for the exact opposite. Therefore, it appears that rich, stimulating environments enhance the **collateral sprouting** of axons and dendrites in all types of animals (Coss, Brandon, & Globus, 1980). People who have spent many years in education tend to have brains with longer and more comprehensive branching of the dendrites than people with less education (Jacobs, Schall, & Scheibel, 1993).

DEVELOPMENTAL ABNORMALITIES

Figure 4.7 shows some of the failures of neural development.

Figure 4.7   *Failures of neural development*

SPINA BIFIDA

As mentioned earlier, one developmental birth defect that is caused by the failure of the embryonic neural tube to close completely is called spina bifida. In the condition, some of the vertebrae that overlie the spinal column are not completely developed, do not fuse and remain open. Part of the spinal cord can extend beyond the bone openings when the aperture is large enough. A fluid-filled sac all around the spinal cord might or might not be present.

There are four categories of spina bifida: spina bifida cystica or myelomeningocele, meningocele, spina bifida occulta and lipomeningocele. Spina bifida cystica (myelomeningocele) is the most complex and severe form of spina bifida and usually involves neurological problems that can be very serious or even fatal. It accounts for 95% of cases of true spina bifida. In meningocele the membrane that surrounds the spinal cord may enlarge, creating a lump or 'cyst'. This is often invisible through the skin and causes few problems with little nerve damage. In spina bifida occulta the defect is not visible ('occulta' means hidden). Spina bifida occulta is rarely linked with complications or symptoms and is usually discovered accidentally when the person has a scan. It is probably the most common form. Lypomeningocele is a mild form of spina bifida where a fatty tumour is present over the spine. There may be urinary and bowel problems.

The terms 'spina bifida' and 'myelomeningocele' are usually used interchangeably. Surgical means can be used to close spina bifida, though normal brain function cannot be restored to the parts of the spinal cord that were affected. The taking of folic acid by the mother (around 4 or 5 mg daily) before and during pregnancy reduces the risk of spina bifida by as much as 75%.

ANENCEPHALY

Anencephaly is a cephalic (head) disorder caused by an abnormality in the neural tube that is the result of the cephalic end of the neural tube failing to close, typically between the 23rd and 26th day of pregnancy. The foetus develops with a major portion of the brain, skull and scalp missing. Individuals born with this disorder have no forebrain; as we have seen, this is the biggest part of the brain, consisting of the cerebral hemispheres, including the neocortex, whose function is high-level thought processing. The brain tissue that is left is usually exposed and not covered with any bone or skin. Most anencephalic foetuses either do not survive birth or die within a few hours or days after birth.

MICROCEPHALY

Microcephaly is a disorder in which the circumference of the head is smaller than normal because the brain has not developed normally or has stopped growing (Abuelo, 2007). The term 'microcephaly' means 'small head' and is assessed by measuring the head's maximum circumference – the occipito-frontal circumference or OFC. Microcephaly occurs in many known conditions

Microcephaly can present at birth or it can develop in the first few years of life. Reduction in OFC usually means that the volume of the brain is also reduced, which may cause mental and physical disabilities. Although severity of symptoms varies, children with microcephaly may have intellectual disabilities, delayed motor functions and speech, facial distortions, short stature, seizures and other neurological problems (Abuelo, 2007). There are many conditions which produce microcephaly in children, such as **foetal alcohol syndrome** (see this chapter) or anticonvulsant foetal syndrome, where the maternal use of anticonvulsant drugs during pregnancy may produce congenital microcephaly. Genetic microcephaly includes multiple syndromes such as Brachmann–de Lange syndrome and Williams syndrome. In Brachmann–de Lange syndrome, individuals have microcephaly with distinct facial features including bushy eyebrows, depressed nasal bridge and upturned nose. Genetically some individuals with this syndrome have a duplication of the q26–q27 band region of chromosome 3 (Kozma, 1996). People with Williams syndrome again have microcephaly with distinct facial features such as prominent lips and subcutaneous tissue around the eyes. They also have cardiac abnormalities. Genetically individuals show deletion of chromosome subunit 7q11.23 (Francke, 1999).

MACROCEPHALY

Macrocephaly is a condition characterised by abnormally large head and brain in relation to the rest of the body, and in most individuals it results in some degree of cognitive problems as well as growth retardation (Olney, 2007). Macrocephaly may be due to many causes such as megalencephaly or an enlarged brain, hydrocephalus or water on the brain, or bone overgrowth called cranial hyperostosis. Many genetic conditions present with macrocephaly, such as Alexander disease, which is one of a group of neurologic disorders collectively referred to as leukodystrophies which are caused by dysmyelination or failure of the maintenance of the myelin sheath in the white matter of the CNS. Alexander disease is caused by mutations in the gene coding for glial fibrillary acidic protein (GFAP), which is important in the function of the astrocytes (Namekawa et al., 2002).

DOWN SYNDROME

Down syndrome is caused by trisomy 21 in which there is an extra whole or partial 21st chromosome present. The British physician John Langdon Down described the syndrome in 1866 and it bears his name. In 1959, Jérôme Lejeune discovered that Down syndrome was caused by a chromosome 21 trisomy. Amniocentesis can identify if the baby will have Down syndrome, or it can be diagnosed at birth. Down syndrome is associated with some impairment of cognitive capability and physical growth, and a specific set of facial features. Individuals with Down syndrome present with a lower than average cognitive ability, and intellectual disability varies from mild to moderate. The median IQ of children with Down syndrome is approximately 50, as opposed to typically developing children who have an IQ of 100. A small number have an extreme intellectual disability. Down syndrome occurs in approximately one in every 733 births, but there is a higher rate with mothers who are older. Several of the common physical characteristics associated with Down syndrome may also be present in individuals with a normal chromosome set, including microgenia (an unusually small chin), a round face, macroglossia (protruding or enlarged tongue), almond-shaped eyes due to an epicanthic fold of the eyelid, up-slanting palpebral fissures (the division between the top and bottom eyelids), shortened limbs, a single transverse palmar crease (the presence of one instead of two creases across one or both palms), poor muscle tone, and an oversized space between the big and second toes. Health issues for people who have Down syndrome include a greater chance of congenital heart defects, reflux ailments, repeat ear infections, sleep apnoea and thyroid problems. Intervention programmes, careful monitoring for common issues, medical attention when necessary, a supporting family and occupational training can help to provide a child with Down syndrome with a better developmental process. Even though there are physical genetic limitations in Down syndrome that are insurmountable, education and good care will help the individual to have a better quality of life.

PHENYLKETONURIA (PKU)

If there is a lack of the enzyme that is required to break down phenylalanine, an amino acid found in many foods, a person will present with a disorder called phenylketonuria (PKU). PKU is an autosomal recessive metabolic genetic disease defined by a lack of the hepatic enzyme phenylalanine hydroxylase (PAH). The body requires this enzyme to facilitate the metabolism of phenylalanine into tyrosine. When there is a PAH deficiency, there is an accumulation of phenylalanine, which turns into phenylpyruvate (or phenylketone); this can be detected with a urine screening. Since PKU was first discovered, there have been great strides in developing effective treatment. This can be self-managed by the patient with minimal problems other than the annoyance of management itself. Without medical attention, the condition can result in developmental disruption of the brain, causing progressive intellectual disabilities, brain damage and seizures.

FRAGILE X SYNDROME

Fragile X syndrome (FXS), or Martin–Bell syndrome, is an inherited X-linked dominant disorder caused by mutations in the FMR1 gene that result in a wide range of characteristic physical and mental problems and psychological and behavioural traits, ranging from severe to mild. Apart from the cognitive problems, the main traits of the syndrome consist of a long face, big ears or ears that stick out, flattened feet, big testes (macroorchidism) and decreased muscle tone. The individual may speak in a cluttered or anxious manner. Characteristic behaviours may also include hand-flapping, as well as abnormal social development, especially shyness, inability to maintain eye contact, poor memory and problems with facial encoding.

Some people who have fragile X syndrome are also autistic. Most women with the syndrome have symptoms to a lesser degree due to their second X chromosome; however, they can develop symptoms just as severe as those of men. Full mutation males usually present with a high level of intellectual disability, but the level of disability in full mutation females ranges from minimal to severe; this could be why males are diagnosed more often than females.

FOETAL ALCOHOL SYNDROME (FAS)

Foetal alcohol syndrome (FAS) is a pattern of mental and physical problems that can develop in a foetus when a woman consumes excessive alcohol while pregnant. FAS is a high risk for children whose mother drank alcohol during pregnancy at specific times and frequently. Alcohol passes through the placenta and can interfere with correct foetal growth; it can cause distinct facial stigmata and damage to nerve cells and parts of the brain, possibly resulting in emotional or behavioural problems, as well as being harmful to the body in other ways. The most profound impact of FAS is permanent damage to the CNS and the developing neurons, leading to a variety of primary cognitive and functional disabilities, including memory problems, attention deficits and impulsive behaviour.

NEURAL PLASTICITY

Many of the higher brain functions such as facets of sensory perception, cognitive function and language are progressively acquired during development. As alluded to in Chapter 2, one of the extraordinary features of the development of the nervous system is that the configuration of specific neural associations and synaptic connections can be dramatically influenced by experience. This experience-dependent modification of connections within the nervous system is called plasticity (Figure 4.8). This section gives a few examples of how plasticity alters the development of connections in the mammalian visual system. Similar mechanisms are believed to underlie the development of other sensory systems and are also likely to play a role in other experience-dependent changes such as various forms of learning, as detailed in Chapter 11.

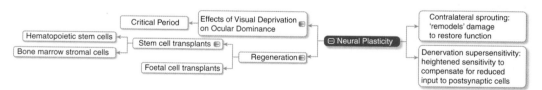

Figure 4.8   *Neural plasticity*

EFFECTS OF VISUAL DEPRIVATION ON OCULAR DOMINANCE

As we will see in Chapter 5, the visual system is not one unified pathway but is segregated at the level of the lateral geniculate nucleus (LGN) into ocular dominance columns in layer 4. This organisational feature is not present from birth but instead forms as a result of visual experience. Visual experience present over time causes axons to divide and gives rise to the pattern of ocular dominance organisation seen in the adult brain.

Hubel and Wiesel (1977) investigated whether this distribution of ocular dominance could be changed by visual experience. They carried out an experiment where they closed one eye of a very young kitten and then left the animal for about six months to mature into adulthood. They subsequently found remarkable changes in the organisation of the visual system. Electrophysiological recordings pointed to the finding that the cells in the deprived eye did not respond to stimuli and the kitten was behaviourally blind in the deprived eye. Other findings indicated that the ocular dominance distribution had shifted so that all the cells were now stimulated by the eye that had stayed open.

The recordings from the lateral geniculate layers of the retina seemed to show that the non-existence of cortical cells in the closed eye was not due to retinal degeneration or a loss of retinal connections to the thalamus. The evidence suggested that the deprived eye had been functionally disconnected from the occipital cortex, and even if the eye that was deprived was left open, little or no recovery occurred. These observations suggested that visual experience could have a dramatic effect on the organisation of ocular dominance columns. Surprisingly, the same procedure of closing one eye had no effect on the response of the cells in the occipital cortex of an adult cat. The closure of one eye of an adult cat for a year or more had little effect on the ocular dominance columns; indeed, the reopened eye showed the same ocular dominance distribution and visual behaviour as normal. Thus, sometime between a kitten first opening their eyes after birth and one year of age, visual experience determined how the occipital cortex is wired up in ocular dominance.

See Box 4.2 for detail on cortical plasticity in blind individuals.

BOX 4.2   Critical period for cross-modal plasticity in blind humans

Background

Blind subjects who learn to read Braille must be able to extract spatial information from subtle tactile stimuli. In order to accomplish this, changes appear to take place in the cortex rewiring the brain to perform such a task. Previous studies have shown that Braille learning appears to be associated with the recruitment of parts of previously 'visual' cortex (V1 and V2) for tactile information processing. However, whether this plasticity and reorganisation were age dependent was unclear. This study (Sadato, Okada, Honda, & Yonekura, 2002) investigated if age was a deciding factor in the reshaping of the cortex.

Method

The researchers measured the change of regional cerebral blood flow using 3.0 tesla functional MRI during passive tactile tasks performed by 15 blind and eight sighted control participants. Nine of the blind participants had lost their sight before the age of 16 years (early blind), and the others after age 16 years (late blind). All blind subjects were blind due to dysfunction at the level of the eye or early optic nerve. All participants were scanned while engaging in a Braille discrimination task.

Results

The study found that, during the tactile discrimination task, there was increased activity in the postcentral gyrus to posterior parietal cortex and decreased activity in the secondary somatosensory area, in blind compared with sighted subjects. In addition

(Continued)

(Continued)

the blind participants, irrespective of their age at onset of blindness, exhibited higher activity in the visual association cortex than did sighted subjects. V1 was activated in early blind subjects whereas it was suppressed in late blind subjects (Figure 1).

Interpreting the findings

The activity in the postcentral gyrus and the decreased activity in the secondary somatosensory area suggest that there is a greater demand for shape discrimination processing in blind subjects. The pattern of activity in V1 suggests that the first 16 years of life represent a critical period for a functional shift of V1 from processing visual stimuli to processing tactile stimuli. This highlights the time-dependent nature of neuronal plasticity and reinforces the idea of a critical period first proposed by Hubel and Wiesel (1977).

References

Hubel, D.H. and Wiesel, T.N. (1977). Functional architecture of macaque monkey visual cortex. *Proceedings of the Royal Society of London, Series B, 198*, 1–59.

Sadato, N., Okada, T., Honda, M., & Yonekura, Y. (2002). Critical period for cross-modal plasticity in blind humans: a functional MRI study. *Neuroimage, 16*, 389–400.

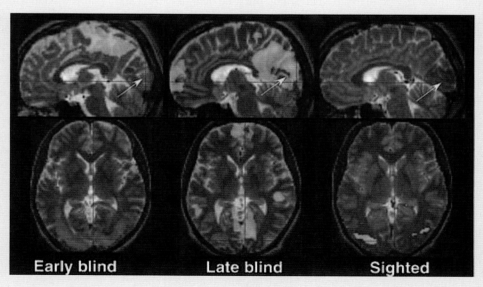

Figure 1   *Statistical parametric maps of individual analysis of neural activity in early-onset blind (left), late-onset blind (middle), and sighted (right) subjects during the Braille discrimination task compared with that during the rest period*

THE CRITICAL PERIOD

By altering the time of monocular deprivation, one can identify a period during which visual experience can influence connectivity in the cortex. Further experiments have shown that the first three months of life seem to be the critical period during which visual experience alters the cellular arrangement. Hubel and Wiesel found that around four weeks of age was the most sensitive time, because as little as three to four days of eye closure during this time was sufficient to alter the ocular dominance profile of the visual cortex. In the cat the critical period lasts for six to eight weeks after birth and in primates it is approximately 16 weeks. As the response from the retina and the LGN seemed normal in these studies, the implication was that the altered circuitry was most likely due to a change in the distribution of the stripe-like patterns of geniculocortical axons which represent the input from the two eyes and from the ocular dominance columns. This assumption was confirmed by subsequently examining the anatomical distribution of geniculocortical axons in layer 4 of the cortex. Monocular deprivation in animals was shown to reduce the number of LGN axon terminals receiving input from the deprived eye and a corresponding increase in the number of axon terminals receiving input from the non-deprived eye.

As already stated, the age at which damage happens in the nervous system is a vital issue in considering the chances of recovery from injury (Prang, Del Turco, & Kapfhammer, 2001). Neurons that have been damaged in the peripheral nervous system have the potential to regrow and build connections to other cells. However, with the exception of the olfactory system and some cells in the retina, you do not see this type of nerve cell regeneration in the central nervous system of adults. We do see evidence of regeneration occurring in embryonic and neonatal nervous systems, and it is likely that the difference is a result of age-related proteins that support the development of axons (Goldberg & Barres, 2000). In adulthood, the brain has a huge capacity for adaptive change and it does this by interaction with the surroundings or environment.

We can view this experience-dependent modification as playing a role in three major areas:

1 the processes that support memory and learning

2 the neurological recovery that occurs after the brain is injured

3 the loss of neural plasticity in the cognitive decline observed in older people.

The nervous system can be injured in a variety of ways, including blows to the head, invasive traumas (like a bullet wound), or the demise of neurons because of infections, toxins and radiation. There can also be damage from illnesses like Alzheimer's or Parkinson's diseases. If the body of a nerve cell suffers damage then the cell dies, since the soma is the metabolic centre of the cells; however, if the axon suffers damage, changes will result that might or might not cause the cell to die. After injury to an axon, deterioration can happen in two ways: its distal part, the part between the injury and the presynaptic terminal, can deteriorate, a process referred to as anterograde degeneration; or it can degenerate back towards the cell body by a procedure called retrograde degeneration. A neuron that is degenerating may additionally harm neighbouring neurons with which it has synaptic relations. The result can be small enough to cause only minimal changes in the network of connections, or it can be so severe that the nerve cells degenerate through a process known as transneuronal degeneration, which can cause comprehensive damage to the nervous system (Johnson and Cowey, 2000).

NEURONAL REGENERATION

This section looks at damage to central and peripheral nervous systems which results in serious and sometimes irreversible injury to neurons. Neurons have very little capacity to divide and replace damaged cells, so any loss of neurons will result in permanent changes in the functional circuitry of the neuron system. In almost every case, neurons have withdrawn from the mitotic cycle and therefore can no longer divide to produce new neurons to replace damaged cells. Regeneration is much more likely in the PNS than in the CNS, and trophic factors play a major role in any neuronal regeneration that occurs. Trophic factors seem to provide an environment which protects PNS axons from degeneration after axotomy. This compares with the general incapability of injured neurons in the CNS to regenerate. Not surprisingly, some of the trophic factors needed for adult neurons to survive after injury are similar to the trophic factors present during neural development. Nerve growth factor (NGF) is one trophic factor which is important for the growth, maintenance and survival of certain neurons (Varon & Conner, 1994). If exogenous NGF is added to a damaged sympathetic neuron, then regeneration and reinnervation occur; and if the NGF is then neutralised with anti-NGF **antibodies**, regeneration is blocked. This indicates that NGF is needed for the regeneration and maintenance of peripheral synaptic connections in the adult PNS. NGF also appears to play a role in the maintenance of cholinergic neurons in the part of the brain called the basal forebrain which has been linked to Alzheimer's disease (Salehi, Delcroix, & Swaab, 2004). Other mechanisms contributing to the regeneration of the nervous system include macrophages and Schwann cells. Macrophages secrete mitogenic factors that stimulate Schwann cell proliferation (Kiefer, Kieseier, Stoll, & Hartung, 2001). This proliferation causes increased glial cell secretion of extracellular matrix molecules, which supports adhesion of the regenerating axons to the support cells.

CONTRALATERAL SPROUTING

Even though the neurons of the fully developed nervous system are unable to regenerate after injury, neighbouring neurons may be able to make up for lost connections via a process known as contralateral sprouting. This is a mechanism whereby these nearby neurons grow new axonal endings to connect to empty receptor sites (Goldstein, Little, & Harris, 1997). Cells within the damaged area respond to the event by giving off neurotrophins to prompt other axons nearby to fill the vacant synapses with new branches or contralateral sprouts. In time, this process slowly fills in and connects several of the synapses and 'restructures' the brain area that has suffered injury in an attempt to regain function.

Sometimes this sprouting can result in completely restored normative functioning, as evidenced by cortical injury and subsequent recovery in rats (Kolb, Stewart, & Sutherland, 1997).

DENERVATION SUPERSENSITIVITY

Denervation supersensitivity is a process that compensates for the reduced input to a post-synaptic cell if the input to that cell is interrupted. For example, a muscle cell which usually only demonstrates a response to neurotransmitter activity at the **neuromuscular junction** will construct more receptors, developing a higher sensitivity to the neurotransmitter over a greater surface area if the axon activating it is inactive or destroyed. The mechanism by which this heightened sensitivity appears following damage involves not only an increase in the amount of receptors but also an increased responsiveness of the receptors, probably due to alterations to their second messenger systems.

REORGANISATION OF SENSORY REPRESENTATIONS

In the brain of a violinist who has played the instrument for a long time, we would see a larger cortical representation for the fingers on their left hand. These changes that we observe in the brain are caused by processes like contralateral sprouting and alter how the sensory system of the brain is constructed. This plasticity causes both cortical and functional changes, as evidenced by the capabilities of a skilled musician. Similar processes happen when the brain is injured and reorganisation occurs in the sensory representations.

A fascinating occurrence associated with the reorganisation of cortical maps is **phantom limb** syndrome (Ramachandran & Rogers-Ramachandran, 2000). People who have had limbs amputated report this condition. Following amputation, people continue to have feelings in the missing limb, such as discomfort in the arm or leg; this may subside after a few days or weeks, but sometimes may last all their life. We can explain phantom limb syndrome by the expansion of the cortical representation map, where local brain areas, each responsible for processing and performing a specific function and reflected in the cortex as 'maps', gain areas of the unused cortex from the phantom map. One study reported that an amputee felt something in their amputated 'phantom' arm when a cotton swab was applied to their face. The amputee underwent a magnetoencephalography (MEG) scan, which showed that the part of the brain that is responsible for facial sensation had spread into the nearby part of the brain responsible for sensation in the arm and hand. After the arm was surgically removed, the arm and hand areas of the cortical brain no longer had any input and, by the process of contralateral sprouting, the phantom area was remapped with the face area in a nearby part of the brain. Typically, phantom limb cases demonstrate a strong relationship between the extent of cortical remapping and the amount of phantom pain, which can fade as the brain starts to reorganise (Ramachandran & Seckel, 2010).

REGENERATING THE NERVOUS SYSTEM: CELL TRANSPLANTATIONS

A number of neurological conditions result from the permanent loss of cell populations from certain areas of the nervous system. In recent years, transplantation of these deleted cells has become widely applicable to treatment of these conditions; however, each condition has specific requirements in both phenotype and quantity of cells.

Methods that are being evaluated for the restoration of lost functions of the nervous system after it has sustained injury include replacement of neural tissue with transplanted material. Here foetal tissue is believed to be the perfect remedy as these undifferentiated cells have the ability to re-establish neural connections. However, many people think there are ethical problems relating to using such tissue for transplants as the cells are gathered from aborted foetuses. Because of these views, foetal transplantation is still highly controversial. However, transplanted foetal stem cells have reportedly improved the ability to move in Parkinson's patients (Freed et al., 2001) and animal studies indicate that this progress is the result of new dopaminergic synapses forming in the basal ganglia. Other areas in which these transplantation approaches have been tried include the synthesis and secretion of nerve growth factor (NGF) in Alzheimer's disease (Li et al., 2008) and the synthesis and secretion of extracellular matrix and adhesion molecules to support regeneration in damaged CNS or PNS tissues (Ourednik & Ourednik, 2005).

Using adult stem cells in research and treatment seems to be less controversial than using embryonic stem cells, as producing adult stem cells does not necessitate destroying an embryo. These cells are located in specific areas of the body, such as haematopoietic stem cells which form the blood cells found in the body. A second population is bone marrow stromal stem cells, often referred to as mesenchymal stem cells or skeletal stem cells. These non-haematopoietic stem cells comprise a small percentage of the bone marrow's stromal cell population, and are able to produce bone, cartilage, fat, cells that promote the formation of blood, and fibrous connective tissue.

SUMMARY

In this chapter we have looked at how the nervous system develops from a single cell into a fully functioning nervous system (Figure 4.9). Cell division starts in the embryo with the ectoderm layer becoming thicker, forming the neural plate. The edges of the neural plate then curl up from 'head' to 'tail' along the developing embryo to form the neural tube, which ultimately becomes the complete central nervous system. The rostral area of the neural tube turns into the brain, and the caudal region turns into the spinal cord. The brain then separates into three ventricles: the forebrain or prosencephalon; the midbrain or mesencephalon; and the hindbrain or rhombencephalon. After further time, the forebrain and the hindbrain divide again: the forebrain forms the telencephalon and the diencephalon, and the hindbrain forms the metencephalon and the myelencephalon. The chapter then went on to discuss the stages of the developing nervous system: (1) induction of the neural plate and formation of the neural tube; (2) proliferation of precursor cells that will give rise to neurons and glia; (3) migration of neurons and glia to the place where they will finally reside; (4) aggregation of neurons into identifiable structures; (5) differentiation into mature neurons; (6) synaptogenesis, which describes the formation of functional synapses with other neurons; (7) selective cell death of many neurons or neuronal precursors; and (8) functional validation of the connections. Neural plasticity was then discussed, and the experience-dependent development of the visual system was explained.

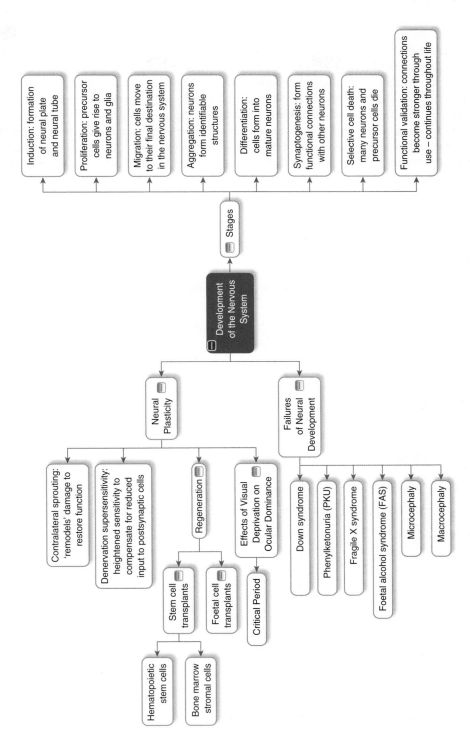

Figure 4.9 *Development and modification of the nervous system*

Space was then given to the problems which can arise during brain development and the developmental birth defects that can result. One of the most exciting aspects of biological psychology was then discussed: the idea that the brain is not completely inflexible but can be changed through experiences, not only in the early stages of development but well into the adult years. One way the brain is modified in the fully developed nervous system is that neurons may be able to make up for lost connections via a process known as contra-lateral sprouting. Another process, called denervation supersensitivity, makes up for an interrupted input to a postsynaptic cell. Our sensory cortex can also be reorganised, and such reorganisation can be seen in skilled musicians and people with phantom limb syndrome. Finally the controversial area of stem cell therapy was discussed and how this technology might be able to treat some neurological disorders.

 FURTHER READING

Johnson, Mark H. (2004). *Developmental cognitive neuroscience* (2nd edn). New York: Wiley-Blackwell.

Nadarajah, B., & Parnavelas, J.G. (2002). Modes of neuronal migration in the developing cerebral cortex. *Nature Reviews Neuroscience*, 3(6), 423–432.

Sperry, R.W. (1943). Visuomotor coordination in the newt (*Triturus viridescens*) after regeneration of the optic nerve. *Journal of Comparative Neurology*, 79, 33–55.

 KEY QUESTIONS

1 Explain the stages of cortical development.

2 Describe two conditions which arise from abnormal cortical development.

3 To what extent is the human nervous system capable of repair?

5 VISUAL SYSTEM

Understanding the visual system in humans requires a grasp of a general principle that applies to all our senses, that of transduction. The physical energy that evokes a visual system response is light, which is a form of electromagnetic radiation. In order for us to see light, energy must be converted or transduced into information that the nervous system is capable of processing, and then it must be transmitted to the primary visual cortex area at the back of the brain. This chapter will trace the path of this visual information into the brain and examine how we see the colour of an object or determine if the object is in motion. However, in order to fully understand how our visual system achieves this, we must first look at the initial transducer of light energy: the eye.

THE EYE

The act of seeing begins in the eye (Figure 5.1). Light passes through the transparent outer layer of the eyeball, called the cornea. After this, the light passes through the aqueous humor, a clear liquid found in the anterior chamber of the eye. From here the light passes through the pupil via the iris. Your eye colour comes from the iris, which consists of a band of muscles covered in coloured tissue and functions as a channel for light to pass through the pupil. The amount of light that is allowed to enter the eye is controlled by the iris, which increases or decreases the size of the pupil. The light passes through the pupil before it gets to the lens. The ciliary muscles, which pull on ligaments either side of the lens, determine the shape of the lens necessary to focus images on the retina. **Accommodation** is the term used to describe how the retina maintains the focus of a particular image. The shape of the lens changes to achieve this accommodation. It flattens out to focus on items in the distance and becomes more rounded (convex) to focus on items that are close. After passing through the lens the light continues through the vitreous humor, a gelatinous liquid, before arriving at the retina.

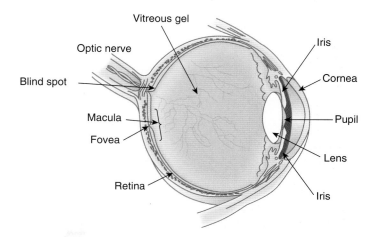

Figure 5.1 *The eye*

THE RETINA

Approximately 70% of the eye's interior surface is covered by the retina, a layer at the back of the eye that is sensitive to light. The retina is formed from a number of specialised cells, each responsible for a part of the visual process. The first layer is composed of photosensitive cells called **rods** and **cones**. These cells transform light energy into signals that the optic nerves transmit to the brain. **Bipolar** cells and ganglion cells form another layer of cells found close to the inner surface of the retina and obtain visual information from the rods and cones by way of two other types of nerve cells, bipolar and amacrine cells. These are the cells that ultimately form the optic nerve. The bipolar cells are located between the photoreceptors and the ganglion cells. Their principal function is to send signals from the photoreceptors to the ganglion cells. The light must first pass through the ganglia and bipolar cells before reaching the rods and cones (see Figure 5.2). This odd,

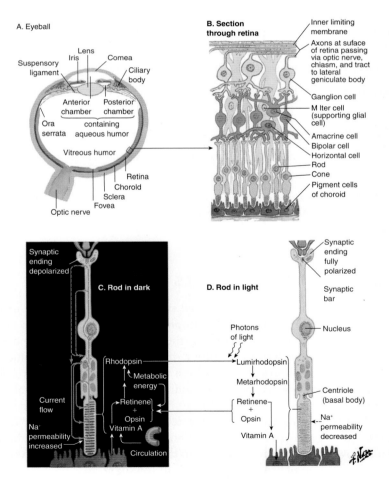

Figure 5.2   *Structure of the retina*

upside-down arrangement results in a significant loss in acuity, so the retina is structurally specialised to address this issue in the form of a **fovea**. This is an area at the central position of the retina; this region has high visual acuity because only photoreceptors are present. The cones are concentrated around the central foveal area and the rods are mainly located at the periphery of the retina.

The layers located nearest to the vitreous chamber are on the inside, and the epithelium and the choroid are on the outside and can be found next to the retinal pigment. The layers, from outer to inner, are:

- *Retinal pigment epithelium*: provides the photoreceptors with supportive and metabolic functions.
- *Receptor layer*: contains the light-sensitive outer segments of the photoreceptors.
- *Outer nuclear layer*: holds the photoreceptor cell bodies.
- *Outer plexiform layer*: here the photoreceptors synapse with the horizontal and bipolar cells.
- *Inner nuclear layer*: contains the horizontal, bipolar and amacrine cell bodies.
- *Inner plexiform layer*: here the retinal ganglia synapse with the bipolar and amacrine cells.
- *Retinal ganglion cell layer*: contains the retinal ganglion cell bodies.
- *Optic nerve layer*: contains the ganglion cell axons which will innervate the optic disc.

Remember that light passing through the cornea, lens and vitreous humor must also go through the majority of the retinal layers prior to arriving at the light-sensitive portion of the photoreceptor, the outer segment in the receptor layer.

PHOTORECEPTORS: RODS AND CONES

Rods and cones (Figure 5.3) are characterised structurally by the shapes of their outer segments. There is also variation in the photopigments found in the rods and cones. A photopigment called **rhodopsin** is present in the rods which can absorb a wide bandwidth of light. The cones differ in the colour of the light their photopigments absorb. There are three types of photopigment which absorb light of different colours: red, green and blue. As each cone receptor can contain only one photopigment, three types of cones therefore exist: red, green and blue. The rods react best when exposed to white light, while the cones are best stimulated by a particular colour of light. The rods' and cones' photopigments also differ in how sensitive they are to light: rhodopsin breaks down at lower illumination levels than do cone photopigments. As a result, the rods have a higher degree of sensitivity, at least in low light.

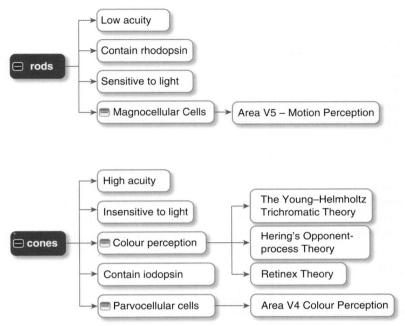

Figure 5.3   *Rods and cones*

Even though cones are able to detect colour, they do not have the same light sensitivity as retinal rod cells. They can also recognise finer detail because fewer cones than rods converge onto retinal ganglion cells, and rods possess a high convergence of information while cones possess a low convergence. Also, cones demonstrate a faster response time to stimuli than do rods. Duplex theory describes the difference between rods and cones and is demonstrated in Table 5.1. One more feature of the retina is that this is the location where the axons relaying visual information join together and exit the eye. This area is called the optic disc, and is sometimes referred to as the blind spot because no receptors are located there (see Figure 5.1).

Table 5.1   *Duplex theory in humans*

Rods	Cones
Relatively sensitive to light	Relatively insensitive to light
Located mostly at the periphery of the retina	Located mostly in the centre of the retina
Operate at low levels of light	Operate under high levels of light
High convergence of information	Low convergence of information
Sensitive to light	Relatively insensitive to light
Low visual acuity	High visual acuity
Around 120 million in each retina	Around 6 million in each retina

TRANSDUCTION OF VISUAL INFORMATION

When light energy signals are transferred into electrical polarisation, we call this trans-duction. Ultimately, this polarisation process results in a neural signal that moves along the optic nerve to the brain.

When light falls on the retina, rhodopsin found in rods or iodopsin found in cones absorbs light; the arrangement of a retinal cofactor inside the protein is converted from the cis form to the trans form, resulting in the retinal cofactor changing shape. This change alters the state of second messenger molecules to their active state, eventually shutting down the sodium channels, which are usually open (Baylor, 1996). As a result, the sodium ions are no longer able to cross into the cell, and hyperpolarisation of the photoreceptor occurs. This hyperpolarisation reduces the amount of glutamate that is transmitted to the bipolar cell, thus decreasing the inhibition of the bipolar cell. Consequently, depolarisation of the bipolar cell occurs; it is graduated, meaning that the greater the depolarisation, the greater the amount of neurotransmitter released. Bipolar cells excite ganglion cells in the retina.

MAJOR TYPES OF GANGLION CELL

In the human eye there are two main kinds of retinal ganglion cells, type M and type P. The following is an outline of their main properties.

Type P: object detectors with colour sensitivity

The P retinal ganglion cells:

- are greater in number than the M ganglion cells
- synapse with cone bipolar cells
- are colour sensitive
- have a small **receptive field**
- generate a sustained, slow **adaptation** reaction that persists while a stimulus is centred on the receptive field
- give a weak response to stimuli that move through its receptive field.

The P cell has a slowly adapting reaction and is well equipped to relay information about the presence, colour and extent of a visual stimulus. Unlike the M cell it is not suited to relay information about the movement of stimuli.

Type M: motion detectors without colour sensitivity

The M retinal ganglion cells:

- are bigger than P ganglion cells
- synapse with many bipolar cells

- are not sensitive to colour

- have a big receptive region

- are receptive to small centre–surround brightness variation

- have a fast adaptive reaction to a constant stimulus

- have the strongest possible response, with high discharge rates.

Their fast adaptive reactions mean that type M cells are well equipped to relay information about temporal variations in the motion of a stimulus.

M and P ganglion cells in the retina form the optic nerve and leave the eye at the optic disc. The majorities of the axons move to and synapse at the thalamus, in the lateral geniculate nucleus.

Behaviour of retinal ganglion cells

Three different categories of retinal ganglion cells have been identified (see Figure 5.4):

1 on ganglion cells that are triggered by bipolar cells reacting to light conditions

2 off ganglion cells that become excited with the removal of the light stimulus and are inhibited by amacrine cells when light is present

3 on–off ganglion cells that become excited by bipolar cells in the presence of a light stimulus and are not inhibited by amacrine cells upon the removal of the light stimulus.

The axon terminals of bipolar cells hook up in the inner plexiform layer to the dendritic processes of amacrine cells and ganglion cells. Here, depolarisation results in neurotransmitter release by the bipolar cell at its axon terminals. Bipolar cells usually release glutamate, which has a depolarising effect on most ganglion cells. The amacrine cells may synapse with bipolar cells, other amacrine cells or ganglion cells. It is the axons of the retinal ganglion cells that exit the eye to form the optic nerve and transmit visual information to the lateral geniculate nucleus of the thalamus as well as to other diencephalic and midbrain structures.

In the absence of light on the centre of the receptive field, the off bipolar cell undergoes depolarisation, causing the release of glutamate and depolarisation of the ganglion cells in the retina, producing an action potential. Thus, the retinal ganglion cells that synapse with off bipolar cells have properties with off-centre/on-surround receptive regions, and are called off ganglion cells. The opposite is true for the on bipolar cell which becomes depolarised when light falls on the centre receptive field. This again causes the release of glutamate and depolarisation of the retinal ganglion cells, which results in the production of an action potential.

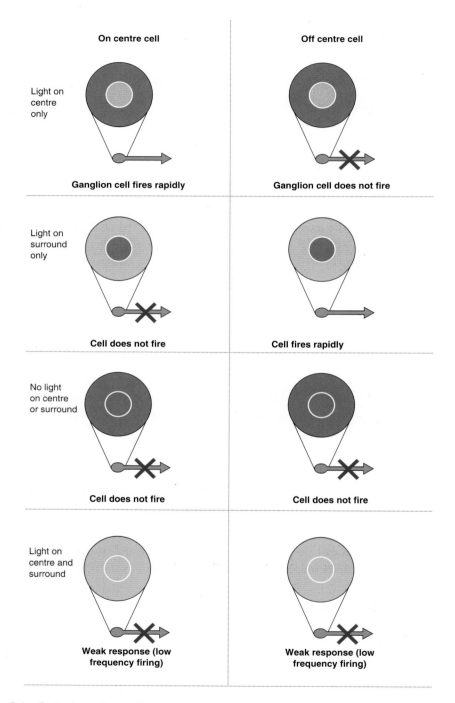

Figure 5.4   *Retinal ganglion cells*

HORIZONTAL CELLS

In the outer plexiform layer, the photoreceptor cells and the horizontal cells form both presynaptic and postsynaptic connections. The reactions of their 'centre' photoreceptors cause the horizontal cells indirectly to produce the bipolar cell receptive field surround effect. This effect, although not as strong as the centre effect, intensifies contrasts in brightness to yield images that are sharper, to make something look brighter or darker depending on the background, and to sustain these contrasts under different lighting conditions.

AMACRINE CELLS

These cells form synaptic relationships with bipolar and ganglion cells and are much like horizontal cells in that they provide lateral connections between the same type of neuron. What makes them unique from horizontal cells is that they also provide the vertical connections which link bipolar and ganglion cells.

PATHWAYS OF THE EYE AND BRAIN

The optic nerve transmits visual information from the retina (Figure 5.6). The second of 12 paired cranial nerves, the optic nerve is considered to be part of the CNS. Because it is in the CNS, the fibres are covered with myelin composed of oligodendrocytes instead of the Schwann cells of the PNS. The optic nerve is formed from the retinal ganglion cells in the retina. It exits the eye through the optic canal, running towards the optic chiasm, where some of the fibres from the inner halves (nasal side) of the retina cross the midline (as seen in Figure 5.5). These nasal fibres move across at the optic chiasm and then move up on the other side of the brain. The axons from the temporal side of the retina stay on the same side of the brain. Most axons (approximately 80%) of the optic nerve end at the lateral geniculate nucleus (LGN), from which information is transmitted through the geniculo-calcarine tract or optic radiation to the primary visual cortex or the striate cortex (V1) in the occipital lobe of the brain. The other 20% of the axons stretch out to a structure in the tectum of the midbrain known as the superior colliculus. The superior colliculus is a paired structure found beneath the thalamus, surrounding the pineal gland in the mesencephalon of the brains of vertebrates. In human beings, the superior colliculus plays a role in facilitating **saccadic** eye movements and eye–head coordination. This pathway has also been associated with a condition called blindsight in which an individual responds to visual stimuli without consciously perceiving them (Cowey, 2010).

The LGN is part of the thalamus, and in humans it is a six-layered structure. We refer to the inner two layers as the magnocellular (M) layers and the outer four layers as the parvocellular (P) layers. Another type of nerve cell in the koniocellular layer is found in a position that is ventral to the M and P layers. A third input to the visual cortex is made up

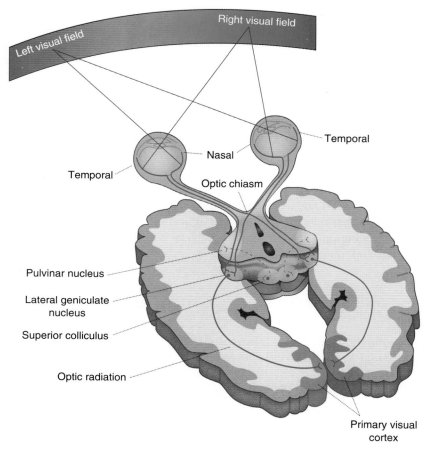

Figure 5.5 *Visual pathways*

of the K cells, which are not similar to the M and P cells. The function of the koniocellular system is at present not known; however there is emerging evidence that it plays a role in colour processing.

ANALYSIS OF INFORMATION: THE VISUAL CORTEX

The visual cortex contains a well-defined map of spatial information, in that the upper bank of visual area 1 (V1) or the calcarine sulcus reacts to stimuli in the lower half of the visual field, and the lower bank of the calcarine sulcus reacts to stimuli in the upper half of the visual field. Theoretically, this **retinotopic** map seen in the primary visual cortex or V1 is the conversion of the visual image from the retina. The correspondence between a specific site in V1 and in the subjective visual field is extremely accurate. A portion of V1 is mapped to the fovea, which as already mentioned is a site in the middle of the retina responsible for excellent vision or sharp acuity, a phenomenon referred to as cortical magnification. Primary visual cortex nerve cells are constructed in such a way that they synapse with axons from either the left or the right eye. These are termed ocular dominance columns and span multiple cortical layers, producing a striped pattern when stained (Hubel, Wiesel, & Stryker, 1977).

The visual cortex is separated into six distinct layers, each of which has a different function, labelled I through to VI. Layer IV gets the most visual feedback from the lateral geniculate nucleus (LGN). The parvocellular pathways of the primary visual cortex are made up of neural groups that are known as blobs (Wong-Riley, 1979), and interblobs are the areas between blobs. These blobs have sensitivity to certain specific colours (Dow, 2002). Other nerve cells located in this parvocellular layer are sensitive to boundaries of stationary objects. Nerve cells located in the magnocellular layer react to motion, orientation and retinal disparity.

The extrastriate cortex, an area that surrounds the primary visual cortex, receives information from the primary visual cortex. The extrastriate cortex, also known as the visual association cortex, divides into two separate visual pathways; one is known as the dorsal stream and the other is known as the ventral stream (Haxby et al., 1991). It is also appropriate to call the division of the dorsal/ventral pathways the 'where/what' streams.

DORSAL AND VENTRAL STREAMS

The dorsal stream starts with V1, travels through V2, then continues to the dorsomedial region of the brain and visual area 5 (V5), also known as the middle temporal (MT) visual area, and to the posterior parietal cortex. The dorsal stream is associated with processing of motion and the representation of objects in space. It is also associated with the organisation of the eyes and arms where it coordinates saccades or reaching movements. Other names for the dorsal pathway include the 'where' pathway or the 'how' pathway.

The ventral stream starts from V1, passes through V2, then through V4, and continues to the inferior temporal cortex. The ventral stream has a role in recognising forms and object representation and is therefore known as the 'what' pathway. It also has a function related to the recollection of long-term memory. Semir Zeki suggested that the nerve cells in V4 were solely dedicated to colour (Lueck et al., 1989). However, this may no longer be the only function of this area, as recent studies indicate that V4 neurons are quite sensitive to the shape and curvature of stimuli (Murphy & Finkel, 2007). Area V4 is found on the fusiform gyrus, and it is commonly held that this area is also involved in how we process face stimuli (Kanwisher, McDermott, & Chun, 1997). We can think about the ventral pathway as follows: V1 → V2 → V4 → inferior temporal area or area IT. See Box 5.1 for detail on the fusiform face area in the brain.

BOX 5.1   Neural mechanism for faces

Background

Evidence from cognitive psychology and neuropsychology suggested that face and object recognition engage dissimilar processes that may occur in separate brain areas. Event-related potential (ERP) had been recorded from separate portions of the fusiform and inferotemporal gyri for faces but not for scrambled faces, cars or butterflies (Ojemann, Ojemann, & Lettich, 1992). In addition reports had described patients who had lost the ability to recognise faces; this was associated with damage in the occipitotemporal region of the right hemisphere (De Renzi, 1997). Thus, several sources of evidence supported the existence of specialised neural 'modules' for face perception in extrastriate cortex. This experiment (Kanwisher, McDermott, & Chun, 1997) investigated whether an area in the occipitotemporal called the fusiform region was specialised for face perception.

Method

The study used an fMRI paradigm to investigate any occipitotemporal areas that might be specialised for face perception. The researchers scanned 15 subjects during the passive viewing of photographs of faces compared to photographs of assorted common objects.

Results

The results indicated that an area in the fusiform gyrus in 12 of the 20 subjects was significantly more active when the subjects viewed faces than when they viewed assorted common objects. In addition, in five subjects tested, the predefined 'face area' also responded significantly more strongly to passive viewing of (1) intact faces than scrambled two-tone faces, (2) full front-view face photos than front-view photos of houses, (3) three-quarter-view, hair concealed face photos than photos of human hands, and (4) on a consecutive matching task, three-quarter-view faces than hands.

Interpreting the results

This study demonstrated the existence of a region in the fusiform gyrus that not only is responsive to face stimuli but is selectively activated by faces compared with various control stimuli. The researchers advocated that a special-purpose cortical mechanism exists for face perception, namely the fusiform face area (FFA) (Figure 1). This finding has been challenged on many occasions, most notably by Gauthier in her Greeble experiments (Gauthier & Tarr, 1997).

References

De Renzi, E. (1997). Prosopagnosia. In T.E. Feinberg & M.J. Farah (Eds), *Behavioral neurology and neuropsychology* (pp. 245–255). New York: McGraw-Hill.

Gauthier, I., & Tarr, M.J. (1997). Becoming a 'Greeble' expert: exploring mechanisms for face recognition. *Vision Research*, *37*(12), 1673–1682.

Kanwisher, N., McDermott, J., & Chun, M.M. (1997). The fusiform face area: a module in human extrastriate cortex specialised for face perception. *Journal of Neuroscience*, *17*(11), 4302–4311.

Ojemann, J.G., Ojemann, G.A., & Lettich, E. (1992). Neuronal activity related to faces and matching in human right nondominant temporal cortex. *Brain*, *115*, 1–13.

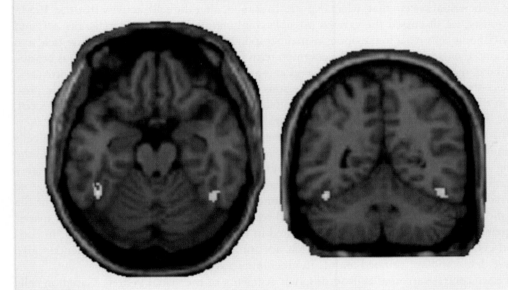

Figure 1   *Fusiform face area*

RECOGNITION OF OBJECTS

Lateral inhibition

The process of object perception starts at a very early point within the visual system, as soon as the retina is exposed to light. As previously discussed, light that reaches the photoreceptors triggers hyperpolarisation and a reduction in how much glutamate neurotransmitter is released. This not only activates the bipolar cells by decreasing their inhibition, but it also activates horizontal cells, which trigger a reduction in the activity of bipolar cells next to the ones that have been activated. We call this decreased activity of bipolar cells outside the centre of the stimulus and the concurrent increased activity of cells at the centre 'lateral inhibition'. Lateral inhibition demonstrates that vision is an active process, more than simply seeing what is physically there; it also explains optical illusions, notably Mach bands. A series of photoreceptors in the eye react differently to

ESSENTIAL BIOLOGICAL PSYCHOLOGY

changing light intensity. When a cell becomes activated as a result of light exposure, it interferes with or stops nearby cells from becoming activated. Because of this, the boundaries between light and dark areas stand out more than they ordinarily would. For instance, in the absence of lateral inhibition, it would be far more difficult to discern the border between a black tile and a while tile.

Receptive fields

Lateral inhibition does not function alone in recognising objects. Receptive fields are areas of cells in the visual system that, when exposed to stimuli, alter the cell's activity (Kuffler, 1953). Previously, we discussed the various possible combinations of ganglion cells: on, off, and on–off. Some cells react in the opposite manner to light in the centre of the receptive field and surround their receptive fields. The common term for this kind of receptive region is centre–surround, meaning that each receptive region is arranged into a central disc, the 'centre', and a concentric ring, the 'surround'. These regions have opposing reactions to light. Light present in the centre of the receptive region might boost the firing of a particular ganglion cell, while light in the surround of the receptive field might dampen the firing of that cell.

The way in which the centre–surround receptive field is organised allows ganglion cells to send information about whether the cells are firing and also about the differences in the firing rates of cells in the centre and surround. This makes it possible for cells to relay information regarding the light and dark (or contrast) inside the visual field. The size of the receptive regions of these centre–surround cells is dependent on the position of the ganglion cells on the retina. Cells with small receptive fields are stimulated by high spatial frequencies, give fine detail, and are situated in the central portion of the retina. In contrast, cells with large receptive fields that are stimulated by low spatial frequencies give coarse detail and are situated mainly in innervate rods in the periphery.

We see centre–surround cells in different segments of the visual system. Ganglion cells can be found in the receptive fields in the lateral geniculate nucleus (LGN), with cells that have a centre–surround system and cells that are either on or off centre. In the visual cortex receptive regions, the cells are larger and have more complex stimuli requirements than the ganglion cells in the retina or LGN. The majority of cells beyond the LGN react to binocular input, and the receptive field does not appear to contain centre–surround cells but rather is responsive to lines and edges.

Using the receptive fields as a basis, Hubel and Wiesel (1979) categorised cells in the visual cortex into **simple cells**, **complex cells** and **hypercomplex cells**. Simple cells are only seen in the primary visual cortex, have elongated receptive fields, and are responsive to lines and edges. These receptive fields have a reaction to stimuli in a particular orientation and are most responsive to vertical light stimulating the on-centre region. Complex cells located in the striate and pre-striate cortex react to a bar of line stimuli in a certain orientation or moving in a certain direction. Hypercomplex cells are similar to complex cells and react to visual stimuli of a specific orientation. Hypercomplex cells do not, however, react if the line stimuli extend beyond a certain point in the receptive region, so a line that extends beyond this point will elicit no activity in the cell. This feature leads us to sometimes refer to hypercomplex cells as end-stopped (see Box 5.2).

BOX 5.2 Receptive fields in visual cortex

Some of the most important research on the structure of the visual system was done by David Hubel and Torsen Wiesel. They were investigating the behaviour of single neurons at various locations in the visual cortex and seeing if they could get the neurons to fire for certain stimuli such as black and white dots or circular spots of light. They took readings from the cat visual cortex via an electrode implanted within a single cell of the cortex. Their efforts were in vain as they failed to get a response from the visual cortex. Oddly however they eventually found that when concentrating on one area of the retina, passing the dot over the area sometimes produced neural firing. They discovered that the response had little to do with the dot and was in fact being produced by the edge of the glass slide (Figure 1). They found that the cells in the visual cortex responded not to the presence of light, but rather to the presence of edges in their region of the visual field. These edge-sensitive cells were called 'simple cells' (Figure 2). They went on to discover 'complex cells' which also responded to edges of a specific orientation at a specific location in the visual field. Observations also suggested that these complex cells obtained their information from simple cells lower in the visual hierarchy. Later cells further up the visual hierarchy were also discovered; these were termed hyper-complex cells and had end-stop properties. Later research has found them to be sub-classes of the simple and complex cells. As a result of this work, David Hubel and Torsen Wiesel won the Nobel Prize for medicine in 1981.

Reference

Hubel, D.H. & Wiesel, T.N. (1959). Receptive fields of single neurones in the cat's striate cortex. *Journal of Physiology*, *148*, 574–591.

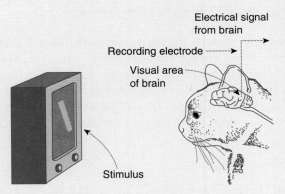

Figure 1   *Receptive field experiment*

(Continued)

(Continued)

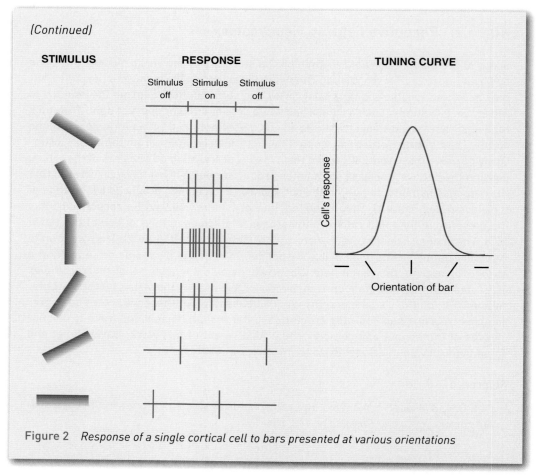

Figure 2   *Response of a single cortical cell to bars presented at various orientations*

As stated earlier, the cells in the visual cortex organise themselves into columns, each of which receives an equal level of input for both the left and right eyes. These columns of cells are referred to as ocular dominance columns. Each cell in a column reacts to the same orientation of stimuli (as seen in Figure 5.6). If monocular deprivation is experienced by the visual system early in life, normal development of the dominance columns does not occur and the non-deprived eye takes over almost all of the cortical cells.

SECONDARY VISUAL CORTEX

The secondary visual cortex, also known as the extrastriate cortex, is the area of the occipital cortex that can be found adjacent to the primary visual cortex. The primary visual cortex comprises Brodmann area 17, while the extrastriate cortex comprises Brodmann areas 18 and 19.

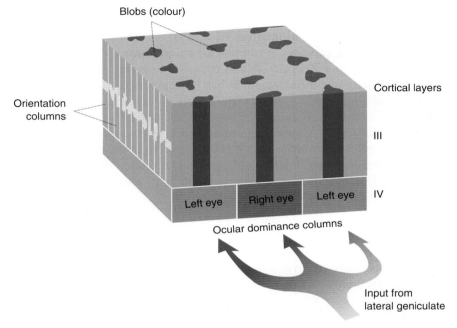

Blobs (colour)

Orientation
columns

Cortical layers

III

Left eye   Right eye   Left eye   IV

Ocular dominance columns

Input from
lateral geniculate

Figure 5.6   *Ocular dominance columns*

Visual area V2

Visual area V2 is the first area within the secondary visual cortex. It gets strong connections from V1 (both forwards and backwards), and also transmits strong forward connections to upstream areas V3, V4 and V5. Area V2 is similar to V1 in several ways. Cells tune into different properties, like orientation, spatial frequency and colour. Also, neurons in this area are controlled by more intricate properties and have been associated with the orientation of illusory contours and figure–ground segmentation (Qiu & von der Heydt, 2005).

Visual area V3

Visual area V3 is a cortical region found directly in front of V2. There is considerable debate as to which section of the cortex contains this area. V3 is separated into two or three distinct sections. Some hypothesise about a 'dorsal V3' in the upper part of the cerebral hemisphere, which is discrete from the 'ventral V3' (or ventral posterior area, VP). We usually consider this dorsal V3, which obtains inputs from V2 and V1 and stretches out to the posterior parietal cortex, to be part of the dorsal stream. Imaging studies indicate that area V3 might be involved in the processing of global movement (Braddick, O'Brien, Wattam-Bell, Atkinson, Hartley, & Turner, 2001).

Visual area V4

Visual area V4 obtains information from V2 and relays information to the posterior inferotemporal cortex. In addition, it obtains inputs from area V1 and is more weakly connected to area V5. Semir Zeki (1977) was the first to suggest that V4 was responsible for the processing of colour information. It has been proposed that this human area is homologous to macaque area V4, which is arguably colour selective. Others have suggested that colour stimuli in humans activate V8 but not V4 (Hadjikhani, Liu, Dale, Cavanagh, & Tootell, 1998). Many studies now report the colour area as V4/V8. In more recent years, it has been discovered that V4 is the first area in the ventral stream to demonstrate strong attentional modulation (Moran & Desimone, 1985). Lesions of V4 in human beings can result in achromatopsia, a condition in which the person only sees in shades of grey (Zeki & Bartels, 1999).

Visual area V5

Visual area V5, or visual area MT (middle temporal), is a part of the extrastriate visual cortex that scientists believe is pivotal to the ability to perceive motion. Area V5 connects to many brain areas; inputs include visual areas V1, V2 and dorsal V3. It transmits information to neighbouring cortex and the **frontal eye regions**. Lesion of V5 may result in akinetopsia, a condition in which the individual is unable to perceive movement (Zihl, von Cramon, & Mai, 1983).

THE PERCEPTION OF COLOUR, MOTION AND DEPTH

COLOUR VISION

We discussed earlier how the cones in the retina play a role in colour vision and how these neurons are the first stage in the process of colour perception. Here we will examine two theories of colour vision to complete the story about our perception of colour.

The Young–Helmholtz trichromatic theory

The **theory of trichromatic** vision was suggested in 1802, more than 50 years prior to the discovery of the three receptors responsible for colour vision. This theory was the formulation of Thomas Young, who suggested that the ability to see colour is the result of the interaction between three different receptors. Later, Helmholtz discovered that people with normal colour vision only require three wavelengths of light to create all the colours of the spectrum. Helmholtz performed colour-matching studies in which individuals would change the quantity of the three different wavelengths of light to correspond with a test colour. Participants were unable to perform colour matching when there were only two wavelengths, but they could do it for any colour when three wavelengths were used. This theory was eventually called the **Young–Helmholtz theory** of colour vision. The Young–Helmholtz theory addresses trichromatic colour vision – the way in which the photoreceptor cells in the eyes of humans and other primates work to enable colour vision.

Helmholtz developed the theory further in the 1850s, and suggested that the three kinds of cone photoreceptor could be classified according to their reaction to the wavelengths of light hitting the retina: short preferring (blue), middle preferring (green) and long preferring (red) (Figure 5.7). The brain thus interprets the relative strengths of the signals at different wavelengths sensed by the three kinds of cones as a detectable colour.

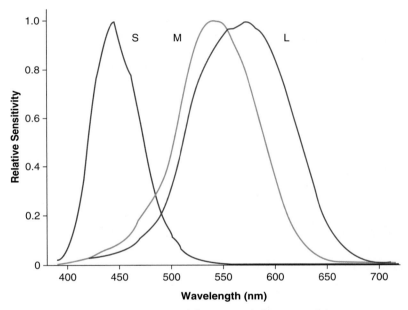

Figure 5.7   *Three wavelengths of light: short (S), medium (M) and long (L)*

Hering's opponent-process theory

The **colour opponent** mechanism postulates that the human visual system interprets information regarding colour by processing signals from cones and rods in an antagonistic way. The three kinds of cones – red, green and blue, or L (long), M (medium) and S (short) – have some overlap in the wavelengths of light to which they react. It seems that the system works best when the visual system processes the differences between the responses rather than the response of an individual cone. Opponent-process theory holds that three opponent channels exist: red versus green, blue versus yellow, and black versus white. The last is not associated with colour and identifies variations between light and dark, or luminance. Reactions to one colour in an opponent channel antagonise the responses to the other colour. This means that, because one colour triggers an excitatory effect and the other triggers an inhibitory effect, the opponent colours cannot be perceived simultaneously (it is not possible for the visual system to be excited and inhibited at the same time). The fact that there are afterimages supports the existence of this arrangement. If you fix your eyes on one colour for a minute or so, then cast your gaze onto a white surface, you will see a negative afterimage which is opposite in brightness and complementary in colour: so blue's afterimage will be yellow, and green's afterimage will be red. This process is the result of the rebound effect of prolonged inhibition or excitation of retinal ganglion cells.

While the trichromatic theory provides a definition for the means by which the retina of the eye lets the visual system detect colour with three kinds of cones, the opponent-process theory accounts for systems that receive and process information from cones. The trichromatic and opponent-process theories were once believed to be in conflict, but it is now thought that the three types of cones signal the mechanisms that are responsible for the opponent process, which then process them at a more complex level.

Retinex theory

There still remains a great deal to understand about the processing of colour information. For instance, let's look at how the visual system perceives the same colour no matter what the illumination is like. A yellow banana appears yellow to us at lunchtime, when the light source is white sunlight, and still appears yellow when the main light source is red in the evening. We refer to this phenomenon as colour consistency (Zeki, 1980). Edwin Land's retinex theory makes suggestions that might account for colour consistency. This proposes that when information is relayed from the retina to the cortex, the cortex compares each of the inputs and decides on how brightness and colour will be perceived for each area (Land, 1977). So, for example, if the cortex picks up a continuous amount of red in what it is viewing, it will deduct a little bit of red from every item to determine its true colour.

MOTION PERCEPTION

It is not easy to explain how we perceive motion in terms of neural processing, but area V5 seems to be pivotal to the processing of visual motion, since we know that damage in this area can disrupt the ability to perceive movement. The pathway from area V1 to area V5 and up to the posterior parietal lobe has a selective responsibility for perceiving motion (Movshon, Lisberger, & Krauzlis, 1990). Individuals who have suffered an injury to this pathway, especially in area V5, find they do not always accurately see movement; as mentioned earlier, this condition is called akinetopsia (Zeki, 1991). V5 in the human is analogous to area MT in primates.

Psychology concerns itself with two types of motion perception – first order and second order. When we talk about first-order motion perception, we are referring to how we perceive the movement of an item that differs in luminance from its background. Second-order motion perception is where the item in motion is defined by some other quality that does not cause an increase in luminance, e.g. contrast, texture or flicker. First- and second-order information appears to be fully shared at the level of area V5/MT of the visual system, and imaging studies indicate that nerve cells in this section of the cortex activate when people view moving objects (Tootell et al., 1995).

Motion-sensitive nerve cells in V1, also known as component direction-selective neurons, only pick up motion in one plane – horizontal, vertical or oblique (Newsome et al., 1989). The cells in area V5 are known as pattern direction-selective neurons; here information from V1 is added together to encode the object moment in multiple planes, so area V5 is able to identify that something is moving down and to the left, for example. How we perceive speed is derived from the firing pattern of nerve cells in area V5. An object moving very rapidly is a direct result of a higher firing rate of neurons in this area (Movshon et al., 1990). Pathways from V5 extend into the brain stem and also the cerebellum, which controls the eye movements that allow us to maintain gaze on items in motion. Furthermore, this magnocellular pathway also projects into the posterior parietal cortex which controls and guides bodily movements towards objects and the environment.

THE BINDING PROBLEM

One question that still remains unanswered is how the fragmented visual processing of shape, colour, motion, etc. unifies into the perception of complete objects. The problem of creating a unified perception from the responses of several different nerve cells is called 'the binding problem'. The binding problem is not only associated with visual perception but is evident in every modality of perception, and several accounts of this occurrence have been documented in the production of language and perception of sound. The binding problem is also an issue in memory research. If we think about all the associations we encode every day, there must be a mechanism for connecting associates with memories of events; but how are we able to remember these associations among different aspects of an occurrence, and how do we retain those associations throughout our lives? The hippocampus and the prefrontal cortex, parts of the brain that are also involved with memory, appear to be important to binding.

One line of research was conducted on the topic of perceptual unification. It examined the connection between gamma-band oscillations of neural activity and visual binding. We sometimes call these oscillations 'oscillatory neural circuits'. The connection between neural oscillations and binding was first found from electrical recordings of single cells in the monkey and cat cortices (Singer & Gray, 1995). Other research has utilised imaging methods, like ERP and MEG, to identify similar events in the human brain. Researchers have discovered that when people see and recognise a face, neurons in the visual cortex generate activity at approximately 30–80 action potentials per second or gamma-band oscillations (Rodriguez, George, Lachaux, Martinerie, Renault, & Varela, 1999). We don't really know what makes this synchronised activity occur or whether it results in binding, but scientists have found it forms in infancy by 8 months of age – the same age at which we see the onset of perceptual binding of spatially separated static visual features (Csibra, Davis, Spratling, & Johnson, 2000).

DISORDERS OF OBJECT PERCEPTION

VISUAL AGNOSIA

Visual **agnosia** is a neurological disorder characterised by the inability to recognise familiar objects. This is distinct from blindness, which is an absence of sensory perception to the brain because of damage to the eye, the optic nerve, or the brain's main visual systems like the optic radiations or the main visual cortex. A stroke or some other serious ailment can damage the posterior occipital and/or temporal lobe(s) in the brain, resulting in visual agnosia. People who have this condition might be able to point to visual objects and describe them in detail but are unable to recognise the entire object. There have also been cases where individuals are able to recognise objects but not faces; this type of agnosia is known as **prosopagnosia**. This dissociation of object and face recognition has led some scientists to think that there is something special about faces and that there is a specific part of the brain dedicated to the processing of faces (Farah, 1996). Individuals diagnosed with prosopagnosia also find it hard to identify animals and plants (Farah, Levinson, & Klein, 1995), so the loss appears to demonstrate a problem with making complex visual discriminations and not a particular deficit involving faces on the whole, as was first believed (Farah, Wilson, Drain, & Tanaka, 1998).

APPERCEPTIVE AGNOSIA

This condition leaves an individual completely incapable of recognising objects. It is hard to distinguish between different shapes, even though other aspects of sight, like the ability to see detail and colour, are fully functional. These individuals have difficulty recognising, copying, and distinguishing between visual stimuli and shapes. Apperceptive agnosics will not be able to perform a task that involves object matching. Since individuals with this condition cannot identify even the most basic shapes, we consider apperceptive agnosia to be a problem in the early part of the visual processing system. This is in contrast to individuals who have received a diagnosis of associative agnosia.

ASSOCIATIVE AGNOSIA

Individuals diagnosed with associative agnosia are unable to assign meaning to an item, animal or structure that they can clearly see. Injury in such cases seems to centre on damage to the temporal and occipital lobes, particularly in the left occipital-temporal area, and sometimes damage to the posterior portion (the splenium) of the corpus callosum. The diagnostic criterion for this disorder is that the individual can copy/draw things that they are unable to identify. The disorder usually presents with other neuropsychological problems such as impaired language or memory and is very uncommon in a 'pure' or uncomplicated form. A person with this condition might not know that they have a problem with their vision and may say that they are 'muddled' when completing everyday tasks. The debate surrounding associative agnosia centres on whether the underlying problem involves disturbances in higher-order visual perception, such as integration of information into complete wholes; whether it is a disconnection syndrome involving a failure in the relation between language and the visual system; or whether it is a problem with the semantic processing system of the brain.

BLINDSIGHT

An individual can sustain damage to area V1 and be unable to experience conscious vision from part of the visual field, yet still be able to experience a response and localise visual objects. This phenomenon – not having conscious vision but being able to 'see' – is known as blindsight. People who have blindsight are not aware of any visual stimuli; however, they are able, often in a forced response, to predict aspects of a visual stimulus, such as location or movement, at levels significantly above chance. In the early 1970s, Lawrence Weiskrantz and colleagues demonstrated this effect, and showed that if forced to guess about whether a stimulus is present in their blind region, some individuals guess correctly many more times than one would expect (Weiskrantz, 1993). The concept of blindsight is still controversial because not everyone experiences it, and the phenomenon varies in degree from individual to individual. However, it is believed that, even after area V1 or the lateral geniculate nucleus (LGN) is injured, visual information can still be transmitted to the superior colliculus in the midbrain and on to the motor control output systems, making it possible for the individual with blindsight to identify the visual stimulation despite the fact that it is not coming into conscious vision (Cowey & Stoerig, 1995). Nevertheless, if the superior colliculus could control unconscious guide movements, we could anticipate that anyone with damage to area V1 would have blindsight. Some do, but more do not, and of those who do show blindsight, it is only in a portion of their visual field (Fendrich, Wessinger, & Gazzaniga, 1992). The region of blindness, also referred to as a **scotoma**, is in the visual region opposite to the damaged hemisphere and can be of different sizes. The other hypothesis is that small portions of the visual cortex do not get damaged and form islands of neural tissue, not sufficient to enable conscious vision but enough for blindsight to happen.

HEMISPATIAL NEGLECT

Hemispatial neglect, also referred to as unilateral neglect or spatial neglect, is a condition in which, after one hemisphere of the brain has been damaged, a deficit in attention to the opposite side of space is observed (see Figure 5.8). Individuals with damaged parietal lobes in the right hemisphere tend to disregard everything that happens on the left side of their bodies and the world (Bartolomeo & Chokron, 2002). Right hemisphere damage is a more frequent and more severe cause of unilateral neglect than left-hemisphere damage (Chatterjee, 1995). In the early stages of the disorder, people with this condition may also disclaim ownership of their contralateral limb and disregard certain parts of their own body.

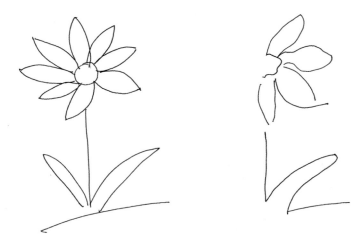

Figure 5.8   *Picture of a flower drawn by an individual with left unilateral neglect*

SUMMARY

This chapter has explored the visual system (Figure 5.9). It began with the structure of the eye, showing that a number of cell layers form the retina and that the photosensitive cells of the retina are referred to as rods and cones – cells that transform light energy into signals that the optic nerves send to the brain. The cones give a different response depending on the colour of light their photopigments absorb: one kind of photopigment absorbs red light, another absorbs green light, and a third absorbs blue light. The rods react best when exposed to white light. Transduction refers to the process of converting light energy signals into electrical polarisation; this polarisation process results in a neural signal that moves along the optic nerve to the brain. In this chapter we have identified three different types of retinal ganglion cells: on ganglion cells that are energised by bipolar cells reacting to light conditions; off ganglion cells that become excited with the removal of the light stimulus, and are inhibited by amacrine cells when light is present; and on–off ganglion cells that become excited by bipolar cells in the presence of a light stimulus, and are not inhibited by amacrine cells upon the removal of the light stimulus. The characteristics of the different ganglion cells were then explained.

Visual information is transferred from the retina inside the eye up the optic nerve into the brain via the LGN. The second of 12 paired cranial nerves, the optic nerve is considered to be part of the CNS. The information reaches the visual cortex, and here we discovered that the visual cortex is divided into visual areas, the primary visual cortex being visual area 1 or V1. The visual cortex is separated into six distinct layers, each of which has a different function. We label these layers 1–6. Layer IV gets the most visual feedback from the LGN. The chapter went on to explore other regions of the visual cortex and detailed the extrastriate cortex, which is an area that surrounds the primary visual cortex

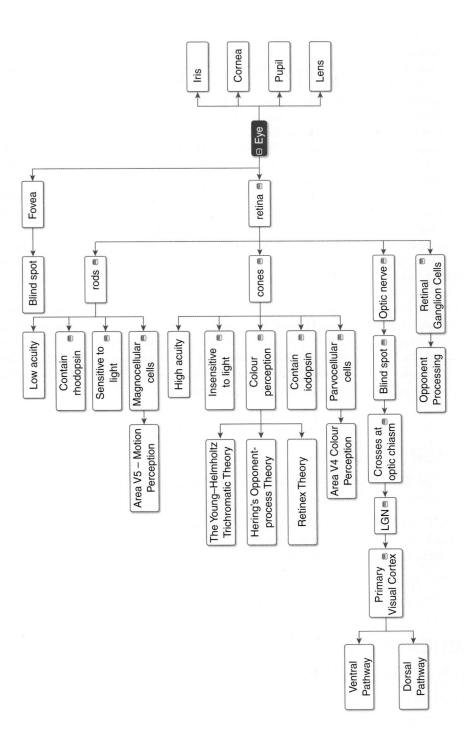

Figure 5.9 *Visual system overview*

and receives information from it. The extrastriate cortex, also known as the visual association cortex, divides into two separate visual pathways: one is known as the dorsal stream and the other is known as the ventral stream. The dorsal stream is sometimes called the 'where' pathway or the 'how' pathway, and deals with motion. The ventral stream, also known as the 'what' pathway, has to do with recognising forms and object representation. We then discussed object recognition and the processes of lateral inhibition and receptive fields. Visual areas from V1 to V5 were detailed.

Three theories of colour vision were explained. The trichromatic theory revealed that three cone photoreceptors are responsible for seeing colour; they are classified as short preferring (blue), middle preferring (green) and long preferring (red), which corresponds with their reaction to the wavelengths of light arriving at the retina. The brain interprets the relative strengths of the signals sensed by the three kinds of cones as a detectable colour. Hering's opponent-process theory shows how a colour opponent mechanism in the human visual system interprets information regarding colour by processing signals from cones and rods in an antagonistic way. The three opponent channels are red versus green, blue versus yellow, and black versus white. Retinex theory was also mentioned; this explains how the visual system perceives the same colour no matter what the illumination is like. Motion perception was then examined by detailing how cells in area V5 detect object motion. One mystery mentioned was the problem of how the fragmented visual processing of shape, colour, motion, etc. unifies into the perception of complete objects. This is called the binding problem, and it has been investigated with ERP techniques. Finally, the chapter ended with a discussion on the various disorders of visual perception including visual agnosia, blindsight and hemispatial neglect.

 ## FURTHER READING

Gauthier, I., & Tarr, M.J. (1997). Becoming a 'Greeble' expert: exploring mechanisms for face recognition. *Vision Research*, 37(12), 1673–1682.

Haxby, J.V., Grady, C.L., Horwitz, B., Ungerleider, L.G., Mishkin, M., Carson, R.E., et al. (1991). Dissociation of object and spatial visual processing pathways in human extrastriate cortex. *Proceedings of the National Academy of Sciences USA*, 88(5), 1621–1625.

Zeki, S. (1980). The representation of colours in the cerebral cortex. *Nature*, 284(5755), 412–418.

 ## KEY QUESTIONS

1   Describe the 'what' and 'where' pathways in visual perception.

2   What are the theories of colour perception?

3   What is the binding problem?

NON-VISUAL SENSORY SYSTEMS

People have broad, less specialised sensory systems compared to those of other animals, mainly due to the fact that a broad range of stimuli is important to us. When we look at our senses, our bodies are perfectly capable of experiencing a broad variety of stimuli and obtaining valuable information, which allows us to maintain appropriate behaviour in a complex environment. In this chapter, we will discuss the biological actions that result in these senses. We also discuss how we use these senses to form perceptions about reality.

SENSORY PROCESSING

Sensory processing is an intricate set of events that allows the brain to understand what is occurring inside your body and in the outside world. Each animal species has a distinct perception of the world, which is founded on their sensory systems being a part of the nervous system and having the responsibility for processing sensory information. A sensory system includes sensory receptors, neural pathways, and areas of the brain used in sensory perception. The most common sensory systems, besides sight, that we will talk about here are those that perceive somatic touch, sound, taste and smell (Hollins, 2010).

Sensory systems work to filter the environment and identify four different features of a stimulus: type or modality, intensity, location and duration. Specific sensory receptor organs are sensitive to specific types of stimuli, relaying information to certain parts of the brain to be processed. The process of sensory perception starts at the receptor cells, which are responsible for converting energy into neural activity. Receptor cells have a receptive field that is a particular part of the sensory nerve cells, which, when exposed to stimuli, will influence the firing of the nerve cell. Generally the system works flawlessly; however, some individuals have an abnormal neuronal connectivity between auditory and visual cortical areas that can leave them with a condition called synaesthesia. Here, a stimulus in one sensory modality triggers an automatic sensation in another; so in 'coloured hearing', hearing words brings about sensations of colour. More information about the neural anatomy of this phenomenon can be found in Box 6.1.

BOX 6.1   Hearing colour

Background

Synaesthesia is a neurological condition in which stimulation of one sensory or cognitive pathway leads to automatic, involuntary experiences in a second sensory or cognitive pathway. In the 'coloured hearing' type of synaesthesia, individuals report colour experiences when they hear spoken words. This study (Nunn et al., 2002) investigated the claim that if the synaesthetic colour experiences resemble the process in normal colour vision, one would expect to observe activation in the human colour centre called V4 (Lueck et al., 1989), sometimes also called V8 (Hadjikhani et al., 1998).

Method

Subjects (all female) were 12 right-handed and one left-handed (by self-report of handedness) word–colour synaesthetes, and 27 right-handed and one left-handed controls. The study employed fMRI to compare the activation pattern elicited by spoken words versus tones in synaesthetes and in controls. The study compared the activation pattern in synaesthetes hearing words to activations in response to actual seen colours, and investigated whether normal subjects imagining colours showed activation of a similar kind to that observed when synaesthetes spontaneously experience colours in response to heard words.

Results

Hearing words compared with tones demonstrated that, in both synaesthetes and controls, there is activation of language areas of the perisylvian regions: the superior temporal gyrus bilaterally, and the left inferior frontal gyrus. Synaesthetes also showed additional activation in the colour-selective areas V4/V8 in the left hemisphere. The location of the activation patterns elicited by colours in the right hemisphere was consistent with activation in colour areas V4/V8. Control subjects showed no activity in V4/V8 when imagining colours in response to spoken words, despite overtraining on word–colour associations similar to those spontaneously reported by synaesthetes. No activity was detected in areas V1 or V2, which suggested that activity in the primary visual cortex is not necessary for colour experiences.

Interpreting the results

These results confirm that V4/V8 was not activated in a colour imagery task when compared to a spatial orientation control task, and thus suggest that the neural substrate of synaesthetic colour experience is closer to that of true colour perception than to colour imagery. In addition, despite extensive overtraining on the relevant word–colour associations, no activation of V4/V8 could be achieved in controls in the imaging tasks, which adds support to the idea of direct connections in brain regions rather than the

(Continued)

(Continued)

alternative account that synaesthesia results from strong associative learning. The authors favour a genetic account of altered developmental processes, given that synaesthesia runs in families and is strongly sex linked (Baron-Cohen, Burt, Smith-Leyton, Harrison, & Bolton, 1996).

References

Baron-Cohen, S., Burt, L., Smith-Leyton, F., Harrison, J., & Bolton, P. (1996). Synaesthesia: prevalence and familiality. *Perception, 25*, 1073–1079.

Hadjikani, N., Liu, A.K., Dale, A.M., Cavanagh, P. and Tootell, R.B.H. (1998) Retinotopy and color sensitivity in human visual cortical area V8. *Nature Neuroscience*, 1, 235–241.

Lueck, C.J., Zeki, S., Friston, K.J., Deiber, M.P., Cope, P., Cunningham, V.J., Lammertsma, A.A., Kennard, C. and Frackowiak, R.S.J. (1989). The colour centre in the cerebral cortex of man. *Nature,* 340, 386–389.

Nunn, J.A., Gregory, L.J., Brammer, M., Williams, S.C.R., Parslow, D.M., Morgan, M.J., et al. (2002). Functional magnetic resonance imaging of synesthesia: activation of V4/V8 by spoken words. *Nature Neuroscience, 5*, 371–375.

THE SOMATOSENSES

Humans have senses that we can draw upon to examine the world – both inside and outside our bodies. There are three separate but interacting somatosensory systems:

⊛ *Exteroceptive system*, which senses external stimuli applied to the skin, i.e. skin sensations. This is divided into three general systems, one for perceiving mechanical touch, one for perceiving thermal stimuli and one for perceiving pain.

⊛ *Proprioception system*, which is the sense of the relative placement of parts of the human body that comes from the receptors in our muscles and joints (see Chapter 7). Proprioception is also an interoceptive sense. It provides us with feedback solely based on the internal condition of the body. This sense monitors body position as well as movement. It ensures that intended movements are accurate. It also determines where the various parts of the body are located, relative to one another. Proprioceptive receptors are situated in the muscles, tendons and joints.

⊛ *Interroceptive system*, which provides information about the internal environment of the body such as temperature and blood pressure.

Figure 6.1 *Skin components*

SKIN RECEPTORS

The skin comprises three layers: the epidermis, which provides protection against environmental factors; the dermis, which is a site for the appendages of the skin; and the hypodermis, which is the subcutaneous fatty tier (Figure 6.1). The epidermis has lots of capabilities, like securing the organs inside the body, keeping water out of the body, and helping maintain the body temperature through perspiration (Figure 6.2).

The distribution of the different receptors found in the skin is shown in Figure 6.3. You will see the Meissner's corpuscles on hairy skin, situated in the elevation of the dermis and stretching out into the layer known as the epidermis. These receptors detect pressure on the skin, and are responsible for sensitivity to light touch: in particular, they have highest sensitivity when sensing vibrations lower than 50 **hertz** (cycles per second; unit symbol Hz). Merkel's discs or the Merkel neurite complex are receptors that also react to pressure and are found in the skin close to the sweat discs. Both the Meissner's corpuscles and the Merkel's discs have small receptive fields and adapt quickly to sensation, so that, for example, you don't constantly sense things such as your clothing or the sofa you're sitting on.

The biggest sensory receptors are the Pacianian corpuscles, located on both hairy and non-hairy (glabrous) epidermis and also some mucous membranes. They are mechanoceptors and register larger variations in pressure and vibrations. The Pacianian corpuscle has only one afferent nerve fibre with a sensitive receptor membrane covering one end. The membrane's sodium channels will open should the membrane become deformed in any way; this results in action potentials being generated, by opening pressure-sensitive sodium ion channels in the axon membrane. This lets the sodium ions in, which creates a receptor potential. The corpuscle has many concentric capsules of connective tissue around it with a viscous gel between them.

The Ruffini ending or Ruffini corpuscle is a class of slowly adapting mechanoreceptors found just beneath the surface of the skin, in the layer known as the dermis. This spindle-shaped receptor is quite sensitive to the stretching of the skin. It is also sensitive to low-frequency vibrations. It is not, however, sensitive to pressure. These sensors may also play a role in controlling finger movements, as well as finger position. They may register mechanical deformation and angle changes within joints. It appears that these

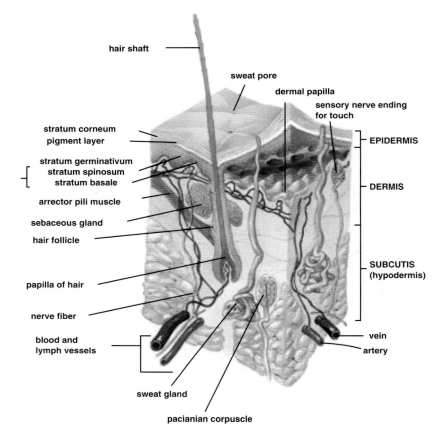

hair shaft

sweat pore

dermal papilla

sensory nerve ending for touch

stratum corneum pigment layer

EPIDERMIS

stratum germinativum stratum spinosum stratum basale

DERMIS

arrector pili muscle

sebaceous gland

hair follicle

papilla of hair

SUBCUTIS (hypodermis)

nerve fiber

blood and lymph vessels

vein

artery

sweat gland

pacianian corpuscle

Figure 6.2 *Skin structure*

receptors also observe slippage of things on the skin's surface, regulating the ability to hold on to an object.

Free nerve endings are an additional kind of somatosensory skin receptor that can be found immediately beneath the top layer of the skin. Free nerve endings are a non-specialised, afferent type that are not encapsulated and do not have complex sensory structures. This is different from those found in Meissner's or Pacianian corpuscles. Free nerve endings pick up changes in temperature as well as pain.

Other kinds of receptors in the epidermis are dubbed **nociceptors**, which are free nerve endings that trigger feelings of pain. Nociceptors don't detect regular stimuli and have a high threshold to sensing chemical, thermal or mechanical stimuli prior to an action potential being made. Internal nociceptors are found in many organs, like the muscle, joint, bladder, stomach and organs in the digestive tract.

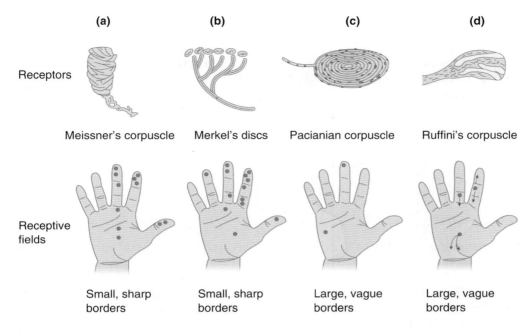

Figure 6.3 *Types of skin receptor*

SPINAL CORD

The spinal cord connects the brain and the rest of the body (Figure 6.4). It begins at the foramen magnum, as an extension of the medulla, and travels to the height of the first or second lumbar vertebrae. It is a pivotal two-way connection between the brain and the rest of the body. The spinal cord is about 40 to 50 centimetres in length and 1 to 1.5 centimetres in width. Two sequential rows of nerve roots come out of each side. The roots of these nerves connect distally, forming 31 pairs of spinal nerves. The spinal cord is a cylindrical structure of nervous tissue. It is composed of both white and grey matter, which is uniformly organised and is divided into four sections: the cervical (C) region, the thoracic (T) region, the lumbar (L) region and the sacral (S) region (see Figure 6.5). Each of these regions comprises several segments. In the spinal nerve, you will find motor and sensory nerves that connect to the rest of the body. Every section of the spinal cord activates a **dermatome**. The pia, arachnoid and dura are the three meninges that protect the spinal cord. The dura is the rough outer sheath, the arachnoid sits under it, and the pia attaches close to the surface of the cord. The lateral denticulate ligaments emanating via the pia folds connect the spinal cord to the dura.

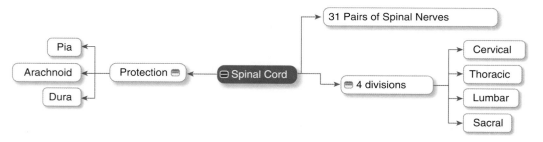

Figure 6.4   *Function of the spinal cord*

DERMATOME

A dermatome is a section of skin which is innervated by peripheral nerve fibres from a single dorsal root ganglion. Thus a severed nerve results in the individual losing all feeling from that particular dermatome. Due to the fact that every part of the cord activates a different part of the body, we can accurately map dermatomes on the body surface (see Figure 6.6). Consequently, loss of sensation in a specific derma-tome can tell us exactly which part of the spine is damaged. As sensory information from the body is transmitted to the central nervous system via the dorsal roots, the axons that develop out of dorsal root ganglion cells are categorised as primary sen-sory axons. Nerve cells in the dorsal root are the first-order sensory neurons. The bulk of the axons in the ventral roots begin from motor neurons located in the **ven-tral horn** of the spine and activate skeletal muscles. Axons also start at the lateral horn and make synaptic connections on autonomic ganglia that activate visceral organs. The peripheral processes of the ventral root axons connect with those of the dorsal root ganglion cells, forming peripheral nerves.

SOMATOSENSORY PATHWAYS

Sensory information travels from the sensory receptor to the brain by its own distinct pathways. These pathways lead into the spinal cord or brain stem, and connect with additional nerve cell clusters (Figure 6.7).

CONSCIOUS SENSATION

A somatosensory pathway will characteristically have three neurons: primary, second-ary and tertiary (or first, second and third). The cell body of the first neuron is located

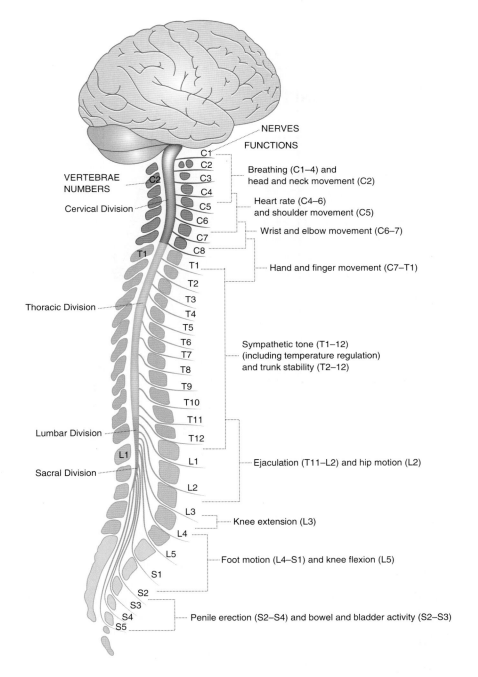

Figure 6.5   *Sections of spinal cord*

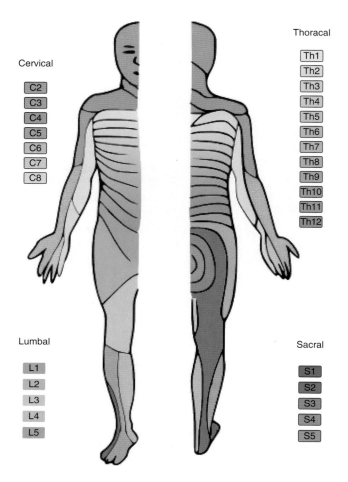

Figure 6.6   *Dermatomes: map showing approximate boundaries*

in the dorsal root ganglion of the spinal nerve, while the cell body of the second neuron is located in either the spinal cord or the brain stem. The ascending axons of this neuron will **decussate** or cross to the opposite side, either in the spinal cord or in the brain stem. The third neuron synapses in the ventral posteriolateral thalamic nuclei. Somatosensory information ascends to the cortex via two major somatosensory pathways: the dorsal-column/medial-lemniscal system which carries information about touch and proprioception, and the anterolateral system which carries information about temperature and pain.

Figure 6.7   *Sensory pathways*

Dorsal-column/medial-lemniscal system

Axons that transmit information about touch and proprioception ascend through the dorsal columns in the spine, which are known as the dorsal-column/medial-lemniscal system, to the nuclei in the medulla. These axons synapse with neurons in the gracile nucleus and cuneate nucleus at the level of the medulla oblongata. The medial nucleus gracilis receives projections from the lower parts of the body; the lateral nucleus cuneatus receives projections from the upper parts of the body. The double dorsal projections then move across the brain and create a cluster of fibres dubbed the medial lemniscus, prior to synapsing with the ventral posteriolateral thalamic nucleus. The third neurons project to the primary somatosensory cortex (see Figure 6.8).

Anterolateral system

The anterolateral system consists of three different tracts (Figure 6.9):

- spinothalamic tract, which projects to the ventral posterior nucleus

- spinoreticular tract, which projects to the reticular formation

- spinotectal tract, which projects to the tectum.

The axons of the secondary cells cross over (decussate) to the opposite side of the spine by way of the anterior white commissure, and to the anterolateral corner of the spine. The axons of the spinothalamic tract and the spinoreticular tract move up along the spine, enter the brain stem and synapse with third-order nerve cells in a number of nuclei of the thalamus. The spinothalamic tract projects to the ventral posterior nucleus, the spinoreticular tract transmits information to the reticular formation, while the spinotectal tract terminates in the inferior and superior colliculi of the tectum.

Pain pathways must also descend from the brain, because if one is not actively aware of the pain, it can hurt less. This is seen in individuals who, when given placebos for pain,

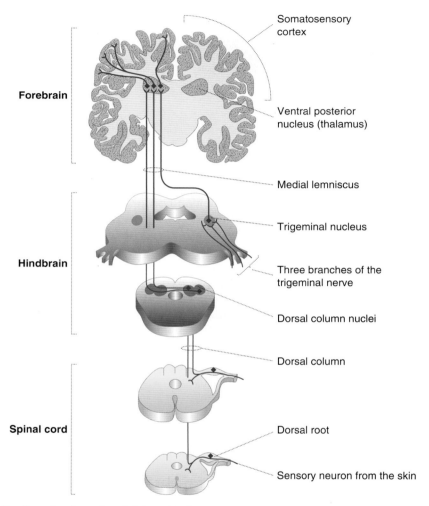

Figure 6.8 *Dorsal-column/medial-lemniscal system*

report their pain has been reduced. The area of the somatosensory cortex which relays to the thalamus and the hypothalamus is where these descending pathways begin. The thalamic neurons move down into the midbrain and synapse via ascending pathways within the medulla and spinal cord. They inhibit ascending nerve signals. Furthermore, if they are stimulated, they produce pain relief (analgesia). The effects of these downward-moving pathways can also cause psychogenic pain (perceived pain with no real external reason). Pain sensation signals can touch off autonomic nervous system pathways as they go

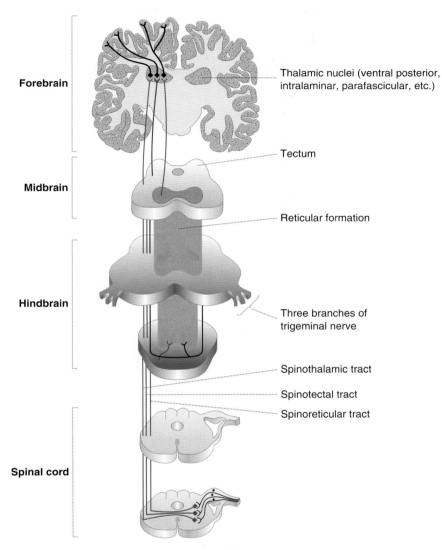

Forebrain

Thalamic nuclei (ventral posterior, intralaminar, parafascicular, etc.)

Tectum

Midbrain

Reticular formation

Hindbrain

Three branches of trigeminal nerve

Spinothalamic tract

Spinotectal tract

Spinoreticular tract

Spinal cord

Figure 6.9 *Anterolateral system*

around the medulla, creating higher heart rate and blood pressure, hyperventilation and perspiration.

The common features of conscious somatosensory pathways are as follows:

❈ All have three neurons from receptor to cortex.

❈ The cell body of the first neuron is situated in the dorsal root ganglia.

❈ The second neuron crosses in the spinal cord or brain stem.

❈ All pathways ascend in the medial lemniscus to the thalamus.

❈ All synapse in the ventral posteriolateral thalamic nuclei.

❈ The third neuron projects to the primary somatosensory cortex.

UNCONSCIOUS SENSATION

There are quite a few pathways for unconscious proprioception; these communicate the information essential for the maintenance of normal muscle tone, posture and coordination. The muscle stretch and tension receptors initiate this from spinal interneurons that contribute in reflexes and regulate motor output. The unconscious proprioception pathways chiefly terminate in the **ipsilateral** cerebellum. The most studied pathways are those of the spinocerebellar tract.

Spinocerebellar tract

The spinocerebellar tract is a group of fibres originating in the spinal cord and terminating in the ipsilateral cerebellum. The dorsal tract conveys information to the cerebellum about limb and joint position (proprioception). This pathway transmits proprioceptive data from the body to the cerebellum. The spinal cord receives proprioceptive information through the dorsal root ganglia (first-order neurons), via the **dorsal horn,** and these synapse in dorsal or Clarke's nuclei with second-order neurons. Axon fibres from the dorsal nucleus send this proprioceptive information via the dorsal lateral funiculus to the cerebellum, where unconscious proprioceptive information processing occurs.

The ventral spinocerebellar tract originates from neurons in the intermediate grey matter of the thoracic and lumbar spinal cord, participates in reflexes and regulates the activity of the motor neurons in the spinal cord. The ventral tract obtains perceptive, fine touch and vibration information from a first-order neuron with its cell body in a dorsal ganglion. The axon travels via the fila radicularia to the grey matter's dorsal horn where it travels to the cerebellum through the superior cerebellum.

GATE THEORY OF PAIN

As already mentioned, thoughts and feelings can have an impact on both ascending and descending pain pathways. There are also other things, both physical and mental, that influence pain perception. To describe the intricate relationships between thoughts, feelings and pain, Ronald Melzack and Patrick Wall (1965) suggested the gate control theory of pain. They discovered a descending tract, which starts in the periaqueductal grey matter (PAG) of the midbrain and synapses with inhibitory interneurons within the dorsal horn of the spinal cord. Small unmyelinated nerve fibres (C fibres) bringing the pain signals, and larger nerves (A$_\beta$ fibres) that hold different sensory information, form a synaptic relationship with inhibitory interneurons inside the dorsal horn. The gate shuts when nociception occurs – when there is more small-fibre stimulation or solely small-fibre stimulation. This makes the inhibitory nerve cell become inactive, and the ascending nerve cell relays signals to the brain telling it to feel discomfort. The gate may be shut at the time of somatosensory input when there is additional large-fibre stimulation (or solely large-fibre stimulation). Although the inhibitory and projection nerve cells receive stimuli, the inhibitory nerve cells inhibit the transmission of pain signals to the brain (the gate closes).

Figure 6.10 shows a schematic representation of gate theory. **A$_\beta$** and **C fibres** coming from the skin stimulate the neuron N which is implicated in transmitting nociception. Pain cannot occur when this signal coming from the skin is weak, as the interneuron (E) is stimulated by the sensory A$_\beta$ somaesthetic fibres inhibiting nociceptive transmission. However, when the stimulus is stronger the small nociceptive C fibres reduce the inhibitory control and pain is felt. This theory doesn't go far enough to explain all that needs to be known about how pain is perceived. However, it does explain why rubbing your arm after you have injured it can diminish the perception of pain.

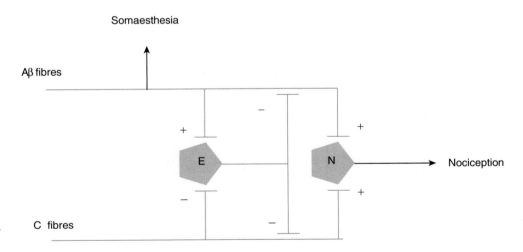

Figure 6.10   *Schematic representation of gate theory*

SOMATOSENSORY CORTEX

The primary somatosensory cortex (SI; Brodmann areas 3, 1, 2) is located in the postcentral gyrus (see Figure 6.11) and obtains **somatotopic** input from the thalamus. The degree

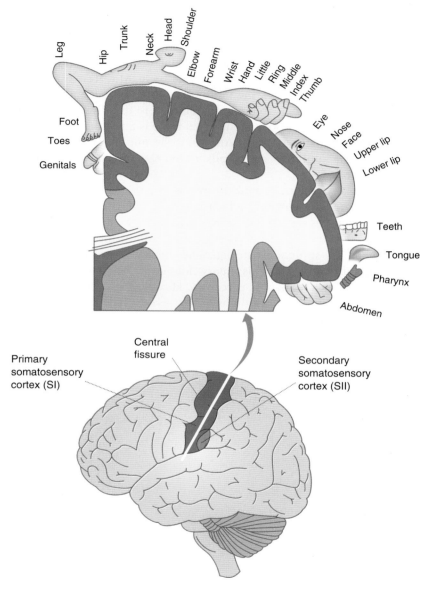

Figure 6.11 *Somatosensory cortex*

of sensory innervation by the cortex is represented on the sensory homunculus. Notice that the very sensitive areas such as the lips and the fingertips have a huge representation.

The secondary somatosensory cortex (SII; Brodmann area 40) is in the lower parietal lobe, and receives connections from the primary sensory cortex and also thalamic nuclei. Although it has much less precision than the primary cortex, this area responds to bilateral sensory stimuli.

The somatosensory association cortex (Brodmann areas 5 and 7) is posterior to the sensory cortex in the superior parietal lobes. This area receives connections from the primary and secondary sensory cortices, and damage to it affects an individual's ability to recognise objects by touch; this is called tactile agnosia.

AUDITORY SYSTEM

Audition, or hearing, is the capability to determine sound by detecting vibrations within the ear. The ear, in humans, is the site where the hearing process begins (Figure 6.12). The sound waves and vibrations are converted into nerve impulses, which the auditory cortex interprets. Sound waves have differences in magnitude and frequency. The amplitude of a sound wave informs us of how intense the sound will be, which we perceive as its **loudness**, while the wave's frequency is perceived as its **pitch**. Not all sounds are audible by every animal, as each species has a range of normal hearing for both volume and pitch. Many animals rely on the sense of hearing to communicate, making it pivotal to their ability to survive and reproduce. The human ear can perceive frequencies between 15 Hz and 20,000 Hz. The parts of the auditory system can be seen in Figure 6.13.

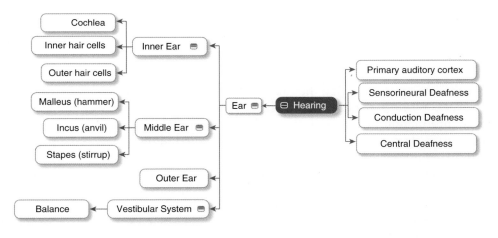

Figure 6.12   *The hearing process*

THE EAR

The ear is a sensory organ that detects sounds. It not only receives sound but, as we shall see, is also pivotal to the ability to maintain balance and body position.

Outer ear

The outer ear is made up of folds of cartilage known as the pinna. This structure not only reflects the sound waves but also alters the reflection of sound waves which provides the brain with information regarding the direction or location of the sound. The sound waves

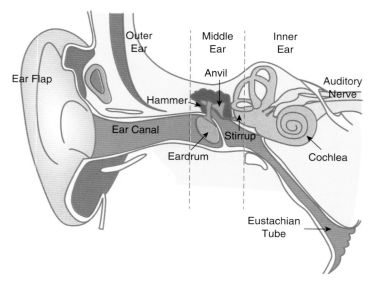

Figure 6.13   *Auditory system*

then travel into the auditory canal and, at the back part of the ear canal, hit the eardrum (or tympanic membrane) in the middle ear.

Middle ear

As sound waves travel through the ear canal, they will ultimately strike the tympanum or eardrum. When a sound wave hits the tympanic membrane, the membrane vibrates and the information then travels across the air-filled middle ear cavity via a series of small bones – the malleus (hammer), the incus (anvil) and the stapes (stirrup) – which send the vibrations to the oval window, a membrane found in the inner ear. The result of this system is that the sound waves are given greater pressure. This increase in pressure is necessary because the inner ear, past the oval window, is filled with liquid rather than air. The sound is not amplified equally through this system and the information remains in sound form; it is transduced into nerve impulses in the cochlea inside the ear. The Eustachian tube links the middle portion of the ear with the back part of the throat and is there to help air pressure stay equal on the two sides of the eardrum.

Inner ear

The inner ear contains the cochlea. The cochlea comprises three fluid-filled sections: the scala vestibuli, the scala media and the scala tympani (see Figure 6.14). The action of the stirrup on the circular window creates vibrations at the opening to the scala vestibuli and sets in motion the liquid within the cochlea. One section, the cochlear duct or scala media, contains the organ of Corti, and converts mechanical waves to nerve impulses. The hair cells of the organ of Corti convert the liquid waves into nerve signals.

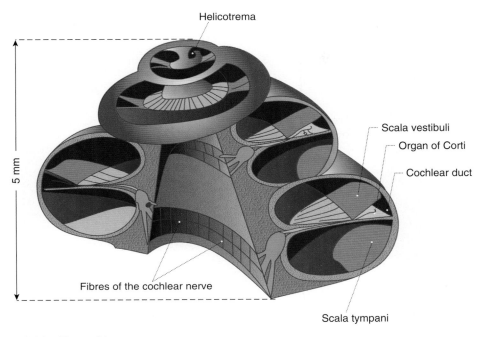

Figure 6.14   *The cochlea*

The cochlear hair cells of mammals are found in two biologically and functionally diverse types: the outer and inner hair cells. The organ of Corti is in the form of columns, each of which has a bundle of 100–200 specialised cilia located at its top, which basically function as the mechanical sensors for the auditory system. Above these cilia is the tectorial membrane which slides back and forth with the sound waves, displacing the hair cells (Figure 6.15). Hair cells have excitatory synapses on the cells of the auditory nerve. Similar to the photoreceptors of the eye, hair cells produce a graded response and not the all-or-nothing reaction that other nerve cells have.

TRANSDUCTION OF SOUND WAVE TO NERVE SIGNAL

Inner hair cells

The resting potential of inner hair cells is typically –60 mV. The cilia bend, causing the K^+ ion channels to open and the membrane to become depolarised. This depolarisation leads to a rapid influx of calcium, triggering the release of glutamate transmitters, which diffuse across the thin space between the hair cell and a nerve terminal. There, they bind to receptors and elicit action potentials in the nerve. In this fashion, the mechanical sound signal is converted into an electrical nerve signal. The hair cells return to their starting point, and the K^+ channels close. There is a brief period in which the membrane is hyperpolarised, and the neurotransmitter fails to be released. Inner hair cell nerve fibres are myelinated.

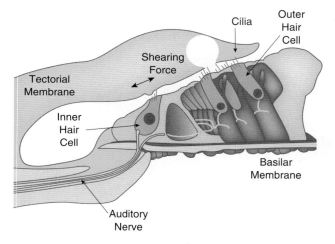

Figure 6.15 *Detail of organ of Corti*

Outer hair cells

Unmyelinated outer hair cells are seen only in mammals, and form a three-row arrangement. They may actively contribute to the tuning sensitivity and frequency selectivity of the cochlea.

NEURAL CONNECTIONS AND THE PATHWAY TO AUDITORY CORTEX

The hair cells synapse with the dendrites connected with the bipolar nerves in the spinal ganglion. The cochlear nerve develops out of the bipolar cells, which join with the vestibular system (balance system) to create the auditory nerve or vestibulocochlear nerve (cranial nerve VIII). Cranial nerve VIII synapses with the cochlear nucleus, which can be found on the dorsolateral side of the brain stem, bridging the area where the pons and medulla meet. In anatomical terms, the cochlea nucleus can be split into ventral and dorsal regions, with the ventral part being subdivided into anterior and posterior segments. Three major projections emerge from the cochlear nuclei. Some of the axons cross the midline and form synaptic relationships with the superior olivary nucleus on the contralateral side, while other fibres synapse with the superior olivary nucleus on the ipsilateral side. The third projection, which is known as the lateral lemniscus, stretches out from the cochlear nucleus straight to the inferior colliculus. The main projection of the inferior colliculus is to the medial geniculate body inside the thalamus. Following this, the medial geniculate projects to the auditory cortex, which is located in the superior temporal gyrus (see Figure 6.16).

PRIMARY AUDITORY CORTEX

Perception of sound, just as with visual perception, happens in the cortical regions related to that particular sense. The primary auditory cortex is about the same as Brodmann

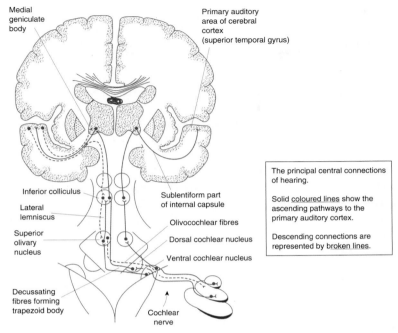

Figure 6.16   *Auditory pathway*

areas 41 and 42 and can be found in the rear half of the superior temporal gyrus (see Figure 6.17). It contains a small gyrus that runs across the superior temporal gyrus. This area is also called **Heschl's gyrus**. Damage to the main auditory cortex leaves an individual unable to perceive sound; however, the capability to act reflexively to sound remains, due to the subcortical processing in the brain stem and midbrain. There is evidence that

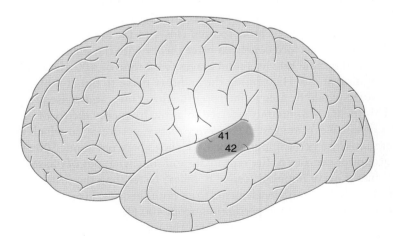

Figure 6.17   *Heschl's gyrus*

nerve cells in the main auditory cortex correlate selectively to sounds of a certain level (Shamma & Micheyl, 2010). They are arranged according to the sound frequency that they are best equipped to respond to. Nerve cells found at one part of the auditory cortex react best to low sounds; nerve cells at the other end react best to high sounds (Weisz et al., 2004). The reason for this frequency map – known as the **tonotopic** map – is unknown, but similar organisations have been discovered in other sensory systems and the motor operation system.

Another common characteristic that the auditory system shares with the visual system is the division of information into 'what' and 'where' pathways. Thanks to work with monkeys and MRI studies in humans, we now know that an auditory 'what' stream originates in the anterior portion of the superior temporal gyrus and is connected to non-spatial frontal areas. The 'where' or spatial stream originates in the posterior part of the gyrus and is connected to spatial areas (Rauschecker, 2011). The amygdala, as it does in the visual system, also receives information from the auditory thalamus (Takahashi, Chan, & Pilar, 2008).

DETECTION OF FREQUENCY

People can detect small changes in sound frequency over the audible frequency range. The pitch of a sound is the term typically used to refer to the sensation of frequencies. A high-pitch sound has a corresponding high-pitch sound wave, and a low-pitch sound correlates to a low-pitch sound wave. The variation in frequency between two individual sounds that can be detected by the average human is as little as 2 Hz. So how do we identify and distinguish between pitches? At this time, there are three main theories. The **place theory** of pitch perception was proposed by Helmholtz. This supports the idea that the inner ear behaves as a frequency analyser. Additionally, the stimulus that reaches our ears becomes decomposed into many sinusoidal components. Each of these components then excites a different place along the basilar membrane. This is the area where hair cells with distinct characteristic frequencies are linked with nerve cells. The receptors located close to the base of the cochlea relay treble sounds, and the receptors located closer to the apex relay bass sounds. In the late 1800s, William Rutherford contested place theory with the suggestion that basal membranes vibrate at the same rate as sound waves, so a tone of 400 Hz would result in the membrane vibrating at 400 Hz, causing the auditory nerve to fire at 400 times per second. The brain, in turn, would be able to interpret the firing rate, and consequently the pitch of the sound. This theory is commonly referred to as the **frequency theory** of pitch perception. In the 1940s Ernest Wever suggested the *volley theory*, according to which the ear changes acoustic vibrations into nerve impulses for frequencies between about 500 Hz and 5000 Hz by causing groups of neurons to fire repeatedly and somewhat out of phase with each other, creating a string of nerve impulses (called a volley) faster than the firing rate of any single nerve cell. Currently, we combine elements from both theories. From 20 Hz to 400 Hz, frequency theory accounts for pitch perception; from 400 Hz to around 4 kHz, volley theory has principal control; and from 4 kHz, place theory comes into play (Bizley & Walker, 2010; Langner, 1997).

PERCEPTION OF AMPLITUDE

Two mechanisms operate within the central nervous system for the purpose of detecting the intensity of stimuli. One is the rate at which nerve cells fire, and the other is the quantity of nerve cells that are firing. With regard to high-frequency sounds, the rate of neuronal firing indicates loudness. However, the loudness of low-frequency sounds is signalled by the number of neurons that are called into play. For this reason, the more neurons that are firing, the louder is the sound signalled (Bizley & Walker, 2010).

MUSIC PERCEPTION

Music perception and cognition are concerned with the brain mechanisms underlying our processing of music. The most researched areas in this field are concerned with the perception and cognition of pitch, and neuroimaging studies to date have generally been concerned with the location and lateralisation of pitch and melodic processing. More recently, studies have identified the task-specific brain regions associated with high-level musical processing such as musical **short-term memory** (Zatorre et al., 1994), musical imagery and music-related semantic retrieval (Halpern & Zatorre, 1999), and absolute pitch processing (Zatorre et al., 1998). In adults, specific neural systems with stronger right-hemispheric activation seem to be necessary to process the components of music such as pitch, melody and harmony and also the structure and meaning of music (Tillmann, Janata, & Bharucha, 2003). Musical training in both adults and children produces stronger activations in the frontal operculum and the anterior portion of the superior temporal gyrus (Koelsch, Fritz, Schulze, Alsop, & Schlaug, 2005). See Box 6.2 for more information on the neural aspects of music perception.

BOX 6.2 Music in newborn brains

Background

Music processing is the integration of a structured and complex pattern of sensory input. Indeed many argue that it has played a role in the evolution of language, and that music making behaviour is associated with vital evolutionary behaviours such as communication as well as social coordination and cohesion (Zatorre & Peretz, 2001). In adults, specific neural systems with stronger right-hemispheric activation seem to be necessary to the components of music such as process pitch, melody and harmony as well as the structure and meaning of music. This study (Perani et al., 2010) investigated the extent of the specialisation of these neural systems by investigating how they function at birth, when auditory experience is small.

(Continued)

(Continued)

Methods

fMRI was used to measure brain activity in one- to three-day-old newborns while they heard excerpts of western tonal music and altered versions of the same excerpts. The altered versions were changes of tonal key or were permanently inharmonious.

Results

Music evoked principally right-hemispheric activations in primary and higher-order auditory cortex. Haemodynamic responses were significantly reduced in the right auditory cortex during presentation of the altered excerpts. Altered excepts also showed activations in the left inferior frontal cortex and limbic structures.

Interpreting the results

These results revealed that the newborn brain shows a hemispheric specialisation in processing music, and indicated that the neural architecture underlying music processing in newborns is sensitive to changes in tonal key as well as to differences in consonance and dissonance, i.e. whether a combination sounds good together or not.

References

Perani, D., Saccuman, M., Scifo, P., Spada, D., Andreolli, G., Rovelli, R., et al. (2010). Functional specializations for music processing in the human newborn brain. *Proceedings of the National Academy of Sciences USA, 107*(10), 4758–4763.

Zatorre, R. and Peretz, I. (eds.) (2001) The biological foundations of music. *Annals of the New York Academy of Sciences*, Vol 930.

HEARING LOSS: DEAFNESS

Conduction deafness

When sound is abnormally conducted through the outer ear, middle ear or both, and is unable to get to the cochlea, the resulting condition is called **conduction deafness**. One common cause of conductive deafness is when the **ossicles** become fused together. Surgery can help in some cases by freeing the structures.

Sensorineural deafness

A hearing loss that is sensorineural may be due to exposure to loud noise. It may also be caused by a metabolic disorder, a genetic disorder or an infection (Pennisi, 1997). The final result is usually seen as a lack of sensitivity in the inner ear (the cochlea). This insensitivity may be mild, moderate or severe. Most hearing loss is because of poor hair cell operation. At birth, the hair cells may be abnormal or they can become damaged during the lifetime of the person due to exposure to loud noises, which shatter and break hair cells. Mutations that occur in the gene GJB2 have been estimated to cause as much as 50% of congenital or early-onset hearing impairment (Martinez, Acuna, Figueroa, Maripillan, & Nicholson, 2009). Human hair cells that have been damaged cannot be replaced, as in amphibians and fish; however, in 2005 a team of researchers successfully produced a regrowth of cochlea cells using guineapigs as test subjects (Izumikawa et al., 2005). With most cell replacement therapy, however, regeneration of hair cells does not mean that hearing sensitivity will be restored, as the cells may not make connections with neurons that carry the signals from hair cells to the processing regions of the brain.

Central deafness

A person suffering from central deafness has lost their hearing due to an injury to the auditory system in the brain. Rarely does this simply result in a loss of auditory sensitivity. Hearing problems can be due to injury to the auditory cortex, the brain stem and the superior colliculus. Bilateral lesions of the auditory cortex lead to a condition known as cortical deafness. Individuals who have suffered central hearing loss usually have irregular hearing, causing them to receive an incorrect diagnosis of 'functional' or hearing disturbances. Central hearing loss is usually considered to be quite uncommon compared to the sensorineural or conductive types of hearing loss, but recent work has observed that central components to hearing loss occur far more frequently than we thought (Gates, Cobb, Linn, Rees, Wolf, & D'Agostino, 1996).

BALANCE: THE VESTIBULAR SYSTEM

The vestibular system, or the balance system, is the sensory system that provides the major input concerning motion and equilibrioception. The system consists of two major parts: the **semicircular canals** and the vestibular sacs (Figure 6.18). The semicircular canal system detects changes in the movement of one's head or rotational motion. The vestibular sacs are made up of the utricle and the saccule. The saccule is the smaller of the two vestibular sacs and contains hair receptor cells. These cells translate head movements into neural impulses which the brain can interpret. The utricle is bigger than the saccule and has hair cells that can identify varying degrees of head tilt.

The semicircular canals are, more or less, orthogonal to each other. They are called the horizontal (lateral), the anterior (superior) and the posterior (inferior) semicircular canals. The anterior and posterior canals may be collectively called the vertical semicircular canals. Any rotational movement activates the fluid within the horizontal semicircular canal, while movement in the transverse plane (elevator movement) is signalled by the anterior and posterior semicircular canals.

The movement of fluid pushes against a structure known as the cupula, where you will find hair cells that convert the mechanical motion into electrical signals. Vestibular hair cells, like the rods and cones in the eyes, synapse with the bipolar cells that make up the vestibular ganglia; these gather together, forming the vestibular nerve. These fibres of the vestibular nerve connect with the cochlear nerve fibres to create the auditory nerve (cranial nerve VIII).

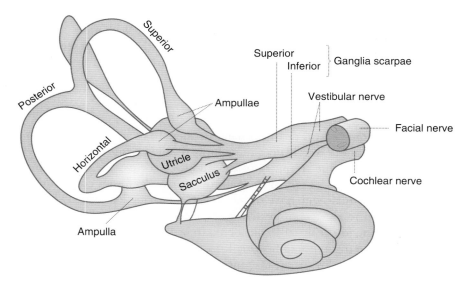

Figure 6.18   *Vestibular system*

CHEMICAL SENSES

The chemical senses of taste and scent have a vital role in life. This section discusses the chemical senses of taste and smell.

TASTE

An appreciation of food flavours demands the diverse interaction of many sensory systems. Distinguishing of flavours is carried out by the two principal systems, taste and smell. Food quality is increased by the tactile, thermal and nociceptive sensory input from the oral mucosa. Saliva is also a key factor in maintaining acuity of taste receptor cells. Saliva acts as a solvent and sends solutes to the taste receptors; it also acts as a buffer for acidic foods and has a reparative action on the **gustatory** system. Signal transduction pathways are now being identified due to recent technical advances in neurophysiology.

Taste bud morphology and types of cell

The taste buds are on **papillae,** which are spread across the tongue's surface (Figure 6.19). The structures are formed like pears and hold around 80 receptor cells placed around a central taste pore. Taste receptor cells are shaped like a spindle; they are modified neuro-epithelial cells that extend from the base to the apex of the taste buds. On the surface of the tongue, the dissolved solutes interact with the taste pores into which extend the microvilli from individual taste cells. The basal lamina is innervated by nerve fibres that are afferent (Figure 6.20).

Five basic tastes – salty, sour, sweet, bitter and umani – can be detected by human beings. Umani is the Japanese name for the taste sensation that results from compounds such as monosodium glutamate (Uneyama, Kawai, Sekine-Hayakawa, & Torii, 2009). This is a savoury, meaty or brothy flavour. There are other influences on your experience

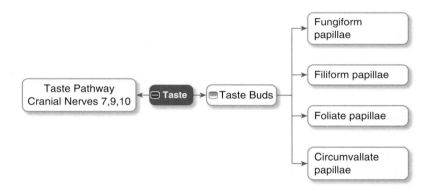

Figure 6.19   *Taste components*

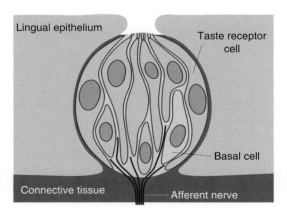

Figure 6.20   *Taste bud*

of food, like how the food smells, which is picked up by the olfactory epithelium in the nose; its texture, which is detected by mechanoreceptors; and how hot or cold it is, which is picked up by thermoreceptors. The distribution of taste buds can be seen in Figure 6.21.

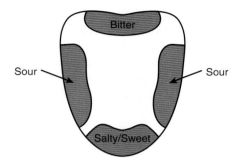

Figure 6.21   *Distribution of taste buds*

As already mentioned, taste buds lie in or around raised protrusions of the tongue's surface known as papillae. Four kinds of papillae are present in the human tongue:

- *Fungiform papillae*. These are mushroom shaped and are found at the tip and the sides of the tongue.

- *Filiform papillae*. These are narrow cones in the shape of a V that are mechanical and are not associated with taste.

- *Foliate papillae*. These are located at the posterior area of the tongue on the lateral borders. They are innervated by facial nerves (anterior papillae) and glossopharyngeal nerves (posterior papillae).

- *Circumvallate papillae*. There are typically just three to 14 of these papillae and they are at the rear of the tongue. They are arranged in a circular-shaped line just ahead of the sulcus terminalis.

Mechanisms of taste perception

The way in which we experience the four main flavours of food is regulated by different mechanisms. Sodium ions (Na^+), which are found in foods that are salty, trigger a taste receptor, resulting in these ions moving through the sodium channels in the cell membrane of the receptor. This results in depolarisation and the release of neurotransmitters. The more sodium inside the food, the more the depolarisation and the bigger the neurotransmitter release. Sour and sweet foods shut down potassium (K^+) ion channels by the action of the hydrogen ions and the sugar molecules respectively. Therefore, just as with salty foods, depolarisation and neurotransmitter release will be modulated by how sour and/or sweet the food is. Bitter tasting things, which contain alkaloid compounds, trigger the movement of calcium (Ca^+ ions) into the cytoplasm, which in turn causes neurotransmitter release.

Taste pathways

The axons of the taste receptors become three branches of cranial nerves 7 (chorda tympani), 9 (glossopharyngeal nerve) and 10 (vagus nerve), and transport the information regarding taste to the CNS. The seventh cranial nerve carries information that starts in the front two-thirds of the tongue, while extensions of the ninth and tenth carry taste information from the rear area of the tongue together with information from the palate and throat. The nerve fibres synapse with the nucleus of the **solitary** tract in the brain stem. Axons then travel to the ventral posteromedial thalamic nucleus via the medial lemnicus, and ultimately synapse with the primary gustatory cortex. This primary gustatory cortex consists of two parts: the frontal operculum on the inferior frontal gyrus of the frontal lobe, and the anterior insula on the insular lobe (see Figure 6.22).

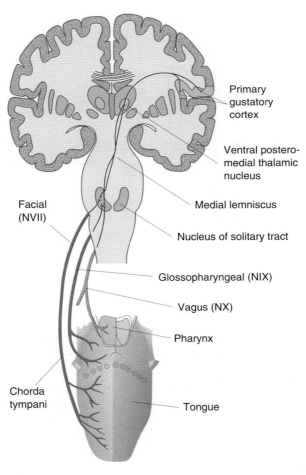

Figure 6.22   *Taste pathways*

OLFACTION

The olfactory function in people is an extremely discriminative and sensitive chemosensory function. People can distinguish between 1000 and around 4000 smells. The process of perceiving smells starts when we inhale and transport volatile scents to the olfactory mucosa, which are situated on both sides of the dorsal posterior area of the nasal cavity. Olfaction, as with taste, is a form of chemoreception. Olfactory sensory neurons in the olfactory epithelium sense the scents or smells we encounter. The quantity of olfactory epithelium found in the top back of the nasal pathway has an area of about 10 cm^2 in humans (Figure 6.23).

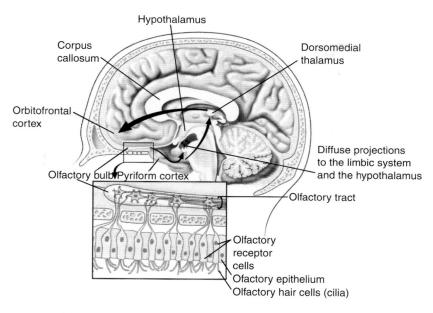

Figure 6.23   *Nasal pathway*

Odour molecules dissolve in the mucus lining of the superior part of the nasal cavity and are detected by olfactory receptors on the dendrites of the olfactory sensory neurons. This process occurs either by passive diffusion or via the binding of the odour to odorant binding proteins, which are present in the fluid part of the olfactory epithelium (Farbman, 1994). The fluid covering the mucous membrane dissolves the odour molecules, and the receptors are activated. In humans, odours stimulate adenylate cyclase to synthesise cyclic AMP (cAMP) via a G protein called Golf. When cAMP is present, it opens Na$^+$ channels, as well as depolarising the receptor membrane. This causes information to be transmitted directly to the brain.

The olfactory pathway

Axons from the olfactory receptor project to the brain within the olfactory nerve (cranial nerve I). These axons then cross the cribriform plate and synapse with the mistral cells of the olfactory bulb. This, consequently, projects olfactory information to the olfactory cortex and other parts of the brain. The mistral cells synapse with the olfactory tract, which synapses on the anterior olfactory nucleus, the olfactory tubercle, the amygdala and the entorhinal cortex. The participation of the orbitofrontal cortex gives conscious perception of the odour, while the entorhinal cortex extends to the amygdala which plays a role in the emotional and autonomic responses to odour and also to the hippocampus which is involved in the memory of odours. The interaction of these systems explains why smell information is easily stored in long-term memory and contains strong connections to emotional memory.

SUMMARY

In this chapter we have discussed sensory processing and detailed how it is a complex set of actions that enable the brain to understand what is going on both inside your own body and in the world around you (Figure 6.24). Explanations were given on the different types of receptors present in the human body. Functions of the skin were highlighted which include protecting the internal organs, waterproofing and helping to regulate the body temperature by producing sweat. The skin also has many receptors on its surface including the Meissner's corpuscles which are sensitive to pressure; the Pacianian corpuscles which detect gross pressure changes and vibrations; and the Ruffini corpuscles which are a class of slowly adapting mechanoreceptors sensitive to skin stretch. The chapter also detailed dermatomes, which are areas of skin supplied by peripheral nerve fibres originating from a single dorsal root ganglion. We discovered that sensory information travels from the sensory receptor to the brain via its own distinct pathway. Axons that convey information such as touch and proprioception ascend through the dorsal columns of the spinal cord, referred to as the dorsal-column/medial-lemniscal pathway. Temperature and pain information ascends via the spinothalamic tract of the anterolateral system, while information about proprioception is transmitted via the spinocerebellar system. The pain sensory system was discussed and the gate control theory of pain was highlighted.

The chapter then went on to examine the sense of hearing with an explanation of how the process of hearing starts with the ear, which not only detect sounds but also plays a major role in the sense of balance and body position. The roles of the outer, inner and middle ear were discussed. Transduction of the sound wave to a nerve signal is achieved by hair cells within the ear, and it is the inner hair cells that convert the mechanical sound signal into an electrical nerve signal. The outer hair cells have evolved only in mammals and may contribute actively to tuning the sensitivity and frequency selectivity of the cochlea. The chapter then moved on to discuss the role of the primary auditory cortex, which occupies Brodmann areas 41 and 42 and lies in the posterior half of the superior

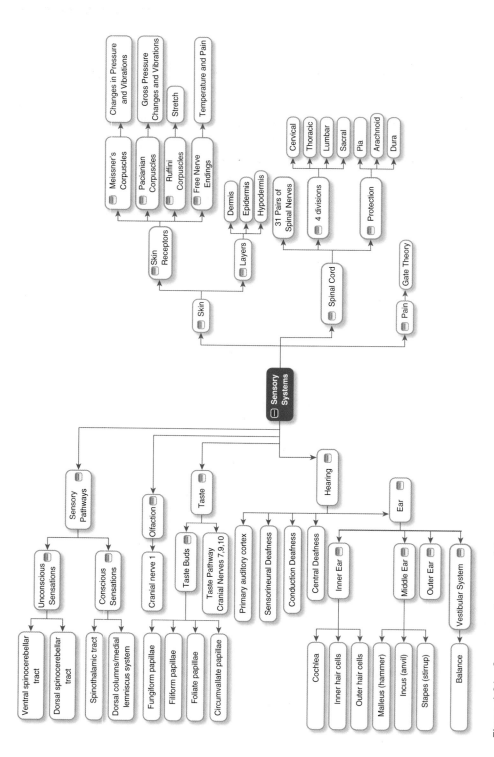

Figure 6.24   Sensory systems overview

temporal gyrus, and includes a small gyrus running transversely across the superior temporal gyrus called Heschl's gyrus. The perception of pitch and loudness were also discussed. It was shown that there are three major causes of deafness: conduction deafness, which occurs when sound is not normally conducted through the outer or middle ear (or both) and is prevented from reaching the cochlea; sensorineural deafness, which results from exposure to loud noise, metabolic disorders, genetic disorders and infections; and finally central deafness, caused by damage to the brain's auditory system.

The chemical senses were discussed, and it was shown that humans can detect five basic tastes – salty, sour, sweet, bitter and umami – with taste buds that lie in or near raised protrusions of the tongue surface called papillae. Four types of papillae are present in the human tongue: fungiform papillae, filiform papillae, foliate papillae and circumvallate papillae. It was also discovered that the mechanism by which food is 'tasted' differs for each of the four basic tastes. The taste pathways were highlighted, and it was explained that the axons of the taste receptors become three branches of cranial nerves 7, 9 and 10, and transmit the information about taste to the CNS. Finally, the olfactory pathway was examined and it was explained that the olfactory function in people is an extremely discriminative and sensitive chemosensory function and that smell information is easily stored in long-term memory and contains strong connections to emotional memory.

 ## FURTHER READING

Hollins, M. (2010). Somesthetic senses. *Annual Review of Psychology*, 61, 243–271.

Pennisi, E. (1997). The architecture of hearing. *Science*, 278(5341), 1223–1224.

Uneyama, H., Kawai, M., Sekine-Hayakawa, Y., & Torii, K. (2009). Contribution of umami taste substances in human salivation during meal. *Journal of Investigative Medicine*, 56(Suppl.), 197–204.

 ## KEY QUESTIONS

1   Explain the route of auditory perception from ear to brain.

2   Detail the sensory spinal tracts involved in sensation.

3   Detail the mechanism of taste perception.

7 MOTOR CONTROL AND MOVEMENT

The human body is in movement all the time, whether or not we are aware of it. Even in apparent moments of stillness, we blink, talk or shift our body position. Many seemingly simple movements actually require lots of cognitive involvement. An example is reaching for a cup without spilling its contents or burning our fingers. The brain has to determine which muscles are involved in the task, estimate the force needed, and then contract the muscles. Also playing a part in the decision process of the brain are other factors such as the material the cup is made of and how much water the cup contains. Consequently, it makes sense that there are several anatomical areas in the brain that play a role in motor function (Figure 7.1).

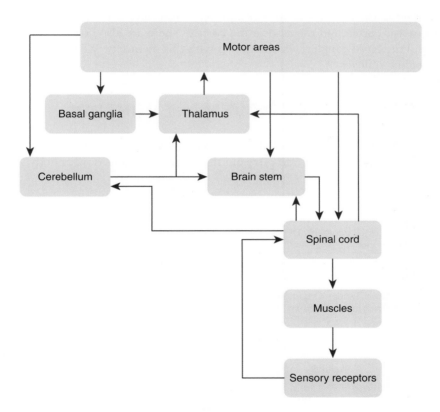

Figure 7.1 *Anatomical areas involved in movement*

A main feature of the motor system is that sensory input is required for the motor system to precisely plan and perform movements. This applies to the low levels of the hierarchy, such as spinal reflexes, right up to the higher cortical levels.

The effortlessness way in which we make movements does not really give an insight into the complexity of our motor system. So how does the brain plan, control and execute movements? Although numerous details are not fully understood, two broad principles emerge which contribute to our understanding:

- *Functional segregation*. A number of different areas of the motor system control different aspects of movement.
- *Hierarchical organisation*. The higher levels within the motor system are concerned with global tasks regarding movement, like planning and sequencing actions. These areas are not concerned with posture or spinal reflexes; such tasks are carried out by the lower levels of the hierarchy.

The hierarchy in the motor system is composed of four levels: the spinal cord, the brain stem, the motor cortex and the association cortex. There are also connections to the cerebellum and the basal ganglia, which interact with this hierarchy. We will first look at the low-level spinal reflexes.

THE MECHANICS OF MOVEMENT CONTROL

There are three types of muscles: cardiac, smooth and striated or skeletal (see Figures 7.2 and 7.3). These muscles help you to carry out the necessary actions of your body. As implied

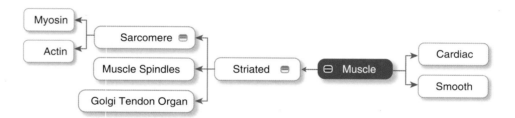

Figure 7.2   *Muscle components*

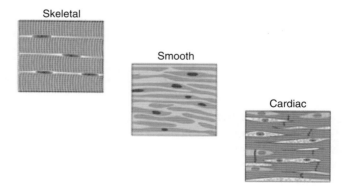

Figure 7.3   *Types of muscle*

by its name, striated or skeletal muscle contains fibres that have a striped appearance when viewed microscopically.

STRIATED OR SKELETAL MUSCLE

Striated muscles make voluntary movement possible. When these muscles contract, they cause the bones that are joined with tendons (or sturdy strips of connective tissue) to move. Typically, these muscles work in pairs that have opposite roles, meaning that while one of the two muscles shortens, the other lengthens, which allows the bone to move. We see this action when a limb is engaged in motion: an extensor muscle generates an extension of the limb and then a flexor muscle triggers flexion, returning the extended limb to its original position near the body. As an example, when the biceps (a flexor muscle) lengthens, the triceps (an extensor muscle) contracts.

The description of muscles working in this manner is sometimes referred to as an *antagonistic pair* of muscles. This means that contraction of one muscle results in forces opposite to those generated by contraction of the other (Figure 7.4). To achieve maximum efficiency, the contraction of opposing muscles has to be inhibited at the same time as muscles with the desired action are stimulated. This reciprocal innervation results in the contraction of one muscle and the simultaneous relaxation of the corresponding **antagonist muscle**.

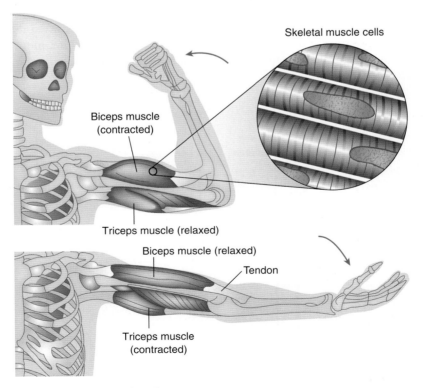

Figure 7.4 *Antagonistic muscle function*

SMOOTH MUSCLE AND CARDIAC MUSCLE

The muscle of internal organs as well as blood vessels consists of smooth muscle. Typically, smooth muscle is involuntary and tonic; its cells can function as a group or on their own (responding to individual nerve endings) and are varied in their shapes. Afflictions involving the voluntary muscle result in weakness, atrophy, discomfort and twitching. The structure of the cardiac or heart muscle is like a branching net and, unlike its counterparts, it contracts rhythmically.

STRUCTURE OF STRIATED OR SKELETAL MUSCLE

Skeletal muscle, as previously mentioned, is made up of individual muscle fibres. These fibres are long, cylindrical, multinucleated cells comprising **actin** and myosin **myofilament** repeated as a **sarcomere** (see Figure 7.5). The other membrane system that surrounds each myofibril is called the sarcoplasmic reticulum. The sarcomere is the working unit of the cell; it is responsible for skeletal muscle's striated look and is necessary for muscle contraction to take place. The sliding of thin filaments, called actin, between thicker filaments, called myosin, allows skeletal muscle to contract, while stretch receptors in the tissue send out feedback, making it possible to perform movements that are smooth and to maintain fine motor control.

   The skeletal muscles are regulated by the motor neurons of the peripheral nervous system; you will find them in the grey matter of the ventral horn of the spinal cord and in various areas of the brain stem (see Figure 7.6). The majority of motor axons have long axons that synapse with individual muscle fibres and are called **alpha motor neurons**. They innervate **extrafusal muscle fibres** of skeletal muscle and are directly responsible for their contraction.

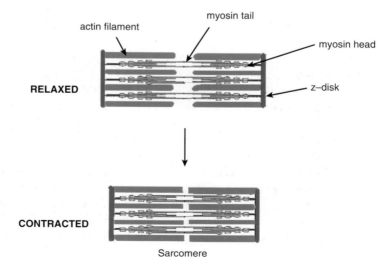

Figure 7.5 *Structure of skeletal muscle*

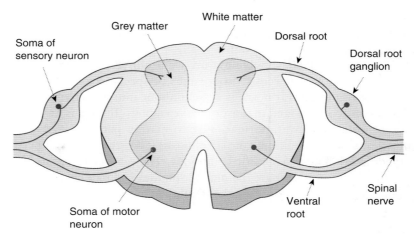

Figure 7.6   *Location of motor neurons*

Alpha motor neurons are distinct from **gamma motor neurons** which innervate the **intrafusal muscle fibres** and generate a sensory proprioceptor. The presynaptic terminal of the alpha motor neuron flattens to form the motor end plate at the point where it meets the muscle fibre. We refer to this synapse or junction of the axon terminal of a motor neuron with the muscle as the neuromuscular junction (see Figure 7.7). It is in this region that the initiation of action potentials across the muscle's surface begins which ultimately causes the muscle to contract. The neurotransmitter acetylcholine facilitates the signal crossing through the neuromuscular junction. We use the term '**motor unit**' to refer to an alpha motor neuron and all the muscle fibres it regulates. Thus, all the fibres of a motor

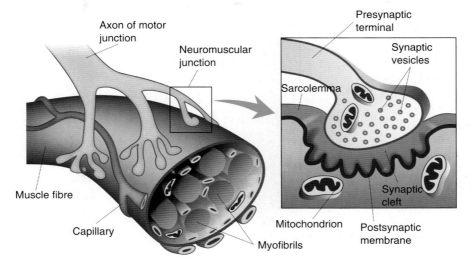

Figure 7.7   *Neuromuscular junction*

unit will contract when it is activated. Often, groups of motor units work in concert to produce single muscle contraction. The group of motor units that coordinate the function of one muscle is called a motor unit pool.

Very few of the nerve fibres supplying a muscle are involved in its contraction. The remaining nerves are either afferent sensory fibres or specialised motor fibres. Afferent sensory fibres notify the central nervous system about muscle activity, and specialised motor fibres govern activity found in sensory nerve endings. If there is any interruption to the feedback of proprioceptive information (information pertaining to body position) from the muscles, tendons and joints, it is still possible for there to be movement, but it cannot be modified to adapt to specific conditions. The sensory receptors that are most actively involved with movement are the **muscle spindles** and tendon organs. Because the muscle spindle is a great deal more complex than the tendon organ, it has been far more intensively studied; nonetheless, it is not as well understood.

TENDON ORGANS

The tendon organ, alternatively referred to as the **Golgi tendon organ,** comprises afferent type Ib sensory fibres that branch and reach their terminus as spinal endings surrounding strands of collagen. This receptor lies near the muscle–tendon junction (see Figure 7.8) or buried deep within the tendon itself.

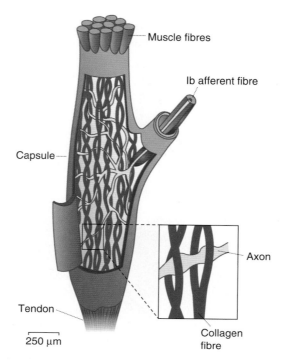

Figure 7.8   *Golgi tendon organ*

The tendon organ measures the amount of force that the muscle exerts upon the bone to which it is attached. Normally, the tendon organs produce a continuous flow of information on the level of muscular contraction. However, when a muscle engages in overexertion, it triggers the protective nature of the tendon organ. During muscle tension, the strands stretch with the changing length of the muscle. Stretching causes the terminals of the Ib afferent axon to become deformed, and transmit the information to the spinal cord where it synapses with interneurons. The main spinal reflex receiving input from the Ib afferent is the autogenic inhibition reflex, which inhibits the alpha motor neurons, reducing the force being provided by the ongoing muscle contractions (Figure 7.9).

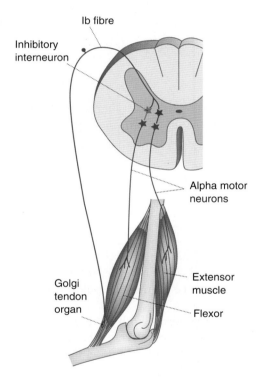

Figure 7.9 *Autogenic inhibition reflex*

MUSCLE SPINDLES

Muscle spindles are mechanoreceptors that are located inside extrafusal muscle fibres, which mainly detect changes of muscle length (see Figure 7.10). The muscle spindle contains intrafusal muscle fibres that extend the length of the spindle; their central positions lack myofibrils and have sensory receptors known as **annulospiral endings** wrapped around them. When there is stretching of the extrafusal muscle fibre, there is also stretching of the intrafusal muscle, triggering the annulospiral endings to fire more rapidly. The

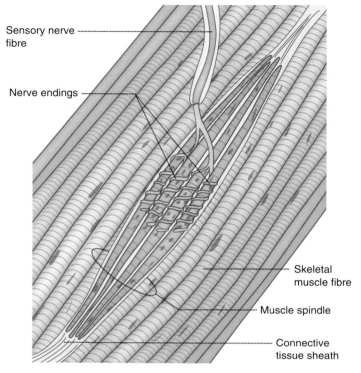

Sensory nerve fibre

Nerve endings

Skeletal muscle fibre

Muscle spindle

Connective tissue sheath

Figure 7.10   *Muscle spindle*

information travels down the axons, the Ia fibres of the annulospiral endings, where it enters the dorsal root of the spinal cord and synapses with the alpha motor neurons. The Ia fibres have an excitatory influence on the alpha motor neurons, causing the extrafusal muscle fibres to contract.

The cerebellum and the cerebral cortex both use the information provided by the muscle spindles. An example of this is kinaesthesia, or the subjective sensory awareness of the position of limbs in space, which relies largely upon the integration of signals within the cerebral cortex emanating from the muscle spindles. Around five intrafusal muscle fibres run throughout the muscle spindles' length; these are several millimetres long and are shorter and thinner than skeletal muscle fibres.

SPINAL REFLEXES

As already stated, movement is triggered by the motor neurons in the CNS, and a certain movement functions on a number of different levels. The most fundamental one functions at the level of the spine. We refer to this as a spinal reflex. The spinal cord works alone in controlling the movement in spinal reflexes. When you pull your hand away from something that is hot (**withdrawal reflex**), you are demonstrating a spinal reflex. We refer to the anatomical pathway of a reflex as the reflex arc, and it comprises an afferent (or sensory) nerve, at least one if not more interneurons in the CNS, and an efferent (motor, secretory or secreto-motor) nerve. Reflexes develop in the womb by about seven and a half weeks, and by birth the sucking and swallowing reflexes are developed. The pupillary light reflex is probably the best-known reflex: the pupils of both eyes contract when a light is flashed in one eye.

Even though reflexes happen immediately with typical reactions, this does not indicate that the reflex reaction is permanent and unchanging. Sensitisation and habituation are the two changes that can happen to the reflex response upon a constant repetition of a stimulus. While sensitisation is an elevation in response to the stimulus, habituation is a reduction in response to the stimulus. Changes in reflexes can also occur by regulation at higher levels of the CNS. For instance, in certain situations, both the cough reflex and the vomiting reflex can be suppressed.

There is also something we refer to as conditioned reflexes, which are actually not reflexes at all but complex acts of behaviour that have been learnt. A well-known example was identified by Ivan Pavlov (1927), who discovered that environmental events that never before had had a relationship to a certain reflex (in this case, the sound of a bell ringing) could, through repeated experience, generate a reflex (in this case, salivation) in dogs.

Reflexes are classified based upon the quantity of neurons or synapses that are located between the primary afferent neuron and the motor neuron. We identify two specific types: the **monosynaptic reflex** and the **polysynaptic reflex**. Monosynaptic refers to the occurrence of a single synapse in the reflex arc; the neural pathway consists of only two neurons, one sensory and one motor. The more common polysynaptic reflex pathways have one or more interneurons and thus synapses connecting the afferent (sensory) and efferent (motor) signals.

Monosynaptic reflex

The monosynaptic stretch reflex is a spinal reflex with a single synapse between the sensory receptor and the muscle effector. One example of this is what we call the knee-jerk reflex. The stretching of a muscle results in the muscle spindles generating impulses which are sent to the spinal cord, where they synapse with motor neurons. This then initiates the contraction of the same muscle so that its original length is restored. Because the reflex action is made up of the transmission of impulses across just one set of synapses, the response is quite rapid at 0.02 s and is described as a monosynaptic reflex.

The stretch reflex also plays a major role in posture. If a person stands up and begins swaying in one direction, the muscles in the legs and torso are stretched. The result is a reflexive response, which is to counteract the swaying. In this way, the higher levels of the motor system can send a simple command, such as 'maintain current posture', without being involved in the implementation of the command. At the lower levels of the hierarchy the command is implemented with mechanisms such as the stretch reflex. This frees the higher levels to perform more complex tasks such as planning the next sequence of movements.

Polysynaptic reflex

A polysynaptic reflex involves an electrical impulse from a sensory neuron being passed through at least one interneuron to a motor neuron in the spinal cord. For instance, when pain receptors in the skin are exposed to stimuli, a withdrawal reflex is triggered (Figure 7.11). This response relies upon several synapses and motor neurons and results in an individual removing their hand or limb away from a stimulus such as a hot object.

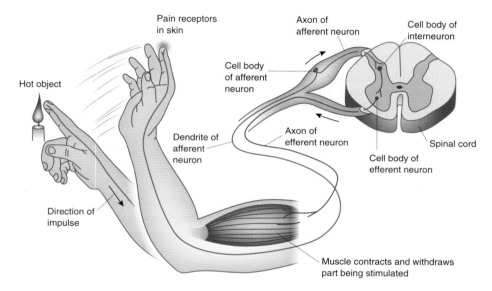

Figure 7.11   *Polysynaptic reflex*

RENSHAW CELLS

Muscle damage can also be as a result of fatigue, especially if it has occurred over a brief period, resulting in poor muscle performance. A set of inhibitory interneurons known as Renshaw cells protect the muscles from developing this fatigue (Renshaw, 1946). Every neuron has a contralateral branch in the spinal cord that synapses with a Renshaw cell. The axon of the Renshaw cell encloses the dendrite of the same alpha neuron, creating a circuit. The Renshaw cell restricts its corresponding alpha neuron once the alpha neuron has a particular rate of firing, thus mitigating muscle fatigue.

GAMMA MOTOR SYSTEM

So far we have discussed how exposing the alpha motor system to stimuli results in skeletal muscle contractions that lead to movement. However, not every muscle contraction results in movement. Actually, muscles can remain contracted at times when there is no movement. This background muscle tension finds its roots in the gamma motor neurons that we collectively refer to as the gamma motor system or **fusimotor** system. This gamma motor system provides the human body with muscle tone all the time except when we are experiencing **REM sleep**. Gamma motor neurons originate in the spine and exit by the ventral horn to synapse with the intrafusal muscle fibre of the muscle spindle (Figure 7.12). Gamma motor neurons are smaller than alpha motor neurons. When stimulated they stretch the centre of the muscle spindle, and conduct impulses more slowly. This stretching triggers the annulospiral ending of the spindle, resulting in a contraction of the extrafusal muscle.

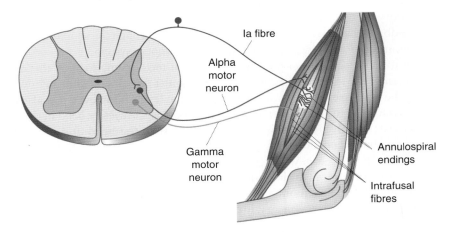

Figure 7.12 *Gamma motor neurons*

In addition to regulating muscle tone, the gamma motor system makes it possible for us to make quick responses and to plan for specific movements. The anticipatory action in the readiness to strike a ball during a game of tennis is the product of the gamma motor system, which is regulating the muscle tone, allowing the player to prepare to hit the ball.

MOVEMENT CONTROLLED BY THE CORTEX

Now let's turn our attention to several structures that are located above the spinal cord. We call these the motor structures. This section focuses on the anatomical and physiological circuits inside each structure and current theories about the role they play in movement.

After reflexes, the next level of control involves the brain stem. Movement that is initiated in these structures travels via the spinal and cranial nerves. By way of the cranial nerves, the brain stem provides main motor sensation to the face and neck and is one segment of the corticospinal tract.

The highest level of movement control is organised and initiated in the cerebral cortex (Figure 7.13). Here the dorsal lateral prefrontal cortex along with the secondary motor cortex

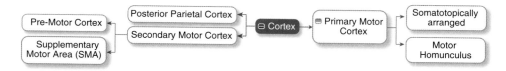

Figure 7.13   *Cortex components*

plan and prepare movement, while the primary motor cortex with other cortical areas such as the somatosensory cortex initiate movement by transmitting signals to the brain stem and spinal cord. Feedback that is sent from muscles and tendons through the somatosensory cortex provides a continuous flow of information regarding the motor system.

The organisation of central nervous system control movement, such as the reciprocal innervations seen in the control of **agonist** and antagonist muscles, is done below the level of the cerebral hemispheres in the brain stem and spinal levels. However, it is also possible to consciously control brain stem reflexes, like when moving the eyes or head in the direction of light or a noise, simply by making the decision to turn the head and eyes and look. Most of the movements coordinated by the cerebral cortex are carried out automatically, but when you are learning a new series of movements, or when a movement is hard to master or has to be precise, planning and internal speech are generally employed. When one is first gaining knowledge about a new movement, the movement at first may be awkward and need a great deal of sensory input and feedback with constant motor adjustments; but as you repeatedly practise the movement it becomes more skilled, reflecting more subcortical control (Haaland, Harrington, & Knight, 2000).

The cerebral hemispheres themselves can organise a discrete series of movements, known as programmed movements; these movements need to be performed so quickly that there is no margin for correcting any error through local feedback. The lateral prefrontal cortex is involved in the planning and initiation of these programmed movements, while the top administrator in dealing with the perception–action cycle is found in the dorsal lateral prefrontal cortex part of the brain (Fuster, 2004). The cells found in this region merge sensory information with motor actions over time. The dorsal lateral prefrontal cortex has connections to other cortical areas; receives information from sensory areas, particularly the parietal lobe; and sends projections to the primary and secondary motor cortex.

PRIMARY MOTOR CORTEX (M1)

The primary motor cortex gets its name because it is directly involved in the control of motor neurons and is located in the precentral gyrus of the frontal lobe. The primary motor cortex is responsible for the generation of neural impulses that regulate movement contralaterally. That is, the right hemisphere of the brain controls the left side of the body and the left hemisphere controls the right. Output from the primary motor cortex crosses the body's midline, activating skeletal muscles on the opposite side.

Each part of the body has its own representation in the primary motor cortex, which is arranged somatotopically. In addition, the amount of brain area devoted to any specific part of the body is representative of how much control the primary motor cortex has over that particular body part, as seen on the **motor homunculus** (Figure 7.14).

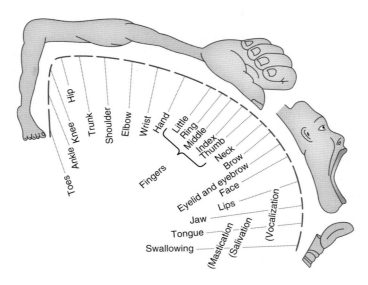

Figure 7.14 *Motor homunculus related to coronal section through primary cortex*

Each location in the primary motor cortex controls movement of that distinct group of muscles, and each gets somatosensory feedback from the somatosensory cortex, from receptors in the muscles and from the joint they influence. However, there is one exception in this pattern for feedback. One of the hand areas of each hemisphere receives input from the skin receptors instead of the receptors from muscles and joints. When the motor cortex sustains damage, a person's ability to move a particular body part (e.g. a finger) will be disrupted and speed, force and accuracy of movement will all be decreased. However, this will not result in **paralysis**.

What makes the primary cortex structure different from other regions of the brain is the lack of granular cells (layer IV), and due to this the primary cortex is sometimes referred to as the agranular cortex. Motor cortex layer V has large neurons called pyramidal cells or Betz cells. These neurons transmit long axons down the spinal cord to synapse onto alpha motor neurons, which then connect to the muscles.

SECONDARY MOTOR CORTEX

The lower end of the precentral gyrus is known as the secondary motor area because it was discovered after the primary motor area and doesn't function in a discrete manner like the primary area.

The secondary motor cortices comprise the premotor cortex and the supplementary motor area (SMA). These locations acquire their information from the dorsal lateral prefrontal cortex and are involved with the preparation and the sequencing of voluntary movements. We find the premotor cortex in front of or anterior to the primary motor cortex. The premotor cortex is involved with the sensory guidance of movement and controls the muscles that are closer to (proximal to) the body, as well as the trunk muscles of the body. Positioned in front of the primary motor cortex, the supplementary motor area is also above and medial to the premotor area. The supplementary motor area plans complex movements and is responsible for the coordination of two-handed movements. The supplementary motor areas and the premotor areas both send information to the primary motor cortex and to the motor regions located in the brain stem. Information from the somatosensory area and posterior parietal cortex is relayed to the SMA, while the premotor cortex receives the majority of its input from the occipital lobe of the visual cortex. A great many connections between the SMA and the premotor cortex are responsible for integrating information.

A certain portion of the premotor cortex, the ventrolateral portion, has been getting a great deal of focus recently. It has been found that this area contains mirror motor neurons (Rizzolatti & Craighero, 2004). These neurons fire in the same pattern regardless of whether they are performing a task or simply observing a task. These mirror neurons might be involved in the process of acquiring motor tasks that rely on hand–eye coordination, and possibly the acquisition of language skills. We still do not have a clear picture regarding the relationship between mirror neural networks and social cognitive tasks.

POSTERIOR PARIETAL CORTEX

The posterior parietal cortex consolidates visual, auditory and skin sense information and transmits it to the dorsal lateral prefrontal cortex, which then uses the information to direct movements. Evidence also suggests that the posterior parietal cortex has strong connections with the cingulate gyrus, as well as the cerebellum and basal ganglia. People who have sustained damage to the right posterior parietal cortex will have problems responding to stimuli presented to the contralateral side of their body. This sensory motor disturbance is referred to as 'neglect'. It is strange syndrome in which patients appear completely unaware of anything occurring on the left side of space and are sometimes unable to acknowledge their surroundings on that side.

MOTOR PATHWAYS

Upper motor neurons are nerve cells that originate in the motor cortex, the cerebellum or various brain stem nuclei, and transmit information to the brain stem and spinal cord to trigger activity in the spinal or cranial motor neurons. Those neurons that actually innervate muscles are known as the lower motor neurons. Whereas upper neurons reside completely inside the CNS, the fibres of lower motor neurons are components of the PNS.

These upper motor neurons are grouped collectively, creating descending tracts in the brain and spinal cord. These tracts usually get their names from the location where they originate and their region of distribution (Figure 7.15, Table 7.1). For example, the rubrospinal tract originates in the red nucleus of the midbrain and goes to the spinal cord, while the corticospinal tract starts in the cerebral cortex and finishes at the spinal cord. Even though we are able to describe the descending motor pathways anatomically, it is still tentative to assume that we have a comprehensive knowledge of how any specific tract contributes to a spontaneous movement.

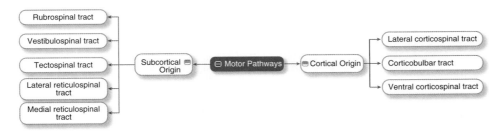

Figure 7.15   *Motor pathways*

Table 7.1   *Major motor pathways*

Pathway	Muscle group
Origin: cortical tracts	
Lateral cortical spinal tract	Fingers, hands and arms
Ventral cortical spinal tract	Trunk and upper legs
Corticobulbar tract	Face and tongue
Origin: subcortical tracts	
Rubrospinal tract	Hands, lower arms, feet and lower legs
Vestibulospinal tract	Trunk and legs: control of posture
Tectospinal tract	Neck and trunk: visual tracking
Lateral reticulospinal tract	Flexor muscles of legs
Medial reticulospinal tract	Extensor muscles of legs

PATHWAYS ORIGINATING IN CORTEX

The corticospinal tracts

We often refer to the corticospinal tracts as the pyramidal tracts due to their formation of enlargements that are shaped like pyramids on the frontal (anterior) surface of the medulla. These tracts are mainly concerned with regulating practised movements of the distal extremities and help the neurons that innervate distal flexor muscles, namely the alpha and gamma motor neurons (see Figure 7.16). The upper motor neurons of these tracts begin in the cerebral cortex (in the precentral gyrus) and travel along until they reach their final destinations in the grey matter of the spinal cord, without synapsing. The fibres descend through the internal capsule and the cerebral peduncles to the basilar portion of the pons where they terminate at the medulla oblongata. Approximately 85% of the fibres cross over in the medulla to join with the opposite side of the spinal cord, where they proceed with their descent in the form of the lateral corticospinal tract (LCST). The corticospinal fibres that do not cross over in the medulla proceed with their descent along the same (ipsilateral) side of the cord, forming the ventral corticospinal tract (VCST).

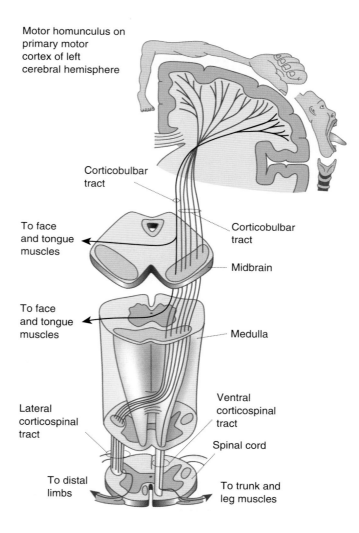

Figure 7.16 *Corticospinal tracts*

Surprisingly, bilateral pyramidal tract lesions leave monkeys still able to normally perform a broad range of motions such as walking and climbing. The principal difficulties are the loss of capability to carry out skilful manipulative tasks using the fingers and hands (Lawrence & Kuypers, 1968a). Unilateral pyramidal tract sections result in the animal experiencing a drastic decrease in the skilled movements of the hand relative to the unaffected hand. However, the animal still maintains the ability to move the entire limb around the joints and displays no apparent problems combining movements of body and limbs. Therefore, it appears likely that the corticospinal system is concerned with the facilitation of movements that require dexterity and skill.

Corticobulbar tract

The corticobulbar tract consists of fibres that originate in the precentral gyrus of the lower section of the motor cortex. As the fibres exit the motor cortex, they travel through the posterior limb of the internal capsule. This is medial and in front of the corticospinal tract. The fibres then travel through the cerebral peduncles, which are medial to the corticospinal tract fibres and finish in the motor nuclei of cranial nerves in the medulla, pons and midbrain. The corticobulbar fibres from one side of the brain project to the motor nuclei on each side of the brain stem (see Figure 7.16). The muscles of the face, head and neck are controlled by the corticobulbar system.

PATHWAYS ORIGINATING IN SUBCORTEX

Rubrospinal tract

The rubrospinal tract begins in the red nucleus of the midbrain prior to crossing the midline and descending in the lateral funiculus of the spinal cord, which is adjacent to the lateral corticospinal tract (Figure 7.17). The posterior part of the red nucleus gives rise to axons affecting motor neurons of the upper limbs and the neck region, while fibres originating from the anterior portion move down to lumbar levels and control lower limb muscles.

Lesion studies conducted on tracts that have been experimentally severed demonstrate that the corticospinal and rubrospinal tracts affect the motor neurons in a similar way. Monkeys with damaged rubrospinal tracts have problems reaching out for and holding on to food and lose skilled control of the distal musculature (Lawrence & Kuypers, 1968b). It comes as no surprise that, since the red nucleus receives inputs from the same area of the cerebral cortex as the corticospinal tracts, lesions in this tract produce similar results.

The ventral medial group

The vestibulospinal tracts

The vestibulospinal tracts, as the name suggests, originate in the vestibular nuclei of the brain stem. The fibres originate in the lateral vestibular nucleus and descend ipsilaterally in the interior funiculus of the spinal cord to form the lateral vestibulospinal tract (LVST) (see Figure 7.17). This helps to maintain an upright and balanced posture by exciting

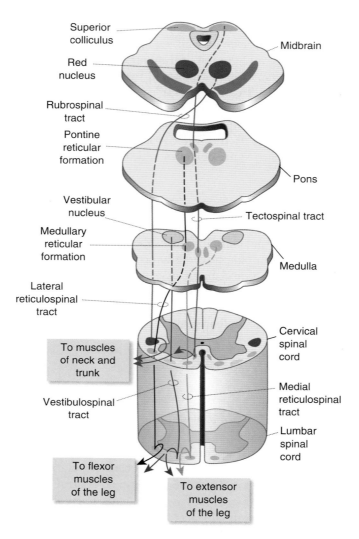

Figure 7.17 *Ventromedial and rubrospinal tracts*

extensor motor neurons in the legs. It innervates the trunk muscles as well, further boosting the posture of the body. The cerebellum (especially the vestibulocerebellum, flocculi and nodulus) sends information to the lateral vestibular nuclei. The cerebellum assists in coordinating postural adjustments.

The medial part of the vestibulospinal tract is smaller, and is mainly composed of fibres from the medial vestibular nucleus. It extends down both sides of the spinal cord and triggers the ventral horn of the cervical spinal circuits and regulates lower motor neurons. The pathway extends to the paramedian pontine reticular assemblage, which controls the posture of the head, neck and eyes as they respond to changes in position.

The reticulospinal tracts

The lateral reticulospinal tract originates in the medullar reticular formation and descends along the spinal cord in the lateral funiculus (see Figure 7.17). It synapses with alpha motor neurons, which are responsible for regulating the flexor muscles in the legs. The medial reticulospinal tract originates in the pons (specifically, in the pontine reticular formation) and synapses with alpha motor neurons that innervate the extensor muscles in the legs. The lateral and medial reticulospinal tracts coordinate their activities to regulate the ability to walk and run.

The tectospinal tract

The tectospinal tract consists of descending fibres, which chiefly arise in the tectum of the superior colliculus. Some of them remain on the same side, while others cross over the midline. In either case they synapse with the spinal cord. The tract is believed to be associated with the mediation of visual reflexes.

CEREBELLUM

Other structures, which are pivotal to creating movement, are the basal ganglia and the cerebellum, each of which is influenced by the activity of the brain stem and primary motor cortex. Maintenance for muscle tone, posture and the refinement of motion falls on the basal ganglia. The cerebellum refines movements that would otherwise be uncoordinated into skilled action and modifies movements to ensure that intent and action correspond.

The cerebellum (Latin for 'little brain') can be found at the back of the brain stem, where it is anchored in place by three cerebellar peduncles (fibre bundles) (Figure 7.18). It comprises two hemispheres that have a convoluted surface similar to the cerebral cortex. Despite the fact that it only accounts for approximately 10% of the brain's mass, it contains about 50% of its neurons; and although practically every sensory input eventually reaches the cerebellum, it is considered to be part of the motor system because injury to the cerebellum results in difficulties with equilibrium, coordinating voluntary movement, and control of one's posture (collectively referred to as movement disorders).

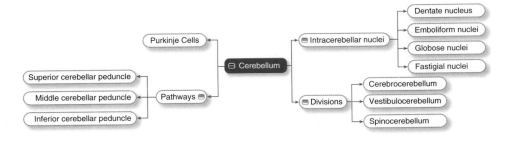

Figure 7.18   *Cerebellum*

The cerebellum appears to function as a comparator in the function of muscle control. The cerebellar cortex receives and analyses a sample of the motor command from the cerebral cortex to the skeletal muscle (see Figure 7.19). After the initiation of the motor activity, the cerebellar cortex starts receiving input by way of the spinocerebellar tracts from the proprioceptors in the muscles, tendons and joints that play a role in the movement. In this way the cerebellum compares the movement that actually occurs with the movement intended to occur. The cerebellar cortex, through the nuclei in the cerebellum and brain stem, is able to make corrections via ascending pathways; and at the spinal cord level, it makes corrective actions via descending pathways. It is important to recognise that this very basic mechanism does not offer a comprehensive explanation about the role the cerebellum plays in motor control, but it is a good place to begin to develop an understanding of the function of the cerebellum.

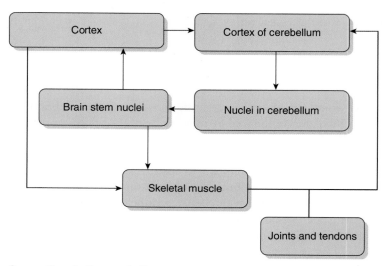

Figure 7.19   *Connections to the cerebellum*

THE STRUCTURE OF THE CEREBELLUM

As with the cortex, the cerebellum is composed of cortical grey matter surrounding a large area of subcortical white matter. Likewise, the surface of the cerebellum is grooved and regular, forming in folds or folia. Some of these grooves are reasonably deep, resulting in the formation of fissures, which divide the cerebral mass into lobules. Furthermore, the cerebellum is made up of two hemispheres divided by the vermis (see Figure 7.20).

The cerebellum and the cerebral hemispheres are also similar in that there are nuclei in the subcortical white matter – often referred to as intracerebellar nuclei when they are present in the cerebellum and basal nuclei when they are present in the cortex. The intracerebellar nuclei are located either side of the midline and are formed as pairs. The dentate nucleus is the biggest, as well as being located the most laterally. In the middle of this, in order approaching the

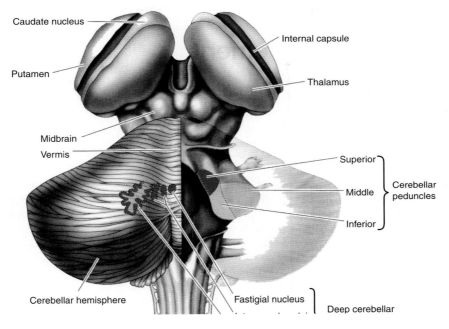

Figure 7.20   *Structure of cerebellum*

midline, are the emboliform, globose and fastigial nuclei. The nucleus interpositus consists of the globose nuclei and the emboliform. The intracerebellar nuclei act as critical relay centres, passing information between the cerebellar cortex and other sections of the brain, brain stem and spinal cord. Damage to the cerebellum can lead to an inability to perform rapid alternating movements, e.g. clapping hands, termed dysdiadochokinaesia. Box 7.1 details a study investigating cerebellum involvement in the coordination of hand movements.

BOX 7.1   Cerebellum involvement in the coordination of hand movements

Introduction

The cerebellum is thought to be an important neural component in coordination of the joints of one limb, between two limbs, and between eye and leg movements. This study (Miall, Reckess, & Imamizu, 2001) investigated the cerebellum's contribution to coordination between eye and hand movements in a visually guided tracking task.

(Continued)

(Continued)

Methods

The study used a tracking task in which participants followed a moving target with their eyes while simultaneously moving a joystick to control a cursor. This paradigm allowed variation of the degree of coordination between eyes and hand. In addition the target trajectories followed by eye and hand were identical, allowing maximal cooperation between the two control systems. The investigators used fMRI to detect brain regions activated by eye and hand movement performed alone or together. In a second experiment they investigated regions whose activity covaried with the degree of coordination between the eye and manual tracking movements.

Results

The study showed that the cerebellum was significantly activated in coordinated eye–hand tracking compared to isolated eye and hand movements, and that the cerebellum and only the cerebellum varied its activity with varied eye–hand coordination.

Interpreting the results

Miall and colleagues highlighted that the cerebellum was strongly activated in a task involving ocular pursuit of a target with simultaneous joystick control of a cursor. They also showed that the time offset between eye and hand motion allowed control of the degree of eye–hand coordination. Only the cerebellum showed activity changes, which covaried with time offset. The study also provided the most direct evidence from functional imaging that the cerebellum supports motor coordination. Its activity is consistent with roles in coordinating and learning to coordinate eye and hand movement.

Reference

Miall, R.C., Reckess, G.Z., & Imamizu, H. (2001). The cerebellum coordinates eye and hand tracking movements. *Nature Neuroscience, 4,* 638–644.

INPUTS AND OUTPUTS TO THE CEREBELLUM

There are three major subdivisions of the cerebellum; these divisions are based on differences in the input sources. The cerebrocerebellum is bigger than the other subdivisions. It takes up the majority of the lateral cerebellar hemisphere and gets input from several parts of the cerebral cortex. The cerebrocerebellum regulates movements that require a high degree of skill, particularly the planning and performance of complicated spatial and temporal sequences of motion. The vestibulocerebellum is phylogenetically the oldest and obtains input from the vestibular nuclei located in the brain stem. Mainly, it is involved with moderating movements that underlie posture and equilibrium. The spino-cerebellum comprises the median and paramedian zones of the cerebellar hemispheres, and this represents the only part that receives input directly from the spinal cord. The main function of the lateral part of the spinocerebellum is the movement of distal muscles, like moving the limbs in order to walk. The vermis, which is located in the middle, is associated with proximal muscle movement and additionally controls eye motion responding to vestibular inputs.

As mentioned earlier, the connections between the cerebellum and other areas of the nervous system occur by way of three large pathways called cerebellar peduncles. The neurons in the superior cerebellar peduncle that give rise to this pathway are found in the deep cerebellar nuclei, and their axons project to upper motor neurons in the red nucleus, the deep layers of the superior colliculus, and, following a relay in the dorsal thalamus, the primary motor and premotor areas of the cortex. This pathway is efferent. The middle cerebellar peduncle starts in the base of the pons or the pontine nuclei and is an afferent pathway that leads to the cerebellum. The pontine nuclei obtain input from several different sources, which include virtually every part of the cerebral cortex and the superior colliculus. The axons of the pontine nuclei are known as transverse pontine fibres, which transverse the median line and join the cerebellum by way of the middle cerebellar peduncle. The smallest of the cerebellar peduncles is the inferior cerebellar peduncle, but its various afferent and efferent pathways make it the most complex. Efferent pathways in this peduncle project to the vestibular nuclei and the reticular formation. The afferent pathways are composed of axons from the vestibular nuclei, the spinal cord and various parts of the brain stem tegmentum.

THE CEREBELLUM CIRCUITS

The Purkinje cell is a distinctive cell type found in the cerebellar cortex, and it is the final destination of the afferent pathway. These cells are one of the largest neurons in the human brain (only the pyramidal cells are larger), with intricately elaborate dendrites marked by numerous dendritic spines. In the cerebellum, you will find Purkinje cells located in the Purkinje layer. Their large dendrites form layers through which pass parallel fibres from the deeper layers pass. This produces a structure so that each Purkinje cell is in line to obtain input from several parallel fibres, each of which can contact several Purkinje cells.

The Purkinje cells project in turn to the deep cerebellar nuclei. The cerebellar cortex does not have other output cells. The cerebellar cortex output is inhibited due to the fact that Purkinje cells are GABAergic. It is best to explain this circuitry while referring to the Purkinje cells. The climbing fibres provide excitatory input to the Purkinje cells which obtain input indirectly by way of the parallel fibres of the granule cells. The Golgi, stellate and basket cells are involved in regulating how information flows through the cerebellar cortex. An inhibitory feedback is created by the Golgi cells that may limit the duration of the granule cell input to the Purkinje cells. The basket cells offer **lateral inhibition** to the Purkinje cell activity. The Purkinje cells regulate the activity of the deep cerebellar nuclei from the direct excitatory input of the mossy and climbing fibres.

Modulation of information through the cerebellum provides the basis for both real-time control of movement and the long-term changes in control that underlie motor learning (Ito, 2002). Dysfunction of the cerebellum cause symptoms which include muscle weakness (asthenia), decreased muscle tone (hypotonia), back-and-forth eye motions (nystagmus), muscle tremor when completing voluntary movements (intention tremor), and an overall reduction in muscle coordination (**ataxia**).

BASAL GANGLIA

The basal ganglia, or basal nuclei, are a group of nuclei located in the brain that interconnect with the brain stem, thalamus and cerebral cortex (Figure 7.21).

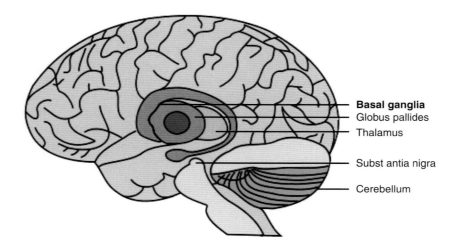

Basal ganglia
Globus pallides
Thalamus

Subst antia nigra

Cerebellum

Figure 7.21   *Location of basal ganglia*

The functions normally associated with the basal ganglia include: control of motion, memory, emotional response and learning ability. Included in this structural name are: caudate, putamen, nucleus accumbens, globus pallidus, substantia nigra, subthalamic nucleus, and traditionally the amygdala (Figure 7.22).

However, the amygdala is not involved with movement and is not interconnected with the rest of the basal ganglia, and as such does not feature much in this section. The basal ganglia adapt movement on a moment-to-moment basis and function in conjunction with the cerebellum. The motor cortex transmits information to the two structures, and they both relay information back to the cortex by way of the thalamus (don't forget, you cannot get to the cortex without crossing the thalamus). When the cerebellum provides excitatory output, the basal ganglia provide inhibitory outputs. When these two systems are balanced with one another, there can be smooth, well-coordinated movement. Any disturbance in

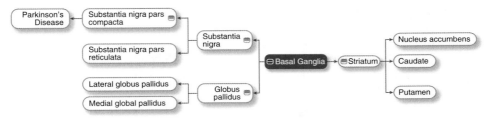

Figure 7.22 *Components of basal ganglia*

either system will present in the form of a movement disorder. We frequently talk about the basal nuclei in groups: the caudate, the putamen and the nucleus accumbens form the striatum; the striatum and the globus pallidus are collectively known as the corpus striatum; and the putamen and the globus pallidus together form the lenticular nucleus.

The putamen and caudate are equally connected with the substantia nigra, receive input from the cerebral cortex and send most of their output to the globus pallidus (Figure 7.23). The substantia nigra pars reticulata (SNpr) and the substantia nigra pars compacta (SNpc) make up the two parts of the substantia nigra. The SNpc gets information via the caudate and putamen, and relays information back. Input is delivered to the SNpr via the caudate and putamen which is sent outside the basal ganglia for the purpose of controlling the movements of the head and eyes. The SNpc produces dopamine, a substance that is necessary for normal movement; if it degenerates, Parkinson's disease results.

The globus pallidus may be separated into two distinct sections: the lateral globus pallidus (external) and the medial globus pallidus (internal). Both sections are in communication

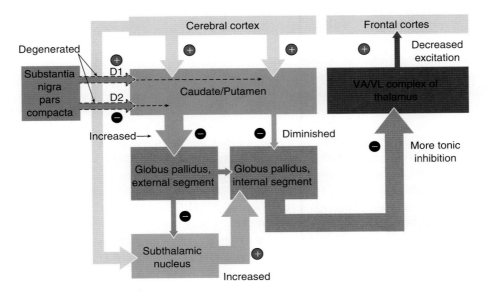

Figure 7.23 *Pathways of basal ganglia*

with the subthalamic nucleus and both receive input from the putamen and caudate. However, it is the medial globus pallidus that carries the major inhibitory output from the basal ganglia to the thalamus (Figure 7.23).

The most common and, consequently, best-known basal ganglia disorder is Parkinson's disease, which results from the slow and steady loss of dopaminergic neurons in the substantia nigra pars compacta. Individuals suffering from Parkinson's disease will demonstrate actual **rigidity**, unlike the spasticity (increased tone of a muscle) observed in patients with disorders of the brain stem. The tremor present is a **tremor at rest**; the intensity of the tremor will decrease with active movements, but typically it does not disappear. Parkinson's patients generally either move little (**akinaesia**) or move slowly (**bradykinaesia**). For more detail on the condition, see Chapter 13. Box 7.2 describes another motor disorder called developmental coordination disorder or DCD. In this condition some children have difficulty learning to coordinate their movements and may show clumsy behaviour.

BOX 7.2 Developmental coordination disorder (DCD)

Some children have great difficulty learning to coordinate their movements and may show awkward or clumsy behaviour. These children often struggle with sports or physical education at school and have issues in other subjects such as art or music that require handling items in lessons. They also have problems learning new motor skills, especially those that require coordination of their bodies in relation to moving objects such as balls. Children with these types of difficulties may have a condition called developmental coordination disorder (DCD). Depending on the definition, motor awkwardness occurs in around 5–15% of children. DSM-IV suggests that DCD is not caused by conditions such as muscular dystrophy or cerebral palsy.

DCD presents chiefly as impairment in locomotor, manual and sporting skills (Wilson & McKenzie, 1998). Furthermore, emotional and social problems are widespread in these children, and problems such as low self-esteem and social isolation also occur. The long-term outcomes for these children are not particularly heartening, with around 50% of children showing continual motor and associated difficulties into adulthood (Rasmussen & Gillberg, 2000). What obscures our understanding of the causes and prognosis of DCD is the comorbidity of motor difficulties and difficulties in other, non-motor areas. Numerous children with DCD also show problems with concentration and attention, and some present with specific learning disabilities such as dyslexia and specific language impairment (SLI). Although the comorbidity issue is well recognised, up to now few research studies have selected pure samples of DCD; thus the research is far from conclusive. Attempts have been made to explain such comorbidity phenomena: the minimal brain dysfunction (MBD) theory refers to a non-specific problem in brain function, basically similar in kind to the damage connected to cerebral palsy or mental retardation (Rutter, 1984). More recent theories such as the atypical brain development hypothesis and the deficits in attention, motor control and perception (DAMP) hypothesis (Gillberg, 1998) attribute the problems to some form of diffuse brain dysfunction.

References

Gillberg, C. (1998). Hyperactivity, inattention and motor control problems: prevalence, comorbidity and background factors. *Folia Phoniatrica et Logopaedica, 50*(3), 107–117.

Rasmussen, P., & Gillberg, C. (2000). Natural outcome of ADHD with developmental coordination disorder at age 22 years: a controlled, longitudinal, community-based study. *Journal of the American Academy of Child and Adolescent Psychiatry, 39*(11), 1424–1431.

Rutter, M. (1984). *Developmental neuropsychiatry*. New York: Churchill Livingstone.

Wilson, P.H., & McKenzie, B.E. (1998). Information processing deficits associated with developmental coordination disorder: a meta-analysis of research findings. *Journal of Child Psychology & Psychiatry, 39*(6), 829–840.

SUMMARY

The various mechanisms of movement control have been discussed in this chapter (Figure 7.24). The organisation of movement control was detailed and the spinal reflexes at the lower level of this hierarchy were explained. The different kinds of muscles were highlighted, and it was shown how they are composed of individual muscle fibres. The contraction of skeletal muscle is achieved by the sliding of thin filaments (of actin) between thick ones (of myosin); stretch receptors in the tissue provide feedback, allowing smooth motion and fine motor control. We learnt how tendon organs monitor the amount of force muscles exert and how under normal circumstances the tendon organs provide a continuous flow of information on the level of muscular contraction. If a muscle exerts too much force the protective nature of the tendon organ comes into play. The chapter also described the muscle spindle located within extrafusal muscle fibres which primarily detect changes in the length of the muscle. The chapter then explained the different types of reflex and how fatigue is combated by a set of inhibitory interneurons called Renshaw cells.

The chapter detailed the gamma motor system which provides us with muscle tone, other than in a stage of sleep called REM, as well as allowing us to react quickly and anticipate certain movements. The cerebral hemispheres can organise a sequence of movements called programmed movements; these actions are performed so rapidly that there is no time for correction of error by local feedback. The primary and secondary motor cortex were discussed, as was the role of the primary motor cortex in generating neural impulses that control the execution of movement. Impulses from the primary

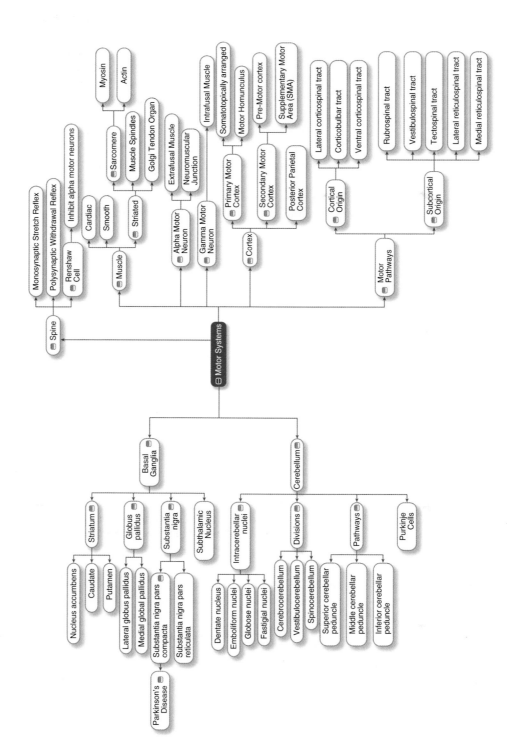

Figure 7.24   *Motor systems overview*

motor cortex cross the body's midline to activate skeletal muscles on the opposite side. Thus the left hemisphere of the brain controls the right side of the body, and the right hemisphere controls the left side of the body. In addition the body is represented in the primary motor cortex, and these representations are arranged somatotopically. The secondary motor area is located at the lower end of the precentral gyrus, and is secondary because it does not function in a discrete manner and also was discovered after the primary motor area.

Motor pathways were then discussed. These are pathways which originate in the brain or brain stem and descend down the spinal cord to control the alpha motor neurons. The best-known pathway is the so-called 'pyramidal system', which begins with the large pyramidal neurons of the motor cortex, travels through the brain stem and facilitates the alpha and gamma motor neurons which innervate the distal flexor muscles.

The cerebellum was discussed as part of the motor system. It is located posterior to the brain stem and is anchored by three cerebellar peduncles. It has two hemispheres with a convoluted surface like the cerebral cortex. Damage to the cerebellum causes problems in equilibrium, coordination of voluntary movement and postural control. Finally the basal ganglia were discussed; this is a group of nuclei in the brain interconnected with the cerebral cortex, thalamus and brain stem. The basal ganglia are associated with a variety of functions: motor control, cognition, emotions and learning. Lesions in specific nuclei in the basal ganglia tend to produce characteristic deficits, and loss of dopaminergic neurons in the substantia nigra pars compacta leads to a condition known as Parkinson's disease.

 ## FURTHER READING

Haaland, K.Y., Harrington, D.L., & Knight, R.T. (2000). Neural representations of skilled movement. *Brain*, *123*, 2306–2313.

Rizzolatti, G., & Craighero, L. (2004). The mirror-neuron system. *Annual Review of Neuroscience*, *27*, 169–192.

Wilson, P.H., & McKenzie, B.E. (1998). Information processing deficits associated with developmental coordination disorder: a meta-analysis of research findings. *Journal of Child Psychology & Psychiatry*, *39*(6), 829–840.

 ## KEY QUESTIONS

1 Describe the organisation of the cortex motor and describe its relationship with other areas of the brain.

2 Describe the three types of muscle found in humans.

3 Name and describe the motor tracts and the movements they control.

8 THE BIOPSYCHOLOGY OF MOTIVATION

CHAPTER OUTLINE

Studying motivation involves examining the factors in an individual that influence goal-oriented behaviour. It has long been the object of psychological studies, Charles Darwin, for example, posited that animal behaviour is based on instinct, while Freud believed that irrational instinctive urges or unconscious motivation governed much of human behaviour. This chapter focuses on the brain mechanisms of motivation, paying special attention to eating and drinking, sexual behaviour, and the relationship between reinforcement and biology (Figure 8.1).

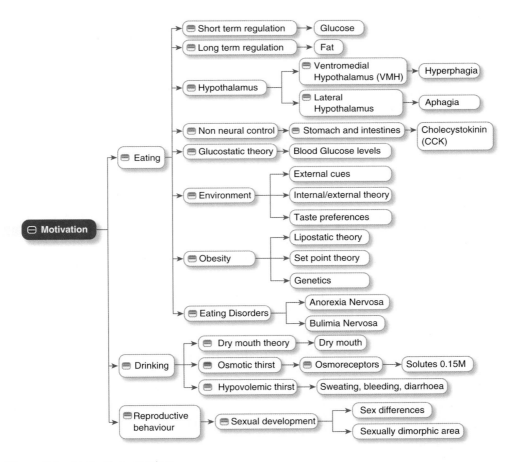

Figure 8.1 *Motivation overview*

MOTIVES

Walter Cannon (1871–1945) first suggested that basic human drives played a role in the homoeostasis of animals by decreasing physiological tension. Others see a motive as a sensitisation to a particular behaviour: a hungry person, for example, will see food differently from a person who is not hungry, so people tend to fill up the shopping basket more if they shop when they are hungry as opposed to after eating a good meal.

Two types of motives are often described: unlearnt primary or basic motives, which both animals and humans display; and secondary or learnt motives, which vary among individual people. The biological motives or primary motives are based on physiological actions and are necessary for survival of the individual or species. These generally include hunger, thirst, pain, sleep and air. Motives can be described as either 'push' or 'pull' motives. Push motives are involved with internal changes that trigger certain motivational states. Pull impulses are associated with external objectives that affect the subject's behaviour directed at them. Generally, most motivational situations are really a blend of push and pull conditions. Hunger, for example, may be signalled by internal changes in blood glucose, but the motivation to eat is also greatly influenced by what foods are accessible. Hence, motivational behaviour is often a complicated mix of both internal and external impulses.

EATING

The reasons people eat involve two different mechanisms (Figure 8.2). The first mechanism, which we refer to as short-term regulation, tries to obtain enough energy to compensate for what is being expended. This is a short-term mechanism that dictates our meal size and our meal times. Longer-term regulation is a second mechanism which is concerned with the storing of enough energy for later use if the short-term mechanism should fail in some way. The energy for this long-range usage is stored as fat contained in the fat cells of our body. Short-term control methods involve monitoring blood glucose or blood sugar levels in the body and eating only when levels fall below some predetermined optimum. Long-term regulation involves monitoring the fat levels of the body and again eating when fat stores fall under some optimal level.

The human digestive process starts in the mouth, where chewing mixes saliva into the food, adding moisture and an enzyme called amylase, which starts to convert any starches that are found in the food. The tongue then forms the food into something called a bolus, a small mass, which is then swallowed. Through the process of peristalsis, the bolus moves through the pharynx and oesophagus and ultimately reaches the stomach, where the food is combined with gastric acid (HCl). A hormonal substance called gastrin stimulates the secretion of gastric acid by the parietal cells of the stomach. The food is now in a semi-liquid state, known as chime, and moves along into the duodenum, where the bulk of the digestive process occurs (see Figure 8.3).

When carbohydrates in the form of glucose are absorbed by the duodenum, the blood glucose level rises and triggers the pancreas to release the hormone insulin. Insulin boosts the glucose uptake from the blood into the liver, where the glucose not required for

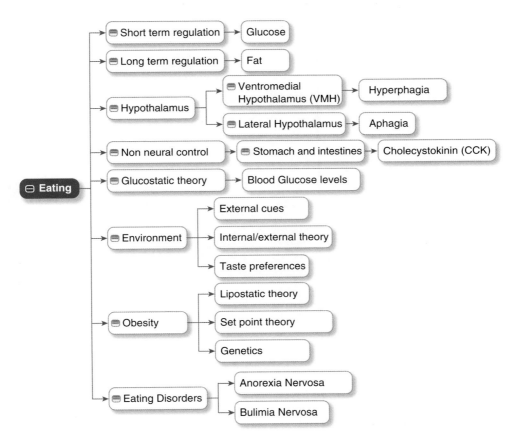

Figure 8.2 *Eating*

immediate energy is converted into glycogen and stored; later this can be converted back into glucose as needed. Any excess glucose not stored as glycogen is stored as fat in adipose tissue, making it available for future energy needs (see Figure 8.4). Trypsin is an enzyme that is secreted by the pancreas for the purpose of assisting in the breakdown of simple amino acids and complex proteins. In the stomach trypsin takes over the work begun by pepsin and completes the breakdown of the protein into single amino acid molecules. After the process of protein breakdown has taken place, the amino acids are moved to the small intestine. Thousands of finger-like projections known as villi are found lining the inside of the small intestine. These projections provide the small intestine with additional surface area for completing the digestive process and absorbing nutrients. Lymph vessels and a network of blood capillaries are present within each villus. Once the proteins have been broken down into amino acids, they can then make their journey across the intestinal lining and enter the walls of the capillaries. Amino acid molecules are then transported via the circulating blood in the body's capillary system.

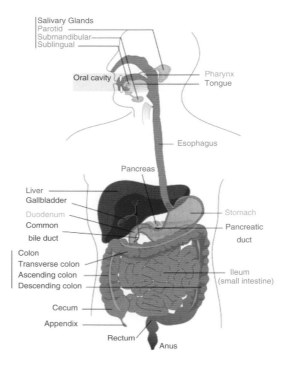

Figure 8.3 *The digestive system*

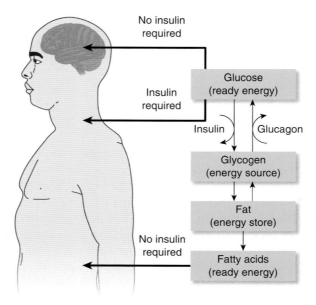

Figure 8.4 *Glucose processing*

THE ROLE OF THE HYPOTHALAMUS IN HUNGER AND SATIETY

The local theory of hunger proposes that signals that cause hunger and thus trigger eating begin in the digestive tract, namely in the stomach. Hunger pangs are thought to stem from contractions of the stomach. However, this theory is not believed to be an adequate explanation of hunger, as other factors such as motivation play a role. It has for example been found that when a large amount of the stomach is removed, there is no loss of hunger motivation. Likewise, it has been shown that elimination of stomach contractions resulting from cutting the vagus nerve does not suppress the sensation of hunger.

In the 1940s, it was discovered that bilateral lesions to the ventromedial (lower, middle) region of the hypothalamus (VMH) lead to **hyperphagia**, a condition in which animals overeat resulting in huge weight gain (Hetherington & Ranson, 1940). Lesions to another region, called the lateral hypothalamus (LHA) (sited on the sides of the hypothalamus), give rise to **aphagia**, which is a total lack of eating (York & Bray, 1996), as well as **adipsia**, which is a lack of drinking (Anand & Brobeck, 1951).

These findings gave rise to the dual centre hypothesis, in which the LHA is the satiety centre and the VMH is the hunger centre. This dual centre model was widely accepted, but it cannot fully explain all behaviour. Following a lesion to the ventromedial region, an animal exhibits a pattern of hyperphagia known as the 'dynamic phase' and during this period, it becomes fat and gains weight. However, this over-consumption and motivation to eat eventually subsides leaving the animal with a new but much higher than normal weight. This so-called 'static-phase' of not eating would not be expected if the VMH is a hunger centre and whose destruction increases an animal's motivation for food. This observation has led to the idea that what causes this VMH syndrome is the destruction of the area of the brain causing the animal to store its energy in the form of fat. Therefore, animals consume more food to satisfy their metabolic needs. VMH lesions lead to large increases of insulin in the blood and subsequently can elicit feeding responses, as well as promoting the conversion of nutrients into fat. Thus, bilateral lesions of the VMH increase the likelihood of the body producing and storing more fat and reduce the likelihood of releasing this fat into the bloodstream.

Because the calories that VMH-lesioned rats eat are converted to fats at such a high rate, the rats must continue eating to make sure that they have sufficient calories in their blood to meet their immediate energy needs (see Figure 8.5). Evidence against the notion of LHA being a dedicated feeding centre has come from studies on aphagia and adipsia caused by LHA lesions.

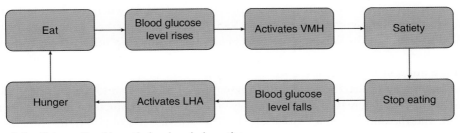

Figure 8.5 *Schematic of hypothalamic role in eating*

Subsequent findings demonstrated that LHA lesions yielded a variety of motor disturbances and a general lack of reactivity to sensory input, even though we know that the LH contains nerve cells that are responsive to the positive incentive properties of food and not the food itself (Rolls, Rowe, & Rolls, 1982).

PARAVENTRICULAR AND ARCUATE NUCLEI

The original dual centre hypothesis, which identified the ventromedial hypothalamus as the centre for satiety and the lateral hypothalamus as the centre for hunger, has been recently revised to take into account the responses caused by hypothalamic lesions. Two areas that have been investigated are the arcuate and paraventricular nuclei. The arcuate nucleus contains nerve cells that produce neuropeptide Y (NPY) and project to the ventromedial hypothalamus and the nucleus of the solitary tract. The paraventricular nucleus (PVN) contains nerve cells which release corticotrophin releasing hormone that projects to the arcuate nucleus and locus coeruleus.

Stimulation of the PVN alters eating behaviour. Microinjections of noradrenaline directly into the PVN increase carbohydrate consumption (Leibowitz, 1975). Likewise, repeated stimulation of the PVN with NPY has triggered an increase in the daily intake of carbohydrates and fat resulting in dramatic weight gain in female rats (Stanley & Leibowitz, 1985). Predictably, NPY neurons are hyperactive in genetically obese mice (Williams, Cai, Elliott, & Harrold, 2004).

The arcuate nucleus plays a key role in the regulation of feeding behaviour. Neuropeptide neurons which are located in the arcuate nucleus manufacture and release a neurotransmitter often referred to as agouti-related protein (AgRP); food intake is strongly stimulated by AgRP. Other neuron groups produce two substances that can cause an appetite suppressing response; these are cocaine and amphetamine regulated transcript (CART) and pro-opiomelanocortin (POMC). The gut peptides also signalling to the hypothalamus act via the arcuate nucleus and provide appetite modifying neurotransmitters, like the opioid peptides and alpha-melanocyte stimulating hormone (α-MSH) (see Figure 8.6).

Oral sensations and stomach cues are associated with hunger and eating; oral sensations like the taste and quality of food appear to regulate the persistence and maintenance of eating (Teitelbaum & Epstein, 1962). Satiety is also affected by oral cues and suppressed food intake. Because satiety occurs prior to the body absorbing the food, stopping the intake of more food is dependent on peripheral and metabolic signals. Two things occur in the stomach that stops feeding. First, the stomach is distended, triggering pressure detectors; and second, nutrient detectors suppress feeding when there is food already in the stomach (Janowitz & Hollander, 1955). The stomach conveys feelings of being satisfied to the brain by way of the vagus nerve, which supplies information concerning the stretching of the stomach wall, while the splanchnic nerve transmits information about the nutrient contents of the stomach (Deutsch & Ahn, 1986).

The duodenum is also involved in the regulation of meal size and the sensation of feeling satisfied. This is achieved in two primary ways: first, the sphincter muscle between the stomach and the duodenum is closed, causing the stomach to hold on to its contents; and

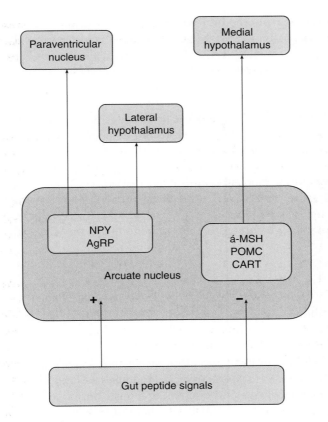

Figure 8.6   *The arcuate nucleus*

second, cholecystokinin (CCK) is released which stimulates the vagus nerve, which then signals the satiated message to the hypothalamus via the nucleus of the solitary tract (Crawley & Kiss, 1985). CCK infusions have been found to result in greater suppression of food intake in older people than in younger ones. It has been suggested that increased CCK activity may play a role in the **anorexia** that is associated with ageing (MacIntosh, Sheehan, Davani, Morley, Horowitz, & Chapman, 2001).

GLUCOSTATIC PRINCIPLE

Findings indicate that blood sugar levels, i.e. glucose, also play a part in appetite and feelings of fullness. Food begins its journey into the bloodstream as glucose, and a low level of glucose in the blood creates hunger. Specialised glucoreceptors probably located in the hypothalamus initiate eating behaviour when there are low blood glucose levels, whereas higher blood sugar levels result in feelings of fullness. When the body has a high level of blood glucose (hyperglycaemia), the pancreas responds by secreting insulin into the blood.

This triggers a response from the liver which turns some of the excess glucose into glycogen, and fat cells turn a quantity of it into fat. If the glucose levels start to drop, the liver takes glycogen and turns it into glucose. In this manner, glucose levels remain constant for most people, most of the time. Individuals who have insufficient insulin to remove glucose from the blood have a condition called diabetes mellitus.

One noticeable problem with the glucostatic theory is that diabetics report excessive hunger in spite of their high blood glucose levels. This is because diabetics are unable to change their blood glucose into energy, as insulin is required for glucose uptake into the cells and for it to be metabolised. This observation led to the original glucostatic theory being modified to suggest that the key factor is the availability of glucose for metabolism, rather than its level in the bloodstream (Mayer, 1995).

Higher blood sugar levels cause the paraventricular system to suppress eating. Increased blood sugar levels increase activity in the VMH accompanied by a reduction in appetite, but the satiety glucoreceptors are to be found in the liver rather than the VHM (Russek, 1976).

GHRELIN

Although the hormone ghrelin is mainly produced by P/D1 cells lining the fundus of the stomach, other ghrelin producing cells have also been found in the small and large intestines (Sakata et al., 2002) and in the pancreas (Wierup, Svensson, Mulder, & Sundler, 2002). The levels of ghrelin increase before meals and decrease after meals, and unlike leptin, which is produced by adipose tissue and induces satiation when present at higher levels, ghrelin is often labelled as the circulating hunger hormone.

Ghrelin is present in the arcuate nucleus, where its action is to stimulate the anterior pituitary gland to secrete growth hormone. Receptors for ghrelin are found in the arcuate nucleus and the lateral hypothalamus and also in the sensory ending of the vagus nerve present right through the gastrointestinal tract. One theory is that ghrelin could play a role as a peripheral appetite modulator by affecting the sensitivity of the sensory endings of the vagus nerve, making them less sensitive to distension of the stomach resulting from overeating.

ENVIRONMENTAL FACTORS IN EATING

Hunger cannot be understood just as a biological process. As humans, we cannot ignore the psychological aspect and the characteristics of hunger that have been learnt or are cognitively based. Therefore, in addition to the peripheral and metabolic cues, we must also take into account the effects of environmental cues, like the smell and sight of food, on hunger and satiety.

Hunger and eating based on learning

For some individuals, thinking about certain foods they crave is all that is needed to trigger hunger; for others it might simply be because the clock says it is lunchtime or dinnertime.

Appetite that stems from external stimuli is referred to as conditioned hunger. This hunger is triggered by learnt behaviours as well as the smell, taste or texture of food. I am sure you have experienced this when you smell your favourite food. If you like chips, just the smell of potatoes being cooked as you pass a chip shop could trigger your hunger. Further, an animal's motivation to eat is boosted by salivation and gastric secretion (cephalic reflexes); palatable food produces greater cephalic responses than non-palatable food.

Individuals (whether or not they are obese) who react to external cues of hunger tend to experience greater increased levels of insulin in their bloodstream than individuals who respond to internal cues. Rodin (1981) reported increased insulin levels in externally triggered hungry individuals who were exposed to external cues such as the sights and the smells of steak grilling. The internal–external theory regarding hunger and eating has also been investigated by measuring participants' food intake and altering the actual time by moving the clock ahead or back. The hypothesis was that if hunger in an obese person was triggered by the time on a clock rather than the real time, then the individual would consume more food when the clock indicated dinnertime. The results supported this, with obese people reacting to external cues of hunger, such as what time it is, more than non-obese people, who tended to react more to internal cues of hunger (Schachter, 1971).

Dietary habits are additionally affected by acquired likes and dislikes of taste. Animals learn to like tastes that are followed by an infusion of calories and avoid tastes that are followed by sickness. Humans develop food preferences that are based on cultural experiences as well as their knowledge about food. Past positive experiences with selected foods also influence what people eat and as such people generally learn to change their food preference to eating 'good' food (Franken, 2001). Box 8.1 details an fMRI study on the motivation to eat one of the 'bad' foods, chocolate.

BOX 8.1   Brain activity for chocolate

Introduction

Many studies have investigated the motivational aspects of feeding behaviour. This study (Small, Zatorre, Dagher, Evans, & Jones-Gotman, 2001) investigated brain activity when individuals ate chocolate to beyond satiety. The procedure was based on the premise that people, if given enough chocolate, would eventually lose the desire to eat. At the start of the experiment, the eating of chocolate would be consistent with individual motivation; but as the chocolate was eaten to beyond satiety, the behaviour would become inconsistent with individual motivational behaviour. So in essence, the experimental paradigm is both rewarding and punishing at the same time.

Methods

Pilot testing was initially carried out to determine which chocolate to use. Nine healthy volunteers, five women and four men, who claimed they were 'chocoholics' took part in

(Continued)

(Continued)

the study. Participants were scanned after being given one square of chocolate and instructed to eat it by letting it melt in their mouths, this process was repeated until they had consumed between 16 and 74 squares of chocolate (or about 40 to 170 grams). Measurements of brain activity were taken as participants became satiated and then beyond satiated to the point where they ate despite no longer wanting to.

Results

Different brain areas were active according to whether the individual was very motivated to eat chocolate and had a pleasurable experience or whether they ate chocolate despite being satiated. When individuals were motivated there was activity in the subcallosal region, caudomedial orbitofrontal cortex (OFC), insular/operculum, striatum and midbrain. When they were satiated the parahippocampal gyrus, caudolateral OFC and prefrontal regions were found to be active. The posterior cingulate cortex was active during both conditions.

Interpreting the results

The results highlight the role of the OFC, insular and caudomedial regions as cortical chemosensory areas, suggesting that the reward value of food is represented in these regions. The lateral and medial OFC activity in the two conditions showed opposite patterns of activity, which may indicate functional segregation of the neural representation of reward and punishment system in the brain. Thus, there may be two motivational systems in the brain, one coordinating approach behaviour and another avoidance behaviour.

Reference

Small, D.M., Zatorre, R.J., Dagher, A., Evans, A.C., & Jones-Gotman, M. (2001). Changes in brain activity related to eating chocolate: from pleasure to aversion. *Brain, 124,* 1720–1733.

Obesity and long-term control of body weight

Obesity results when an individual is carrying too much body fat for their height and sex. An individual is considered obese if they have a body mass index (BMI) of 30 or greater. People become obese for a number of reasons. Traditionally, we have looked at eating too much and not getting enough exercise as the main causes of weight gain, with fat storage increasing when there is more energy consumed than used. This explanation is accurate but does not give a full explanation of the matter, as willpower, environment and exercise habits also have a high degree of influence on eating. In addition, certain biological factors have been identified that are involved with weight management. Box 8.2 details an fMRI study on obesity.

BOX 8.2   Brain activation in response to pictures of high-calorie foods

Background

This experiment (Stoeckel, Weller, Cook, Twieg, Knowlton, & Cox, 2008) built on the understanding that the reward effect of an addictive drug and natural reinforcers such as foods are possibly mediated by a common neural substrate. The current models of addiction propose that drug-related cues may trigger drug-seeking behaviour by causing hyperactivity in the reward areas of the brain, such as the ventral tegmental area, amygdala, nucleus accumbens/ventral striatum, orbitofrontal cortex and ventral pallidum. This study asked whether food cues could act in a similar way in the development and maintenance of obesity and that stimuli associated with high-calorie foods may have a greater than normal force for activating the reward system.

Methods

This study used fMRI to investigate the activation of reward system and associated brain structures in response to pictures of high-calorie and low-calorie foods in 12 obese compared to 12 normal weight women. Participants were scanned while viewing stimuli divided into low-calorie and high-calorie items, each consisting of 84 unique images. Images of steamed vegetables and boiled fish were used as representations of low-calorie foods, while high-calorie foods were represented by items mainly high in fat. Control stimuli consisted of car images.

Results

Analysis of the fMRI results showed that pictures of high-calorie foods produced significantly greater activation in a number of brain areas including the medial and lateral orbitofrontal cortex, amygdala, nucleus accumbens/ventral striatum and hippocampus of the obese group when compared to normal weight controls. The obese group also had generally more activation when viewing high-calorie food than when viewing low-calorie food.

Interpreting the results

In summary, when compared to normal weight controls, obese women showed greater activation in response to pictures of high-calorie foods in a number of brain regions believed to play a role in the motivational effects of food cues. These results robustly support the hypothesis suggested by behavioural studies that overeating in obese individuals is triggered by exaggerated reactivity to stimuli associated with high-calorie foods.

Reference

Stoeckel, L.E., Weller, R.E., Cook, E.W. III, Twieg, D.B., Knowlton, R.C., & Cox, J.E. (2008). Widespread reward-system activation in obese women in response to pictures of high-calorie foods. *Neuroimage, 41*, 636–647.

THE LIPOSTATIC THEORY

The lipostatic theory proposes that the byproducts of fat metabolism circulating in the blood act as a signal to the hypothalamus. A reduced amount of lipids in the bloodstream results in the sensation of hunger, and the mammalian hormone leptin acts to maintain body weight. In typical metabolism, high leptin indicates sufficient energy reserves and low amounts indicate hunger mode. Research has shown that obese people have more leptin, and the leptin levels are strongly correlated with percentage of body fat, suggesting that the cells of obese people show little sensitivity to leptin levels (Considine & Caro, 1996).

The hormone leptin is concerned with long-term weight control, as the levels of leptin do not increase immediately following a meal. Leptin is manufactured primarily in the adipocytes of white adipose tissues, while leptin receptors are found in various tissues like the muscles and the gut, and in particular in the ventromedial hypothalamus (VHM). Reacting to leptin levels, the arcuate nucleus will produce varying levels of neurotransmitters and neuropeptides that regulate the quantity of food that is eaten. Leptin also minimises the impact of NPY, which as we have seen is an eating stimulant, and promotes alpha-melanocyte stimulating hormone (α-MSH) which also reduces appetite. Leptin might also suppress melanin concentrating hormone (MCH) which stimulates feeding and reduces the stimulating properties of endocannabinoids. In addition leptin could also increase the effects of cocaine and amphetamine regulated transcript (CART), which is an appetite suppressant, and other known appetite reducers like bombesin and corticotrophin releasing factor (CRF). In addition to regulating food intake, leptin also controls the burning of fatty acids in skeletal muscle, with high levels increasing metabolism. In addition circulating leptin levels are directly proportional to the total amount of fat in the body, and the rate at which leptin is produced is dependent on fat cell size. Although leptin appears to be a substance that reduces appetite, it is believed that obese people in general have a resistance to high leptin levels and the presence of large fat stores leads to leptin desensitisation, resulting in the malfunction of the satiety pathways. Leptin also intensifies the effects of insulin and thus further inhibits the use of fat as an energy source by inhibiting the release of glucagon (Friedman, 2002).

SET POINT THEORY

According to set point theory, the body tries to maintain a set weight point determined by the hypothalamus (Keesey & Powley, 1986). Dieting fails because the person has their own set weight point, and the body itself works to maintain that set point. Therefore, the fewer calories a person consumes, the more determined the body becomes to maintain the weight set by the hypothalamus. It is suggested that damage to the VHM might raise the critical set weight point. Indeed, animals with a lesion to the VMH become obese, with their excessive eating being attributed to storing enough fat to reach the new higher set point of the hypothalamus.

GENETICS AND OVERWEIGHT

Evidence indicates that there is a genetic component to being overweight. As stated earlier, leptin, the **protein hormone** encoded by the ob gene, is secreted mainly from adipose tissue and plays a key role in controlling the intake of food. The level of circulating leptin in the body has a positive correlation with the amount of fat in individuals without any mutations in their ob genes. This is an indicator that people who are obese have more leptin in their bodies and that they might be resistant to the proposed anti-obesity action of leptin. For instance, mice with mutations on both ob genes (ob/ob mice) are unable to synthesise leptin. In these animals, a lack of leptin results in overactive neuropeptide Y neurons and hyperphagia and obesity, which mirrors VMH or PVN damage. There is also a decrease in appetite and weight loss after injecting leptin into these animals (Halaas et al., 1995).

Genetic mutations that cause defects in leptin synthesis and leptin receptors give rise to db/db mice and fa/fa Zucker rats (Beck, 2000). In fa/fa Zucker rats that have defective leptin receptors, endogenous administered leptin has little influence on food consumption, which suggests that weight gain may be because of the incapability of leptin to inhibit neuropeptide neurons in these animals. Conversely, ob/ob mice cannot produce leptin despite having intact leptin receptors. These mice are sensitive to the satiety effect of leptin, and react to exogenous leptin being injected into the brain, reversing hyperphagia obesity syndrome. It is quite unusual to find a homozygous mutation for the leptin or leptin receptor genes in humans. Nonetheless, those who do have this condition, like the ob/ob and db/db mice, are generally found to be obese. Moderate obesity can be caused by heterozygous mutations.

EATING DISORDERS

ANOREXIA NERVOSA

Individuals suffering from anorexia nervosa are severely underweight, and have a distorted body image and an obsessive fear of putting on weight. It is well known that anorexic individuals control their body weight by voluntarily starving themselves, engaging in excessive exercise, or undertaking other extreme weight control measures like taking diet pills or diuretic drugs. While the condition primarily affects teenage females, almost 10% of individuals diagnosed are male (Becker, Grinspoon, Klibanski, & Herzog, 1999).

Anorexics usually have a body weight that is 85% or less of what it should be for their height, age and sex, but do not have a distorted image of their weight and physique. Usually, they believe their severely underweight bodies to be fine and sometimes possibly even overweight. They usually eat an extremely restricted and rigid diet, and are obsessively fearful of putting on weight. Along with the weight loss, women also experience amenorrhoea (absence of menstruation for a minimum of three consecutive months).

The mortality rate varies, but approximately 5–20% of individuals with this disorder die from starvation or medical complications resulting from low weight and such a rigid, restricted diet (Steinhausen, Seidel, & Winkler Metzke, 2000). Even though we do not know the precise origins of anorexia nervosa, the underlying causes of the disorder are multifaceted and include genetic and physiological risk factors and developmental factors that may give these individuals a negative biased body image. Other factors have also been implicated, such as lack of internally driven emotions and a familial pattern of eating. Psychological factors present in these individuals might encompass a range of influences, like an anxious temperament, tendencies towards perfectionism or being obsessive, a co-occurring psychological disorder (e.g. depression), and either chronic or acute stress. There is a greater risk for individuals who have a family history of alcohol or substance dependence, any form of abuse, mental disorders, or parents who are frequently in conflict. Usually, anorexia is preceded by a period of strict dieting that moves into extreme restriction of intake and deliberate starvation.

A variety of psychotherapies and nutritional therapies have been used to treat the condition, and there has been some success using cognitive behavioural therapy (Bowers, 2001). With adolescents, family therapy with parents and even siblings and a family-based treatment (FBT) approach called Maudsley therapy seem to help (FBT was first used in the 1980s at the Maudsley Hospital in London). Other treatments include behavioural systems family therapy (BSFT) and multiple-family day treatment (MFDT). In anorexia, treatment with medication plays a much less prominent role than it does for many other psychiatric disorders. That said, it appears that treating the condition with selective serotonin reuptake inhibitors (SSRIs) may be generally effective in preventing relapse. Zinc supplements are suggested as part of the treatment protocol for anorexics since large weight gain has been observed after treatment with zinc. The results point to the greater effectiveness of neurotransmission in different parts of the brain such as the amygdala (Birmingham & Gritzner, 2006).

BULIMIA NERVOSA

Bulimia nervosa refers to the act of binge eating followed by some compensatory behaviour like self-induced vomiting, excessive exercise or fasting. Even though some individuals with anorexia nervosa will engage in binge eating followed by purging, the body weight of an individual who has bulimia nervosa usually stays near or above normal. Women constitute 90% of all those diagnosed with bulimia nervosa, with most reporting that the illness began somewhere between the ages of 12 and 25 (Barker, 2003).

As with anorexia, bulimia nervosa generally starts in adolescence or early adulthood with chronic dieting. Genetic and biological factors, and a general lack of internal feelings, seem to contribute to the development of this disorder. Several mental disorders often coexist including depression and certain personality disorders. In addition, a family history of eating issues or body image, as well as a predisposition towards self-judgement based on outside standards rather than internal ones, is often present. Bulimia may be caused by a hormone imbalance. People suffering from the disorder secrete abnormally low levels of cholecystokinin (CCK) in response to a meal; this leads to them being less satisfied than normal. Cognitive behavioural therapy seems to be the most successful therapy for bulimia nervosa.

DRINKING

Processes similar to the physiological control mechanisms of hunger are believed to control thirst motivation. On average, we drink more water than our body can use, and the excess is eliminated through our kidneys. This kind of drinking, where we anticipate how much fluid we need, is called secondary drinking; conversely, where we drink as a reaction to a loss of or deleted intracellular or extracellular fluid, we are engaging in what is called primary drinking. When a person's fluid levels are lower than they should be, urine is concentrated, sweat is decreased, and the person feels thirsty. The sensation of thirst and the desire to replenish fluids by drinking seems to be triggered by loss of fluids in specialised brain cells called **osmoreceptors** as well as by fluid loss outside the cells. A number of different circumstances can motivate someone to consume liquids; some are physiological but, as with hunger, there are also some external influences (Figure 8.7).

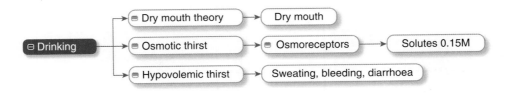

Figure 8.7   *Drinking*

DRY MOUTH THEORY

In 1934, Walter Cannon suggested a theory of drinking which advocated that people feel thirsty because their mouths get dry. Recent evidence has challenged this and shown that in animal studies where the animal can drink but the water does not enter the stomach, thirst is only temporarily reduced, thus indicating other factors must be involved in determining how much water we drink.

We experience the sensation of thirst in several ways. Eating salty food results in osmotic thirst, and losing fluid through eating or bleeding results in **hypovolemic** thirst.

OSMOTIC THIRST

The concentration of all solutes in the human body maintains a nearly constant level of 0.15 M (molar or moles per litre); this concentration can be regarded as a set point. Any deviation from this set point activates a mechanism that restores the concentrate to this

208 ESSENTIAL BIOLOGICAL PSYCHOLOGY

0.15 M level. Body fluids contain sodium chloride (NaCl), otherwise known as table salt. So eating salty foods will increase the NaCl concentration in the extracellular fluid, which will then develop a higher osmotic pressure than the intracellular fluid. This causes water to be pulled out of the cell, equalising the osmotic pressure across the cell membrane and resulting in cell shrinkage. The resulting cellular dehydration stimulates the kidneys to concentrate the urine and the person becomes thirsty; this is called osmotic thirst.

Osmoreceptors are neurons which display sensitivity to osmotic pressure. When these sensory neurons are stimulated, the individual feels thirsty, causing the posterior pituitary to release antidiuretic hormone (ADH) or vasopressin, which results in the kidneys retaining more water and concentrating the urine (see Figure 8.8). It was proposed that osmoreceptors could be found in the lateral preoptic section of the hypothalamus (Blass & Epstein, 1971),

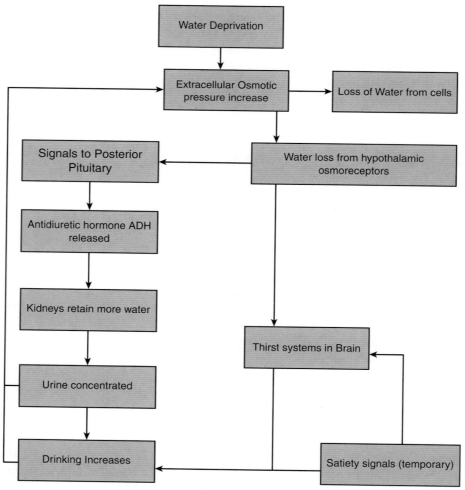

Figure 8.8   *Schematic of drinking behaviour*

but subsequent to that, osmoreceptors have been found in the subfornical organ (SFO) which resides in the dorsal part of the third ventricle, and the organum vasculosum lamina terminalis (OVLT) which is interconnected with the medial preoptic nucleus of the hypothalamus (Figure 8.9).

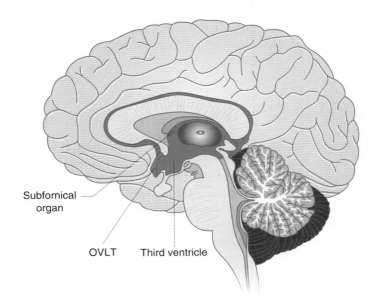

Subfornical organ

OVLT   Third ventricle

Figure 8.9   *Location of osmoreceptors*

Other information on sodium levels travels to the brain from receptors in the periphery including the stomach, allowing the brain to make an anticipatory reaction to osmotic needs even before the body experiences them. Information from the SFO, the OVLT and the stomach travels to the superoptic nucleus and the paraventricular nucleus (PVN) of the hypothalamus, which regulates the rate at which the posterior pituitary releases ADH. Information is also transmitted to the lateral preoptic area of the hypothalamus, which regulates drinking behaviour. When we consume water, it is absorbed through our gastrointestinal system and the osmotic pressure is restored, thus quenching thirst. Drinking activity is also inhibited by the monitoring of swallowing and how much fluid is in our stomach and intestines (Huang, Sved, & Stricker, 2000).

HYPOVOLEMIC THIRST

Hypovolemic thirst results from losing extracellular fluid from sweating, bleeding or diarrhoea. Decreased blood volume, otherwise known as hypovolemia, leads to a decrease in blood pressure which in turn stimulates mechanoreceptors or **baroreceptors** in the large blood vessels. These receptors send signals to the brain to release antidiuretic hormone (ADH), which leads to the concentration of urine in the kidneys. In addition, low blood pressure triggers receptors in the kidneys to release an enzyme called renin or angiotensinogenase, which changes the protein angiotensinogen into the hormone angiotensin created by the liver to give angiotensin I, which is then further converted to become angiotensin II by the angiotensin converting enzyme (ACE). Angiotensin II constricts the flow of blood, increases the release of ADH (which increases the amount of fluid retained) and the hormone aldosterone (which increases the amount of sodium retained), and triggers the hypothalamus to activate the thirst reflex, each resulting in a higher blood pressure.

REPRODUCTIVE BEHAVIOUR

The process of reproduction in animals encompasses all occurrences and activities that are directly involved in the organism creating at least one replacement of itself. Speaking in evolutionary terms, when an organism reproduces its chief goal is to create offspring that have a maximum representation of its own genetic traits. Regardless of the fact that it is easier for an animal to just divide into two or more individuals, and there are several living things that do this, it is more common to reproduce sexually, not asexually (Figure 8.10). Contrary to asexual reproduction, sexual reproduction allows the genetic material to be reorganised both within and between the offspring of a generation, leading to a wide range of offspring, each of whom will have their own unique genetic composition, one that differs from that of its parents.

Figure 8.10   *Reproduction*

DEVELOPMENT OF THE REPRODUCTIVE ORGANS

As you may be aware, humans are dimorphic, which means that we develop into two models, males and females. Sexual differentiation in mammals begins at fertilisation and changes with our development and ageing. These changes occur very quickly during puberty, but become slower and more gradual at other times. As seen in Chapter 3, the sex chromosomes of people are delineated by an X and a Y. Gender chromosomes consist of a single paired set among the 23 total pairs in human beings. Gender is determined by X and Y chromosomes: two X chromosomes (XX) for females and X and a Y (XY) for males.

In the first eight weeks of development, termed the neutral or indeterminate phase, the embryo shows no outward signs of its gender. In the early stages, embryos for both genders are very much alike in the duct systems they possess, including the **Müllerian** ducts and **Wolffian** ducts. The Y chromosome in males includes SRY (the sex determining area on the Y chromosome) gene, which results in the primitive gonads developing into testes; these then produce the hormone testosterone which causes the Wolffian ducts to differentiate into four associated structures: a duct of the epididymis, a ductus deferens, an ejaculatory duct and a seminal vesicle. A **peptide hormone**, Müllerian inhibiting hormone (MIH), results in the degeneration of the Müllerian ducts which, in women, continue to develop into the fallopian tubes, the uterus and part of the vagina.

The external genitalia undergo a transformation around this time, too, with the genital projections developing into either a penis in males or a clitoris in females. In the female body, the channel beneath the clitoris remains open, forming the vulva, and the folds on the two sides of the groove develop into the inner lips of the vulva, or the labia minora. In males, these folds fuse, creating the urethral tube of the penis. In women, swellings on either side stay apart and comprise the large labia (labia majora), whereas in the male they grow together to form the scrotal sac. There is development in the reproductive organs during childhood and, as puberty begins and the secondary sexual characteristics develop, we observe more activity in the reproductive system. The male sex hormones or androgens produced by boys result in additional muscular development, facial hair and changes in voice. In female youths, oestrogen hormones produce breast formation, menstruation onset and feminine build.

Males may develop both the behaviour and the anatomy of a female if they lack androgen receptors or have been castrated. In addition, factors that interfere with the effects of the male androgen or testosterone tend to lead to the development of more feminine characteristics. Alcohol, marijuana and cocaine are all known to interrupt the normal male pattern of development. The female androgen **oestradiol** does not give a male feminine characteristics in the way that testosterone gives females more masculine characteristics. If testosterone is present in the early stages, a male will be produced; if there is no testosterone, a female is produced no matter how much oestradiol or other oestrogens are present. As a result, in effect the 'default setting' for all humans is the feminine gender. Research in this area has suggested that testosterone results in the development of the masculinised brain (Gorski, 2002).

The hormones continue being important to the adult. A deficiency of androgen will cause a decrease in a man's sexual responsiveness. Additionally, a lack of oestrogen will negatively affect a woman's fertility and cause a condition of atrophy of the genitalia. Androgen appears to have a correlation with aggression and sex drive in both genders. When female animals are given testosterone, they become more aggressive and display behaviour usually associated with males, whereas oestrogen will increase their sexual responsiveness and intensify their female behaviour.

SEX DIFFERENCES IN THE BRAIN

The areas of the brain that seem to play a role in sexual responses are the hypothalamus and the limbic system, but no specific 'sex centre' in the brain has been identified. Sex hormones seem to affect the development of the cerebral cortex because they control the rates of apoptosis, leading to size difference in regions of the brain (Goldstein et al., 2001).

In females, the density of nerve cells in the temporal area is greater than that of males, while males tend to have a greater amount of white matter than females.

Structural differences can be seen in the preoptic regions of the hypothalamus, known as the sexually dimorphic nucleus (SDN). Males have more SDN than females, mainly because they have a larger volume of cells and a larger cell size in their SDN. In rats, the region that might not be analogous is called the sexually dimorphic nucleus in the preoptic area (SDN-POA). More male SDN correlates with a higher concentration of foetal testosterone levels in males than would be found in females. Humans are born with approximately 20% of the SDN cells that will be present at four years of age. After this, males experience a higher rate of cell formation than females, resulting in the sexual differentiation of the structure. The number of cells in the SDN drops significantly in males over the age of 50.

Some sex differences that have been reported in the literature have turned out to be controversial. One study reported sex differences in the corpus callosum, finding greater connectivity between the two hemispheres of the brain in women (de Lacoste-Utamsing & Holloway, 1982). There was disagreement not only regarding the cognitive and neuropsychological implications of the anatomical difference, but even over whether such a difference actually exists. A meta-analysis of 49 published papers conflicted with de Lacoste-Utamsing and Holloway, discovering that when making adjustments for the larger brain sizes, the corpus callosum in males is bigger than that in females (Bishop & Wahlsten, 1997). Recent imaging techniques have been used and have found differences in morphology, but whether these differences relate to differences in cognitive processing is still not clear (Shin et al., 2005).

ROLE OF SDN IN THE MANAGEMENT OF MALE SEXUAL BEHAVIOURS

Male sexual behaviour occurs in two phases. First, there is the appetitive stage, in which a highly variable sequence of activities occurs, like attracting a mate and courting her. Next, there is the consummatory stage, in which highly stereotyped copulatory activities occur. It is thought that the **medial preoptic region** of the brain is involved in controlling the expression of both male copulation and male appetitive sexual behaviour.

Indeed, lesions to the SDN-POA cause extreme disruption to the copulatory activities of rats, and lesions of the sexually dimorphic area (SDA) pars compacta in gerbils severely disrupt male copulatory behaviour (Commins & Yahr, 1984). A number of **sexual dimorphisms** or differences have been discovered in areas not necessarily associated with reproduction. For instance, rats have sexually dimorphic patterns of cortical and hippocampal asymmetries. In human males, there seems to be greater functional asymmetry and a greater brain asymmetry in the temporal planum (Wada, Clarke, & Hamm, 1975).

SUMMARY

This chapter explored the topic of motivation and explained the notion of primary biological drives. It was also explained how motives can be described as either 'push' or 'pull' motives. Push motives are involved with internal changes that trigger certain motivational states. Pull impulses are associated with external objectives that affect the subject's behaviour directed at them. Eating was discussed and short-term regulation and long-term regulation of eating was explained. Short-term control methods involve monitoring blood glucose or blood sugar levels in the body, while long-term regulation involves monitoring the fat levels of the body and eating when fat stores fall under some optimal level. The role of the hypothalamus was discussed and how it is involved with the dual centre hypothesis, namely identification of the ventromedial hypothalamus (VMH) as the hungry centre and the lateral hypothalamus (LHA) as the satiety centre. The chapter then discussed the paraventricular and arcuate nuclei, indicating the important role of these areas in the regulation of feeding behaviour. Non-neural control of feeding behaviour was discussed and it was emphasised that oral sensations like the taste and quality of food appear to regulate the persistence and maintenance of eating. The duodenum releases cholecystokinin (CCK) which is involved in regulating the sensation of feeling satisfied. In addition, it was indicated that blood sugar levels, i.e. glucose, also play a part in appetite and feelings of fullness. Specialised glucoreceptors, probably in the hypothalamus, initiate eating behaviour when there are low glucose levels in our blood. Higher blood sugar levels cause the paraventricular system to suppress eating. Ghrelin is a hormone produced mainly by P/D1 cells lining the fundus of the human stomach, and increase before meals and decrease after meals. In contrast to leptin, produced by adipose tissue, which induces satiation when present at higher levels, ghrelin is often seen as the circulating hunger hormone.

The chapter then went on to discuss the environmental factors of eating, highlighting that hunger cannot in reality be understood with just the biological component, as we cannot ignore the psychological aspects and the characteristics of hunger that have been learned or are cognitively based. In addition to the biological cues, we must also take into account the effect of environmental cues, like the smell and sight of food, on hunger and satiety. The lipostatic theory was discussed, which proposes that the product of fat metabolism circulating in the blood acts as a signal to the hypothalamus. The hormone leptin was then detailed, explaining that it is manufactured primarily in the adipocytes of white adipose tissues and is concerned with long-term weight control, as the levels do not increase immediately following a meal. Although leptin is a circulating indicator that reduces appetite, obese people appear to develop a resistance to these high levels; their large fat store leads to leptin desensitisation, resulting in the malfunction of the satiety pathways which function correctly in non-obese individuals. The genetics of obesity were discussed along with the relevance of genetic mutations that cause defects in leptin synthesis and leptin receptors, giving rise to db/db mice and fa/fa Zucker rats. In fa/fa Zucker rats with defective leptin receptors, administered leptin has little influence on consumption, whereas ob/ob mice cannot produce leptin even with intact leptin receptors. The eating disorders of anorexia nervosa and bulimia nervosa were discussed, highlighting the biological and environmental factors that have been implicated in contributing to the conditions.

Theories that explain the control mechanisms of drinking were presented; dry mouth theory was detailed, as was osmotic and hypovolemic thirst. It was highlighted that there are two ways in which we experience the sensation of thirst. Eating salty food results in osmotic thirst, and losing fluid through eating or bleeding results in hypovolemic thirst.

The chapter finished by discussing the motive to reproduce, and it was explained that the process of reproduction in animals encompasses all occurrences and activities that are directly involved in the organism creating at least one replacement of itself. Although a controversial area, some male and female biological differences were highlighted. Finally, the role of the sexually dimorphic nucleus was examined, where structural differences can be seen between sexes. Males have more SDN than females, because they have a larger volume of cells and a larger cell size in male SDN. Other studies have reported sex differences in the corpus callosum, leading to greater connectivity between the two hemispheres of the brain in women. This has caused disagreement not only regarding the cognitive and neuropsychological implications of the anatomical difference, but even over whether such a difference actually exists.

 ## FURTHER READING

Bishop, K.M., & Wahlsten, D. (1997). Sex differences in the human corpus callosum: myth or reality? *Neuroscience and Biobehavioral Reviews*, 21(5), 581–601.

Franken, R.E. (2001). *Human motivation* (4th edn). Pacific Grove, CA: Brooks/Cole.

Friedman, J.M. (2002). The function of leptin in nutrition, weight and physiology. *Nutrition Reviews*, 60, S1–S14.

 ## KEY QUESTIONS

1 What is the role of the stomach in regulating food intake?

2 Describe the biological processes of short-term and long-term hunger.

3 What is the SDN and how does it influence sexual behaviour?

9 SLEEP AND BIOLOGICAL RHYTHMS

Sleep is a natural restful state that occurs in humans and other animals. During sleep, the person or animal is less able to react to external stimuli in the environment. While it seems that regular sleep is necessary for many animals to survive, a great deal of research is being done to determine why we spend so many hours of our lives sleeping. In this chapter, we will review the key theories attempting to explain the need for sleep and an overview of the biological mechanisms of sleep.

BIOLOGICAL RHYTHMS

These periodic biological fluctuations in an animal correspond to, and are in response to, environmental changes that occur. The cyclic environmental variations include changes in the relative position of the earth to the sun and to the moon, as well as the effect of these variations, such as the day following night and the position of tidal heights. 'Biological clock' refers to the internal bodily mechanism that maintains these fluctuations even when environmental cues are not present. When one travels across time zones, the environmental cycle moves out of alignment with the body's internal cycle, and the body's internal clock continues to function for a while in concert with the original environmental cycle. When this happens, a person may feel fatigued and tired for a few days following the trip, during which time the person is said to be suffering from a condition called jet lag.

A rhythm with a 24 hour cycle is referred to as a **circadian rhythm**. 'Circadian' comes from the Latin *circa* 'about' and *di* 'day'; thus 'about a day'. Human performance competence also demonstrates biological and behavioural variation over a 24 hour period. Disturbed circadian cycles have also been linked to a range of mental and physical problems, whether the disturbance is due to voluntary behaviours, like shift work, or circumstances not under a person's control, like an illness (Toh, 2008). Regular periods or cycles repeated throughout a 24 hour day such as hormonal release, urination and appetite are termed ultradian rhythms; cycles which have periods longer than a day are termed infradian rhythms.

There is variation in body temperature during a 24 hour period, with the lowest temperature occurring during the early morning hours and the highest temperature occurring in the late afternoon and early evening. A drop in body temperature around midnight and an increase in the early morning are responsible for the sleep and wake cycle. Body temperature has also been found to impact mood (Kerkhof, 1998). Hormone levels also fluctuate during the day, as seen in the secretion of both melatonin and growth hormone which increases at night.

Humans generally experience sleep disturbances linked to jet lag, shift work or sleep disorders. Sleep disturbances are a symptom of a number of mental and physiological disorders, especially affective disorders, but it is still a matter of speculation as to how sleep disturbances affect illnesses (Kamdar, Needham, & Collop, 2011).

THE SUPRACHIASMATIC NUCLEUS (SCN)

The hypothalamus is the region of the brain that controls circadian rhythms. It integrates the rhythmic information, thereby establishing sleep patterns. Endogenous circadian

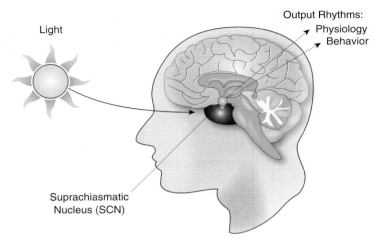

Figure 9.1   *Suprachiasmatic nucleus*

rhythms are controlled by a small area of the hypothalamus referred to as the suprachias-matic nucleus (SCN) which is located in a shallow impression in the optic chiasm (Moore, 2007). Regulation of various bodily functions over the course of a 24 hour period is effected by its neuronal and hormonal activities (see Figure 9.1).

After light has stimulated the photoreceptor cells in the retina, messages are transmitted to the SCN by neurons in the retinohypothalamic path. These signals then travel to a small, cone-shaped structure attached to the posterior end of the third cerebral ventricle called the pineal gland and then connect directly to the cholinergic basal forebrain which influences cortical arousal. Melatonin is produced in the pineal gland and the light reaching the retina decreases the production of melatonin, waking the individual up. In comparison, darkness causes an increase in the production of melatonin, and the body starts preparing for sleep. The sleep state is then induced by actions such as lowered body temperature and blood pressure; these take place because of melatonin binding to receptors in the SCN. For this reason, circadian rhythms are dependent upon the cyclical variations of melatonin. The human body is capable of functioning in cycles of between 18 and 28 hours, but even in parts of the world with no darkness, like the subpolar twilight zone, the body has normal cycles of wakefulness and sleep. A certain readjustment period is required when extreme changes in the circadian cycle occur.

It is believed that circadian rhythms permit animals to anticipate and get ready for par-ticular and regular changes in the environment. It appears that the rhythmicity is critical in the regulation and coordination of internal metabolic processes, as well as in coordinat-ing with the environment. The term 'jet lag' is commonly used when people's circadian rhythms are disrupted as they travel across several time zones.

The fruit fly has regularly been used as an animal model for the examination of bio-logical clocks. These experiments have discovered that the rhythms have a hereditary component to them. It is possible to create three mutant fly lines that exhibit variations in their biological clocks – one with a shorter period, one with a longer one, and the third with none. The same gene, the period or PER gene, is involved in all three mutations (Stanewsky, 2003). Mammals also carry the same gene, but it is referred to as the clock gene (King & Takahashi, 2000).

INFLUENCE OF LIGHT–DARK CYCLE

Circadian rhythms are strongly connected to cycles of light and dark. Animals and people that remain in complete darkness for a long time develop free-running rhythm. Every 'day' their sleep cycle is adjusted backward or forward in line with their endogenous period which may be shorter or longer than 24 hours. The rhythms are reset daily by the environmental cues provided by light and dark. These exogenous cues are referred to as **Zeitgebers**, German for 'time givers'. Although blind animals, such as the mole rat, cannot see the environmental stimuli, their photoreceptors still function and they come to the surface from time to time to 'reset' their circadian rhythms.

HOW MUCH SLEEP DO PEOPLE REQUIRE?

Although the physiological bases for the need for sleep are still a matter of debate, a great deal of evidence is available regarding the amount of sleep that people actually get. Possibly the most significant conclusion that we can draw from this evidence is that there is wide variation in the total sleep time for different individuals (see Table 9.1). In addition to heredity and circadian rhythms, the stage of life is an important variable that helps determine how much sleep a person requires each night. There has been a consistent link between age and the changing amount, quality and pattern of electro-physiologically defined sleep. Newborn babies need to sleep for 16 to 18 hours daily, but by the time children are a year old they normally sleep 13 to 14 hours, and that number of hours steadily decreases until they are adolescents. In general, adolescents need at least eight and a half hours of sleep daily, and some researchers believe that they need even more than that. Most adults require approximately eight hours of sleep for proper functioning.

Pregnancy and menopause can both create large alterations in sleep patterns in women. Pregnant women in the first trimester need much more sleep than normal. Decreased sleep quality tends to occur when women enter menopause, and insomnia and sleep apnoea may occur (Dursunoglu, 2009). It is possible that these changes are related to hormonal function or the psychological issues linked to menopause (Shin & Shapiro, 2003). In addition, other possible causes include physiological factors involved in the process of ageing and weight gain which commonly occur during this time in a woman's life.

While older people do not require less sleep than younger people, the elderly tend to have a more difficult time sleeping and frequently take naps during the day. Reduced sleep time in the elderly may also be caused by illness and utilisation of medications, rather than natural physiological reduction in sleep (Roepke & Ancoli-Israel, 2010).

Table 9.1 *Patterns of sleep and wakefulness*

Age and condition	Average amount of sleep per day
Newborn	Up to 18 hours
1–12 months	14–18 hours
1–3 years	12–15 hours
3–5 years	11–13 hours
5–12 years	9–11 hours
Adolescents	9–10 hours
Adults, including elderly	7–8 (+) hours
Pregnant women	8 (+) hours

MEASURING SLEEP

Sleep is measured in a variety of ways:

- *Electroencephalogram (EEG)*: measures the spontaneous electrical activity of the brain from the scalp produced by the firing of neurons within the brain. The equipment takes the form of electrodes which are attached to the scalp while the individual sleeps.

- *Electrooculogram (EOG)*: measures eye movements. An electrode placed near the eye records a change in voltage as the eye moves.

- *Electromyogram (EMG)*: measures electrical activity of the muscles. In humans, sleep researchers usually record from under the chin, as this area undergoes dramatic changes during sleep.

- *Actigraphy*: a non-invasive method of monitoring human rest/activity cycles. The sensors are generally wristwatch-like units worn on the non-dominant hand. The unit continually records the movements as the individual goes about daily activities including sleeping.

SLEEP STAGES

Sleep normally involves five stages: 1, 2, 3, 4 of non-rapid eye movement (NREM) sleep, and rapid eye movement (REM) sleep (see Figures 9.2, 9.3). Beginning with stage 1, the stages progress in order through to REM, at which time they start again with stage 1. A full sleep cycle will last roughly 90 to 110 minutes. The initial sleep cycles each night are characterised by relatively short periods of REM sleep and longer periods of deep sleep; however, as the night progresses, the periods of REM sleep get longer and the periods of deep sleep get shorter.

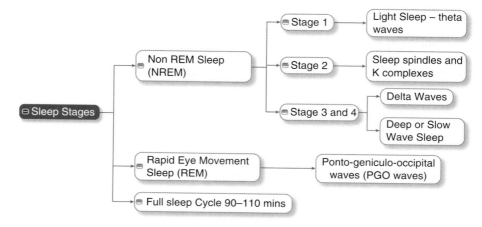

Figure 9.2   *Sleep stages*

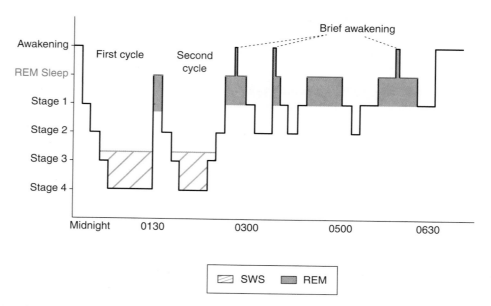

Figure 9.3   *Sleep cycles*

In the first phases of sleep, people are still fairly alert and awake. Small, fast **beta waves** are produced by the brain. Slower waves, called **alpha waves**, are produced as the brain starts to relax. At this point, when sleep has not yet arrived, some individuals experience strange sensations call hypnagogic hallucinations (Manni, 2005). When experiencing this phenomenon, people may feel as if they are falling or they may hear someone saying their name. A further common example of this is a myoclonic jerk. You have experienced this unusual behaviour if you have ever startled suddenly for no apparent reason.

Based on EEG criteria, stage 1 refers to the transition of the brain from alpha waves (see Figure 9.4) and is defined as a light sleep characterised by awakening easily and drifting in and out of sleep. During this stage, muscle activity slows and the eyes move slowly. **Theta waves** (theta activity) characterise this stage. During stage 2 sleep, there is no eye movement or theta activity. There are sleep spindles of 1 to 2 second bursts of 12–14 Hz activity, and **K complexes** consisting of a single large negative wave (upward spike) followed by a single large positive wave (downward spike). Very slow brain waves (**delta waves**) that have a frequency of 1 to 4 Hz are a characteristic feature of stage 3 sleep. In stage 4, delta waves predominate for a deeper level of sleep. Stages 3 and 4 are known as deep sleep or **slow-wave sleep** (SWS) and it is quite difficult to rouse people when they are in these stages of sleep. No eye movement or muscle activity occurs during deep sleep, and this is when bedwetting, sleep walking and night terrors take place.

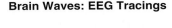

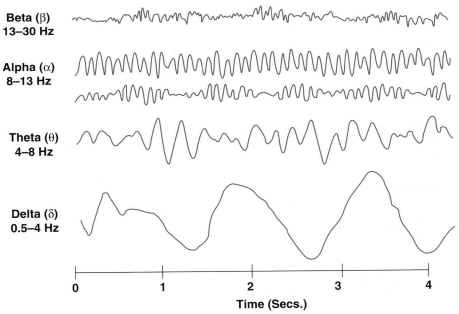

Figure 9.4   *EEG tracings during sleep*

REM SLEEP

Eugene Aserinsky and Nathaniel Kleitman first referred to REM sleep in 1953. REM sleep was found to exhibit traits very different from the model of sleep where there is recuperative deactivation of the central nervous system. The physiological aspects of REM sleep provide a pattern of brain activity that bears more similarity to wakefulness than to sleep. It is now accepted that REM (**paradoxical**) sleep and non-REM (NREM or 'orthodox') sleep are qualitatively different.

In the REM period, breathing accelerates, becoming irregular and shallow, the eyes twitch rapidly, and temporary paralysis affects the muscles of the limbs. During this time, the individual's brain waves increase to waking levels and the body may lose some of its ability to regulate temperature, blood pressure will rise, heart rate will increase, and, in males, erections will occur. This is when the majority of **dreams** take place, and if a person is woken during REM sleep they can usually recall their dreams. Typically, there are somewhere between three and five REM sleep periods each night. Unlike newborns who normally experience REM immediately, adults very seldom experience REM when first falling asleep.

PONTO-GENICULO-OCCIPITAL (PGO) WAVES

The appearance of ponto-geniculo-occipital (PGO) waves is the initial sign that REM sleep has begun. These are phasic electrical bursts of neural activity that begin in the pons, move on to the lateral geniculate nucleus in the hypothalamus and terminate in the occipital primary visual cortex (Laurent, Guerrero, & Jouvet, 1974). PGO waves are observed just before REM sleep and are therefore considered to be linked with dreaming and responsible for the rapid eye movement and vivid visual experience of dreams that are typical during REM sleep.

SEQUENCES OF NREM AND REM SLEEP

The normal chronological series of the two types of sleep in the adult human is for a period of about 70–90 minutes of NREM sleep to come prior to the first period of REM sleep, which may last between 5 and 15 minutes. The initial NREM sleep takes place in a set series of stages and is ordered 1–2–3–4–3–2. Then approximately equal total duration of NREM–REM cycles recur during the night, with the REM portion becoming somewhat longer and the NREM portion becoming correspondingly shorter as sleep progresses. REM sleep makes up nearly 25% of the entire sleep cycle and NREM sleep takes up the other 75%, which is generally spent in stage 2 sleep.

NEURAL MECHANISMS OF SLEEP

PASSIVE SLEEP THEORY

The first influential theory regarding the physiology of sleep was introduced by Bremer in the 1930s (Figure 9.5). His hypothesis was that sleep happens as a result of decreased sensory input to the forebrain. To investigate this hypothesis, he carried out several experiments in which he severed the brain stems of cats between the inferior colliculi and the superior colliculi to disconnect the cortex from the ascending sensory input. Cerveau isolé preparation (literally meaning isolated forebrain) is the term used to describe this surgical

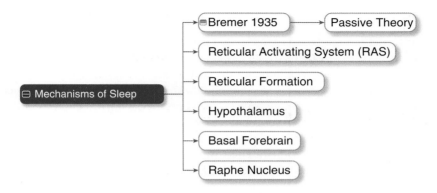

Figure 9.5 *Mechanisms of sleep*

procedure. Bremer discovered that the cortical EEGs of the cat forebrains that were examined showed an almost uninterrupted slow-wave sleep. The waveform could only be modified to a desynchronised EEG when strong visual or olfactory stimuli were available. Bremer also demonstrated that transection of the caudal medulla (an encéphale isolé), although resulting in paralysis requiring mechanical ventilation, produced an animal that remained alert, with normal sleep–wake cycles. Bremer's discovery formed the foundation for the passive theory of sleep (Bremer, 1935).

ACTIVE RETICULAR ACTIVATION SYSTEM THEORY

Bremer's passive theory gave way to the theory that sleep is actively regulated by an arousal mechanism that is referred to as the reticular activating system (RAS). Low levels of activity in the reticular formation result in sleep, while high levels result in wakefulness (Moruzzi & Magoun, 1949). This theory caused many to rethink the existing principles of sleep. One of these theories was that sleep is a condition of general neural stillness. This has since been contradicted by neural recording, which has shown that although many neurons are less active in the sleep cycle, in REM sleep many are more active than during times of wakefulness. Indeed, with the notable exception of the ventrolateral preoptic (VLPO) nucleus, overall electrical activity in most regions of brain is decreased during NREM sleep.

Around this time, it was also discovered that sleep promoting circuits exist in the brain, so stimulation of certain structures can induce sleep, while sleep can be disturbed by brain lesions. It appears that the caudal brain stem is such a structure, and sleeping cats awaken when the area is anaesthetised or cooled (Berlucchi, Maffei, Moruzzi, & Strata, 1964). The neural mechanisms associated with the sleep state seem to work independently to control different aspects of sleep, and the correlates of sleep are dissociable. Research suggests that a single neural mechanism is not responsible for controlling REM sleep, slow-wave sleep and wakefulness; rather, each sleep state occurs as a result of the interactions of several brain mechanisms, each of which can operate independently of each other.

Reticular activating system

The reticular formation is a group of nuclei that can be found in the brain stem. These nuclei receive input from the majority of sensory systems of the body as well as other parts of the nervous system such as the cerebellum and the cortex, and are often referred to collectively as the reticular activating system (RAS) (Siegel, 2004). The RAS neuronal circuits connecting the brain stem to the cortex are believed to be concerned with wakefulness, arousal and consciousness. A number of other neuronal pathways project from the reticular formation to the motor neurons found in the spinal cord. These neurons influence functions such as the control of respiration and cardiovascular function. Some of the network links are discussed below and the neurotransmitters involved in sleep are detailed in Box 9.1.

BOX 9.1   Neurotransmitters and neuromodulators of sleep

- *Serotonin*. Promotes wakefulness, inhibits REM sleep, processing sensory information, generation of waking-related motor activity; serotonergic cells in dorsal raphe nucleus of brain stem (reticular formation).

- *Noradrenaline*. Inhibits REM sleep; locus coeruleus (pons) noradrenergic neurons excite spinal motor neurons; in cataplexy locus coeruleus neurons cease discharging.

- *Acetylcholine*. Promotes REM sleep and EEG arousal; medial pontine reticular formation ACh release increases in REM sleep.

- *Adenosine*. Promotes slow-wave NREM sleep by inhibiting cholinergic neurons; basal forebrain structures important; possibly builds up when awake to sufficient quantities to promote sleep.

- *Dopamine*. Systems promote wakefulness, vigilance and performance enhanced by dopamine agonists; dopamine antagonists impair performance, more likely to fall asleep; complex interactions poorly understood.

- *Histamine*. Neurons from posterior hypothalamus promote wakefulness; antihistamines produce drowsiness.

- *Hypocretin/orexin*. A peptide produced by cells whose bodies are located in the lateral hypothalamus; involved with regulating the sleep on/off cells in the ventrolateral preoptic area (VLPA); cell destruction leads to narcolepsy.

Reticular formation

The pontomesencephalon is one area involved in the reticular formation that is concerned with arousal (Woolf, 1997). Obtaining input from a number of sensory systems, axons travel from here to the forebrain where they release acetylcholine and glutamate which stimulates the hypothalamus, thalamus and basal forebrain, causing the pontomesencephalon to maintain arousal.

HYPOTHALAMUS

The hypothalamus has a number of different pathways that have an effect on levels of arousal. Some of these pathways release histamines causing comprehensive excitatory activity in the brain and making the individual feel more awake (Haas & Panula, 2003). A peptide neurotransmitter named orexin is released by other pathways. This causes stimulation of cells that release acetylcholine which results in increased alertness (Kiyashchenko et al., 2002). In addition, pathways from the lateral hypothalamus extend to regular cells located in the basal forebrain.

BASAL FOREBRAIN

The basal forebrain is a collection of structures located just anterior and dorsal to the hypothalamus. Cells from here extend to the cerebral cortex and thalamus. Acetylcholine (ACh) is secreted by many of these cells and appears to have a great influence on arousal. When these cells are damaged as in Alzheimer's disease, sleep is not induced, but alertness and attention are diminished (Cummings & Back, 1998). Additionally, ACh antagonists, which interfere with the function of ACh, reduce EEG indicators of arousal.

GABA, the primary inhibitory neurotransmitter of the brain, is released by other axons in the basal forebrain. GABA is vital and sleep would not be possible without it (Gottesmann, 2004). It appears that GABA prevents synaptic activity, which lessens brain excitation and therefore promotes sleep.

RAPHE NUCLEUS

The raphe nucleus is a subgroup of the reticular nuclei of the brain stem and is where serotonin is synthesised. It is present in narrow longitudinal sheets along the midline of the caudal reticular formation. The raphe nucleus projects to the thalamus, hypothalamus, basal ganglia, hippocampus and neocortex, and when it is stimulated, locomotion and cortical arousal occur. When you are awake, serotoninergic neurons are the most active. Their activity decreases quickly during slow-wave sleep, and comes to almost a complete stop during REM sleep (Monti, 2010).

THEORIES REGARDING REASONS FOR SLEEP

Since the environment is dangerous and there is a great deal of competition for limited resources, only those that are the fittest live long enough to reproduce. However, all the most advanced creatures, which are usually alert and vigilant, abandon their defences to rest and sleep. For about two-thirds of our lives we are awake, but the remainder of the time we are virtually in a paralysed state as we sleep. So given the grave risk that animals are subjected to by sleeping, sleep must provide some evolutionary benefit to natural selection or we would have evolved to a point where we do not need to sleep. If we do not get enough sleep we become sleep deprived, as detailed in Box 9.2.

Although modern advances now allow us to study sleep and related phenomena, not all researchers share the same opinion as to why we sleep. There are many theories about the purpose of sleep; three are discussed below.

BOX 9.2   How long can you stay awake?

In 1965 during a science fair Randy Gardner, a 17-year-old high school student, set a record of 264 hours (about 11 days) for remaining awake. Reportedly on the 12th day he slept for 14 hours before returning to a normal 8 hour sleep pattern. He also experienced no serious medical, neurological, physiological or psychiatric problems from his ordeal. However, during his time awake he showed deficits in perception, cognition and motivation. Prolonged sleep deprivation in individuals can effect states of consciousness in which they appear awake but are experiencing 'micro-sleeps'. These are characterised by involuntary instances of attention loss that can be associated with behaviour such as prolonged eye closure or staring blankly into space. Randy Gardner was 'awake' but basically cognitively dysfunctional at the end of his ordeal.

Rats deprived of sleep for around two weeks or more may die. Rechtschaffen and Bergmann (1995) did a series of experiments on sleep deprivation and used a rotating disc over a pool of water to keep animals awake. The cause of death in these animals is associated with whole body hypermetabolism (the physiological state of increased rate of metabolic activity). In a rare human autosomal dominate disorder called fatal familial insomnia (FFI) in which individuals cannot sleep, death usually occurs after about six to 30 months. However, this so-called FFI death results from multiple organ failure rather than sleep deprivation.

Reference

Rechtschaffen, A., & Bergmann, B.M. (1995). Sleep deprivation in the rat by the disk-over-water method. *Behavioural Brain Research*, 69, 55–63.

EVOLUTIONARY THEORY OF SLEEP

According to the evolutionary theory, sleep is advantageous as the animal is immobilised for an extended period, and this increases its safety as it is less noticeable to potential predators. The need for immobilisation in humans can be considered to be a remnant of our evolutionary past, since this appears to be no longer a relevant explanation for sleep.

However, evolutionary theory can explain the long sleep cycles of babies as protecting their caregiver from exhaustion, and thus increasing their own survival chances (Meddis, 1975).

Hibernation theory (Webb, 1974), a variation of evolutionary theory, suggests the main reason that elaborate sleep mechanisms have evolved is to keep at rest when it is dark. In general, animals that conserve energy are more likely to survive than animals that do not. Therefore hibernation has several functions: it saves energy, keeps animals away from danger, and slows down the ageing process. Hamsters that hibernate for longer periods have longer life expectancies (Lyman, O'Brien, Greene, & Papafrangos, 1981).

Evolutionary theory would have to be capable of explaining why different modern species have very different lifestyles and sleep at various times of the day and night. Regardless of lifestyle, mammals as a whole seem to be able to find enough time for the bare minimum of sleep. The sleeping habits of animals are governed by a variety of factors including the number of hours per day they forage for food and the level of danger they feel from predators. Dolphins, along with several other species, have developed the ability to let half their brain sleep at any given time. Here, the two hemispheres alternate responsibility for sleeping and controlling other activities, such as swimming, breathing, etc. (Rattenborg, Amlaner, & Lima, 2000). These adaptations lead us to believe that sleep has become essential in our physiology, regardless of any evolutionary influences. It seems to be necessary for the proper function of the brain, thus supporting the next theory, the restorative theory.

REPAIR AND RESTORATION THEORY OF SLEEP

This theory suggests that sleep is critical for revitalising and restoring the physiological processes that enable the body and mind to function in a correct and healthy manner (Oswald, 1966). According to this theory, NREM sleep governs restoration of biological functions, while REM sleep is responsible for restoring mental abilities. Studies have shown that longer durations of REM sleep occur after periods of sleep deprivation and demanding physical activity (Dement, 1960). While sleeping, the body undergoes a heightened rate of cell division and the production of proteins, which is another indicator that repair and restoration take place while we are asleep in addition to reinforcing the memories and learning of wakefulness (Roffwarg, Muzio, & Dement, 1966).

The body requires a certain amount of REM. When deprived of REM, an individual will spend 50% more time than usual the following night in the REM stage of sleep. This phenomenon is referred to as REM rebound. Cats and other animals will also experience more REM sleep after sleep deprivation (Endo, Schwierin, Borbely, & Tobler, 1997). REM sleep in humans correlates with age (Kahn, 1970), with babies spending up to 18 hours a day asleep. Obviously environmental and maturational factors both play a role here, but it could also be that the developing brain requires protein synthesis for the production and growth of cells, and REM sleep helps this to occur (Empson & Clarke, 1970). Activation–synthesis theory is another interpretation of the purpose of REM sleep: it refutes the notion that dreams are meaningful, and suggests that dreams result from random neuron firing and reduced sensory input during REM sleep. During REM sleep, the pons in the brain stem produces electrical activity that travels to main brain areas, such as those associated with motor and sensory activities. The activation–synthesis theory suggests that one result of this activity is to create and transmit images and feeling to the frontal brain areas. This is termed the 'activation' period in the theory. The theory then suggests that the forebrain tries to make sense of these disconnected inputs and creates a narrative in the form of a dream. This is the 'synthesis' stage of the theory (Hobson & McCarley, 1977).

INFORMATION CONSOLIDATION THEORY OF SLEEP

This theory is based on cognitive research. It suggests that sleep enables individuals to process information acquired during the day and permits the brain to ready itself for the events of the next day (Stickgold, Whidbee, Schirmer, Patel, & Hobson, 2000). When an individual learns something and is subsequently tested, their performance is usually better on the second day after learning the task than it was on the first day after, with one caveat: this only holds true if they get enough sleep the night before the test. According to some studies, sleep allows us to re-evaluate facts and events experienced during the previous day (Wagner, Gais, Haider, Verleger, & Born, 2004). This theory is based on several sleep deprivation studies that indicated that a lack of sleep seriously impacts a person's ability to recall and remember information (Stickgold, 2004).

It is thought that REM sleep plays a role in **consolidation** of memory. According to one hypothesis, REM sleep is instrumental in the storage of memory as well as in the elimination of unnecessary connections between neurons that have been formed while a person is awake (Crick & Mitchison, 1983). REM sleep brings about increased neuronal activity following a deep encoding (or discrete) waking incident, thus increasing neural plasticity which subsequently plays a necessary part in consolidating memories. In addition, it is thought that induction of hippocampal long-term potentiation (LTP) during waking causes increased extrahippocampal Zif268 (early growth response protein 1) expression while REM sleep takes place (Ribeiro, Mello, Velho, Gardner, Jarvis, & Pavlides, 2002).

According to the consolidation hypothesis, memory formation is impaired when a person is deprived of REM sleep. However, it has been shown that when individuals are deprived of REM sleep using drugs, namely monoamine oxidase (MAO) inhibitors, they do not report any memory impairment (Vertes & Eastman, 2000). So, how or indeed whether REM sleep affects memory consolidation remains inconclusive.

SLEEP DISORDERS

The primary diagnostic resource for clinicians and researchers in the field of sleep is the International Classification of Sleep Disorders (ICSD) and sleep medicine (ASDA, 2005). This gives the following classifications (see also Figure 9.6):

- ✴ insomnia
- ✴ hypersomnias of central origin

- sleep-related breathing disorders

- circadian rhythm sleep disorders

- parasomnias: disorders of arousal (NREM); REM sleep parasomnias; other parasomnias

- sleep-related movement disorders

- isolated symptoms/normal variants/unresolved

- other.

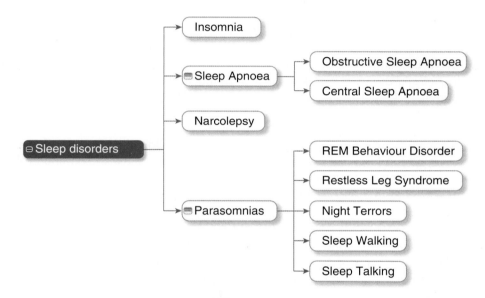

Figure 9.6 *Sleep disorders*

INSOMNIA

When insomnia causes sleep deprivation, it is known as dyssomnia or a sleep disorder, and can be characterised as either transient, chronic or acute. Insomnia can be defined as difficulties initiating and/or maintaining sleep which lead to associated impairments of daytime functioning or marked distress for more than one month (Morin, Blais, & Savard, 2002). Laboratory animals have died after long-term sleep deprivation, with REM sleep deprivation in rats causing death in about five weeks (Kushida, Bergmann, & Rechtschaffen, 1989). A constant state of sleep deprivation can result in fatigue, feeling tired during the day, clumsiness and weight gain. Sleep deprivation can also cause sensory hallucinations as well as an inability to concentrate. Lack of sleep causes accidents, and it has been speculated that driving while drowsy is as dangerous as driving drunk (Falleti, Maruff, Collie, Darby, & McStephen, 2003). Poor sleep hygiene, noise, temperature, stress, pain, diet and medications are among the various causes of insomnia. Sleep problems can also be caused by various psychiatric and neurological disorders.

SLEEP-RELATED BREATHING DISORDERS: SLEEP APNOEA

Sleep apnoea is a sleep disorder in which a person is unable to breathe while sleeping. As people age, it is not uncommon for them to experience occasional periods during which they do not breathe for as much as 9 seconds while they are sleeping, usually occurring during REM sleep (Culebras, 1996). However, those who suffer from sleep apnoea are troubled with periods of disrupted breathing that take place more often and last for longer periods. A sleep apnoea event is said to have occurred when at least a 10 second interval occurs between breaths, along with at least a 3 second shift in EEG frequency and/or a blood oxygen desaturation of 3–4% or more. The brains of people with sleep apnoea exhibit loss of neurons in several areas, which results in these people experiencing issues with cognition, including attention, learning and reasoning (Macey et al., 2002). Rats that experience low levels of oxygen while asleep exhibit neuronal loss in the hippocampus and the cerebral cortex (Gozal, Daniel, & Dohanich, 2001).

Two kinds of sleep apnoea exist, as described in the following. However, no matter which kind a person has, they usually do not realise that they have a breathing problem and their sleep partners are usually the ones who notice the issue. It is possible for a person to experience symptoms for months or years without being identified or treated.

Obstructive sleep apnoea (OSA)

The most common form is obstructive sleep apnoea (OSA), which is caused by a breathing obstruction that impedes the flow of air in the mouth and nose. Typically in obstructive sleep apnoea, the throat closes up, blocking the passageway and stopping the air from flowing to the lungs (Tabba & Johnson, 2006).

There are a number of risk factors for OSA, including: being obese or overweight, having abnormally large tonsils or adenoids, nasal congestion or blockage (due to cold, sinusitis, allergies, smoking, etc.), and having throat muscles and a tongue that become overly relaxed during sleep, possibly because of the use of alcohol or sedatives, or because of advanced age. Hereditary medical conditions or anatomic abnormalities do not seem to be implicated in obstructive sleep apnoea. OSA can be treated by surgically removing the obstruction. Alternatively, in some cases a continuous positive airway pressure mask (CPAP) can be used, which is placed over the nose and mouth while the person sleeps and delivers air at a fixed pressure to keep the breathing passages open.

Central sleep apnoea (CSA)

Central sleep apnoea (CSA) is rarer than OSA, and is mostly found in individuals suffering from specific illnesses. CSA can result from injury to or disease of the brain stem, like stroke, brain tumour, viral brain infection or chronic respiratory disease. Even though

CSA and OSA apnoea are brought on by different things, they present in the same way and both cause sleep and oxygen deprivation. Some kinds of CSA can be treated by utilising CPAP (Eckert, Jordan, Merchia, & Malhotra, 2007).

HYPERSOMNIA: NARCOLEPSY

Narcolepsy is a chronic sleep disorder in which a person experiences excessive daytime sleepiness (EDS). This is characterised by severe fatigue and may cause the person to fall asleep at inappropriate times (Aldrich, 1992). In people with this condition, you might also see cataplexy, paralysis during sleep and hypnagogic hallucinations. A person with narcolepsy will probably have interrupted sleep at night as well as odd sleep patterns in the daytime, which sometimes can be mistaken for insomnia. Particular genes have been linked to the condition and a portion of chromosome 6, referred to as the HLA complex, can be modified in narcoleptics. However, other genes besides the HLA complex may govern the development of narcolepsy, because there are many people who have HLA complex variations who do not develop narcolepsy.

Some narcolepsy symptoms can be associated with the neurotransmitter orexin. It appears that individuals afflicted with narcolepsy do not have hypothalamic cells which are responsible for producing and releasing hypocretins (orexins). As previously mentioned, orexin maintains wakefulness, so if this neurotransmitter is lacking, sleepiness will result. It is not known why some people do not have these cells, but some suggest the autoimmune system may play a role (Kroeger & de Lecea, 2009).

CIRCADIAN RHYTHM SLEEP DISORDERS

Circadian rhythm sleep disorders affect mostly the timing of sleep behaviour. Individuals with the condition are not capable of sleeping or are unable to sleep. These individuals wake at the times required for normal work, school and social requirements but have problems with the associated tasks. Some of these people are able to get the required amount of sleep if allowed to sleep and wake at the times dictated by their body clocks. Sleep quality for these people is generally of normal quality.

PARASOMNIAS

Parasomnia is a type of sleep disorder that includes abnormal and unnatural movements, behaviours, emotions, perceptions and dreams that take place while a person is in the process of falling asleep or waking up from sleep, or during the sleep state (Matwiyoff & Lee-Chiong, 2010).

Arousal disorders: night terrors, sleep walking and sleep talking

Night terrors usually occur during non-rapid eye movement sleep and cause severe terror as well as a temporary inability to fully regain consciousness. They differ from nightmares,

which are merely unpleasant dreams. Children generally experience night terrors more frequently than adults. In the middle of a night terror, the person wakes fast, usually along with moaning or shouting. Often these sleepers cannot be fully awakened and will just settle back to sleep. People do not normally remember a night terror.

Sleep walking usually occurs in families and in children between two and five years of age. It happens mostly during stage 3 or stage 4 non-REM sleep and generally in the early part of the night. For the most part, sleep walking is harmless. Waking a person while they are sleep walking is not dangerous, although they may be a bit confused when they are awakened.

Sleep talking is a condition that occurs quite frequently in the normal population, but unless someone else is listening, generally the individual is unaware of it. Sleep talking takes place in REM and non-REM sleep periods (Arkin, Toth, Baker, & Hastey, 1970).

REM behaviour disorder

People who present with rapid eye movement behaviour disorder (RBD) physically act out what is occurring in their dreams during REM sleep. This could manifest as kicking and punching or simply moving about while asleep. Yelling and groaning are also characteristics of RBD. RBD is related to other sleep disorders that include motor activity, like sleep walking and periodic limb disorder. Individuals with this condition can end up getting hurt, injuring others or causing damage to property (Olson, Boeve, & Silber, 2000).

Restless leg syndrome

Restless leg syndrome (RLS) is a neurological disorder in which uncomfortable feelings occur in the legs, causing an uncontrollable urge to move them in an attempt to alleviate these feelings. The sensations that occur in RLS are frequently referred to as paraesthesias (abnormal sensations) or dysaesthesias (unpleasant abnormal sensations). These feelings can be merely uncomfortable, or they can be annoying or painful to the point that the person will sometimes wake up. The majority of people who have RLS also experience a more common condition referred to as periodic limb movement disorder (PLMD). A person with PLMD experiences involuntary leg twitching or jerking movements while sleeping. These usually occur every 10 to 60 seconds and cause severe sleep disruption.

Usually the treatment for RLS involves dealing with the associated medical condition, like diabetes or peripheral neuropathy. Treatment for those who suffer from idiopathic RLS focuses on alleviating symptoms; treatments include improved sleep hygiene routines and elimination of alcohol and caffeine from the diet.

Other parasomnias

These include:

- *Exploding head syndrome*: presents as individuals experiencing a very loud noise originating from within their head, usually described as the sound of an explosion.

⊛ *Sleep enuresis*: more commonly known as bedwetting, this refers to the lack of ability to maintain urinary control during sleep. Sometimes called nocturnal enuresis.

⊛ *Sleep groaning (catathrenia)*: a rapid eye movement sleep parasomnia. Here the sound is produced during exhalation, as distinct from sleep apnoea and snoring which involve inhalation.

SUMMARY

This chapter started with an explanation of biological rhythms, which are periodic biological fluctuations in an animal that correspond to, and are in response to, environmental changes that occur (Figure 9.7). The term 'biological clock' refers to the internal bodily mechanism that maintains these fluctuations even when environmental cues are not present. A rhythm with a 24 hour cycle is referred to as a circadian cycle. Here biological and behavioural functioning vary over a 24 hour period. A disturbed circadian cycle in humans has been linked to a number of mental and physical issues. The hypothalamus was then highlighted and it was explained that endogenous circadian rhythms are controlled by a small area of the hypothalamus referred to as the suprachiasmatic nucleus (SCN). The chapter then went on to examine how much sleep people require, emphasising that there has been a consistent link between age and the changing amount, quality and pattern of electrophysiologically defined sleep. In addition, electroencephalography (EEG) has demonstrated that there are several different sleep stages, and that the proportion of sleep time spent in the various sleep stages differs depending upon the age of the individual. Sleep stages were then explained and it was detailed that sleep normally involves five stages: 1, 2, 3, 4 of NREM sleep and REM sleep. Beginning with stage 1, the stages progress in order through to REM, at which time they start again with stage 1, with a full sleep cycle lasting roughly 90 to 110 minutes. The appearance of PGO waves is the initial sign that REM sleep has begun. These are phasic electrical bursts of neural activity that begin in the pons, move on to the lateral geniculate nucleus in the hypothalamus and terminate in the occipital primary visual cortex.

The section on the neural mechanisms of sleep discussed Bremer's passive theory of sleep as well as the location of a collection of nuclei called the reticular formation. These nuclei receive input from the majority of the body's sensory systems and are often referred to collectively as the reticular activating system (RAS). The chapter went on to discuss the evolutionary theory of sleep, which suggests that sleep is advantageous, as the animal is immobilised for extended periods. Hibernation theory, a variation of evolutionary theory, was also discussed. The repair and restoration theory of sleep suggests that sleep is critical for revitalising and restoring the physiological processes that permit the body and mind to function in a correct and healthy manner, while the information consolidation theory of sleep suggests that people sleep so that they can process information that they have gained during the day.

Sleep disorders were discussed, including the conditions of insomnia, sleep apnoea, narcolepsy and parasomnias. Parasomnias are a type of sleep disorder that includes abnormal

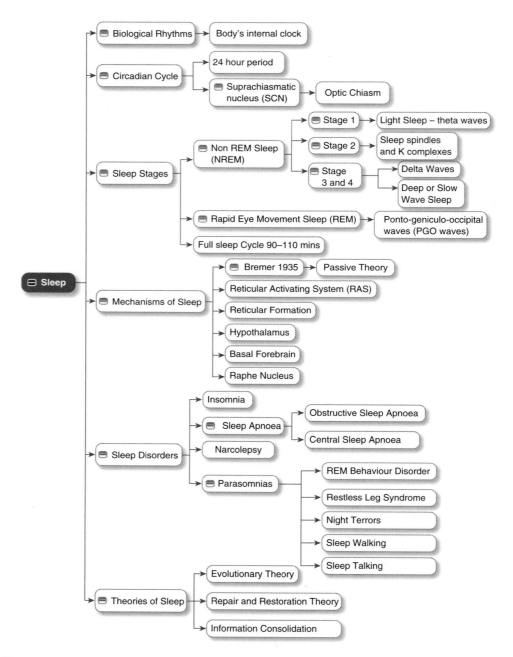

Figure 9.7 *Sleep overview*

and unnatural movements, behaviours, emotions, perceptions and dreams that take place while a person is in the process of falling asleep or waking up from sleep, or during the sleep state. Parasomnias detailed included REM behaviour disorder in which people physically act out what is occurring in their dreams during rapid eye movement (REM) stage sleep, and the more common parasomnias of night terrors, sleep walking and sleep talking.

 FURTHER READING

Crick, F., & Mitchison, G. (1983). The function of dream sleep. *Nature, 304*(5922), 111–114.

Meddis, R. (1975). On the function of sleep. *Animal Behavior, 23*(3), 676–691.

Moore, R.Y. (2007). Suprachiasmatic nucleus in sleep–wake regulation. *Sleep Medicine Reviews, 8*(Suppl. 3), 27–33.

 KEY QUESTIONS

1 What are the stages of sleep, and what are the characteristics of each stage?

2 Describe some of the disorders of sleep.

3 Outline the theories of why we sleep.

10 BIOPSYCHOLOGY OF EMOTIONS, STRESS AND HEALTH

Emotion is entirely subjective and associated with several different aspects of a person. Mood, temperament and personality all play a part in how we interpret and express emotion. We define emotion in several different ways; here we are going to look at the theoretical standpoint of emotion and the outcomes from experiencing that emotion. In this chapter, functional accounts of the emotional experience will be discussed and the neural mechanism responsible for these behaviours will be examined. The chapter will conclude with a discussion of stress and health.

BIOPSYCHOLOGY OF EMOTIONS

DARWIN'S THEORY

The early theories regarding emotion (Figure 10.1) actually began with the publication in the late nineteenth century of Darwin's book *The expression of emotions in man and animals*. Darwin proposed that survival of the fittest had necessitated an evolution in emotions and this would be found in cultures around the world. Additionally he said that animals have feelings just like humans.

Darwin's theory aimed to explain behaviour and give a meaning to almost all involuntary gestures and movements which humans and animals employ to show their emotions. The primary idea was that the display of feelings had developed from behaviours that show how the animal will react next, and that the signals associated with the feelings gave survival benefits to the animal who was displaying them. Darwin concluded that this mechanism would evolve to enhance the communication behaviour of animals.

Researchers have examined Darwin's theory in relation to various kinds of animal behaviour. For example, threat expressions have evolved to the point where animals

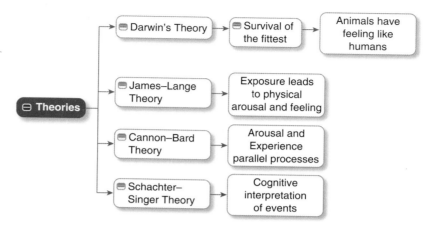

Figure 10.1   *Theories of emotion*

obtain survival advantage by effectively communicating their aggression to intimidate other animals without having to engage in a fight. Therefore, aggression displays can be quite elaborate, leading to a reduction in actual fighting between animals.

JAMES–LANGE THEORY

In 1884, researchers James and Lange devised the very first psychological theory of emotion. The theory posits that when an individual experiences an emotional stimulus, they become physically aroused, leading to certain emotions (see Figure 10.2). Therefore, exposure to a stimulus will set off a physical change in an individual's body, and, in turn, the individual's brain will interpret these changes and convert them into an emotion. For instance, imagine you are on a hike in the forest and encounter a bear. Your autonomic nervous system produces physical responses, like tensing of the muscles, elevated heart rate, sweating and dry mouth. The James–Lange theory suggests that people experience these physical responses and infer from them that they are scared ('I am shaking, so I must be scared').

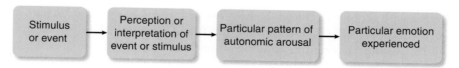

Figure 10.2   *James–Lange theory*

In 1987, Cannon developed his own theory of emotion. Cannon disregarded the James–Lange theory, most of which is rooted in the linkage between internal structures, the viscera, the CNS, and the perception of emotions. Cannon's main argument was that visceral modifications make themselves known in many different kinds of emotional situation, ranging from non-emotional to highly emotional. Today the James–Lange theory is disregarded as too simple a model to explain complex emotions, and is

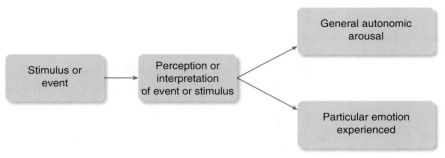

Figure 10.3 *Cannon–Bard theory*

generally referred to out of historical interest rather than as an explanation of human behaviour.

CANNON–BARD THEORY

As mentioned, Cannon suggested a different take on the James–Lange theory of emotion, which was later expanded upon by Bard to form the Cannon–Bard theory (Figure 10.3). This theory claims that stimuli and feelings have two separate excitatory reactions: the sensation of an emotion in the central nervous system, i.e. the brain of the individual, and the expression of the emotion in the somatic and autonomic nervous systems.

Cannon–Bard theory thus suggested that the experiencing and expressing of emotions were simply parallel processes which did not have a cause–effect relationship. In contrast, the James–Lange theory proposed that the experience of emotion is completely caused by the feedback provided by the autonomic and somatic nervous systems. Both these theoretical statements have fundamental problems in their explanation of emotional behaviour as seen in observations of natural behaviour. The autonomic nervous system, for example, does not appear to be required for experiencing emotion: individuals who have lost feedback of the somatic and autonomic systems as a result of injuries, like a broken neck, still have a complete range of emotions. Nevertheless, we have seen evidence that supports the idea that somatic and autonomic reactions to emotional stimuli have an impact on a person's emotional experiences.

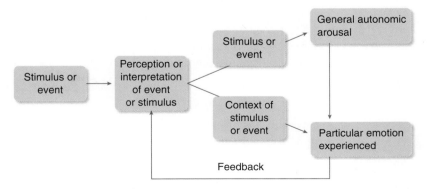

Figure 10.4 *Schachter–Singer theory*

SCHACHTER–SINGER THEORY

This model assumes a two-factor mechanism, suggesting that emotion is the cognitive interpretation of a physiological response. Schachter and Singer argued that previous theories based in physiology did not account for the wide variety of emotions, moods and feelings, and that these were not matched by the same variety and number of visceral patterns.

This inconsistency in previous theories led them to believe that cognitive factors might be involved in the experience of emotion. Their model of emotional experience was founded on the perception of cognitive labels as a reaction to physical excitement. People sense the specific emotional stimuli that trigger an autonomic reaction, but along with this pattern of bodily excitation a certain cognitive label is created, allowing the person to put a name to the bodily feeling (Figure 10.4). See Box 10.1 for details of the original experiment.

The theory takes a look at the function of feedback mechanisms, too, as an individual's past experience creates a framework within which they can interpret and name their emotions. For a lot of people, this is the most favourable explanation of emotion. Most people think of this as the common-sense theory to explain the physiological alterations that result from their emotion.

BOX 10.1   Role of cognitive and social situations on emotion

Background

Studies on emotions had shown that the same psychological reactions were present for most emotions displayed. In this study it was suggested that the emotional state may be considered a function of the status of physiological arousal and these emotions as interpreted by past experience, and may provide a framework within which one labels and understands one's feelings. Specifically, do people induce a physiological change to their body according to the emotional state they cognitively assign? In other words, do people react emotionally only when they experience physiological changes?

Procedure

The experimental procedure (Schachter & Singer, 1962) involved telling participants that the experimenters were testing the consequence of a vitamin supplement on vision. Some participants received an injection of noradrenaline which stimulated the sympathetic nervous system; other participants were given a placebo.

Information was given to the participant according to the three conditions:

1   *Adrenaline informed.* These participants were told that the drug would have some side effects like increased heart rate, face warm and flushed, etc.

2   *Adrenaline ignorant.* This group was given no information.

3   *Adrenaline misinformed.* These individuals were told that they would feel numbness, an itching sensation, and a mild headache.

After the injections were given, the emotional state of the participants was manipulated by being introduced to a room with a confederate who behaved in alternative ways:

1 They behaved euphorically, making paper aeroplanes and shooting bits of paper into the bin; or

2 They behaved angrily over filling out the questionnaire.

Observations were then carried out of participants under these two conditions.

Results

Physiologically, the adrenaline had the effect of raising heart rate as rated by the participants on adrenaline versus the placebo. In addition, compared to other groups, the misinformed people did not experience any sympathetic symptoms of headaches or itchiness.

In the euphoria condition, the participants were more vulnerable to the mood of the confederate and consequently became more euphoric. Participant rankings for feelings of low euphoria to high euphoria in each condition were found to fall into the following order: adrenaline informed, placebo, adrenaline ignorant, adrenaline misinformed. These results were also confirmed by the observers who rated the participants' behaviour in the same way.

The participants' reported data in the anger condition was difficult to interpret because they did not want to express anger about taking part in the experiment. However, it was observed that people who were ignorant of the effects of the drug did become much angrier than those informed and the placebo group.

Interpreting the results

The results indicate that individuals seem to assign an emotion to a physiological change based on the available information about available emotions in the social situation.

Reference

Schachter, S., & Singer, J. (1962). Cognitive, social, and physiological determinants of emotional state. *Psychological Review, 69*, 379–399.

SHAM RAGE

Pretend or sham rage is a quasi-emotional state marked by manifestations of fear and anger in the presence of barely significant provocation, which can be produced in animals by removing the cerebral cortex (decortication). Bard (1929) first recognised this occurrence when he observed that cats that no longer had a cortex still had an aggressive reaction to stimuli. He discovered you could remove the cortex down to the hypothalamus and still trigger sham rage in the cats. Aggressive behaviour was not seen if the hypothalamus was removed, which led Bard to conclude that the hypothalamus must play a role in expressing aggressive responses.

ANATOMY OF EMOTIONS: THE LIMBIC SYSTEM

The limbic system is a group of brain structures that includes the hippocampus, amygdala, anterior thalamic nuclei and limbic cortex, all of which work together to fulfil a variety of functions, like experiencing and expressing emotion, engaging in certain behaviours, long-term memory and the sense of smell. Animals as far back on the evolutionary timeline as reptiles have limbic systems; for them, this area is very involved in smell and is pivotal to the tasks of defending territory and hunting for food. The amygdala and the hippocampus appear to be most connected to emotion. The amygdala is connected to the hippocampus along with the medial dorsal nucleus of the thalamus.

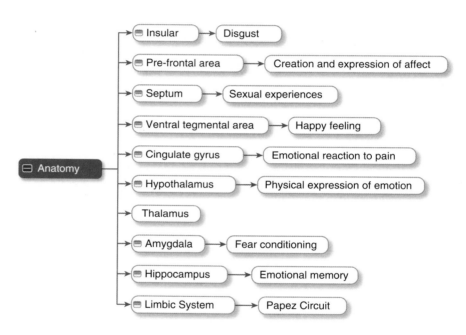

Figure 10.5 *Anatomy of emotions*

LIMBIC SYSTEM AND PAPEZ CIRCUIT

In 1937 James Papez introduced the Papez circuit of the brain, which is a major pathway of the limbic system and is mainly involved in the cortical regulation of emotion. The circuit constitutes a long pathway in the forebrain of mammals that leads from the hippocampus via the fornix to the mammillary body. From this point, it returns to the hippocampus via the anterior thalamic nuclei, cingulate gyrus and parahippocampal gyrus (Figure 10.6). Papez suggested that emotional expression was governed by the integrative action of the hypothalamus.

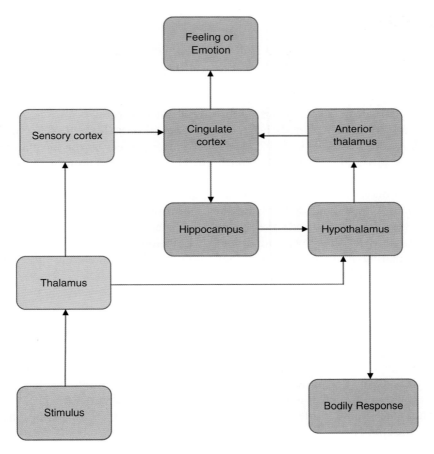

Figure 10.6 *Papez circuit*

HIPPOCAMPUS

The hippocampus plays a role in memory formation and the process of long-term potentiation (LTP). When the hippocampus suffers a major injury, the individual can have serious problems forming new memories (anterograde **amnesia**) and can occasionally have
difficulty retrieving memories formed before the injury (retrograde amnesia). The hippocampus and the amygdala are connected, and in times of great emotion they work together
in small but important ways. In particular, the amygdala is able to adapt the encoding as
well as the storage of memories that are dependent on the hippocampus. The hippocampal
complex influences the amygdala reactions whenever emotional activities occur, by bringing together occasional actions of emotionally meaningful occurrences. Even though these
are stand-alone memory systems, they work as a unit when emotion encounters memory
(Phelps, 2004).

AMYGDALA

The amygdala (plural amygdalae) is almond-shaped groups of nuclei found deep in the medial temporal lobe. The structure forms connections with the hippocampus, the septal nuclei, and the prefrontal area, as well as the medial dorsal nucleus of the thalamus. The amygdala plays a role in forming and storing memories connected with emotional occurrences, including the developmental process known as fear conditioning, during which animals learn to fear new stimuli (Dalzell, Connor, Penner, Saari, Leboutillier, & Weeks, 2010). Sensory stimuli project to the basolateral complexes of the amygdala, mainly the lateral nucleus, where they join or associate with memories of the stimuli.

The central nuclei of the amygdala are integral to the expression of fear responses, i.e. freezing (unable to move), tachycardia (heart beating rapidly), increased respiration (breathing hard) and stress-hormone release. Studies have shown that the disintegration of the amygdala structures lowers an animal's aggression, causing the animal to become non-discriminating about sex and oblivious to harm, while stimulating these structures brings about violent behaviour (Aggleton, 2000).

THALAMUS

The thalamus, which is located between the cerebral cortex and the midbrain, is a midline paired symmetrical structure within the brain. It is responsible for transmitting sensations and motor signals to the cerebral cortex. Lesion or stimulation of the medial dorsal and anterior nuclei of the thalamus has been associated with altered emotional behaviour. The thalamus is also a key player in the regulation of sleep and wakefulness.

Thalamic nuclei play a role in emotional processing not by eliciting emotions but by managing the connections to other aspects of the limbic system.

HYPOTHALAMUS

The hypothalamus consists of several small nuclei that perform various tasks. Lesions of the hypothalamic nuclei disrupt both sleep and wakefulness along with motivational behaviours, body temperature, sexual behaviours, fight reaction, appetite and thirst (Flament-Durand, 1980).

On top of the other tasks it performs, the hypothalamus is also involved in the physical expression of emotion. Specifically, its lateral area appears to be associated with pleasure and anger, while the median area is believed to be associated with aversion and displeasure, and has also been identified as a main influence on the production of loud, uncontrollable laughter (Dott, 1938). However, the hypothalamus has much greater correlation with the feeling of emotions than with the beginnings of the affective states. The lateral hypothalamus contains neurons that synthesise and respond to opiate-like substances, i.e. encephalins, and is implicated in the pleasure response and reinforcing effects of opiate use (Britt & Wise, 1981).

CINGULATE GYRUS

The cingulate gyrus is located in the middle of the cingulate sulcus and the corpus callosum in the middle of the brain. The cingulate gyrus obtains inputs from the anterior nucleus of the thalamus and the neocortex, as well from somatosensory areas located in the cortex. It extends to the entorhinal cortex by way of a collection of white matter fibres termed the cingulum. The anterior cingulate gyrus appears to be involved in unconscious priming (e.g. the pairing of sights and smells with pleasurable episodic memories) and is involved in the emotional reaction to pain as well as the control of aggressive behaviour (Vogt, 2005).

VENTRAL TEGMENTAL AREA

The ventral tegmental region is located in the mesencephalic part of the brain stem. In this area we find a small group of dopamine releasing nerve cells, whose axons terminate at the nucleus accumbens (mesolimbic dopaminergic pathway). This area is associated with the experience of happy feelings and intense romantic love (Xu, Aron, Brown, Cao, Feng, & Weng, 2011).

SEPTUM

The septal region is located anterior to the thalamus. This area has been connected to various types of pleasant feelings, mainly those to do with sexual experiences (Chozick, 1985).

PREFRONTAL AREA

The prefrontal area represents the non-motor anterior section of the frontal lobe. Even though it is not really part of the traditional limbic circuit, it is made up of bidirectional links to the thalamus, amygdala and other subcortical structures. It is critical to the creation and expression of affect, and disruption of dorsomedial prefrontal cortical-amygdala connectivity has recently been implicated in postpartum or postnatal depression (Moses-Kolko, Perlman, Wisner, James, Saul, & Phillips, 2010).

INSULA

This area has been found to be responsible for processing tastes and may be pivotal to the experience of feeling disgust (Phillips et al., 1997: see Box 10.2). The insular cortex has also been linked to other areas of the brain that regulate the body's autonomic functions, such as heart rate and breathing.

BOX 10.2   Neural substrate of disgust

Background

Recognition of facial expressions is a vital process for humans if we are to appreciate our social environment, and this perception must take into account the wide range of emotions and the different facial features used to express these emotions. Research conducted on the neural substrates of emotional processing has shown amygdala activation with fearful faces. This study (Phillips et al., 1997) examined brain activation while participants perceived facial images conveying disgust.

Methods

The study employed functional magnetic resonance imaging (fMRI) and scanned seven right-handed healthy volunteers (five female and two male; mean age 27 years) while they viewed emotional and neutral facial stimuli for a total of four 5 minute experiments. The facial stimuli consisted of faces of eight individuals transformed to create two levels of intensity of expressed fear and disgust. Brain activity in response to these stimuli was contrasted with that for neutral faces.

Results

Brain activity for the fear condition was in line with previous PET findings showing amygdala involvement, while both the mild and strong disgust expressions activated anterior insular cortex but not the amygdala. The limbic cortico-striatal-thalamic circuit was also activated by the strong disgust condition.

Interpreting the results

The study demonstrated that the perception of the emotion of disgust involved the anterior insula area of the brain. No activation was seen in the amygdala, which had previously been recorded to be active for the fear emotion. Interestingly the disgust expression is very much associated with foodstuffs, so it was not unexpected that the anterior insula is connected to the ventro-posterior-medial thalamic nucleus, which in primates is part of the gustatory cortex containing neurons that respond to pleasant and unpleasant tastes.

Reference

Phillips, M.L., Young, A.W., Senior, C., Brammer, M., Andrew, C., Calder, A.J., et al. (1997). A specific neural substrate for perceiving facial expressions of disgust. *Nature*, *389*, 495–498.

CEREBRAL HEMISPHERES AND EMOTION

Biological theories of emotion are concerned with different areas of the brain and their activity while certain emotions are being experienced. Several theorists have argued that two general motivational systems underlie emotional behaviour. A behavioural activation system (BAS) based on the left hemisphere (especially in the frontal and temporal regions) is believed to regulate appetitive motives, in which the goal is to move towards something desired. A behavioural avoidance (or inhibition) system (BIS) based on the right frontal and temporal regions is said to regulate aversive motives, in which the goal is to move away from something unpleasant. The BIS/BAS assessment scale was developed to assess individual differences in the sensitivity of these systems (Carver & White, 1994). An imbalance in BIS and BAS levels is reportedly related to a variety of forms of psychopathology (Scholten, van Honk, Aleman, & Kahn, 2006).

EMOTIONS AND FACIAL EXPRESSIONS

One form of non-verbal communication which conveys our emotion state is our facial expressions, which result from one or more motions or positions of the muscles of the face. This close link between emotion and expression was investigated by Paul Ekman and colleagues who collected cross-cultural data to formulate a basic menu of human emotions (Ekman, 1992; Ekman & Friesen, 1986) (Figure 10.7). This menu of basic emotions was constructed because of the observation that people from different cultures were able to reliably recognise emotions being depicted in photos of people from cultures that they had no experience of. Furthermore, they were able to connect facial expressions to the circumstances that evoked them. Using this information, Ekman and Friesman came to the conclusion that six primary expressions could be seen on a person's face: anger, disgust, fear, happiness, sadness and surprise. These primary emotions are the foundation of the Facial Action Coding System, a research tool devised to measure facial expressions by defining the muscular movement underlying brief alterations in facial expression. Each observable component of facial movement is called an action unit. All facial expressions can be decomposed into their constituent action units (AUs) and descriptions can be made of how AUs appear in combinations of expressions (Ekman & Friesen, 1977).

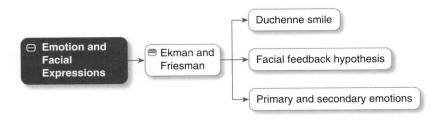

Figure 10.7 *Emotions and facial expressions*

PRIMARY AND SECONDARY FACIAL EMOTIONS

As previously discussed, Ekman and Friesman suggested that there are six primary emotions, and they went on to suggest that every other emotion we express is a predictable combination of these six primary emotions. For example, a person may feel ashamed as a result of becoming anxious or sad. Secondary emotions are often caused by the beliefs we have about experiencing certain emotions.

FACIAL FEEDBACK HYPOTHESIS

The idea of facial feedback is that any facial movement or expressions you make can have a direct effect on your emotional experience (Buck, 1980). For instance, someone who makes themselves wear a smile at a party will enjoy it more and feel more positive emotions. Charles Darwin was one of the earliest proponents of the notion that emotions not only cause physical reactions but are also affected by physical actions.

The facial feedback hypothesis was recently supported by the use of the botulinum toxin (commonly called botox) to paralyse facial muscles on a short-term basis. Botox discriminately prevents muscle feedback by inhibiting neuromuscular presynaptic acetylcholine receptors. Therefore, although motor commands to the facial muscles do not change, there is a reduction in output from the extrafusal muscle fibres, and maybe even from intrafusal muscle fibres as well. In a recent fMRI study, people undertook a facial expression imitation task while being scanned in an fMRI scanner prior to and following botox injections in the corrugator supercilii muscle, which is used to form a frown. Results showed that when compared to prior activation, injections of botox reduced the activation of brain areas associated with emotional processing and experience; this reduction was particularly evident in the amygdala and the brain stem when subjects imitated angry facial expressions (Hennenlotter, Dresel, Castrop, Ceballos-Baumann, Wohlschlager, & Haslinger, 2009).

DUCHENNE SMILE

It appears that there are two ways to differentiate genuine facial expressions from expressions that are fake (Ekman, Davidson, & Friesen, 1990). First, we look for 'microexpressions', which are brief, involuntary facial expressions shown on the faces of humans according to emotions experienced, which are hard to fake; and second, there are noticeable differences in the muscles used in forming false and true facial expressions. Duchenne, in 1862, noticed two specific types of smile, one fake and one genuine. A genuine Duchenne smile requires that you contract both the zygomatic major muscle (the muscle that lifts the corners of the mouth) and the orbicularis oculi muscle (the muscle that lifts the cheeks and allows crow's feet to form around the eyes). A fake or non-Duchenne smile uses only the major zygomatic muscle. Duchenne believed that one could voluntarily control the zygomaticus major while most individuals are unable to voluntarily contract the outer part of the orbicularis oculi muscle, which is therefore only contracted when the individual feels genuine pleasure.

FEAR, ATTACK AND ESCAPE BEHAVIOURS

Fear as an emotion occurs when threat is present, and it is the major method of protection afforded to animals whose lives are in danger. Conversely, aggressive or attack behaviours are performed for the purpose of scaring or injuring an enemy. The majority of dynamic behaviours in animals are categorised as either attack or defensive behaviours, which is why the function of the sympathetic nervous system is referred to as the 'fight-or-flight' system.

ATTACK BEHAVIOURS

As mentioned, attack or aggressive behaviours refer to any actions that aim to cause harm or inflict pain. We classify aggression into two general categories: hostile, affective or retaliatory aggression; and instrumental, predatory or goal-oriented aggression (McElliskem, 2004). The main kind of aggression viewed in the animal kingdom is that between a predator and the hunted. In evolutionary terms, a living thing that is protecting itself from a predator behaves aggressively to stay alive and to keep its offspring alive. Animals use aggression to assist them in obtaining and maintaining territory, as well as obtaining other needs essential for survival like food, water and mating possibilities.

HEREDITY AND AGGRESSION

The genetics of aggression have been studied in several different animal strains, and it has been shown that selective breeding for specific genes can result in more aggressive behaviour (Nelson, Trainor, Chiavegatto, & Demas, 2006). Furthermore, this aggression can be influenced by the age of the animal. For example, mice bred with a high degree of aggression have demonstrated more hostility during the middle period of their lives by attacking other mice (Brain & Benton, 1981).

The latest studies have focused on manipulation of candidate aggression genes in mice and other creatures to trigger effects which may potentially act out in humans. The majority of this research has centred on serotonin and dopamine receptors as well as neurotransmitter metabolising enzymes (Figure 10.8). Serotonin (5-HT) has been connected to impulsive aggressiveness; mice who do not have certain genes for 5-HT have demonstrated more aggressive behaviours than normal mice, and are quicker and exhibit more

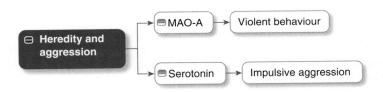

Figure 10.8   *Heredity and aggression*

violence when they strike (Nelson & Chiavegatto, 2001). Research focusing on mutations of the enzyme monoamine oxidase A (MAOA) have indicated that these mutations lead people to have a tendency towards certain behaviours, including violence and impulsiveness (Tremblay et al., 2005). A genetic variant that causes deficiency of MAOA has been associated with violent behaviour in men (Brunner, Nelen, Breakefield, Ropers, & van Oost, 1993). Additionally, low levels of MAOA have been found in people who express antisocial behaviour. This is also true of many who have been mistreated as children (Caspi et al., 2002).

NEUROTRANSMITTERS AND HORMONES

Many neurotransmitters and hormones are known to have an impact on aggression (Figure 10.9). The amount of testosterone present is particularly correlated with aggression in humans. Testosterone levels in the bloodstream of males convicted of violent crimes are higher than those of males with no criminal records or who were convicted of non-violent crimes (Bernhardt, 1997), with the highest levels being observed in males who were incarcerated for rape or murder (Bernhardt, 1997). While testosterone does not trigger violent behaviour, it can change the manner in which a person will react to various stimuli. Furthermore, we have learned that aggression in rats, which has been triggered by stimulating the hypothalamus, is enhanced by androgens (Bermond, Mos, Meelis, van der Poel, & Kruk, 1982), and research using animal and human participants demonstrates that competitive aggression rises near puberty, can be decreased by castration, and is further increased by administering testosterone injections (Booth & Mazur, 1998).

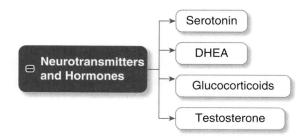

Figure 10.9   *Neurotransmitters and hormones*

TESTOSTERONE

Testosterone acts as a pro-hormone, a chemical compound that is a precursor to an actual hormone. This pro-hormone is converted into 5-alpha-dihydrotestosterone (5a-DHT) which acts on androgen receptors. If it is converted into oestradiol by the enzyme aromatase, it acts on oestrogen receptors. Some evidence suggests that there may be a key period during development when testosterone 'sensitises' certain neural regions (like the amygdala and hypothalamus), and it is this sensitisation that allows for the effects of testosterone that become prominent in adulthood.

Even though there is a persuasive relationship between testosterone and aggression, generally speaking hormones are not able to cause a particular behaviour. They are only able to facilitate or inhibit the likelihood that the behaviour will occur. Biology does not work on its own; there are other variables, such as environment and social factors, that need to be considered when looking at aggressive behaviours. For instance, we have seen evidence that social status has a great deal of influence over the existence and extent of aggression in both animals and people (Olweus, Mattsson, Schalling, & Low, 1988).

Just as we have observed in males, female aggression appears to be influenced by testosterone, with the degree of influence depending on the dosage. Studies have been carried out where female rats have had their ovaries removed and they have been injected every day with either testosterone, oestradiol or a placebo. The rats showed much more aggressive behaviours such as fighting when given testosterone, whereas oestradiol and the placebo had little influence on their conduct (Van de Poll, Taminiau, Endert, & Louwerse, 1988). Typically, the patterns of aggressive behaviour we observe in females are just like those we observe in males, i.e. ovariectomy with no hormone replacement reduces physical aggression while replacing testosterone triggers it.

GLUCOCORTICOIDS

Glucocorticoids are a group of fat-soluble hormones that connect to the glucocorticoid receptor and seem to play a role in hostile behaviour and are released during aggressive interaction between animals. Studies on glucocorticoids do not suggest that the hormone plays an active role, but corticosteroids may be required for an individual to fully express aggression. Some researchers have theorised that glucocorticoids influence the development of aggressiveness and the formation of hierarchies in animal societies (Summers et al., 2005).

DEHYDROEPIANDROSTERONE (DHEA)

DHEA is an androgen and can swiftly be metabolised into strong androgens and oestrogens. It has been found that birds have an elevated level of DHEA during the non-breeding season, which supports the idea that non-breeding birds combine adrenal and/or gonadal DHEA synthesis with neural DHEA metabolism. In this way, they are able to maintain territorial behaviour even when gonadal testosterone secretion is low (Soma, Wissman, Brenowitz, & Wingfield, 2002). In humans, levels of DHEAS, the sulphated ester of DHEA, increase as activity in the adrenal glands also increases during adrenarche, the period just prior to puberty (at approximately nine years of age). During this time there are fairly low levels of testosterone, so if aggressive behaviour is observed in children before puberty, it is generally caused by the plasma DHEAS level and not plasma testosterone.

SEROTONIN

A lack of serotonin has consistently demonstrated a relationship with impulsive aggressive behaviour over several different research paradigms. Serotonin is pivotal to the regulation of moods like impulsive aggressiveness during social decision making, which suggests that serotonin is also very important in social decision making by typically keeping aggressive social responses under control (Crockett, Clark, Tabibnia, Lieberman, & Robbins, 2008).

STRESS AND HEALTH THEORIES RELATING TO STRESS

Nearly every individual experiences stress at some time in their lives. One way to look at stress is to say it triggers a number of negative emotions and responses when people are in frightening or difficult circumstances. However, not every stress reaction is a negative one. We actually need some stress in order to stay alive. Indeed, we have defined stress as neurological and physical responses that allow us to cope (Franken, 1994). Research into stress generally has been focused on the body's reaction to stress and the cognitive mechanisms that affect the perception of stress. When talking about stress we must keep in mind that individuals going through similar things may not experience them the same way, so we must also take into account the social aspects of the stress reaction (Pearlin, 1982).

'Stress' is a difficult term to define, and there are several different factors that cause one to feel stress. Hans Selye observes that few individuals share the same definition of stress. Selye (1982) states that an important feature of stress is that there are so many varied circumstances that can trigger a stress reaction, like being overtired, feeling pain, being uncertain and even achieving success. For this reason, people have defined stress in various ways. One model that encompasses and explains stress thoroughly is the biopsychosocial model of stress (Bernard & Krupat, 1994). This model suggests that stress is made up of an external component and an internal component, which are connected in some way. The external component of stress can be thought of as environmental events that precede a person's recognition of feeling stressed but can elicit a stress response. People are usually aware of these external stressors when they feel frustrated or annoyed at something. The internal components of the model consist of the internal biological mechanisms such as the neurological and physiological reactions associated with the feeling of stress.

Hans Selye suggested that stress is 'non-specific' and so can result from a variety of stimuli or situations. He also stated that the stress response goes through three phases: alarm reaction phase, resistance phase and exhaustion phase. He called this generic set of responses a general adaptation syndrome (GAS) (Selye, 1951). In this framework, the alarm reaction is equivalent to the fight-or-flight response in which the sympathetic nervous system is aroused and other systems like the adrenal cortex and pituitary gland might also become involved. The resistance phase is a continuous state of alertness, which if the threat is not removed leads to the exhaustion phase. During this phase breakdown occurs as the body's energy reserves are finally exhausted. Selye's model highlights the fact that the functions of the body will return to normal if the stressor is removed and the body can begin growing and healing again. However, if the threat is drawn out and long lasting, the sympathetic nervous system arousal stays active, and it is in situations like these that health can be adversely affected. Exposure to prolonged or chronic stress depletes the immune system, making a person more susceptible than usual to illness (Cohen, Tyrrell, & Smith, 1993). The three phases of the model are expanded upon as follows.

GENERAL ADAPTATION MODEL

Alarm phase

Stress prepares an individual to deal with the threat, and puts the body in a state to deal with the stressor; this is known as the fight-or-flight response. During this time activation of the hypothalamic-pituitary-adrenal (HPA) axis, the sympathetic nervous system and the adrenal glands takes place. When the stressor ends, the parasympathetic nervous system takes over. To summarise, events are:

- Sympathetic nervous system arousal.

- Body prepares for 'fight or flight'.

- Reaction lasts minutes to hours.

- When stressor ends, parasympathetic nervous system takes over.

Resistance phase

In this second phase the source of stress may be known and the body shifts back to normal. Homoeostatic mechanisms of the body begin to restore functions and a period of recovery can take place. The events are generally:

- Release of adrenocorticotropic hormone (ACTH).

- Triggers the release of glucocorticoid hormone.

This results in:

- Conversion of non-sugars to sugars.

- Enhancement of glycogen storage.

- Increased effectiveness of adrenaline and noradrenaline.

- Systems not involved in stress resistance are inhibited.

⊛ Suppression of inflammatory system.

⊛ Reduction in ability to fight illness.

Exhaustion phase

If the body reaches this phase it has been around for some time. This is the phase of chronic stress and subsequently this phase is dangerous to health. Chronic stress can not only cause high blood pressure and stress-related illnesses but also damage the nerve cells of organs and tissue. The events of this phase are:

⊛ Depletion of physiological resources.

⊛ Failure of electrolyte balance.

⊛ Exhaustion of lipid reserves.

⊛ Inability to produce glucocorticoids.

⊛ Damage to vital organs.

⊛ When no resources remain, death ensues.

HOW THE BODY REACTS TO STRESS

There are two major physical reactions to stress, one that addresses immediate (or acute) stress, and one that addresses long-term (or chronic) stress (Figures 10.10 and 10.11).

Acute stress: the sympathomedullary pathway

Interpretation of the source of stress activates the sympathetic nervous system, which prepares the body for 'fight or flight' by triggering the adrenal medulla to release adrenaline and noradrenaline. Adrenaline and noradrenaline speed up your heart rate and blood pressure, and prepare fat and body sugars for use, all of which get the body ready to engage in sudden activity.

Chronic stress: the pituitary-adrenal system

We also refer to this system as the hypothalamic-pituitary-adrenal (HPA) axis, which reacts to ongoing or acute stress. Continuous exposure to stress causes the hypothalamus in the midbrain to synthesise hormones like corticotrophin releasing factor (CRF), which triggers the anterior pituitary to emit adrenocorticotropic hormone (ACTH), which in turn stimulates the adrenal cortex in the adrenal gland. The adrenal cortex releases around 20 different hormones. One well-studied hormone that has a range of biological effects is cortisol. The effects of cortisol can be beneficial, e.g. a rise in one's energy level and a decrease in one's intensity of discomfort, although other effects can be more negative, such as decreased immunity. Moderate cortisol levels can help to improve memory formation (Abercrombie, Kalin, Thurow, Rosenkranz, & Davidson, 2003), while temporary

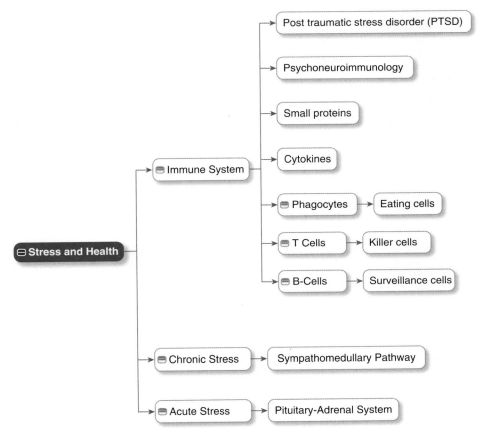

Figure 10.10 *Stress and health*

rises in cortisol levels augment the function of the immune system (Benschop et al., 1995). Continuous rises, however, can damage the immune system.

THE IMMUNE SYSTEM

Many conditions have been attributed to stress, ranging from headaches and asthma to head colds, ulcers and cancers (Glaser & Kiecolt-Glaser, 2005). One reason for this is that long-term stress can have a negative effect on the immune system as corticosteroids suppress its activity, thus making it more vulnerable to infection. Exposure to stress can also result in a person making unhealthy choices and can ultimately be an indirect cause of ill-health. People who are experiencing stress are more prone to smoking and consuming alcohol, exercise less, and get less sleep than people who are not under stress.

The immune system, which defends the body from illness, mainly comprises antibodies and leukocytes, or white blood cells. A number of different leukocytes have been identified, including B cells, T cells and natural killer cells.

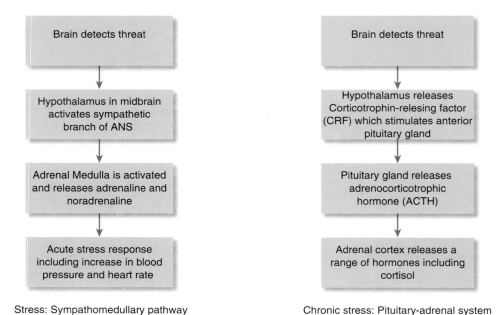

Figure 10.11   *The sympathomedullary pathway and the hypothalamic-pituitary-adrenal system (HPA axis)*

B cells

B cells grow to maturity mainly in the bone marrow and release Y-shaped proteins that link specifically to certain **antigens**. Antigens are substances that, when introduced into the body, trigger the production of an antibody by the immune system. The body produces various kinds of B cells on a regular basis, which travel through the blood and lymphatic system and essentially perform the role of immune monitoring. Each cell's surface contains its own unique receptor protein (known as the B cell receptor or BCR) that binds to a specific antigen. Plasma B cells are sometimes known as plasma cells. These cells are large B cells that have been exposed to an antigen and manufacture and secrete antibodies. These antibodies assist in the destruction of bacteria and/or foreign particles by binding with them, making it easier for phagocytes to ingest the bacteria and/or foreign particles. Memory B cells develop out of activated B cells that are specific to the antigen encountered during the primary immune response.

T cells

T cells or T lymphocytes are distinguishable from other lymphocyte types, such as B cells and natural killer cells, because they have a special receptor on their cell surface, referred to as a T cell receptor (TCR). Researchers have identified a number of different subsets of T cells, each of which plays a specific role. Natural killer T cells, or NKT cells, are a specific type of lymphocyte that play a big part in the body's rejection of tumour cells and cells that are infected by viruses. Natural killer cells differ from B and T cells in that they do not just attack one specific intruder, they attack all of them. Other types of T cells assist other T cells or B cells to grow in number.

Phagocytes

Phagocytes or white blood cells guard the body by 'eating' (phagocytosing) damaging non-natural particles like bacteria or dead or dying cells.

Cytokines

To counter infection, leukocyte and other cells produce small proteins known as cytokines. These fight infection and communicate with the brain to let you know that you are ill (Maier & Watkins, 1998). When these substances are released, common symptoms of sickness are experienced like feverishness, feeling sleepy and poor appetite.

PSYCHONEUROIMMUNOLOGY (PIN)

Psychoneuroimmunology is concerned with the interaction between biological processes and psychological state. A traditional view, still held by many, is that the immune system is autonomous, can regulate itself, and is quite efficient at defending the body. However, in recent years it has been shown that the immune system can be modulated by a person's psychological state and whether a person is stressed. Indeed, it seems that stressful events lead to cognitive and affective responses which can induce sympathetic nervous system and endocrine system changes, which in turn impair immune function (Houldin, Lev, Prystowsky, Redei, & Lowery, 1991).

POST-TRAUMATIC STRESS DISORDER (PTSD)

Post-traumatic stress disorder (PTSD) is a severe anxiety disorder in which a person develops symptoms subsequent to experiencing a horrifying or life-threatening event. Individuals with PTSD experience symptoms such as recurring, distressing flashbacks and bad dreams about the event. In addition they may avoid situations that remind them of the incident and they may have a heightened response to external stimuli (Murray, 1992). For a formal diagnosis of PTSD the symptoms have to be present for more than 30 days following the event, and the event must have caused significant damage in social, occupational or other important areas of functioning, like the ability to form relationships. A recent review of the literature indicated prevalence rates of PTSD in the general population ranging from 7% to 12%, together with high rates of secondary mood, anxiety and substance use disorders (Seedat & Stein, 2001). People with PTSD secrete low amounts of cortisol and high amounts of noradrenaline, suggesting that individuals with low cortisol levels may have a higher risk of developing PTSD (Meewisse, Reitsma, de Vries, Gersons, & Olff, 2007). One research study observed that military personnel with low salivary cortisol levels prior to entering the service had a higher risk for developing the symptoms of PTSD after being exposed to war trauma than soldiers who had pre-service levels that were more typical (Aardal-Eriksson, Eriksson, & Thorell, 2001). It appears that hyperarousal of the amygdala is involved in PTSD, in which there is a lack of top-down control from the medial prefrontal cortex and the hippocampus, most especially during extinction (Koenigs et al., 2008).

SUMMARY

This chapter explored the subject of emotion, stress and wellbeing by first explaining the basic theories of emotion (Figure 10.12). In the James–Lange theory, exposure to a stimulus sets off a physical change in an individual's body, and the brain will read these changes and convert them into an emotion. The Cannon and Bard theory of emotion suggested that stimuli to feelings have two separate parallel excitatory reactions, general autonomic arousal and the emotional experience; while the Schachter and Singer theory postulated a two-factor theory of emotion, suggesting that emotion is the cognitive interpretation of a physiological response.

The chapter then detailed sham rage and the decortification experiment carried out by Bard, and explained how the limbic system contains structures which work together to fulfil a variety of functions like experiencing and expressing emotion. Two of these structures, the amygdala and the hippocampus, appear to be most connected to emotion. The chapter then moved on to discuss the Papez circuit, which is one of the major pathways of the limbic system and is mainly involved in the cortical regulation of emotion.

The chapter then detailed the brain areas associated with emotions. The amygdala was highlighted as the area that is able to adjust the encoding as well as the storage of memories that are dependent on the hippocampus. The hippocampus also influences the amygdala reactions whenever emotional activities occur, by bringing together occasional actions of emotionally meaningful occurrences. Other areas that were detailed include the thalamus, which acts as a relay station and is responsible for transmitting sensations and motor signals to the cerebral cortex. The ventral tegmental area is involved in the experience of happy feeling, while the cingulate gyrus appears to be involved in unconscious priming and is involved in the emotional reaction to pain as well as the control of aggressive behaviour. The prefrontal cortex is critical to the creation and expression of affect. The behavioural inhibition system (BIS) and the behavioural activation system (BAS) are two theoretical neural motivational systems that regulate sensitivity to punishment (BIS) and reward (BAS). It has been suggested that an imbalance in these systems can lead to some forms of psychopathology.

Emotions and facial expressions were discussed and the work of Paul Ekman was highlighted. The facial feedback hypothesis was introduced, the idea being that any facial movement or expressions you make can have a direct effect on your emotional experience. The genuine or Duchenne smile was explained, which requires that you contract

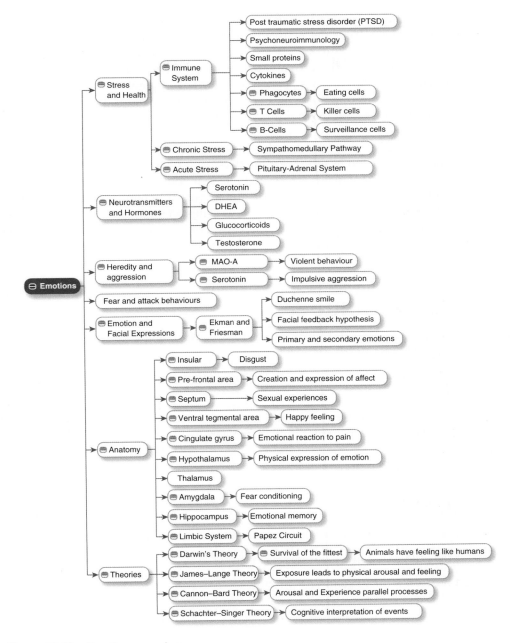

Figure 10.12 *Emotions overview*

both the zygomatic major muscle (the muscle that lifts the corners of the mouth) and the orbicularis oculi muscle (the muscle that lifts the cheeks and allows crow's feet to form around the eyes).

Fear and attack behaviours were then discussed as well as the link between heredity and aggression, showing that the majority of the research has centred around serotonin and dopamine receptors as well as neurotransmitter metabolising enzymes. The hormones were discussed, with particular emphasis on the role of testosterone. It was highlighted that although there is a persuasive relationship between testosterone and aggression, generally speaking hormones are not able to cause a particular behaviour. They are only able to facilitate or inhibit the likelihood of aggressive behaviour occurring.

The final section of this chapter detailed the various emotional implications of and the theories relating to stress and health. There are two major physical reactions to stress: one that addresses immediate (or acute) stress, and one that addresses long-term (or chronic) stress. The immune system was then described and post-traumatic stress disorder was detailed, explaining that an individual experiences symptoms subsequent to a horrifying or life-threatening event. Individuals with PTSD experience such symptoms as recurring distressing flashbacks and bad dreams about the event.

FURTHER READING

Glaser, R., & Kiecolt-Glaser, J. (2005). How stress damages immune system and health. *Discovery Medicine*, 5(26), 165–169.

Oatley, D., Keltner, D., & Jenkins, J. (2006) *Understanding emotions* (2nd edn). Chichester: Wiley-Blackwell.

Phelps, E.A. (2004). Human emotion and memory: interactions of the amygdala and hippocampal complex. *Current Opinion in Neurobiology*, 14(2), 198–202.

KEY QUESTIONS

1   With reference to the theories of emotion, what is the role of the environment?

2   What is the HPA axis and what is its role in stress?

3   Explain the role of the BIS and BAS systems.

11 MEMORY, LEARNING AND AMNESIA

In psychological terms, memory is the capability to encode, store and recall information. Researchers have paid a great deal of attention to the cognitive aspects of memory along with the different divisions of information processing. With new imaging techniques becoming available, cognitive neuroscience has allowed us to look at the **neuroanatomy** of memory and join the cognitive field of psychology with the neuroanatomical world. This chapter examines the different types of memory, the formation of memories, and the neuroanatomy of information processing.

PROCESSING OF INFORMATION

Different types of memory are defined by the nature of what is remembered and over what period the memory functions. The Atkinson–Shiffrin (1968) model was a theory of human memory that proposed human memory could be broken down into three different memory stores (Figure 11.1):

* sensory memory

* short-term memory

* long-term memory.

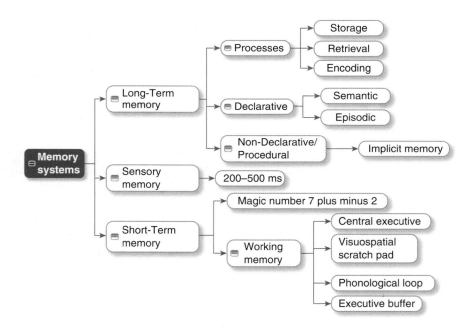

Figure 11.1 *Memory systems overview*

Sensory memory is defined as the capability to hold ongoing knowledge and experiences in mind for a few milliseconds. Short-term memory has the capability to hold information on line for seconds to minutes. Working memory also comes under this category; working memory combines the ability to hold information on line while allowing the management and planning of that information.

Long-term memory allows the retention of information for days, weeks or even a lifetime. There are three major phases in forming and retrieving memory from long-term memory:

⊛ encoding (obtaining and processing information)

⊛ storage (producing a record of the encoded information)

⊛ retrieval, recall or recollection (retrieving the information that has been stored).

SENSORY MEMORY

Sensory memory corresponds to about the first 200–500 milliseconds after the perception of an item (Baddeley, 1999). An instance of sensory memory is being able to look at one thing and remember its appearance using just one second of observation. In very brief presentations, subjects frequently report that they appear to 'see' more than they are able to report. George Sperling (1979) ran the original research studies that looked at this form of sensory memory, utilising the 'partial report paradigm'. Participants looked at a grid that had 12 letters presented on it, which were organised into three rows of four. After looking at it for a short time, the participants then heard a high, medium or low tone that cued them on which of the rows to report. With these partial report studies as a foundation,

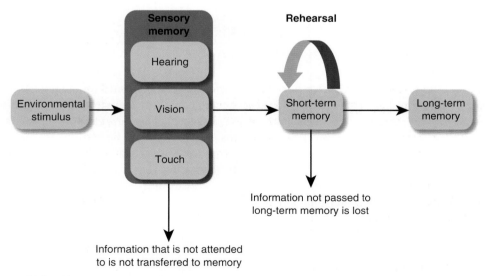

Figure 11.2   *Memory system interconnections*

Sperling demonstrated that the sensory memory could retain about 12 items, but that it deteriorated quite rapidly (in a few hundred milliseconds). As this form of memory is so fleeting, subjects would view the display, but could not report what all 12 items were before it was lost. One key finding was that this skill cannot be extended with practice. A diagrammatic representation of sensory and short-term memory is shown in Figure 11.2.

The definition of sensory memory can be thought of as a number of sensory memory systems, one for each sense. For example, the sensory memory for vision is called iconic memory, while that for hearing is called echoic memory.

SHORT-TERM MEMORY

Short-term memory makes it possible to remember a small amount of information in an active state for a short period (Figure 11.2). It has been demonstrated that short-term memory cannot hold many items at one time and its capacity is fairly minimal. Work done by George Miller (1956) demonstrated that the store of short-term memory was only seven plus/minus two items. Today, we are aware that memory capacity can be expanded through a process known as chunking, where items are organised into familiar manageable units. For instance, when remembering a phone number, an individual might break the digits into groups: the area code, then three digits, and finally a four-digit segment. That way the individuals work with three defined segments rather than a string of individual numbers.

Some decline in memory is normal as we age and often takes the form of memory lapses such as forgetting where you left your keys. Older memories and memories of personal information tend to survive well into old age, but short-term memory and executive function can be impaired. Box 11.1 highlights a review on the subject.

BOX 11.1   Age-related memory loss: a review

Background

It may be perfectly normal behaviour to sometimes forget things such as a phone number or where you parked your car. However, ageing can affect memory by altering the way the brain stores and retrieves information. Research has shown that older adults typically perform at a lower level on many types of memory tasks when compared with younger adults. An issue is whether the performance of elderly subjects is due to the ageing process or to some factor other than advancing years. The purpose of this review paper (Luszcz & Bryan, 1999) was to look at three current views that might explain the relationship between age and memory. These were the processing speed hypothesis, the executive function hypothesis, and the common cause hypothesis.

Methods

The paper reviewed the behavioural studies that related to each hypothesis. The paper did not review imaging studies.

Results

The review found that the speed of information processing plays a major role in the memory difficulties associated with ageing. In addition, cognitive functions such as working memory, executive function and sensory input are important to memory processes.

Interpreting the findings

Despite the depth and breadth of research into age-related memory loss, much work still remains to understand why it occurs. Phenomenological approaches to the subject are important for shaping the direction and nature of future research.

Reference

Luszcz, M.A., & Bryan, J. (1999). Toward understanding age-related memory loss in late adulthood. *Gerontology, 45*, 2–9.

WORKING MEMORY

Working memory is defined as the part of memory used for the manipulation and temporary storage of information. It has limited capacity and deals with a range of cognitive tasks such as language comprehension and reasoning. Short-term memory, which stores information but does not have the ability to manipulate, is generally considered as the storage side of the working memory model. Working memory, in contrast to short-term memory, takes on both the manipulation and the storage of information, and plays a role in the execution of complex cognitive tasks. Working memory also has a different function from long-term memory. Long-term memory has an enormous capacity for storing information and holds the information over longer periods.

The working memory model has three subcomponents. The first is the central executive, which is generally seen as the attention controlling system and is important in planning and monitoring action. The central executive controls two slave systems: the visuospatial sketch pad, which manipulates visual images; and the phonological loop, which stores and rehearses speech-based information (Baddeley & Hitch, 1974; Baddeley, 1999) (see Figure 11.3).

A fourth component was added to the model, which Baddeley called the 'episodic buffer'. This constitutes a third slave system in the model devoted to linking information across sensory domains to create integrated units of sensory information combining visual, spatial and verbal information with chronological ordering or time sequencing. The episodic buffer is also thought to have an association with long-term semantic memory. The reason for the addition of the episodic buffer was the observation that patients with amnesia, who generally have problems with encoding new information, still retain good short-term

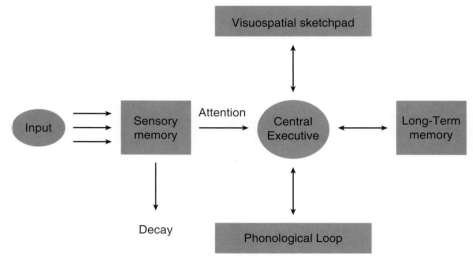

Figure 11.3   *Working memory model*

recall of conversations and stories and bring to mind more than would be available in the phonological loop (Baddeley, 2000).

Neural substrate of working memory

Research in this field has concentrated on two aspects: individuals with specific lesions; and normal individuals through the application of imaging technology. Generally the results support a three-component model, which indicates that the phonological loop is localised to the left hemisphere with storage occurring in part of the temporoparietal junction (Brodmann area 40), while rehearsal or inner speech is more associated with the area for speech or Brodmann area 44 (Paulesu, Frith, & Frackowiak, 1993). It seems that the visuospatial sketchpad is localised to a few regions of the right hemisphere: one area is for the processing and storage of visual stimuli; a second area is located more towards the parietal regions of the brain and is most likely associated with spatial aspects of the stimuli; while control functions have been associated with two frontal areas of activation (Fletcher & Henson, 2001). It is generally accepted that the frontal cortex is critical to executive control, but there is still debate as to whether these functions can be localised to one area of the cortex (Duncan & Owen, 2000). Little evidence exists regarding the localisation of the episodic buffer, and it appears to reflect a widely distributed system that may not trigger activation in any particular area (Baddeley, 2000).

LONG-TERM MEMORY

Researchers have broken down long-term memory systems into two broad classifications: declarative and non-declarative (Figure 11.4). The declarative memory system is

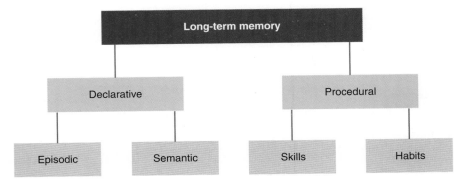

Figure 11.4 *Long-term memory*

conscious and it includes memories of facts and occurrences (Eichenbaum, 1997). Non-declarative memory, also known as implicit or procedural memory, is very important even though the brain is not aware of it. It includes the memories for skills and habits like bike riding, driving an automobile, playing a sport and playing a musical instrument. Declarative long-term memory is further separated into episodic memory and semantic memory. Episodic memory is our memory of events and experiences, and it is this memory that gives us our autobiographic story. Semantic memory in contrast consists of facts and concept and skills that we have acquired throughout our lives.

Rehearsal of short-term information leads to long-term storage of information. Repeated rehearsal or exposure to a piece of information or stimulus leads to transfer into long-term storage. The failure to retrieve information is generally called forgetting, and this is usually as a result of either decay of or interference in information. However, forgetting something may not just be caused by retrieval failure. Information retrieval can be achieved in two ways: by recall and by recognition. In the process of recall, the information is reproduced from memory. Recognition in contrast is the identification of something that has been seen before or is already known; thus it is less difficult than recall because information is available as a cue. Recall can also be assisted by provision of cues, enabling faster and more accurate retrieval of information.

REINFORCEMENT

CLASSICAL CONDITIONING

Classical conditioning (sometimes referred to as Pavlovian conditioning) is a form of associative learning first demonstrated by Ivan Pavlov (1927), a Russian psychologist (Figure 11.5). The usual guideline for triggering classical conditioning consists of giving a neutral stimulus alongside a stimulus of some meaning. A neutral stimulus is something that does not trigger any noticeable behavioural reaction from the animal. Conditional stimulus or CS is the term used to describe this stimulus. The unconditional stimulus (US) is just the

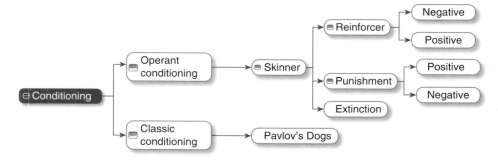

Figure 11.5 *Conditioning*

opposite. It is a significant stimulus that triggers an innate, often reflexive reaction known as the unconditioned response (UR). After continuously pairing the CS with the US, the stimuli become associated and the animal develops a behavioural response to the CS.

The salivary conditioning of Pavlov's dogs was the first recorded instance of classical conditioning. Pavlov observed that the dogs were producing saliva every time they saw the person who normally brought their food, even when they had no food. He referred to this as salivation psychic secretions. Pavlov believed that if a stimulus accompanied a dog being served its meal, the dog would associate the stimulus with the food and would salivate in its presence without the food. In his future research, Pavlov demonstrated that a neutral stimulus, like a noise, became a conditioned stimulus (CS) by constantly coupling it with the unconditioned stimulus (US), as seen in Figure 11.6.

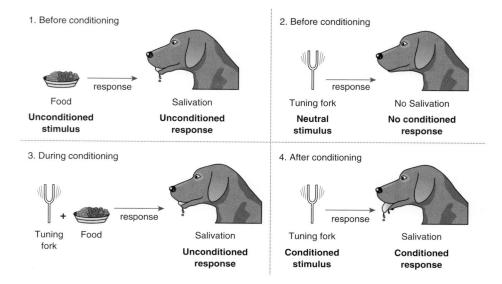

Figure 11.6 *Pavlovian conditioning*

INSTRUMENTAL OR OPERANT CONDITIONING

Unlike classical conditioning, operant conditioning involves altering 'voluntary behaviour' or operant behaviour. Skinner (1953) developed the concept of operant conditioning based on the idea that learning involves overt behavioural changes. He believed that a person's reaction to events or stimuli in the environment is reflected in their behavioural change. The process of operant conditioning has a few main concepts associated with it. A reinforcer is something that supports or increases the behaviour that it comes after, whereas a punisher causes behaviour to occur with less frequency. Extinction is when there is a lack of consequence following a particular behaviour; thus neither favourable nor unfavourable consequences follow the behaviour and as such it will occur with less frequency. Shaping was a term given to the process of guiding current behaviour towards some desired outcome through what Skinner called successive approximation, whereby the successive responses reinforced are more and more accurate approximations of the response desired by the trainer. When a previously reinforced behaviour is no longer reinforced with either positive or negative reinforcement, it leads to a decline in the response or extinction.

Reinforcers can be one of two types:

⚙ *Positive reinforcers*: positive outcomes follow the behaviour. When positive reinforcement occurs, behaviour is strengthened as a result of that behaviour being directly rewarded.

⚙ *Negative reinforcers*: unfavourable things are taken away after a behaviour. The reaction is made stronger by taking away something that is disliked or seen as unpleasant.

Two types of punishment exist:

⚙ *Positive punishment*: consists of presenting an unfavourable event such as to weaken the subsequent response.

⚙ *Negative punishment*: a favourable event or outcome is taken away following a specific behaviour.

Examples of operant conditioning are observable around us all the time. Children can be rewarded for finishing their homework, or an adult might receive a bonus at work for completing a project. In both these cases, desired behaviour increases on the promise of reward. The process of operant conditioning could also decrease the behaviour. The removal of undesirable outcomes or the use of punishment can be used to decrease or prevent undesirable behaviours. For example, a child may be told they will lose their privileges if they do not tidy their bedroom.

NEURAL MECHANISMS OF REINFORCEMENT

Although studies have highlighted that stimulation of many brain regions can be reinforcing (Olds & Forbes, 1981), there are a few regions that require special attention. One is called the medial forebrain bundle (MFB) which runs along the anterior–posterior axis from the midbrain to the anterior basal forebrain, passing through the lateral hypothalamus. Electrical stimulation in regions of the lateral hypothalamic area are positively reinforcing and induce eating in satiated animals. The mesolimbic dopamine pathway, which begins in the ventral tegmental area (VTA) of the midbrain and projects to the amygdala, hippocampus and nucleus accumbens, plays a major role in reinforcement; studies have shown that the natural reinforcers such as water, food and sex stimulate release of dopamine in the nucleus accumbens (Nakahara, Ozaki, Miura, Miura, & Nagatsu, 1989). In addition, these pathways seem to be involved in the biological mechanisms of drug addiction and dependency. The cocaine and amphetamine reward system includes the dopamine neurons of VTA, and the alcohol reward system involves the VTA and the nucleus accumbens (Koob, 1992).

HEBBIAN THEORY

According to Donald Hebb's (1949) theory, a necessary mechanism for synaptic plasticity is an increase in synaptic efficacy that results from the presynaptic cell's constant and recurring stimulation of the postsynaptic cell. To put it another way, when one neuron is active and produces repeated firing, the activity contributes to the firing of another cell. This relationship between cells means that what may start as little more than a chance association between the firing of two nearby neurons becomes contributory, and the relationship between these neurons becomes causal. We also refer to this process as Hebb's rule. We typically use Hebbian theory to describe some facets of associative learning where simultaneously activating cells causes the synapses to strengthen, sometimes called Hebbian learning.

The theory states that the cell assemblies are the most basic unit of memory. Experiencing an event triggers activity in a neural circuit within the central nervous system, which continues to reverberate throughout the circuit, providing temporary storage for the memory until consolidation and storage can occur in permanent memory. Hebb referred to these as neural circuit cell assemblies. These basic units of memory may regulate simple reflexive behaviours, while more complex processes, for example voluntary behaviours, are controlled by interconnected cell assemblies. Cell assemblies that are active at the same time become interconnected into a phase sequence to regulate more complex processes. Individuals produce weak memories or no memories at all when reverberation is disrupted in the early stages of the consolidation process. Consequently, for strong memories to form there must be biological changes in the cell assemblies and the neural activity must not be interrupted. Interfering with the reverberatory activity late in the consolidation process does not have much effect on the subsequent formation of memory (Leisman & Koch, 2000). Recent studies now suggest that Hebbian theory can explain learning and short-term memory, but does not account for long-term memory formation (Bailey, Giustetto, Huang, Hawkins, & Kandel, 2000).

LEARNING IN *APLYSIA*

In the 1980s, Eric Kandel investigated the learning-related changes in synaptic responses in the sea slug *Aplysia californica*, a mollusc with no shell (Kandel, 2009) (see also Chapter 3). *Aplysia*'s breathing apparatus comprises a gill contained in a protective chamber or mantle shelf, which ends in a spout or siphon. Usually when the siphon or mantle is disturbed in *Aplysia*, a reflex defensive mechanism triggers the delicate siphon and gill to retract. This is called the gill and siphon withdrawal reflex (GSWR). The siphon is served by 24 sensory neurons (touch receptors), the cell bodies of which are located in the abdominal ganglion; six motor neurons serve the gill.

This defensive withdrawal reaction can be sensitised or habituated by experience and is believed to parallel withdrawal responses observed in vertebrates. Three different types of non-associative learning have been studied in *Aplysia*:

⚙ *Habituation* occurs when a stimulus is repeatedly presented to an animal and there is a progressive decrease in response to that particular stimulus.

⚙ *Dishabituation* occurs when the animal is presented to another novel stimulus and a partial or complete restoration of a habituated response occurs.

⚙ *Sensitisation* is the increase of a response due to the presentation of a novel, often noxious, stimulus.

The gill and siphon withdrawal reflex of *Aplysia* can undergo classical conditioning of amplitude and duration when the siphon is stimulated (the conditioned stimulus, CS) at the same time as there is shock to the tail or mantle (the unconditioned stimulus, US).

The neural components regulating the defensive reflex are serotonergic. Facilitatory interneurons send out serotonin, thus making the duration of the action potential in the sensory neuron longer by lengthening the closure of potassium (K^+) ion channels (Hawkins, Kandel, & Siegelbaum, 1993). This generated an action potential with an increased duration, which consequently makes it possible for greater Ca^{2+} ion movement into the presynaptic membrane of the sensory nerve cell and then an increased release of neurotransmitters at the synapse, creating a bridge between the sensory and motor neurons, thus strengthening the withdrawal response.

BRAIN AREAS INVOLVED IN MEMORY

THE HIPPOCAMPUS

The hippocampus is a component of the limbic system and is integral to spatial navigation and long-term memory function (Bird & Burgess, 2008) (Figure 11.7). In primates, including humans, the hippocampus can be found inside the medial temporal lobe below the cortical surface, with parts on the left and right areas of the brain (Figure 11.8). Those with extensive hippocampal damage may experience the inability to form or retain new memories; this is generally called amnesia (Kesner & Goodrich-Hunsaker, 2010; Squire, Ojemann, Miezin, Petersen, Videen, & Raichle, 1992).

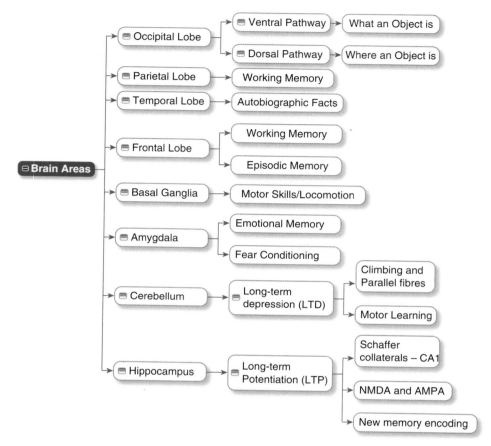

Figure 11.7   *Brain areas involved in memory*

Damage to the hippocampal region leads to difficulties in forming new memories, termed anterograde amnesia. Damage can also affect memories created before injury, termed retrograde amnesia. People with anterograde amnesia can have intact older memories, which suggests that consolidation of memories over time results in the transfer of memories from the hippocampus to other parts of the brain. Procedural memory, like being able to learn new motor skills, is not affected by damage to the hippocampus, suggesting other areas of the brain are associated with this type of memory.

In addition, individuals with amnesia frequently hold onto implicit memory for experiences despite having no conscious awareness of the experience (Machado et al., 2008). Studies on rats and mice have indicated that the large number of hippocampal neurons called 'place' cells fire when the animal moves into particular areas of their surroundings. In primates, these 'place' cells have fired as a reaction to the place a monkey is seeing or

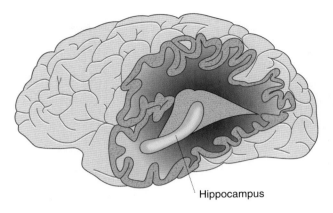

Hippocampus

Figure 11.8   *Location of hippocampus*

looking at instead of the place where the monkey is located at the time (Rolls & Xiang, 2006). These hippocampal place cells are believed to be the main cells that code for spatial awareness, and they produce complex firing when a creature moves through a specific place in an environment. The area where a cell does the most firing is known as that cell's 'firing field' or 'place field' (O'Keefe & Dostrovsky, 1971). Place cells fire at a rate of around 20 Hz in the place field, and at a rate as low as 0.1 Hz when away from the place field. Using these place fields it is believed that place cells are capable of detailing or 'mapping' any environment or maze (O'Keefe & Nadel, 1978). See Box 11.2 for an explanation of the types of mazes used in animal experiments.

BOX 11.2   Mazes and rats

Rats are the animal of choice when it comes to investigating memory. Many studies have used rats in different type of mazes to examine spatial learning and memory. The following gives a brief description of the mazes used.

The classic maze

The classic maze (Figure 1) consists of high walls with no ceiling so the rat can see out of the top. The rat is placed in the maze at one location and moves around the maze where it will generally find a reward. The time the rat takes to get to the reward is observed, as are the errors over trials. Plotting the data gives a learning curve for a particular rat for certain conditions set up.

(Continued)

ESSENTIAL BIOLOGICAL PSYCHOLOGY

(Continued)

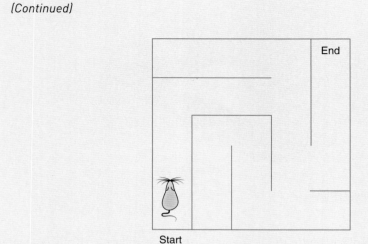

Figure 1   *Classic maze*

The T-maze

As the name implies, this maze is T shaped (Figure 2). Rewards are located in one or both arms of the maze. This maze is used to ask questions such as which side the rat has a preference for, or how it explores the environment if food reward is offered. The maze gives the investigator more control as there are only two options for the rat to choose between, so behaviour can be manipulated in a systematic manner.

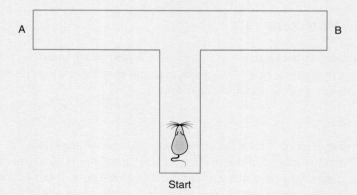

Figure 2   *T-maze*

The Y-maze

As with the T-maze, exploration studies and short-term memory studies can be done using this type of maze (Figure 3).

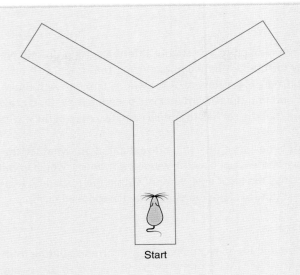

Figure 3 *Y-maze*

The multiple T-maze

Behaviour in this maze (Figure 4) can be easily recorded as there are only two options at each intersection. However, exploring the environment is rather challenging for rats.

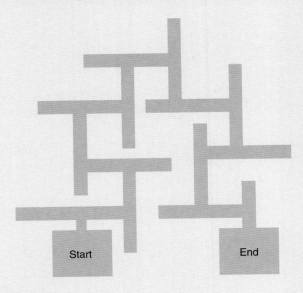

Figure 4 *Multiple T-maze*

(Continued)

(Continued)

This type of maze is used to investigate **latent** learning. In this type of learning, a delay is generally introduced between exploring the maze with no reward and then some time after introducing a reward. A rat who is familiar with the maze will explore the maze quicker and find the reward quicker because it has had previous exploration time. This indicates that the rat has formed a cognitive map of the environment (Tolman & Honzik, 1930).

Other aspects of behaviour that can be investigated are whether the rat responds to markers in the environment such as the windows or doors, which is called place learning; or whether it uses the local environment within the maze and learns responses to the maze like turn left, turn right, which is called response learning.

The radial arm maze

The radial arm maze (Figure 5) is constructed with arms radiating from the centre. The number of arms varies according to the study. Studies with this maze will investigate short-term memory for food in one of the arms. The maze can be rotated to probe place and response learning.

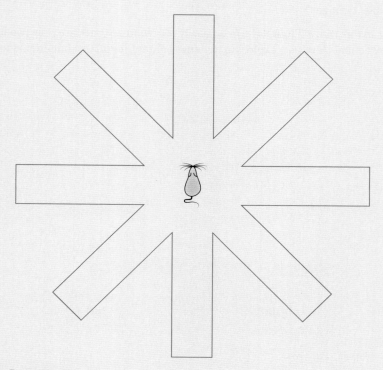

Figure 5   *Radial arm maze*

The Morris water maze

The Morris water maze (Figure 6) is rather like a large round bath filled with milky water. The milk added to the water makes the water opaque, so the rat cannot see a platform just submerged under the surface of the water (Morris, Garrud, Rawlins, & O'Keefe, 1982). This maze is used to investigate spatial learning and place learning. The rat is placed into the tank at various points and the time taken to find the platform is recorded. The rat will take refuge on the platform once it is found. The water maze is a very popular tool and has been used for the effects of transplantation as well as the manipulation of brain areas by lesion techniques to study the effect of brain damage on spatial awareness.

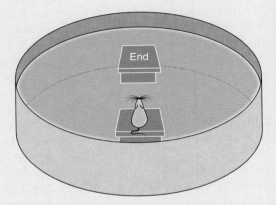

Figure 6   *Morris water maze*

References

Morris, R.G., Garrud, P., Rawlins, J.N., & O'Keefe, J. (1982). Place navigation impaired in rats with hippocampal lesions. *Nature, 297,* 681–683.
Tolman, E.C., & Honzik, C.H. (1930). 'Insight' in rats. *University of California, Publications in Psychology, 4,* 215–232.

The firing rate of rat hippocampal cells relies not only on location but also on other variables, like the direction in which the subject is travelling and the subject's destination (Smith & Mizumori, 2006). Research using brain imaging technology has demonstrated that a variety of spatial cognitive tasks are associated with activity in the hippocampus. Using computer simulations of the visual navigation tasks, we see increased activity in the hippocampus and evidence that the area is involved in identifying new routes between familiar places.

Recent research has demonstrated that part of the hippocampus is bigger in London taxi drivers, whose job involves navigating through a maze of streets, than in the rest of the population, with the most experienced drivers having the largest hippocampi. The study looked at the relationship between the size of the grey matter and how long the subject had worked as a cab driver, and discovered there was a positive correlation between the length of time a person held this job and the size of the right hippocampus (Maguire et al., 2000). They also discovered that the total size of the hippocampus remained unchanged when compared with normal controls, so even though the posterior section of the hippocampus in cab drivers was larger, the anterior section was found to be smaller. The study's conclusions have posed some problems: for example, is it that a bigger hippocampus makes someone more likely to become a taxi driver, or is it that driving through the streets of London makes someone's hippocampus increase in size?

SECOND MESSENGER SYSTEMS AND MEMORY

There are two types of synaptic transmission: one that results in temporary changes in the postsynaptic neurons, and one that results in longer-lasting changes in the postsynaptic cells. The first type works by way of ion-channel-linked receptors. The second type works by way of G-protein-linked receptors and second messenger systems, sometimes referred to as 'metabotropic' receptors in contrast to the other main family of receptors, which are known as 'ion channel' receptors.

Second messengers are molecules that transmit information from receptors on the surface of the cell to target molecules located in the cytoplasm or nucleus of the cell. Second messengers are synthesised as a response to a neurotransmitter and a G-protein-linked receptor binding together. After these second messengers have been created, they can lead to permanent changes in neural structures and function, and because of this they have been associated with the creation of memory (Krasne & Glanzman, 1995). The main second messenger in the brain is cAMP (cyclic adenosine monophosphate), which is involved in the sensitisation of *Aplysia*'s gill withdrawal reflex discussed earlier. Serotonin is released which, in turn, releases cAMP in the siphon sensory neuron buttons. This cAMP triggers another enzyme, protein kinase A, which closes some of the potassium (K^+) channels; this consequently lengthens the duration of each action potential, which increases the influx of calcium (Ca^{2+}), which in turn increases neurotransmitter delivery at each touch of the siphon.

Long-term memory storage relies upon the second messenger system to trigger the production of protein, a requirement that is not necessary in short-term memory. The creation of protein results in structural changes to the neuron, like increases in the size and number of synaptic contacts (Glanzman, Kandel, & Schacher, 1990), while inhibitors of protein production in the neuron keep structural changes from occurring and block the development of long-term memory (Castellucci, Blumenfeld, Goelet, & Kandel, 1989).

THE CELLULAR BASIS OF MEMORY: LONG-TERM POTENTIATION

It has long been thought that the cellular mechanisms of learning and memory in the mammalian brain involve changes to the synaptic connections between neurons (Hebb, 1949). Long-term potentiation (LTP), a process that elicits changes in the nervous system, has been very widely studied, and is defined as the ongoing facilitation of synaptic transmission that happens after the presynaptic neurons undergo intense stimulation (Lynch, 2004). One area of the brain where LTP has been extensively studied is in the hippocampus.

Although studies have involved recording LTP in both humans and animals, the mechanism of LTP has been extensively studied using *in vitro* slices of hippocampus (Sastry, Maretic, Morishita and Xie, 1990).

The NMDA-type glutamate receptor has a key role to play in some types of LTP, especially LTP around the CA3–CA1 synapse in the hippocampus. (CA refers to cornu Ammon, a Latin name for Ammon's horn – as the hippocampus is said to resemble the shape of a ram's horn.) The pyramidal cells in the CA1 region process dendrites, which receive synapses from the axons of pyramidal cells in the CA3 region, otherwise known as the Schaffer collaterals. The postsynaptic CA1 cells have two kinds of receptors. One is known as the NMDA-type glutamate receptors; the other is the AMPA-type glutamate receptors. Na^+ and K^+ can permeate both receptors, but the NMDA type has two extra characteristics: it possesses a significant permeability to Ca^{2+} as well as being permeable to Na^+, and the receptor channel is usually obstructed by Mg^{2+}.

When the Schaffer collaterals are excited by a single electrical stimulation they generate excitatory postsynaptic potentials (EPSPs) in the postsynaptic CA1 cells but without influx of K^+, Na^+ and Ca^{2+} due to the channel being blocked by the Mg^{2+}, and therefore will remain in this closed state when stimulated by a weak signal. Thus when stimulation of the Schaffer collaterals only occurs two or three times per minute, the size of the evoked EPSP in the CA1 neurons remains constant. If however a brief high-frequency train of stimuli (a tetanus) is delivered, there will be summation of the EPSPs. As a result of this temporal and spatial summation of EPSPs, the membrane potential of the postsynaptic neuron undergoes significant depolarisation, even greater than the depolarisation that results from an individual afferent stimulus. With the large synaptic input the inside of the cell becomes positive and the positively charged Mg^{2+} is then repelled by the positive charge present inside and is 'pushed' out of the channel. The channel now has no Mg^{2+} ion, making it possible for Ca^{2+} to enter by way of the unblocked NMDA receptor. When the Ca^{2+} enters the cell, it triggers different protein kinases, such as an enzyme known as calcium-calmodulin-dependent kinase II (CaMKII). Kinases serve to bind phosphate compounds with protein and thus change their mode of operation. CaMKII phosphorylates another glutamate receptor called α-amino-3-hydroxy-5-methyl-4-isoxazole-propionate or AMPA, making these receptors more permeable to sodium ions (Na^+), and therefore reducing the resting potential of the cell and increasing its sensitivity to subsequent incoming impulses. There is also some evidence that the activity of CaMKII raises the number of AMPA receptors at the synapse, therefore contributing to LTP (Figure 11.9).

Another enzyme that is activated is adenylate cyclise. This synthesises cyclic adenosine monophosphate (cAMP), which then triggers another protein, kinase A (or PKA), to become active. PKA phosphorylates the AMPA receptors, which again makes it possible for the receptors to stay open for more time after they bind with glutamate. Consequently, the postsynaptic neuron depolarises even more. Other proteins like CREB (cAMP response element binding) protein have also been found to engage with PKA. CREB is pivotal to the transcribing of protein genes, and when it is activated, new AMPA receptors that are able to further increase synaptic efficiency are formed. Thus, following this process, the transmitter released from the presynaptic neuron is able to stimulate a greater number of receptors on the postsynaptic neuron. A bigger (potentiated) EPSP (i.e. LTP) will be created if additional receptors are bound and thus opened. Along with an increase in the number of postsynaptic

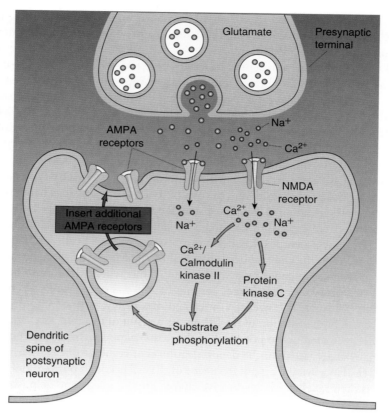

Figure 11.9   *Long-term potentiation*

AMPA receptors, there also seems to be a greater amount of transmitter released from the presynaptic neurons. Presynaptic and postsynaptic effects, when combined, have a synergistic effect, thus enlarging the size of the synaptic potential in the postsynaptic neuron.

Along with all of the postsynaptic mechanisms associated with establishing LTP, it has been proposed that some presynaptic alterations happen during the maintenance stage. However, modifications would necessitate the presence of a retrograde messenger that goes back to this neuron and changes it. Nitric oxide (NO) is well suited to perform this role since it is naturally a gas and can therefore pass through cell membranes. This view is founded mainly upon the fact that there is no LTP present when slices of the hippocampus are incubated with inhibitors of NO synthase (NOS) or of NO scavengers (Bennett, 1994).

OTHER BRAIN STRUCTURES ASSOCIATED WITH MEMORY

Cerebellum and long-term depression

If synapses in the nervous system LTP just increased the connections of neurons they would eventually reach some level of maximum efficacy, making it tricky to encode new information. Therefore, to make synaptic strengthening realistic, other neural processes are necessary to weaken specific synapses. One of these processes is called long-term depression (LTD). While LTD was found to occur at the synapses in the hippocampus, the process of cerebellar LTD has been suggested to be important for motor learning, which mediates the coordination, acquisition and storage of complex movements (Thach, 1998).

Purkinje neurons in the cerebellum obtain excitatory input from two sources, one from the climbing fibres and the other from the parallel fibres. Cerebellar LTD happens when the climbing fibres and parallel fibres are stimulated together. Activity of the climbing fibres and parallel fibres leads to activation of two processes in the postsynaptic Purkinje cell (Figure 11.10):

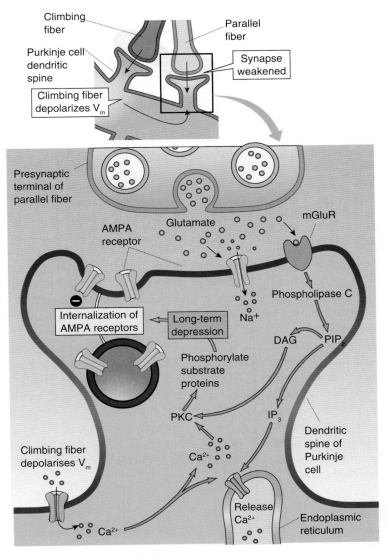

Figure 11.10 *Long-term depression (LTD)*

1   Parallel fibres release glutamate which triggers two receptors, AMPA receptors and glutamate receptors. Glutamate binding to the AMPA receptor triggers membrane depolarisation, and the activation of the glutamate receptor causes a second messenger process to take place that produces inositol trisphosphate (IP3) and activates an intracellular enzyme, protein kinase C (PKC).

2   Activation of the climbing fibres causes an increase in intracellular Ca^{2+} concentration. as a large influx of Ca^{2+} takes place through **voltage-gated channels**.

This simultaneous activation of these pathways leads to Ca^{2+} interacting with PKC. This decreases the postsynaptic activity of AMPA to glutamate and ultimately leads to LTD.

Amygdala

The amygdala is a mass of grey matter located in the anterior-medial portion of the temporal lobe, situated anterior to the hippocampus. It consists of a number of distinct subnuclei and is connected to other parts of the brain in three functional subdivisions. The medial group of subnuclei connects with the olfactory bulb and the olfactory cortex; the basolateral group of nuclei connects with the orbital and medial prefrontal cortex; and the central and anterior group of nuclei connects with the brain stem and hypothalamus and with various visceral sensory structures.

There are two amygdala in the brain, one in each hemisphere. In humans, the amygdalae perform principal roles in forming and storing memories associated with emotional events (Phelps, 2004). Several behavioural paradigms have been used to investigate the role of the amygdale; one based on the conditioned fear responses in rats has been extensively studied. When an initially neutral stimulus is repeatedly paired with an inherently aversive one, a behaviour called conditioned fear develops, and over time the animal will respond to the neutral stimulus with behaviours comparable to those elicited by the threatening stimulus. Studies have demonstrated that, while the animal is undergoing fear conditioning, sensory stimuli are communicated to the basolateral complex of the amygdala, most especially the lateral nuclei, where they become associated with memories of the stimuli (Dalzell, Connor, Penner, Saari, Leboutillier, & Weeks, 2010). These emotional experiences mediated by lateral nuclei trigger fear behaviour by way of connections with the central nucleus of the amygdala and the bed nuclei of stria terminalis (BNST). The central nuclei of the amygdala play a role in many fear reactions, including freezing (inability to move), tachycardia (rapid heartbeat), increased respiration, and stress-hormone release. Furthermore, if the amygdala is removed or damaged there is an impairment in the ability to acquire and express fear conditioning (Cousens & Otto, 1998). Besides fearful emotional learning, the amygdala is also responsible for pleasurable emotional learning (Herbert et al., 2009).

Motor memory and the basal ganglia

The basal ganglia are a collection of nuclei found in the medial temporal lobe (MTL). The basal ganglia consist of the subthalamic nucleus, the substantia nigra, the globus pallidus, the ventral striatum and the dorsal striatum, which comprises the putamen and the caudate nucleus (Suvorov, 1998). The basal ganglia area of the brain has traditionally been regarded as composed of motor structures that regulate the initiation of movements. However, recent research has determined that the area is also involved with unconscious memory processes like motor skills, locomotion and implicit memory (Wilkinson, Khan, & Jahanshahi, 2009). When the basal ganglia are damaged, the individual has difficulty learning motor and perceptual-motor skills (Boyd & Winstein, 2004). A lack of dopaminergic cells in the substantia nigra leads to the neurological disorder of Parkinson's disease which is related to impaired motor function (Santens, Boon, Van Roost, & Caemaert, 2003).

Frontal lobe

The frontal lobe is located at the front of each cerebral hemisphere and positioned anterior to the parietal lobes and superior and anterior to the temporal lobes. The frontal region has been linked to the coordination of information and working memory and can also be separated into different areas with specific functional outputs. For example, a small region of the frontal lobe called the lateral prefrontal cortex has been linked to the encoding and retrieval of episodic memory (Lee, Robbins, & Owen, 2000). The frontal lobes also play a role in prospective memory, which is defined as that capacity to remember events in the future and upcoming actions (Basso, Ferrari, & Palladino, 2010).

Temporal lobe

The temporal lobes are located under the Sylvian fissure on the left and right brain hemispheres. They are involved in the memory of autobiographical facts (Rosenbaum et al., 2008) and play a role in recognition memory (Squire, Wixted, & Clark, 2007). Damage to the temporal lobes leads to a range of disturbances including attention and perceptual disturbances, and problems with organisation and language comprehension. In addition individuals with **temporal lobe epilepsy** frequently experience general cognitive impairment (Helmstaedter & Kockelmann, 2006).

Parietal lobe

The parietal lobe of the brain lies between the frontal lobe anteriorly and the posterior occipital lobe. The parietal lobe has traditionally been associated with mediating attention when required and providing spatial awareness and navigational skills. Recent functional imaging work, however, has found that the parietal lobe activations are associated with memory processes and that individuals with parietal lobe damage exhibit both working memory and long-term memory deficits (Haramati, Soroker, Dudai, & Levy, 2008; Olson & Berryhill, 2009). It has been suggested that parietal activations during recognition memory tasks might reflect processes such as the storage of retrieved information in a working memory buffer for further cognitive processing (Haramati et al., 2008).

Occipital lobe

The occipital lobe or visual cortex is located dorsally to the cerebellum and posterior to the parieto-occipital sulcus. As we now know, the visual cortex of the brain is the part of the cortex responsible for processing visual information. The occipital lobe transmits information to two primary pathways, called the dorsal stream and the ventral stream. The dorsal stream is associated with motion and representation of object locations, while the ventral stream is associated with form recognition and object representation and seems to play a role in the storage of long-term memory.

DISORDERS OF MEMORY: AMNESIA

Amnesia is a condition which involves difficulties with learning new information or recalling old information. Amnesia is defined as a severe disruption of memory without deficits in intelligence, attention, perception or judgement, and generally occurs following damage to any of several brain structures which are critical for memory (Squire & Zola, 1997).

Amnesia can be either neurological or functional in nature and can be divided into four types (Figure 11.11):

1 *anterograde amnesia*, which is seen as an impairment in storing new memories

2 *retrograde amnesia*, which is a loss of old memories

3 *psychogenic or functional amnesia*, which involves a functional loss of memories

4 *temporary amnesia*, which is a temporary loss of memory which can follow the use of certain drugs such as benzodiazepines (e.g. Valium).

Damage or injury to the medial temporal lobe or medial diencephalon is characterised by a loss of declarative memory, while non-declarative memory or the collection of non-conscious knowledge systems generally remains intact. Individuals with this type of neurological amnesia have difficulty learning new facts and events (anterograde amnesia) and also usually experience some difficulty remembering facts and events that were acquired prior to the onset of amnesia (retrograde amnesia). Injury restricted to the hippocampus is enough to result in fairly serious amnesia in human subjects (Spiers, Maguire, & Burgess, 2001).

ANTEROGRADE AMNESIA

Individuals with anterograde amnesia are severely impaired in learning new information following an incidence of brain injury. Generally, their memories for events that occurred before the injury are largely spared, and some individuals with circumscribed damage only to the medial temporal lobe or midline diencephalon have intact intellectual and perceptual functioning (Levy et al., 2005; Shrager et al., 2006). In some cases amnesia can also be accompanied by visual perceptual deficits (Lee et al., 2005).

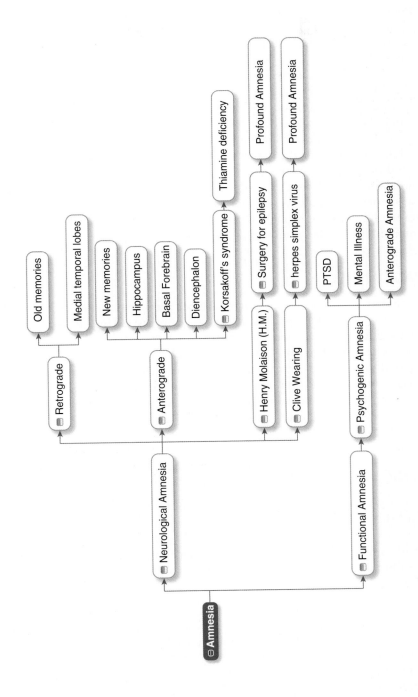

Figure 11.11 *Amnesia*

Due to the nature of memory, damage to different brain areas can lead to the condition of anterograde amnesia. Damage to the hippocampus and associated areas in the medial temporal lobes of the brain leads to the disruption of new memory formation and as a result no memories can enter long-term memory. Damage to these areas can occur following a stroke or aneurysm, carbon monoxide poisoning or hypoxia (Yamaoka et al., 1993). Anterograde amnesia can also occur as a result of injury, usually an aneurysm to the basal forebrain. This area is located ventrally to the striatum; it is considered to be the major cholinergic output of the brain and plays a major role in memory and learning. Finally, anterograde amnesia can sometimes occur following damage to the structures of the diencephalon which include the thalamus, the hypothalamus, the optic tracts and the mammillary bodies, the posterior pituitary gland and the pineal gland. **Korsakoff's syndrome** is a good example of this type of amnesia. This condition is generally seen in individuals who consume excessive amounts of alcohol and results from a deficiency of thiamine (vitamin B1) which is thought to cause damage to the medial thalamus and possibly to the mammillary bodies (Sullivan & Pfefferbaum, 2009).

RETROGRADE AMNESIA

Individuals with damage to the medial temporal lobes may also experience impairment of the memories that were obtained prior to the onset of amnesia. This kind of memory loss is known as retrograde amnesia. Generally, retrograde forms of amnesia are assessed on a temporal basis, where information obtained far back in time (remote memory) is not affected compared to the more current memory (Jarrard, 2001). The effects of retrograde amnesia can last a brief period, disappearing within one or two years, or can be far more enduring, spanning decades. Interestingly, even in cases of severe retrograde amnesia, patients can still recall the facts and events of their childhood and teenage years (Kirwan, Bayley, Galvan, & Squire, 2008).

PSYCHOGENIC OR FUNCTIONAL AMNESIA

Psychogenic amnesia can happen as the outcome of an emotional trauma. The symptoms associated with this type of amnesia are different from those of anterograde and retrograde memory loss. Psychogenic amnesia is marked by severe retrograde amnesia with little anterograde amnesia and is not caused by damage to a specific brain structure. As a result, some people recover well from psychogenic amnesia.

CASE STUDY: CLIVE WEARING

One of the most documented cases of severe amnesia is that of the English musician Clive Wearing, who at the age of 46 was infected with the herpes simplex virus, which destroyed his hippocampus bilaterally and left him profoundly amnesic. Wearing's procedural and semantic memory is largely intact and he can recognise his wife and family. He also retains a normal vocabulary, and can still play the piano. However, his episodic memory is extremely impaired. He has sufficient short-term memory ability to be able to hold a conversation, but quickly forgets about the subject matter of which he spoke moments earlier. The nature of the amnesia seen in Wearing perfectly illustrates the distinction between semantic memory and episodic memory (Tulving, 1983). Desperate to grasp something, Wearing started to keep a journal of his memories and events. However, his journal entries consisted essentially of the statements 'I am awake' or 'I am conscious', entered again and again every few minutes. He would write, '2:15 p.m.: this time properly awake … 2:30 p.m.: this time finally awake … 2:40 p.m.: this time completely awake', with earlier statements crossed out as he had no recollection of writing them. In essence he repeatedly has the feeling that he has just woken up; his conscious experience is entirely of the present, as he cannot remember anything further back than a few seconds ago. His wife Deborah has written a book about her husband's case entitled *Forever today* (Wearing, 2005).

CASE STUDY: HENRY GUSTAV MOLAISON

A classic case study on the localisation of memory was the result of surgery performed on Henry Molaison, an individual who, until his death in 2008, was known to the scientific community only as an anonymous patient by the name of H.M.

H.M. originally suffered from intractable epilepsy and was referred for treatment to William Beecher Scoville, a neurosurgeon at Hartford Hospital, Connecticut. H.M.'s epilepsy was localised to his left and right medial temporal lobes (MTLs) and he was recommended to undergo surgical resection of the MTLs as a treatment. In 1953 Scoville removed parts of H.M.'s MTL on both sides of his brain, resulting in the loss of two-thirds of his hippocampus, parahippocampal gyrus and amygdala. The operation resulted in severe damage to the hippocampus and the entorhinal cortex as well as damage to a portion of the anterolateral temporal cortex. Prior to the operation H.M. had a fully functional memory, but following the surgery he experienced profound anterograde amnesia. In particular, he retained procedural memory but was unable to complete tasks that require recall from short-term memory. The pattern of deficit suggested at the time that recall from these memory systems may be mediated, at least in part, by different areas of the brain (Scoville & Milner, 1957).

H.M.'s case was significant in the history of neuropsychology not only for the information it provided about memory impairment and amnesia, but also for the insight it gave into how particular areas of the brain may be linked to specific memory processes (Corkin, 2002). In particular it showed that old and new memories are functions of different brain regions: the hippocampus processes new memories, while older memories are retrieved from other parts of the brain such as the frontal cortex.

SUMMARY

This chapter began by highlighting the three temporal classes of memory: sensory memory, which has the ability to hold ongoing experiences in mind for a few milliseconds;

short-term memory, which can hold information online for seconds to minutes; and long-term memory, which allows the retention of information for days, weeks or even a lifetime (Figure 11.12). The three major phases in forming and retrieving memory from long-term memory were detailed; these are encoding, storage and retrieval. Classical conditioning, sometimes referred to as Pavlovian conditioning, was then explained, in which an unconditioned behaviour is paired with a conditioned response. This pairing subsequently leads to a new conditioned response as the subject forms an association between the unconditioned stimulus and the conditioned stimulus. Operant conditioning was also explained, which unlike classical conditioning involves altering voluntary or operant behaviour. The process of operant conditioning is associated with a reinforcer which is something that supports or increases the behaviour, and a punisher which causes a behaviour to occur with less frequency.

The chapter then detailed how Hebbian theory explained learning and short-term memory, but does not account for long-term memory formation. Studies on the sea slug *Aplysia californica* were detailed, explaining that this animal displayed three different type of learning: habituation, dishabituation and sensitisation. It was then explained that second messenger systems were a vital process in memory formation and that long-term memory storage relies upon the second messenger system to trigger the production of proteins. The chapter then discussed the brain areas involved in memory. The hippocampus is a component of the limbic system and is essential to spatial navigation and long-term memory function. Damage to the hippocampal region leads to difficulties in forming new memories, termed anterograde amnesia. The process of long-term potentiation (LTP) was explained, which is believed to be the cellular mechanisms of learning and memory in the mammalian brain and involves changes to the synaptic connections between neurons. LTP has been extensively studied in the hippocampus. The role of the cerebellum was then highlighted, detailing how this structure is involved in the learning of procedural memory and motor learning. Long-term depression (LTD) was explained, which is the neural process to weaken specific synapses. It has been suggested that LTD is important for motor learning, which mediates the coordination, acquisition and storage of complex movements.

The chapter then moved on to discuss other brain regions associated with memory. It was explained that the amygdala is linked to the conditioned fear response, and when it is removed or damaged there is an impairment in the ability to acquire and express fear conditioning. The amygdala is also responsible for pleasurable emotional learning. The basal ganglia are involved with unconscious memory processes like motor skills, locomotion and implicit memory, while the frontal lobe is linked to prospective memory. The temporal lobe is associated with autobiographic and recognition memory. The parietal lobe plays a role with short-term and episodic memory, and damage to the parietal lobe leads to problems with working memory and long-term memory. Finally it was detailed how the occipital lobe transmits information to two primary pathways: the dorsal stream which is involved in representation of object locations, and the ventral stream which plays a role in object representation.

The chapter ended with a section on amnesia, explaining that amnesia can be as a result of functional and neurological problems. The causes of functional amnesia include psychological factors such as mental disorder and post-traumatic stress,

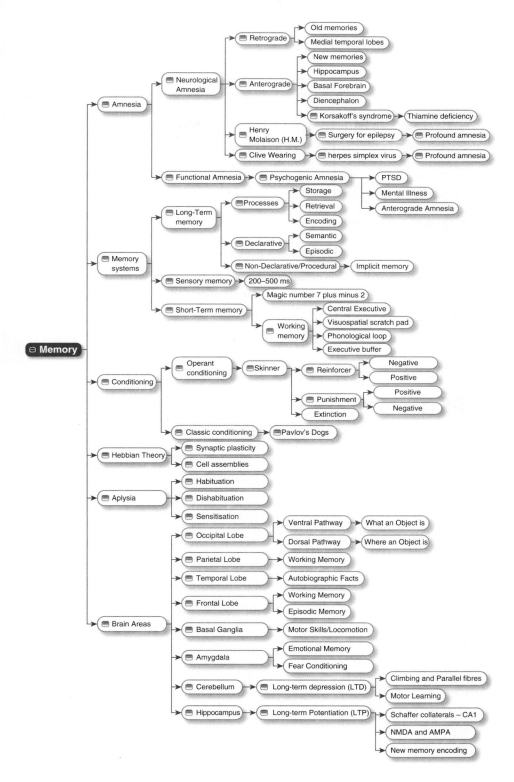

Figure 11.12 *Memory overview*

whereas neurological amnesia results from head injury or a neurological condition. Anterograde amnesia is defined as an impairment in storing new memories; retrograde amnesia is a loss of old memories; and psychogenic amnesia involves a functional loss of memory. Finally, the case of H.M. was detailed, showing that while the hippocampus is important for the construction of new memories, it is not the depository for old memories.

 ## FURTHER READING

Baddeley, A.D. (1999). *Essentials of human memory*. Hove: Psychology.

Bird, C.M., & Burgess, N. (2008). The hippocampus and memory: insights from spatial processing [review]. *Nature Reviews Neuroscience*, 9(3), 182–194.

Squire, L.R., Wixted, J.T., & Clark, R.E. (2007). Recognition memory and the medial temporal lobe: a new perspective. *Nature Reviews Neuroscience*, 8(11), 872–883.

 ## KEY QUESTIONS

1   What role does LTP play in memory formation?

2   Describe the case of H.M. What does he tell us about memory?

3   Describe the role of the different brain areas involved in the working memory model.

12 LATERALISATION AND LANGUAGE

CHAPTER OUTLINE

The human ability to communicate using a complex symbolic language is believed to be fundamentally different from other animals. Human complex symbolic language structure is based on rules with elements that can be combined in countless ways. Research into verbal communication systems of the brain has determined that language is predominantly processed in the left hemisphere while other cognitive functions such as spatial awareness are located in the right hemisphere. Why the brain is lateralised with its cognitive functions dominating on either one side or the other is still unknown; however, we do know that the way the brain is organised and uses information is an essential element in the understanding of lateralisation. In this chapter we will examine the biological aspects of language, and we will discover that different aspects of communication are processed in many different locations in the human brain.

LATERALISATION OF BRAIN FUNCTION

It has been observed that there is a great deal of difference between the two hemispheres of the brain, ranging from the dendritic structure or neurotransmitter distribution to the gross anatomical level. For instance, compared to that in the left hemisphere, the lateral sulcus or Sylvian fissure in the right hemisphere is usually shorter. However, you should note that information provided by experiments shows modest, if any, dependable support for associating functional differences with structural differences (Musiek & Reeves, 1990).

It has been shown in earlier chapters that when the activities of a certain area in the brain, or even a complete hemisphere, are either harmed or damaged, the brain's functions can occasionally be adopted by a neighbouring area. The areas associated with the adoption process can on occasions even be located in the opposite hemisphere, depending on the part of the brain that is impaired and the age of the patient (Helmstaedter, Kurthen, Linke, & Elger, 1994). Injury might also cause problems with the neural pathway from one location to another. In such a case, other associations might be present which can replace the original neural pathway to convey information to a specific targeted location. This type of transmission may be less effective than using the original pathway but it means that some functions of behaviour can be restored. Although in normal development evolutionary processes have modularised brain functions into certain regions, they can be rewired according to an individual's medical history. Indeed, some individuals are limited to the 'left brain' or the 'right brain' as they have undergone a surgical procedure called a hemispherectomy, which is the term for the surgical removal of one of the cerebral hemispheres.

So, how do we determine where a function such as language resides in the brain? One way is to look at handedness. Around 90% of people who are right-handed will have their left hemisphere serving in a dominant way for language functions. However, only a small proportion (18.8%) of left-handed people will have their language functions primarily derived from the right hemisphere; in addition, around 20% of left-handed individuals have bilateral language functions (Taylor & Martin, 1990). Thus, although easy to ascertain, a person's handedness preference is not a sure sign of the location of brain function, even though brain function lateralisation is shown in right or left ear preferences and in right-handedness or left-handedness (Knecht et al., 2000). Furthermore, even within the different language functions, like semantics, syntax and prosody, the two hemispheres are differently specialised in the processing of segmental features of language (Sammler, Kotz, Eckstein, Ott, & Friederici, 2010).

Most research agrees that language functions, like grammar and vocabulary, are frequently lateralised to the left hemisphere of the brain. In contrast to this, prosodic language functions like intonation and accentuation are often localised in the right hemisphere of the brain (Friederici, von Cramon, & Kotz, 2007). The right hemisphere of the brain also appears to process the functions of ocular stimuli, spatial manipulation, facial comprehension and creative abilities (Mihov, Denzler, & Forster, 2010; Vogel, Bowers, & Vogel, 2003). Other integrative processes, like arithmetic, sound localisation and moods, appear to be controlled on both sides (Silberman & Weingartner, 1986).

Some of the best evidence relating to hemispheric specialisation comes from a method called the Wada test, named after Canadian neurologist Juhn Atsushi Wada. The Wada test involves testing each hemisphere of the brain independently by a process of anaesthetising one hemisphere of the brain. In a Wada test, an anaesthetic is administered to a single hemisphere of the brain by way of the carotid arteries. A neuropsychological examination is then performed to identify dominance for producing and comprehending language, and verbal and visual memory processes. Methods that are not quite so invasive or costly, like fMRI and transcranial magnetic stimulation, can also help to identify hemispheric dominance (Medina, Aguirre, Bernal, & Altman, 2004).

Wilder Penfield and colleagues devised a method for mapping the brain that could decrease the side effects resulting from surgical treatment of epilepsy. By administering tiny electrical currents during surgery, they were able to activate discrete regions of motor and somatosensory cortices. They discovered that stimulating one hemisphere of the motor cortex causes the muscles to contract on the opposite side of the body, and additionally these functional maps varied very little between individuals (Penfield & Boldrey, 1937).

SPLIT-BRAIN PATIENTS

The term 'split brain' is used to describe the result when the corpus callosum connecting the two hemispheres of the brain is disconnected (Figure 12.1). The surgical operation to produce this condition is called a corpus callosotomy and is usually used to treat otherwise intractable epilepsy. The surgical method cuts the wide, flat bundle of neural fibres beneath the cortex connecting the left and right cerebral hemispheres, resulting in the disruption of interhemispheric communication. From observations of these split-brain patients, scientists have gained information about the distinct functions of the brain's right and left hemispheres.

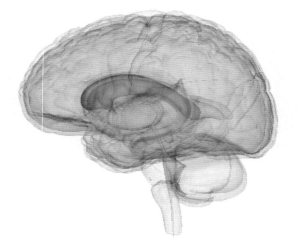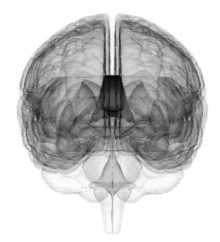

Figure 12.1   *The corpus callosum*

Robert Sperry was the first to investigate the strange behaviour of split-brain patients (Sperry, 1961). He discovered that a person's brain has certain abilities on the right and left sides, and each side can function independently. For a normal brain to function as a whole, the stimulus information is quickly transferred through the corpus callosum from one hemisphere to the other; however, after surgery the two hemispheres of a split-brain patient are unable to communicate with each other. In Sperry's experiments, major differences were apparent between the mental capabilities of the two hemispheres of the brain. The left hemisphere demonstrated involvement in all things logical, analytical, quantitative, rational and verbal, while the right hemisphere was involved in all things conceptual, holistic, intuitive, imaginative and non-verbal.

The extraordinary behaviour of people with split brains has shown there can be a great deal of variation of functions between the two brain hemispheres. Patients who have a split brain will not be able to verbally name images that are presented in their left field of vision (Figure 12.2). The reason for this is that the area associated with speech control, otherwise known as Broca's area, in the majority of individuals is located in the left side of the brain, but the images from the left visual field are only sent to the right side of the brain. Therefore, as the two sides of the brain cannot communicate with each other, the subject is not able to articulate what is seen by the right side of the brain. However, the individual is able to draw the item they have seen using their left hand, because the right side of the brain controls the left hand (Sperry, Gazzaniga, & Bogen, 1969).

Generally, split-brain patients are able to act in a coordinated, purposeful and consistent way, regardless of their hemispheric independence. When both of the hemispheres obtain opposing stimuli simultaneously, the response is generally governed by the task they are engaged with, and it is likely that the brain decides which of the two hemispheres is in charge of behaviour (Levy & Trevarthen, 1976).

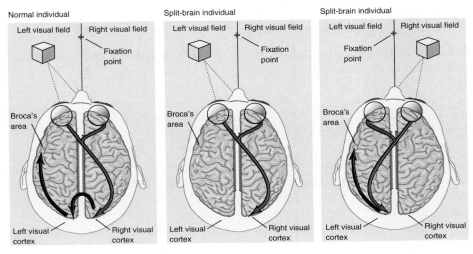

Figure 12.2 *Naming experiments in split brain patients. In a normal individual with an intact brain, visual information about the object crosses to the left hemisphere and the individual is able to name the item. In split brain individuals, the information is confirmed to the one hemisphere, and if shown in the left visual field the information about the object can no longer travel to the language areas in the left hemisphere, so the individual cannot name the object; they can however draw it.*

LANGUAGE

Human language belongs to the most complex cognitive behaviours. It is best described as a method of communication, either spoken or written, consisting of the use of words or symbols structured in a predictable way. Language is not only spoken but can also include gestures and body language, both of which aid communication. The conventional view is that language is an adaptation and that it evolved in response to some selection demands to enhance communication between humans. However, the exact nature of the time course or indeed the mechanism of this evolutionary change is still hotly debated (see Box 12.1).

Spoken language develops relatively early in life. The average 10-year-old comprehends around 40,000 different words, while teenagers have passive vocabularies of over 60,000 (Anglin, 1993).

If we define language as verbal communication, then the question arises of how we join words in order to achieve this communication. Rules are needed so that our thoughts can be conveyed into speech and understood by the receiver. If no rules were present in our speech, it would be a series of meaningless utterances. In linguistics (the scientific study of language), the set of structural rules that govern the composition of words and sentences in a language is called grammar. The subcategories that make up grammar are as follows:

⚙ *Morphology*: specifies the rules for combining words to make longer words, including the addition of suffixes and prefixes.

⚙ *Phonology*: dictates the regulations involved when sound elements and phonemes are combined to form words.

⚙ *Prosody*: consists of the arrangement of intonation and stress which for instance lets us distinguish questions from statements.

⚙ *Syntax*: dictates the way in which words combine to make phrases and sentences in order to make the meaning clear.

BOX 12.1   When was language first produced?

If we are innately capable of producing language, then at what point did the ability evolve? Although specific dates have not been given, some believe the use of language may have started as far back as 2 million years ago (Corballis, 2009). As detailed in the chapter, one important aspect of language is that it is localised to an area in the left hemisphere of the brain called Broca's area. Anthropological evidence from the examination of skulls of our distant relative *Homo habilis* suggests that this language area may have become enlarged as far back as 3 million years ago. In addition, our genetic makeup may also have had an influence on the evolution of speech. The recent discovery of the FOXP2 (Forkhead box protein P2) gene has led to more debate about language acquisition and has raised optimism about understanding the origins of speech and language. In some reports, the FOXP2 has been said to be the language gene, which developed differently in humans and apes. It has been reported that there are two amino acid differences between chimp and human FOXP2 genes and that this difference led to the evolution of language in humans (Enard et al., 2002). However, other studies have been unable to find a clear association between similar mutations in FOXP2 and vocalisations (Scharff & Haesler, 2004). Please bear in mind that, as stated before, the route from the gene to the person is not clear-cut and is influenced by multiple interacting factors such as other genes, developmental processes and the environment. So, although the FOXP2 gene is necessary for speech and has a role to play in fine motor control, the question that remains is whether the separation of the genome of apes and humans some 6–8 million years ago provided enough time for a separate development of language in the evolutionary branch that resulted in human language (Cooper, 2006).

References

Cooper, D.L. (2006). Broca's arrow: evolution, prediction, and language in the brain. *Anatomical Record Part B: New Anatomist, 289*(1), 9–24.

Corballis, M.C. (2009). The evolution of language. *Annals of the New York Academy of Sciences, 1156*, 19–43.

Enard, W., Przeworski, M., Fisher, S.E., Lai, C.S., Wiebe, V., Kitano, T., et al. (2002). Molecular evolution of FOXP2, a gene involved in speech and language. *Nature, 418*, 869–872.

Scharff, C., & Haesler, S. (2004). An evolutionary perspective on FOXP2: strictly for the birds? *Current Opinion in Neurobiology, 15*(6), 694–703.

INVOLVEMENT OF THE RIGHT HEMISPHERE IN LANGUAGE

Prosody refers to the pitch, volume, rate and tempo of speech (Pell, 2006) and is used to convey both emotional and non-emotional information. Emotional prosody communicates the emotion of the utterance and sometimes the emotional disposition of the speaker, such as whether a person is happy or sad (Blonder et al., 1991). Non-emotional prosody communicates the linguistic and other non-emotional aspects of speech, clarifying any syntactic or semantic ambiguity in a sentence (Rymarczyk & Grabowska, 2007).

Although the **dominant hemisphere** (most generally the left hemisphere) is clearly responsible for most linguistic functions, some aspects of language are mediated by the right hemisphere. Initial observations of the utterances of aphasic patients with left-hemisphere lesions showed that their speech still contained emotional intonation despite lacking propositional speech. This notion that the right hemisphere is involved in some aspects of language was further investigated in patients with unilateral temporoparietal lesions of either left or right hemisphere (Heilman, Scholes, & Watson, 1975). Here the results highlighted that during speech with emotional tone only the right-hemisphere group was unable to correctly identify the emotional prosody. Other studies followed which demonstrated that patients with comprehension emotional prosody disturbances show right-hemisphere lesions involving the basal ganglia and the temporoparietal cortex (Starkstein et al., 1994). Based on these and other findings of patients with deficits in understanding or expressing prosody, Ross (1981) suggested that these deficits be called 'aprosodia'. He also proposed that the subtypes of the emotional or affective aprosodias mirror those of the aphasias. The proposed variants of aprosodia are motor, sensory, global, conduction, anomic, transcortical motor, transcortical sensory, and mixed. Baum and Pell (1999) provide a review of this complicated issue.

IS LANGUAGE INNATE OR DO WE LEARN IT?

How much of our ability to produce and understand language comes from our genetic makeup, and how much do we obtain only with environmental stimulus? Obviously language is not completely genetically acquired, as children cannot learn to speak a language without exposure. The question was the subject of a number of seminal books that Noam Chomsky published in the late 1950s (Chomsky, 1986). Chomsky postulated the idea of the language acquisition device (LAD), an innate mechanism for learning symbolic language. The LAD is an aspect of the nativist theory of language, which suggests humans are born with the instinct or 'innate facility' for language acquisition, and children who are socialised but not taught any known language will make up one of their own (Arbib, 2009). The evidence that supports the concept of acquired language is based on the fact that small children who do not use speech (for example, their parents might not be able to hear) learn to speak normally if they are taught before they become teenagers (Schiff & Ventry, 1976). If they are not taught language until after they have reached puberty, their ability to speak correctly is impaired. It can sometimes be the case that if the entire left hemisphere of an infant is taken out, all of the language functions will develop entirely within the right hemisphere, while if the left hemisphere is removed in

Table 12.1   *Phases of language development*

Age	Speech	Sound
1–4 months	Cooing	Vowel sounds
5–10 months	Babbling	Strings of consonant–vowel syllables (e.g. mama mama)
10–15 months	First words	Consistent labels for objects
18–24 months	Two-word utterances	
>25 months	Meaningful speech	Meaningful pairs of words

adulthood, then they lose all language ability for ever (de Bode & Curtiss, 2000). Ultimately, small children learn a variety of languages without any difficulties, but as they get older they experience difficulties, the key signs of which are improper pronunciation and errors in grammar (Rescorla, 2009). This evidence from the nurture standpoint suggests there is a critical period for language acquisition. Neurologically, for language acquisition the developing brain is very plastic in the early years of life and generally develops along the timeline shown in Table 12.1. Gesture may also play a role in the development of language (see Box 12.2).

BOX 12.2   Gestures and language development

Background

Gestures are generally the main form of communication before children are able to speak, with the typical child producing their first gestures between 9 and 12 months of age. The actions generally start with pointing to objects in the environment, and gesturing continues even after children start to speak and involves gesture–word combinations. This study (Iverson & Goldin-Meadow, 2005) asked whether gesturing is related to the development of language.

Methods

The study observed 10 typically developing children, five males and five females. All the children were from monolingual English-speaking families and all had middle- to upper-middle-class backgrounds. The study was a longitudinal study and children were followed between the ages of 10 and 24 months. The focus of the study was on the period between the onset of one-word speech (range 10–14 months) and the emergence of two-word combinations (range 17–23 months). The children were observed on average eight times (range 5–12). All sessions were videotaped and lasted approximately 30 minutes. Coding of the video was done by two independent coders. Two independent coders were also used to record results, and the reliability between them was assessed for 10% of the 80 sessions. Coder agreement was 93% for isolating gestures and 100% for classifying gesture-plus-word combinations.

Results

The observations showed that many of the lexical items that each child produced initially in gesture later became available to the child in verbal form. In addition, the children who were first to produce gesture-plus-word combinations were also the first to produce two-word combinations.

Interpreting the results

The study suggested that changes in gesturing not only come before language but also predict changes in language. The researchers propose that early gestures may prepare the way for future language development.

Reference

Iverson, J.M., & Goldin-Meadow, S. (2005) Gesture paves the way for language development. *Research Report: Psychological Science, 16*(5), 367–371.

SPEECH PRODUCTION

A neurologist from France, Pierre Paul Broca, is thought to be the father of brain localisation of language function (Figure 12.3). Some say Broca expanded on a theory proposed by Franz Joseph Gall, which indicated that feelings associated with faith, goodwill and lack of openness are distributed across 35 or more divisions of the cortex (Zola-Morgan, 1995). Gall referred to these as cortical 'organs' which became larger as they were used, just as muscles do when you work them, and caused bumps and ridges to develop on the skull. This was the beginning of the science known as phrenology. In contrast, Broca advocated investigating the brains of people with clinical ailments for lesions that might identify the part of the brain and the biological cause of their symptoms. This approach pioneered by Broca laid the foundations of modern neuropsychology and cognitive neuroscience.

In 1861, Broca presented the case of a man named Leborgne, who comprehended language but was unable to produce speech. There were no motor skills reasons for his lack of speech as he was able to whistle a tune, speak isolated words, and sing songs. However, every time Leborgne tried to utter a phrase he could only produce a single repetitive syllable, 'tan'. He could alter the intonation of the sound but he was unable to produce any recognisable words or phrases. Since Leborgne had no productive language, Broca recognised that the behaviour might shed light on the question of language localisation. Leborgne later died of his disorder, and at autopsy a lesion was found on the surface of the left frontal

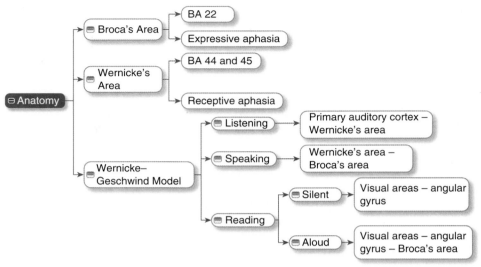

Figure 12.3   *Anatomy of language function*

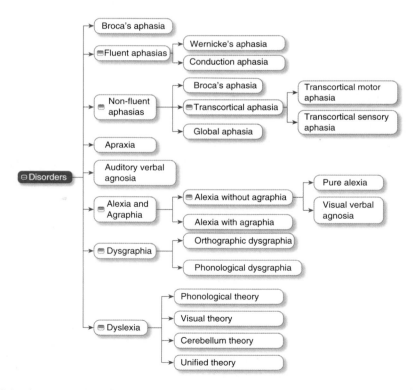

Figure 12.4   *Language disorders*

lobe (Broca, 1861). The finding was the start of the general notion that cognitive functions could be localised to specific areas of the brain. The area that was damaged in Leborgne is today known as Broca's area, and the inability to produce speech is termed Broca's aphasia.

BROCA'S APHASIA

Expressive aphasia is a non-fluent aphasia, also referred to as Broca's aphasia. It is the result of damage to anterior areas of the brain, including but not limited to the left posterior inferior frontal area (Brodmann areas 44 and 45), now called Broca's area. Broca's aphasia is the most prevalent type of non-fluent aphasia and is characterised by the inability to initiate well-articulated conversational speech, which often omits grammatical morphemes and verb tense endings (agrammatical speech). Expressive aphasia is not the same as dysarthria, where an individual cannot correctly move the muscles of the tongue and mouth to create speech.

The most common cause of Broca's aphasia is the result of a stroke in Broca's area or in the immediate location. However, expressive aphasia is also seen in people who have suffered strokes to other parts of the brain (Dronkers, Wilkins, Van Valin, Redfern, & Jaeger, 2004). Individuals who present with acute widespread lesions experience various symptoms which can be diagnosed as global aphasia. Other disturbances to the brain such as extradural haematoma, cerebral haemorrhage or tumours can cause expressive aphasia.

SPEECH COMPREHENSION

Comprehension of speech starts in the auditory system, which detects and analyses the speech sounds. Understanding a speech sound is different from perceiving a speech sound. Recognising a word requires memory for sequences of speech sounds – a task which seems to be performed by the middle and posterior portion of the superior temporal gyrus of the left hemisphere, otherwise known as Wernicke's area.

Wernicke's area took its name from a different sort of aphasia that was characterised by Carl Wernicke (1874). Broca's patient was not able to speak but was able to comprehend language, whereas a patient with Wernicke's aphasia was not able to comprehend language but was able to speak. This was because the locations of the lesions were different in Wernicke's and Broca's patients. Lesions in Wernicke's aphasia are traditionally located in the posterior section of the superior temporal gyrus (STG) in the left cerebral hemisphere. This area is neuroanatomically described as the posterior part of Brodmann area 22 (Figure 12.5).

WERNICKE'S APHASIA

As already stated, damage to the posterior portion of the left hemisphere around the superior and middle temporal gyrus and temporoparietal cortex causes a language disorder called receptive aphasia or Wernicke's aphasia. Individuals with Wernicke's aphasia can speak fluently with the usual grammar, syntax, intonation and stress; however, their language content is less meaningful. Their speech may include incorrect words, words that do not exist, or normal words randomly strung together. A person may also substitute verb tenses or have difficulty using the correct pronoun or preposition; this is called paragrammatical speech. They still have the capacity to sing songs and recite memorised words. Recovery from the disorder is sometimes possible where it is the result of a stroke, because the brain has a capacity for recovery as previous discussed; however, where the disorder is longer lasting or permanent, individuals can still communicate with gestures and facial expression.

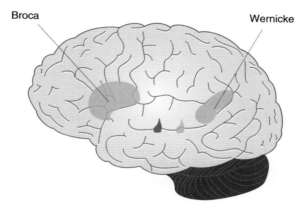

Figure 12.5 *Wernicke and Broca areas*

THE WERNICKE–GESCHWIND MODEL

Wernicke suggested that spoken words involve the separation of motor and sensory programmes, which are not situated in the same cortical areas. The motor programme, located in Broca's area anterior to the motor area, regulates the use of the mouth, tongue and vocal cords. Wernicke's area is associated with the sensory programme, which combines visual, auditory and somatic sensations.

The model that arose from this idea on how the brain produces and evaluates spoken language was first presented in the 1870s by Carl Wernicke. It was formalised and augmented 90 years later by Norman Geschwind, and is known as the Wernicke–Geschwind model. Its elements are as follows (Figure 12.6):

⚙ For listening to and understanding spoken words, the sounds of the words are transmitted through the auditory pathways to the primary auditory cortex (Heschl's gyrus) and on to Wernicke's area, where the meaning of the words is extracted.

⚙ To speak, the information about the meanings of words is transferred from Wernicke's area via the arcuate fasciculus to Broca's area, where morphemes are assembled. It is assumed that Broca's area holds a representation for articulating words. Information about speech is then sent from Broca's area to the facial area of the motor cortex, and on to the facial motor neurons in the brain stem, which transmit movement sequences to facial muscles.

⊛ To read, information about the written text is relayed from visual areas 17, 18 and 19 to the angular gyrus and on to Wernicke's area, for silent reading or, in conjunction with Broca's area, for reading out loud.

This model provides an explanation for the aphasias seen with Broca and Wernicke area lesions. Broca's patients were not able to create words because their Broca's area was impaired, which means that the articulatory phonetics related to the words they wished to pronounce were impaired or non-existent. The Wernicke's areas were unaffected, so they were still able to understand speech. Wernicke's patients do not have any trouble speaking; however, because the Wernicke area is disrupted they do not have a clear understanding when other people are speaking, and their personal speech is meaningless.

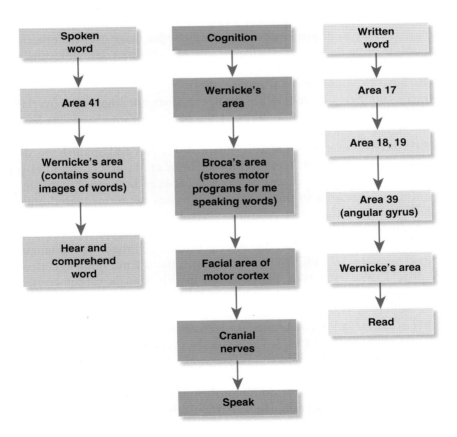

Figure 12.6   *The Wernicke–Geschwind model*

Although this model is a little dated it has been very useful in directing research into language functions. Today, the general view is that the ability to process language will most likely involve parallel processing pathways, rather than serial pathways as in the Wernicke–Geschwind model (Chater & Manning, 2006).

THE BILINGUAL BRAIN

The central issue of cerebral organisation of languages in bilingual people is essentially concerned with the question of whether two different languages are localised in the same area or in distinct areas of the brain. There have been many reports of various patterns of bilingual aphasia which has made the task of applying general rules of organisation about language areas in bilingual speakers very problematic (Aglioti, Beltramello, Girardi, & Fabbro, 1996). Most neuroimaging studies have found no laterality differences between monolingual speakers and bilingual speakers (Hernandez, Dapretto, Mazziotta, & Bookheimer, 2001). Recent evidence has suggested that first and second languages share the same brain regions, as 65% of bilingual aphasia patients showed recovery and similar improvement in both languages (Fabbro, 2001). In other words there is no evidence that brain damage is likely to disproportionately affect one language over the other language, and injury to the brain will give the same pattern of cognitive-communication problems evident in monolingual speakers. In addition bilingual speakers who have left hemisphere damage also have a risk of aphasia (Paradis, 2004).

Just because bilinguals share lateralisation, this does not suggest an overlap of languages or the sharing of the same areas of the brain. Although studies have shown overlap, the extent of the overlap is the topic of much debate. A recent MEG study has shown subtle differences in brain activations, with English and Spanish words activating different regions of the left temporal lobe (Simos et al., 2001). Another proposed factor that may influence the extent of overlap between languages is the age of language acquisition. Research in this area generally uses the terms 'early' and 'late' to describe bilingual speakers' language competency. Individuals that have acquired their languages prior to adolescence are termed early bilingual speakers. The assumption here is that early speakers will have a greater proficiency in their second language than late bilingual speakers or individuals who acquire the second language after adolescence (Ardila, 1998). However, the research in this area is rather contradictory. Although some studies have found no activation differences between languages, others have found similar activation for both languages in some areas but dissimilar activation in other areas for late second-language learners in silent sentence generation tasks (Kim, Relkin, Lee, & Hirsch, 1997). The results of this study do suggest that the age of acquisition plays a role in the pattern of intrahemispheric cerebral activation. In summary, studies over the years have concluded that bilingual speakers seem to have language lateralised within the left or dominant hemisphere, with small variations in the localisation of first or second languages, particularly if the individual is more proficient in or an early speaker of the second language.

OTHER DISORDERS OF SPEECH PRODUCTION

FLUENT APHASIAS

Conduction aphasia

An individual with conduction aphasia has difficulties with repeating orally presented information and makes mistakes during spontaneous speech, including interchanging or transposing sounds. Conduction aphasia is suspected to occur as a result of disconnection between the brain regions involved in the understanding of speech (Wernicke's area) and production of speech (Broca's area), caused by damage to the arcuate fasciculus, a deep tract of white matter. Recent work however has challenged this idea, and at present the ultimate pathophysiology of conduction aphasia remains elusive (Bernal & Ardila, 2009).

Transcortical sensory aphasia

A person with sensory transcortical aphasia has symptoms similar to those of Wernicke's aphasia along with a tendency to repeat verbal stimuli someone has just said, sometimes referred to as echolalia. Individuals with this condition can repeat words or sentences they hear others speak but they have problems in understanding what the words or sentences mean. Injury to Wernicke's language area and surrounding tissue is generally implicated in this disorder type (Kertesz, 1993).

NON-FLUENT APHASIAS

Transcortical motor aphasia

Transcortical aphasia is generally classified into transcortical motor aphasia and transcortical sensory aphasia. Transcortical motor aphasia is a non-fluent language disorder that is very similar to Broca's aphasia, where an individual cannot produce spontaneous speech. This type of aphasia is generally caused by a cardiovascular incident, otherwise known as a stroke, just in front of Broca's area.

Global aphasia

As the name suggests, an individual with global aphasia possesses all of the symptoms of Broca, conduction and Wernicke aphasias. They have poor speech comprehension and difficulty repeating or remembering words; in addition their speech is often limited to a nonsense phase they repeat in all contexts.

Global aphasia is the result of injury to the anterior language region, basal ganglia, and insula (as with Broca aphasia), posterior language region (as with Wernicke aphasia), and superior temporal gyrus (as with conduction aphasia). Global aphasia generally results from injury to Wernicke's and Broca's areas and strokes involving the internal carotid or middle cerebral arteries; however, cases of global aphasia have been reported as a result of a left thalamic haemorrhage (Ozeren, Koc, Demirkiran, Sonmezler, & Kibar, 2006).

APRAXIA OF SPEECH

Apraxia of speech is also known as dyspraxia, and is a language disorder that is the result of dysfunction of the frontal lobe area, including Broca's area. An individual with apraxia of speech has trouble saying what they want to say correctly and consistently due to weakness or paralysis of the muscles of the face, tongue and lips. Acquired apraxia of speech can affect a person at any age, whereas developmental apraxia of speech (DAS) presents in children and is present from birth. Children with DAS often have a family history of communication disorders, which highlights possible genetic factors playing a role in the disorder, as does the observation that it affects more boys than girls (Shriberg, Aram, & Kwiatkowski, 1997).

VERBAL AUDITORY AGNOSIA

Verbal auditory agnosia or pure word deafness is characterised by an inability to comprehend and repeat speech but with intact reading, writing and speaking ability. Individuals also retain the ability to identify non-verbal sounds (Shoumaker, Ajax, & Schenkenberg, 1977). The condition is very rare in its pure form, and usually develops from or in the direction of Wernicke's aphasia (Kirshner, Webb, & Duncan, 1981). It has been identified in patients with lesions deep in the left temporal lobe (Gazzaniga, Glass, Sarno, & Posner, 1973). However, most case reports point to bilateral temporal lesions occurring independently over time (Brick, Frost, Schochet, Gutman, & Crosby, 1985).

READING

As you will know from your own experience, reading is learnt over many years, starting in childhood and gradually developing into a skill that we use almost automatically, with very little conscious effort (Bashir & Hook, 2009). During reading there are many cognitive functions taking place, but initially the actual words must be processed visually. Reading causes our eyes to make a lot of rapid movements back and forth over the words; this movement is referred to as saccades (Rayner, 1998). Our eyes are not simply focused on the details of the text; rather we are applying parafoveal vision. According to studies that have tracked eye movements, it appears that we usually see about two or three words ahead when we read aloud. Therefore, our eyes scan a block of text instead of one word or one letter at a time. This is termed 'perceptual span'.

But reading is not just about seeing; we still have to link patterns on a page to meaning. It is believed that there are two separate pathways for reading. One pathway accounts for the vast majority of reading comprehension and is involved in whole word reading where we convert groups of letters into words. The second pathway comes into play whenever we encounter a rare and unfamiliar word. This kind of reading, called phonological reading, requires recognition of individual letters and knowledge of the sounds the letters make. These two different kinds of reading – whole word and phonological – seem to involve different brain areas, as individuals with phonological dyslexia can generally read by whole word methods but have difficulty sounding words out.

Evidence from imaging studies between different languages and individuals suggests that whole word and phonological reading start with activation in pathways that link the primary visual cortex to the posterior inferior temporal cortex (PITC). From there, whole word reading seems to follow the ventral or 'what' stream to the fusiform gyrus, whereas phonological reading appears to follow the dorsal or 'where' stream to the temporoparietal cortex and then on to the inferior frontal cortex around Broca's area for articulation of sounds. Once the words have been identified it is believed the pathways converge to other unknown areas involved in the syntactic structure and semantics of the words (Sakurai et al., 2001).

WRITING

Writing depends on our word knowledge and our ability to use proper grammatical structure to form sentences. Not surprisingly we see disorders of writing in individuals who have problems with spoken language, and damaged regions of the brain associated with aphasia will produce impairment in writing very similar to those seen in speech. The motor aspects of writing are controlled by the motor cortex with involvement of the dorsal parietal lobe and the premotor cortex, and there is evidence that the left superior parietal lobe is essential for writing behaviour (Menon & Desmond, 2001). As with reading, there is imaging evidence that writing involves the posterior inferior temporal cortex (PITC) (Nakamura et al., 2000). The PITC seems not to be involved in the motor aspects of writing but is concerned with the knowledge associated with irregularly spelt words. As with other aspects of language, writing seems to be organised in the speech dominated hemisphere, which in most people is the left hemisphere. The inability to spell words can also hinder writing. Individuals who are unable to spell out words phonetically as a result of damage to the superior temporal lobe have a condition termed phonological **dysgraphia**, whereas damage to the inferior parietal lobe causes orthographic dysgraphia or an impairment in whole word writing ability. In the next section we will look at the disorders associated with reading and writing.

DISORDERS OF READING AND WRITING

ALEXIA AND AGRAPHIA

Alexia and agraphia are defined as the inability to read and write respectively. They are generally associated with damage to the angular gyrus, an area of the cerebral cortex located in the posterior parietal lobe. The conditions can present in an individual on their own, together, and mixed with aphasia. Alexia without agraphia – sometimes referred to as pure alexia – is associated with disconnection of the inferior parietal lobule from visual input. Word blindness results from this disconnection from the word memory centre, and reading aloud and the understanding of written words are lost; however, individuals retain the ability to name and recognise objects (Imtiaz, Nirodi, & Khaleeli, 2001). Alexia with agraphia is generally the result of damage to the angular gyrus (Sakurai, Asami, & Mannen, 2010).

DYSGRAPHIA

Dysgraphia is characterised by writing disabilities, of which there are two subcategories. Individuals with orthographic dysgraphia have difficulties in using visually based writing; while they can spell out regular words such as 'our' that sound as they are spelt, they have difficulties spelling irregular words such as 'hour'. In contrast, individuals with phonological dysgraphia can write familiar words such as 'glasses' but have difficulty writing unfamiliar words such as 'spectacles' which require the word to be sounded out phonetically. Orthographic and phonological dysgraphia both seem to have a neurological cause. Orthographic dysgraphia results from damage to the inferior parietal lobe, while phonological dysgraphia is associated with damage to the superior temporal lobe (Benson & Geschwind, 1985).

DYSLEXIA

Dyslexia or developmental dyslexia is a condition that interferes with the ability to read. Dyslexia is traditionally defined as a discrepancy between an individual's ability to read and their overall intellectual skills even though they have been given sufficient instruction in reading, and affects 10–30% of the population. Although diagnosis is based purely on behavioural reports, it is now fairly well established that dyslexia is a neurological disorder with a genetic origin (Grigorenko, 2001). The condition has lifelong persistence and, despite research in this area, the underlying cognitive and biological causes of the reading difficulties are still an issue for debate. Although there is no definite known cause of dyslexia there are a number of theories, which are detailed below.

Phonological theory

The phonological theory suggests that individuals with dyslexia are specifically impaired when attempting to represent, store and/or retrieve word sounds. This explains the dyslexic person's impaired reading skills by relying on evidence that the ability to learn how to read the alphabet demands an understanding of grapheme–phoneme correspondence, i.e. the relationship between letters and the sounds that comprise speech. The process of learning grapheme–phoneme correspondence, which is the basis of reading for alphabetic systems, will be affected if sounds are not clearly represented, stored or recalled (Snowling, 1981). Although not everyone is in agreement as to the nature of these phonological problems, the literature seems to agree on the central and causal role phonology plays in the development of dyslexia (Tree, 2008). This theory also suggests a link between behavioural problems and cognitive deficit in a straightforward manner. Neurologically, it is commonly believed that the disorder is caused by a congenital malfunction of left-hemisphere perisylvian brain areas that are associated with orthographic and phonological representations (Beland & Mimouni, 2001).

Visual magnocellular theory

The visual theory suggests that dyslexia is a visual disorder that makes it difficult to process alphabetical letters and sentences on a page, with a central claim that the problems are strictly biological (Stein & Walsh, 1997). The anatomical and functional separation of the visual system into two separate pathways, namely the magnocellular and the parvocellular pathways, is at the foundation of theory. It is hypothesised that there is disruption in the magnocellular pathway in some dyslexic individuals, leading to deficiencies in visual processing and to abnormal binocular control (Stein & Walsh, 1997). Support for the theory comes from studies on dyslexic individuals which have demonstrated abnormalities in the magnocellular layers of the lateral geniculate nucleus (Livingstone, Rosen, Drislane, & Galaburda, 1991) and unstable binocular fixations (Stein, Riddell, & Fowler, 1987). A phonological deficiency is not ruled out with the visual theory, but greater emphasis is placed on the role of vision in a reading problem.

Cerebellar theory

The cerebellar theory of dyslexia suggests that the cerebellum of a dyslexic individual is slightly dysfunctional, resulting in several cognitive deficits (Nicolson & Fawcett, 1990; Nicolson, Fawcett, & Dean, 2001). As the cerebellum is the area of the brain responsible for motor control, and therefore speech articulation, it has been suggested that retarded or dysfunctional articulation would result in a deficit in phonological representations. In addition, the cerebellum plays a role in the automatisation of overlearned tasks, such as driving, typing and reading. The cerebellar theory is supported by observations of insufficient dyslexic performance in several automated and implicit motor tasks (Barnes, Hinkley, Masters, & Boubert, 2007; Fawcett, Nicolson, & Maclagan, 2001). Other studies have found differences in the grey matter volume of the posterior sloping portion of the monticulus of the vermis of the cerebellum, otherwise known as the cerebellar declive (Pernet, Poline, Demonet, & Rousselet, 2009).

Unified theory

The unified theory tries to combine all of the research information previously mentioned. The magnocellular theory (Stein and Walsh, 1997), which is a generalisation of the visual theory, puts forth the idea that the magnocellular dysfunction is not simply restricted to the visual pathways, but is widespread and affects all modalities. Additionally, since the cerebellum is provided with extensive information from a variety of magnocellular systems located in the brain, it is likewise assumed that it will be influenced by the basic magnocellular defect (Stein, 2001). This theory, via one singular biological irregularity, tries to account for every known symptom of dyslexia, including auditory, visual, tactile, motor and also phonological.

SUMMARY

This chapter explored the topic of language, and started with a discussion about the lateralisation of brain functions (Figure 12.7). Language functions such as grammar and vocabulary are frequently lateralised to the brain's left hemisphere, whereas prosodic language functions are frequently localised in the right hemisphere. The chapter then went on to explain that some compelling evidence relating to hemispheric specialisation comes from an experimental method called the Wada test, in which an anaesthetic is administered to a single hemisphere of the brain by way of the carotid arteries. After the hemisphere is anaesthetised, a neuropsychological examination is administered to identify dominance for producing and comprehending language. The extraordinary behaviour of people with split brains was then highlighted. These patients, after undergoing a commissurotomy, show variations of function between the two brain hemispheres. However, split-brain patients are generally able to act in a coordinated, purposeful and consistent way, regardless of their hemispheric independence. Language was then discussed in more detail, highlighting the set of structural rules that govern the composition of words and sentences in a language, or grammar. The subcategories that make up grammar are morphology, phonology, prosody and syntax. There is also involvement of the right hemisphere in language processing. Some individuals have problems using the correct stress or intonation on words in their sentences; this seems to be caused by right-hemisphere lesions involving the basal ganglia and the temporoparietal cortex. The innate and developmental aspects of language were then examined and the critical period in language acquisition was highlighted.

The chapter then moved on to discuss the localisation of language and the contribution of Paul Broca to the topic of language. Broca had a patient who could only produce a single repetitive syllable 'tan', and at autopsy a lesion was found on the surface of the left frontal lobe. The area damaged in his patient is now known as Broca's area, and the inability to produce speech is termed Broca's aphasia. A different sort of aphasia called receptive or Wernicke's aphasia was then described. In this condition a person can speak correctly but has problems understanding what is said to them. Wernicke's area is traditionally located as the posterior section of the superior temporal gyrus (STG) in the left cerebral hemisphere, and Broca's area is located in the posterior inferior frontal gyrus of the brain. The Wernicke–Geschwind model of language was illustrated, and the three routes of language processing – spoken words, listening and reading – were detailed. It was also highlighted that bilingual speakers appear to have language lateralised within the left or dominant hemisphere, with minimal differences between first- and second-language localisation, particularly if the individual is more proficient or an early speaker in the second language.

The chapter then moved on to discuss language disorders. Individuals with conduction aphasia have difficulties with repeating orally presented information and make mistakes during spontaneous speech including interchanging or transposing sounds. Transcortical motor aphasia is characterised by an inability to produce spontaneous speech, and is typically caused by a stroke just in front of Broca's area. In contrast, sensory transcortical aphasia has symptoms similar to those of Wernicke's aphasia with the tendency to repeat verbal stimuli, referred to as echolalia. Global aphasia, as the name suggests, encompasses all of the symptoms of Broca, conduction and Wernicke aphasias. Individuals with this condition

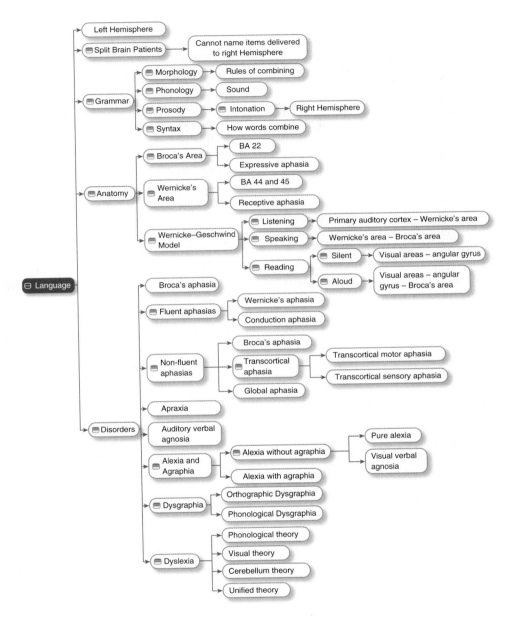

Figure 12.7 *Language overview*

have poor speech comprehension and difficulty repeating or remembering words; in addition, their speech is often limited to a nonsense phase. Apraxia or dyspraxia was then highlighted; this is a language disorder caused by a dysfunction of the frontal lobe area, including Broca's area, which is responsible for the planning and programming of speech production.

Verbal auditory agnosia or pure word deafness is characterised by an inability to comprehend and repeat speech, with an intact ability to identify non-verbal sounds as well as intact reading, writing and speaking ability. Alexia and agraphia are defined as the inability to read and write respectively; they result from damage to the angular gyrus, an area of the cerebral cortex located in the posterior parietal lobe. Dysgraphia is a disorder characterised by writing disabilities, of which there are two subcategories. Individuals with orthographic dysgraphia have difficulties in using visually based writing; by contrast, individuals with phonological dysgraphia can write familiar words but have difficulty writing unfamiliar words. Orthographic dysgraphia results from damage to the inferior parietal lobe, while phonological dysgraphia is associated with damage to the superior temporal lobe.

Finally the current theories of dyslexia were discussed. This final section first detailed the phonological theory, in which it is hypothesised that individuals with dyslexia are specifically impaired when attempting to represent, store and/or retrieve word sounds. Neurologically, it is believed that the disorder is caused by a congenital malfunction of left-hemisphere brain areas that underlie phonological representations. The visual theory of dyslexia was then highlighted, which postulates that dyslexia is a visual disorder that causes difficulty in processing alphabetical letters and sentences on a page, with a central claim that the problems are strictly biological. The cerebellar theory also makes the biological claim that the cerebellum of a dyslexic person is slightly dysfunctional, resulting in several cognitive deficits. Lastly, the magnocellular theory was detailed. This tries to unify the theories by combining all of the research findings previously mentioned and is in essence a generalisation of the visual theory, putting forth the idea that the magnocellular dysfunction is not simply restricted to the visual pathways but is generalised to all modalities.

FURTHER READING

Chomsky, N. (1986). *Knowledge of language: its nature, origin and use*. New York: Praeger.

Corballis, M.C. (2009). The evolution of language. *Annals of the New York Academy of Sciences, 1156*, 19–43.

Nicolson, R.I., Fawcett, A.J., & Dean, P. (2001). Dyslexia, development and the cerebellum. *Trends in Neurosciences, 24*(9), 515–516.

KEY QUESTIONS

1 What can split-brain patients tell us about the functional architecture of the brain?

2 Describe and evaluate the Wernicke–Geschwind model of language.

3 Describe the disorders of speech comprehension and speech expression.

13 BIOLOGICAL BASIS OF BEHAVIOUR DISORDERS

Mental and neurological disorders are caused by various factors. Different frameworks including the biological, psychological and social offer many differing explanations. Today it is generally accepted that factors in all three areas can contribute to the development of behavioural disorders. In this chapter we will look at affective and neurological disorders, which have well-defined biological components that contribute to the behavioural manifestations of the disorder. However, please bear in mind that this chapter is not a definitive guide to biological illness, nor will it detail all biological aspects of the conditions highlighted; it aims to give an insight into the biological abnormalities that have been discovered. Please remember also that there are many psychological explanations for affect disorders. Individual conflict, stress and trauma may lead to the development of depression and schizophrenia, while social explanations suggest that mental illness is caused by significant effects in the environment.

This chapter is divided into two broad areas. The first will discuss the diagnosis of affective disorders and then detail two examples of affect illness: depression and schizophrenia. The second will detail two neurological disorders: **dementia** as found in Alzheimer's disease, and movement as seen in Parkinson's disease.

DIAGNOSIS OF AFFECTIVE DISORDERS

The *Diagnostic and Statistical Manual of Mental Disorders*, 4th edition, known as the DSM-IV, is the main guide to the categorisation of psychiatric diagnoses. The manual covers all adult and child mental health disorders and is published by the American Psychiatric Association (APA). It details all the known causes of the disorders and gives a statistical breakdown in terms of age of onset, gender and prognosis; research findings on treatment are also provided.

DSM-IV assesses five dimensions:

* *Axis I: clinical syndromes.* This refers to the principal disorder that needs immediate attention (e.g. schizophrenia or depression).

* *Axis II: developmental disorders and personality disorders.* This refers to developmental disorders, e.g. autism; and personality disorders, i.e. clinical syndromes such as antisocial and borderline personality disorders.

* *Axis III: general medical conditions.* This covers any medical conditions which may affect axis I and II disorders.

* *Axis IV: severity of psychosocial stressors.* This deals with stressful events in an individual's life which may impact on the disorders listed in axes I and II.

* *Axis V: global assessment of highest level of functioning.* This supports the assessment of the functioning of the individual both at the present time and at the highest level within the previous year.

DEPRESSION

Everybody experience happiness and sadness, and usually these mood changes are part of a healthy emotional life. However, sometimes the emotional state of an individual interferes with their normal daily functioning to such an extent that they may have an affective disorder or a mood disorder. Depression is characterised by an intense and continuing feeling of sadness and worthlessness, and is a general term used to indicate the presence of the disorder; however, it is also used to refer to other forms of depressed mood (Remick, 2002; Keller, Schatzberg, & Maj, 2007). There is no definitive test for diagnosing depression; the basis of the diagnosis is the patient's self-reported experiences during clinical interviews. Physicians use rating scales and questionnaires to help evaluate the patient's symptoms and get a clear understanding of their mental status prior to formulating a diagnosis (Richter, Werner, Heerlein, Kraus, & Sauer, 1998). The most typical time for the symptoms to begin is between 20 and 30 years of age, with a later peak after 40 years of age, most especially affecting women. Depressed people have a tendency to die younger than people who are not depressed, partly because they are more vulnerable to sickness. In addition, being depressed may cause some people to kill themselves; it is estimated that 80% of all people who commit suicide suffer from a severe form of depression (Rihmer, 2001).

DSM-IV identifies 10 symptoms of depression:

* depressed mood (sadness)

* loss of energy or fatigue

* diminished ability to think or concentrate

- sleep disturbances

- weight loss

- feelings of worthlessness

- anhedonia (lack of pleasure in activities)

- suicidal thoughts

- agitation

- psychomotor retardation.

There are two types of depressive disorder: major depression and dysthymia (Figure 13.1).

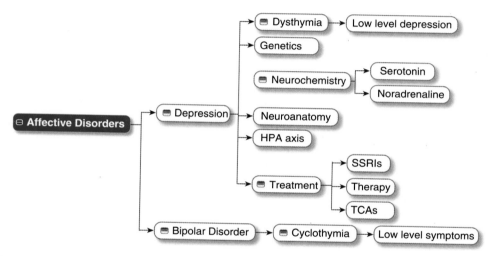

Figure 13.1   *Affective disorders*

MAJOR DEPRESSION

Major depression is characterised by a depressed mood for a duration of at least two weeks, together with other symptoms such as weight loss or weight gain, sleep disturbances, agitation or lethargy, and a feeling of hopelessness. The disorder is hard to predict and periods of depression can last from two weeks up to six months, after which normal mood and behaviour return. Individuals generally have repeated episodes of depression, with biological and psychosocial factors contributing to a higher vulnerability in women (Desai & Jann, 2000).

DYSTHYMIA

Whereas major depression has rapid onset and involves intense feeling, dysthymia is characterised by chronic low-level depression. During these times individuals can have days where they feel okay, then bad days when the feeling of depression returns. They are also less likely to seek help as they may consider the depression to be a personality trait rather than a recognised condition.

BIPOLAR DISORDERS

Individuals with bipolar disorder experience alternating episodes of mania and depression. Mania is a state of abnormally highly elevated or irritable mood, arousal, and/or energy levels. In a sense, it is the opposite of depression. The following are the DSM-IV symptoms of mania:

- inflated self-esteem or grandiosity
- decreased need for sleep
- more talkative than usual or pressure to keep talking
- flight of ideas or subjective experience that thoughts are racing
- distractibility, i.e. attention too easily drawn to unimportant or irrelevant external stimuli
- increase in goal-directed activity (at work, at school, or sexually) or psychomotor agitation
- excessive involvement in pleasurable activities that have a high potential for painful consequences (e.g. engaging in unrestrained buying sprees, sexual indiscretions, or foolish business investments).

Rather than occurring by itself, mania is usually one element of a cycle of mood swings which involves periods of elevated or irritable mood (mania) alternating with periods of depression; this condition is known as bipolar disorder.

CYCLOTHYMIA

This condition is similar to bipolar disorder, but the episodes of mania and depression are less intense. The symptoms usually appear in adolescence or early adulthood, during which a person has mood swings over a period of years that alternate from mild depression to euphoria. Symptoms of cyclothymia as described in DSM-IV include episodes of hypomania and mild depression occurring for at least two years in adults with no more than two symptom-free months in a row.

CAUSES OF DEPRESSION

Over time, our understanding of the nature and causes of depression has changed. Psychological, psychosocial, evolutionary, biological and genetic factors all may contribute to a person's acquisition of depression (Riso, Miyatake, & Thase, 2002).

GENETICS

Genetic research on depression has indicated that there exists a powerful hereditary contribution: identical twins demonstrate a concordance rate of approximately 50%, much greater than that of fraternal twins which is approximately 15% (Kringlen, 1985). Adoption studies have consistently demonstrated these numbers, regardless of whether the twins are raised together or separately. We have not isolated any one gene that causes depression; instead, it appears that several genes make someone vulnerable to the environmental factors and life events that can determine if depression will result. The genetic contribution may be greater for bipolar disorder than for depression, as relatives of individuals with bipolar disorder are more likely to show symptoms of affection disorders than relatives of individuals with major depression (Bearden, Hoffman, & Cannon, 2001); in addition, studies in the 1990s found linkages on chromosomes 18, 21q, 12q and 4p (Potash & DePaulo, 2000).

NEUROCHEMISTRY AND DEPRESSION

Disruption of the monoamine group of neurotransmitters has been linked to affective disorders. This has become known as the monoamine hypothesis of depression (Syvalahti, 1987). The two neurotransmitters which are major contributors to depression are noradrenaline (a catecholamine) and serotonin (an indoleamine). There have been reports of disrupted neurotransmitter systems in the locus coeruleus (noradrenaline) (Leonard, 1997) and 5-HT systems (Arranz, Eriksson, Mellerup, Plenge, & Marcusson, 1994). A disruption in the production and metabolism of noradrenaline, no matter the cause, will interfere with limbic and cortical functioning and arousal; it will also decrease the neuroendocrine activity, and reduce the organism's ability to defend itself against stress and adverse experiences (Brunello et al., 2003). Low levels of a serotonin metabolite (5-HIAA) have been found in individuals with major depression and recently linked to a greater suicide risk (Mann, Oquendo, Underwood, & Arango, 1999). In addition, low levels of a noradrenaline metabolite (MHPG) have been found in the cerebral spinal fluid of major depressive individuals (Maas, Dekirmenjian, & Fawcett, 1974) and patients with depression and bipolar disorder who show increases in D2 dopamine receptors will look more like they have a psychotic disorder and less like they have a mood disorder (Pearlson et al., 1995).

NEUROANATOMY OF DEPRESSION

Affective disorder can cause or be caused by modifications in the brain's functional neuroanatomy. It is believed that depression can result in structural modifications to the brain, and structural abnormalities in the brain can cause depression. Affective disorders are associated with structural changes in the brain, including reduced grey matter in the prefrontal cortex (Haldane & Frangou, 2004) as well as reduction in the hippocampus, amygdala, entorhinal cortex and thalamic nuclei. In addition, some studies have found a reduction in the grey matter ventral to the beginning of the corpus callo-sum in individuals with familial affective disorders (Drevets, Ongur, & Price, 1998). The underlying pathology in the prefrontal cortices and striatal circuits which regulate the limbic system and mediate emotional behaviour may also produce depressive symptoms (Soares & Mann, 1997).

The medial frontal, left frontal and left temporal lobes have all been implicated in depression (Werner & Covenas, 2010). Individuals with disruption to their temporal lobe and amygdala activity frequently experience depression and other psychological problems which can lead to them having frequent thoughts of suicide or self-harm (O'Brien, Holton, Hurren, Watt, & Hassanyeh, 1987). Behaviours that are more apathetic are seen in patients suffering from frontal depression (Tekin & Cummings, 2002).

Disruption of function in the left frontal lobe is associated with crying, excitability and feelings of depression. There is an increase in the activity of the right frontal lobe during episodes of negative mood, while at the same time left frontal activity declines (Bench, Frackowiak, & Dolan, 1995). Temporal lobe abnormalities are often complicated by behaviours associated with personality, emotional mood and sexual disturbances. These people may become paranoid, hysterical and depressive, or experience hyposexuality (Shukla, Srivastava, & Katiyar, 1979).

Seasonal affective disorder (SAD) is a category of depression associated with disruption to the hypothalamus and has been linked to the suprachiasmatic nucleus (SCN) (Howland, 2009). The symptoms of SAD usually recur during the winter months and continue until spring. They mimic those of dysthymia or even major depressive disorder; in addition there can be an increased risk of suicide among SAD suffers (Sher, 2002). SAD has been related to a lack of serotonin (Johansson et al., 2001). It has been suggested that individuals have a delayed and reduced response to corticotrophin releasing factor (CRF), which can be normalised by bright light treatment; this stimulates the neurons of the paraventricular nucleus of the hypothalamus which receive extensive input from the SCN (Partonen, 1995).

THE ROLE OF THE HPA SYSTEM IN DEPRESSION

The hypothalamic, pituitary gland and adrenal system (or HPA axis) is associated with the ability to adapt to new internal or external situations that are stressful; this is in contrast to hyperactivity of the adrenal gland, which is more associated with symptoms of major depression. The adrenal glands can grow during a major depressive episode and then shrink back to normal size when it passes (Rubin, Phillips, Sadow, & McCracken, 1995). This may partly be secondary to stress as well as an abnormality in the HPA feedback regulatory system.

As a reaction to fear, anger or anxiety, the hypothalamus starts to produce corticotrophin releasing factor (CRF) which triggers the adenohypophysis into secreting adrenocorticotropic hormone (ACTH), thus stimulating the adrenal cortex to secrete cortisol. It appears that these events are modulated by norepinephrine, so as the level of stress rises, noradrenaline levels decline, thus activating the HPA axis (Kathol, Jaeckle, Lopez, &

Meller, 1989). Cortisol secretion is increased which can indirectly reduce the production of noradrenaline. These substances, together with ACTH, work to maintain a feedback system. Additionally, cortisol and noradrenaline levels keep a balancing relationship with the circadian rhythm, i.e. in an oppositional manner they rise and fall throughout the day and night. In depressive individuals, it seems that there is a disruption to this entire feedback regulatory system and, consequently, to the HPA axis (Antonijevic, 2008). This causes ACTH and cortisol to be excessively secreted while noradrenaline decreases, which leads to depression. These findings resulted in the creation of the Dexamethasone suppression test, which tests for excessive amounts of cortisol in depressive individuals (Kalin, Risch, Janowsky, & Murphy, 1981).

TREATMENT OF DEPRESSION

The two main treatments for depression are talking therapies such as counselling, and antidepressant medicines. There are several different type of medication. Tricyclic antidepressants (TCAs) delay the absorption of noradrenaline and serotonin; however they are not without side effects, including weight gain and dizziness. Selective serotonin reuptake inhibitors (SSRIs) such as Prozac and Zoloft are probably the most popular of these drugs; they increase the level of serotonin in the brain (Wilson, 2007). SSRIs generally tend to cause fewer side effects. Lithium has been found to be effective in manic depressive disorder. The precise mechanism of lithium as a mood stabilising agent is currently unknown, but it is thought to decrease norepinephrine release and increase serotonin synthesis. Psychological therapies for the treatment of depression include cognitive behavioural therapy (CBT) and psychodynamic psychotherapy (Peng, Huang, Chen, & Lu, 2009).

SCHIZOPHRENIA

Schizophrenia is a psychiatric disorder in which the individual develops symptoms that lead them to misinterpret reality (Freudenreich, Holt, Cather, & Goff, 2007) (Figure 13.2). The characteristic symptoms of schizophrenia include delusions, hallucinations, and disorganised thought (Keith & Matthews, 1991). Individuals diagnosed with the condition usually experience a combination of positive symptoms (hallucinations, delusions, intrusive thoughts), negative symptoms (apathy, lack of emotion, poor social functioning), and cognitive symptoms (memory problems, attention problems).

Kurt Schneider (1957) produced one of the most significant clarifications of the clinical definition of schizophrenia. He considered specific symptoms to be especially indicative of the disorder, like certain types of auditory hallucinations, and referred to these symptoms as 'first-rank symptoms'. Schneider's theory of schizophrenia is the most widely accepted, but it does have its flaws; the first-rank symptoms are not observed in every schizophrenic, nor do they conclusively establish the disorder is present.

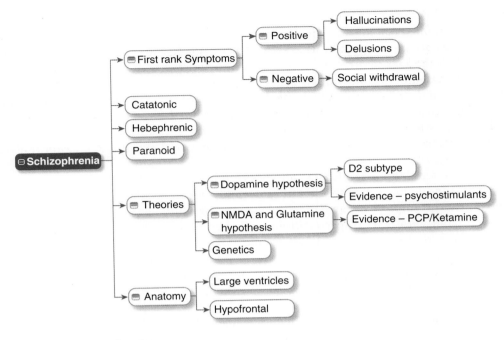

Figure 13.2   *Schizophrenia*

Schneider's first-rank schizophrenia symptoms include:

- auditory hallucinations, such as: hearing thoughts spoken aloud; hearing voices referring to himself/herself, made in the third person; or hearing a commentary
- thought withdrawal, insertion and interruption
- thought broadcasting
- somatic hallucinations
- delusional perception
- feelings or actions experienced as made or influenced by external agents.

COURSE OF SCHIZOPHRENIA

Three stages of schizophrenia are recognised:

- prodromal phase – social withdrawal
- active phase – acute symptoms
- residual phase.

Hallucinations can be defined as perceiving something that has not been caused by an external stimulus. Any of the senses can be involved in a hallucination, but in schizophrenia they are typically auditory (David, 1999). A delusion is a belief that is fiercely held despite the fact that there is no evidence to support it or there is evidence that refutes it. A number of individuals also formulate thought disorders, which show up in the form of distorted or illogical speech because there is an inability to produce and use logical, coherent language. As already stated, though this is not part of the diagnostic criteria for schizophrenia, most schizophrenics have various cognitive or intellectual problems such as deficits in working memory and executive function (Ojeda et al., 2007).

There are a number of different subtypes of schizophrenia based on the symptoms exhibited. Individuals diagnosed with paranoid schizophrenia present with prominent positive symptoms, particularly delusions or hallucinations, which often go hand in hand with fears of persecution; while people with the hebephrenic subtype, also known as disorganised schizophrenia, have a flat or incongruous affect, an absence of goal-oriented behaviour, and prominent thought disorder. Catatonic schizophrenia is diagnosed when there are ongoing observations of abnormal motor behaviour including stupor, excitement, posturing or rigidity (Schultz, North, & Shields, 2007).

The symptoms of schizophrenia usually begin in adulthood, and rarely ever occur in children. Males are at a slightly higher risk of developing this disorder (Bardenstein & McGlashan, 1990); they seem to experience the first symptoms at a younger age than females; and the symptoms appear to be more severe, with more negative symptoms, a lower chance of complete recovery, and usually a worse outcome (Jablensky, 2000). Research indicates that schizophrenia happens more frequently with people born in cities, and the bigger the city and the greater the time the individual resides there, the higher the risk (Pedersen & Mortensen, 2001). Some environmental and social factors such as loss of social support can be contributory, while schizophrenia can be disproportionally represented among ethnic minorities (Boydell et al., 2001). See Box 13.1 for further discussion of risk factors.

BOX 13.1 Risk factors of schizophrenia

There is a genetic component that predisposes an individual to schizophrenia, because although the general population has less than a 1% risk of developing the disorder, first-degree relatives of schizophrenics have around a 5% risk, and identical twins of affected individuals have a 40% risk (Tsuang, 1998) (Figure 1). Recently, gene neuregulin 1 and associated variants have been found to be linked with schizophrenia in an Icelandic sample (Stefansson et al., 2002). However, there are many candidate genes for causing schizophrenia, each of which has a minor effect and each of which is commonly found in the general population. For this reason many investigators believe that schizophrenia is polygenetic or caused by an interaction of many genes. In schizophrenia there is close to a 40% likelihood that both identical or monozygotic twins are affected; the fact that this concordance is not 100% implies that there are epigenetic changes (changes in gene function occurring without changing the DNA sequence) with possibly environmental factors involved. A recent meta-analysis of research findings suggested that schizophrenics are more likely to have complications with pregnancy and child-birth, especially premature birth, low birth weight and hypoxia (Clarke, Harley, & Cannon, 2006). Smoking cannabis has also been identified as a possible factor in pre-disposing an individual to schizophrenia, with studies estimating a twofold to fourfold increased risk of developing the disorder (Semple, McIntosh, & Lawrie, 2005).

References

Clarke, M.C., Harley, M., & Cannon, M. (2006). The role of obstetric events in schizo-phrenia. *Schizophrenia Bulletin, 32*(1), 3–8.

Semple, D.M., McIntosh, A.M., & Lawrie, S.M. (2005). Cannabis as a risk factor for psy-chosis: systematic review. *Journal of Psychopharmacology, 19*(2), 187–194.

Stefansson, H., Sigurdsson, E., Steinthorsdottir, V., Bjornsdottir, S., Sigmundsson, T., Ghosh, S., et al. (2002). Neuregulin 1 and susceptibility to schizophrenia. *American Journal of Human Genetics, 71*(4), 877–892.

Tsuang, M. T. (1998). Genetic epidemiology of schizophrenia: review and reassessment. *The Kaohsiung Journal of Medical Sciences*, 14(7), 405–412.

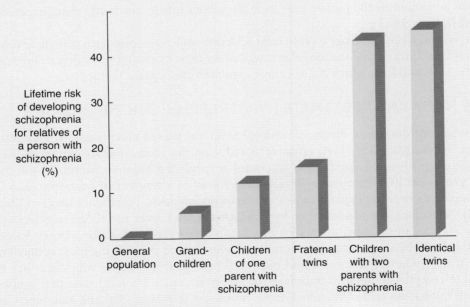

Figure 1   *Risk of developing schizophrenia*

THE DOPAMINE HYPOTHESIS OF SCHIZOPHRENIA

As detailed in Chapter 1, dopamine is classified as a catecholamine neurotransmitter and is a precursor of adrenaline and noradrenaline. The dopamine hypothesis is the most established of the schizophrenia hypotheses, and proposes that hyperactivity of dopamine transmission is responsible for the disorder (van Rossum, 1966). Most of the early evidence was based on the observation that dopamine receptors are activated by psychostimulants. Amphetamine use, which elevates the release of dopamine, can trigger delusions and auditory hallucinations in otherwise healthy individuals, while small doses of amphetamines exacerbate psychotic symptoms in schizophrenics. The D1 family and D2 family of dopamine receptors appear to be involved in schizophrenia. The D1 family contains the receptors D1 and D5. The D1 receptors in the brain are linked to cognition, memory and emotion, all of which are disturbed in schizophrenia. The D2 family contains the receptors D2, D3 and D4; since there is a higher density of D2 in the brain of schizophrenics, particularly in the mesolimbic system, blocking the action of D2 receptors is the key target for antipsychotic drugs (Kapur & Mamo, 2003). In particular the elevated rate of dopamine action in the mesolimbic system is a major factor in schizophrenia. There have been suggestions that the impaired dopamine regulation produces hyperawareness and the development of other symptoms. In this theory it is argued that dopamine is responsible for the attribution of personal importance to an event or other stimuli, making them more personally significant and attention grabbing. Consequently, the upregulation of dopamine in the brains of schizophrenics causes more meaning to be linked to unimportant thoughts or perceptions. The result might be the onset of delusional behaviour as the patient tries to make sense of their constantly changing environment (Kapur, 2003).

Some antipsychotic drugs used to treat schizophrenia have long-term complications. An example is Tardive **dyskinaesia**, characterised by motor tics and involuntary movements of the arms and legs, which can continue even after medication is stopped.

THE NMDA AND GLUTAMATE HYPOTHESIS OF SCHIZOPHRENIA

Although the dopamine theory of schizophrenia has gained much support, and antipsychotic medications have been effective at reducing the acute, positive symptoms in this condition, medications are far less successful at regulating negative symptoms and cognitive problems, like the memory impairment found in a number of schizophrenics. The glutamate theory may explain some of these inconsistencies. This theory suggests that the NMDA receptor is underactive or hypofunctioning and gives rise to the negative symptoms and cognitive impairment seen in schizophrenia (Javitt & Zukin, 1991). Evidence for this hypothesis comes from a number of sources, but perhaps the most compelling is that from studies on ketamine and phencyclidine (or PCP). These substances are both NMDA receptor antagonists and have the ability to create a clinical state that is not distinguishable from schizophrenia. The psychosis-like effects of PCP and ketamine can be successfully reduced by administering the antipsychotic drug haloperidol (Giannini, Underwood, & Condon, 2000).

BRAIN DAMAGE AND SCHIZOPHRENIA

The lateral ventricles for many individuals with schizophrenia are enlarged, which suggests less brain matter and a loss of neurons around the amygdala and hippocampal areas (Copolov & Crook, 2000). Neural structural differences have also been seen at postmortem. Individuals with schizophrenia have less dendritic mass in the prefrontal cortex and a reduced neuron count in some areas of the thalamus. Neurons in the hippocampus and connections to the prefrontal cortex are arranged in a disorganised fashion when compared to typical individuals. This disorganisation could be as a result of a failure of normal neural development, through either an abnormal neural migration pattern or an alteration of the pattern at the programmed cell death stage of development (Jones, 1995). Brain imaging has revealed neural tissue loss around the frontal and anterior lobes and in the hypothalamus of schizophrenics (Bogerts et al., 1992) and a decreased metabolic activity in the frontal areas of the brain in a condition called hypofrontality, which can be present before the actual symptoms of schizophrenia have arisen (Whalley et al., 2008). The hypofrontal theory may account for the negative symptoms seen in schizophrenia, as lesions to the prefrontal area leave individuals socially withdrawn and cognitively impaired (Wolkin, Sanfilipo, Wolf, Angrist, Brodie, & Rotrosen, 1992).

NEUROLOGICAL DISORDERS

When an individual is suspected of having a neurological disorder, clinicians carry out a physical examination on the nervous system. The procedure is called a neurological examination, and it evaluates all aspects of the nervous system function including mental status, cranial nerves, motor and sensory nerves, reflexes, coordination, balance and walking (gait). More emphasis is given to some tests depending on the symptoms the patient presents with.

THE NEUROLOGICAL EXAMINATION

The neurological exam is generally divided into seven areas and is performed in a planned, stepwise manner:

1   general appearance, including posture, motor activity and vital signs

2   mini mental status exam, including speech observation

3   cranial nerves I to XII

4   motor system, including muscle atrophy, tone and power

5   sensory system, including vibration, position, pinprick, temperature, light touch and higher sensory functions

6   reflexes, including deep tendon reflexes

7   coordination and gait.

DEMENTIA: ALZHEIMER'S DISEASE

Alzheimer's disease (AD) is the most common cause of dementia in the elderly, accounting for between 60% and 80% of cases (Figure 13.3). The rate rises with age: it is present in 5–10% of the population over the age of 65, and around 42% of the population over 85. AD initially presents with an individual having mild memory lapses; it progresses with neuronal death in various areas of the brain and ultimately leads to dementia. Symptoms include the three As:

⊛ aphasia – language impairment

⊛ apraxia – motor impairment

⊛ agnosia – loss of ability to recognise objects.

Other neurological and personality issues are often apparent in those with AD, including impaired motor coordination and personality change. The *Diagnostic and Statistical Manual of Mental Disorders* (DSM-IV) defines three progressive stages or categories of Alzheimer's disease: (1) suspected Alzheimer's disease, (2) probable Alzheimer's disease, and (3) definite Alzheimer's disease.

A definite diagnosis of Alzheimer's disease can only be done at post-mortem, where morphological pathological inclusions must be seen in the CNS of an individual. The histopathology consists of three main features: (1) neurofibrillary tangles, which are bundles of intraneuronal cytoskeletal filaments; (2) plaques, which are extracellular deposits of an abnormal amyloid protein; and (3) loss of neurons in various areas of the brain. Neurofibrillary tangles are fibre masses in neuron cell bodies consisting of many pairs of helical filaments (PHFs). One theory regarding PHFs is that they are hyperphosphorylated

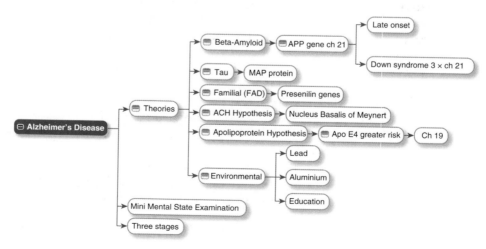

Figure 13.3 *Alzheimer's disease*

microtubule associated protein (MAP) called tau protein. Plaques are the classic sign of AD; they are composed of a core of amyloid-beta protein, are found mostly in grey matter and are thought to be the leftovers of degenerated axon terminals.

CLASSIFICATION OF ALZHEIMER'S DISEASE

Alzheimer's disease is classified as either familial or sporadic in nature. Familial Alzheimer's disease (FAD) or early-onset familial Alzheimer's disease (EOFAD) is an uncommon form of AD which usually begins before the age of 65. It is inherited in an autosomal dominant fashion and appears to involve the presenilin and APP genes. Sporadic Alzheimer's disease usually occurs later in life and appears to be related to the APOE gene found on chromosome 19. The genetic risk for developing Alzheimer's disease is addressed later in this chapter.

ASSESSMENT OF ALZHEIMER'S DISEASE

AD can often be diagnosed through a history and physical exam, including a neurological examination, and administration of the mini mental state examination (MMSE) or Folstein test, which comprises a brief 30-point questionnaire used to screen for cognitive impairment. The test consists of simple questions in a number of areas including arithmetic problems, language use and comprehension, and basic motor skills. The test is scored out of 30 points; a score below 9 points is regarded as severe dementia, between 10 and 20 points as moderate dementia, and between 21 and 24 points as mild dementia (Mungas, 1991).

The Global Deterioration Scale (GDS) is another assessment scale which provides caregivers with an overview of the stages of cognitive function for dementia such as Alzheimer's disease. It is broken down into seven different stages: stages 1–4 are the pre-dementia stages, and stages 5–7 are the dementia stages, where an individual can no longer survive without assistance. The stages are as follows:

1 no impairment

2 mild forgetfulness

3 mild cognitive decline; earliest clear-cut deficits

4 moderate cognitive decline; clear-cut deficits apparent in careful clinical interview

5 moderately severe cognitive decline; patient needs assistance with daily tasks

6 severe cognitive decline; may occasionally forget the name of the spouse upon whom they are entirely dependent for survival

7 very severe cognitive decline; severe loss of motor control; verbal speech lost.

See Box 13.2 for some details of the treatment of Alzheimer's disease.

ESSENTIAL BIOLOGICAL PSYCHOLOGY

BOX 13.2   Treatment of Alzheimer's disease

Although there is no cure for Alzheimer's disease, a variety of drugs is available which help to control the positive symptoms that may occur such as hallucination and thought disorder.

Cholinesterase inhibitors, which manage the symptoms of dementia, are currently used to treat AD. The disease is associated with low levels of acetylcholine. Cholinesterase inhibitors slow down the breakdown of this neurotransmitter so that more is available for use in the nervous system, thus helping to slow down the cognitive impairment.

The four cholinesterase inhibitors approved by the US Food and Drug Administration are: Razadyne® (galantamine), Exelon® (rivastigmine), Aricept® (donepezil) and Cognex® (tacrine).

Namenda®

Namenda® (memantine) is used to treat the symptoms of moderate to severe Alzheimer's disease and is the first class of drug which acts on the glutamate system of the brain. It has been hypothesised that a dysfunctional glutamate neurotransmission system is associated with AD, whereby excessive amounts cause neuronal excitotoxicity and cell death. Administration of the drug seems to protect neurons from the excessive amounts of glutamate which when attached to an NMDA receptor allow the free flow of calcium. Namenda seems to put a stop to this sequence by adjusting the activity of glutamate. The most common side effects of Namenda include dizziness, confusion, headache and constipation.

NEUROTRANSMITTERS AND ACH HYPOTHESIS

The sequence of biochemical decline in Alzheimer's disease has shown an association with deterioration in the following neurotransmitter systems:

- acetylcholine (ACh)
- noradrenaline
- serotonin.

The most studied neurotransmitter is acetylcholine. Cholinergic neurons originate in the basal forebrain in a structure called the nucleus basalis of Meynert and project to the neocortex and hippocampus (Chozick, 1987). The degeneration of this group of neurons significantly decreases the levels of acetylcholine and associated enzymes. Impaired cholinergic system and the administration of cholinergic antagonists in experimental animals produce memory deficits, giving support to the link between memory and acetylcholine and the ACh hypothesis of AD (Levin, 1988).

APP AND AMYLOID-BETA HYPOTHESIS

The fact that there are amyloid deposits in AD suggests that the gene encoding amyloid precursor protein (APP) may be involved. The gene for APP is located on chromosome 21, which as we saw earlier causes Down syndrome. Not only does Down syndrome occur when there is an extra copy of chromosome 21, but individuals with Down syndrome develop clinical and neuropathologic features similar to those of AD but with a much earlier onset (at about age 30 in most cases) (Isacson, Seo, Lin, Albeck, & Granholm, 2002).

The genetic mutation for APP is a 39–43 amino acid fragment which forms the core of the amyloid plaques in AD and is the prime candidate as a main cause of Alzheimer's disease (Gerlai, 2001). The abnormal cleavage of APP results in a product called amyloid-beta peptide (or β-A4), and it is the accumulation of β-A4 that seems to be critical for the pathogenesis of AD (Zhang, Thompson, Zhang, & Xu, 2011), although the density of the β-A4 plaques correlates poorly with the severity of the dementia and is more associated with the density of neurofibrillary tangles.

We do not know the mechanism by which amyloid-beta is toxic to cells. One idea is that it stimulates increased calcium influx, which can then lead to the hyperphosphorylation of proteins such as tau protein. In addition to this, current research shows that amyloid-beta can enhance free radical formations that may destroy neurons.

TAU HYPOTHESIS

The tau hypothesis suggests that irregular processing of the protein tau (hyperphosphorylation) could also be a vital part of AD pathology (Trojanowski & Lee, 2002). Tau is a microtubule associated protein (MAP) and works in the axons of neurons to control the growth and construction of microtubules. In a typical central nervous system, MAPs, with the exception of tau, are responsible for controlling the activity of microtubules in dendrites and the cell soma. Tau seems to be distributed differently in the degenerating neurons of Alzheimer's disease than in the normal ageing process, suggesting it may be one of the key piece of the pathology of AD. This hyperphosphorylation of tau forms neurofibrillary tangles (NFTs) which are interneuronal and disrupt normal cell communication. One finding that links the amyloid-beta and tau hypotheses is that tau's hyperphosphorylation may be induced by the amyloid-beta (Takashima, 2009). As previously stated, the degree of dementia in AD is correlated with the density of neurofibrillary tangles.

PRESENILINS

Alzheimer's disease can also be inherited in an autosomal dominant pattern in a tiny fraction (<1%) of patients. The cause of specific forms of familial AD (FAD) has been linked to the mutations that happen between two genes, presenilin-2 (PS2) located on chromosome 1 and presenilin-1 (PS1) located on chromosome 14. Over 40 different PS1 mutations plus two PS2 mutations have been identified in FAD, and these mutations account for nearly half of all early-onset FAD (Cruts & Van Broeckhoven, 1998). One possible altered function of mutated presenilin genes is that they aid in the different processing of APP to form abnormal amyloid-beta. Recent studies have revealed that forebrain-specific conditional knockouts of PS1 and PS2 genes cause both neuronal degeneration and memory loss without evidence of formation of amyloid plaques (Elder, Gama Sosa, De Gasperi, Dickstein, & Hof, 2010).

APOLIPOPROTEIN E HYPOTHESIS

There are three different variations or alleles of apolipoprotein E: E2, E3 and E4. Each of these variants has different abilities to perform neuronal maintenance and repair functions in the CNS and seems to differentially affect the risk of developing neurodegenerative disorders (Iurescia, Fioretti, Mangialasche, & Rinaldi, 2010). Studies have shown that ApoE4 impacts on amyloid-beta production, mitochondrial functions and tangle formation, leading to neuronal damage. The frequency of occurrence of these alleles varies in the population: around 75% possess E3, and around 15% possess E4. However, the frequency of allele E4 is much larger in late-onset familial AD patients, around 50%, indicating it to be a risk factor for late-onset AD. This translates into individuals who are homozygous for E4 being about eight times more likely to develop AD compared to individuals homozygous for E3, and around 90% of individuals with two copies of E4 develop AD by the age of 80.

MOVEMENT DISORDER: PARKINSON'S DISEASE

Parkinson's disease is a degenerative disease affecting the central nervous system, resulting in impaired motor skills, cognitive processes and other functions (Figure 13.4). The motor symptoms are the most apparent, including tremor, rigidity, slow movement and balance problems (Santens, Boon, Van Roost, & Caemaert, 2003). The non-motor symptoms include autonomic dysfunction, sensory problems, insomnia and in some cases visual hallucinations (Barnes & David, 2001). When the disease becomes more advanced, cognitive and neurobehavioural difficulties and dementia can also be present. We also refer to Parkinson's disease as 'primary parkinsonism' or 'idiopathic Parkinson's disease' (which means there is no known cause), although some Parkinson's cases are genetically based.

A number of risk and protective factors are associated with PD: for example, there may be an elevated risk of PD in people who have had exposure to pesticides (Berry, La Vecchia, & Nicotera, 2010) and a decreased risk for those who smoke (Shahi & Moochhala, 1991). The neurological basis of PD results from the decreased formation and action of dopamine created in the dopaminergic neurons of the substantia nigra. The pathology of the disease is typified by the collection of Lewy bodies, alpha-synuclein protein forming inclusions, and as with AD a formal diagnosis of PD can only be done at post-mortem.

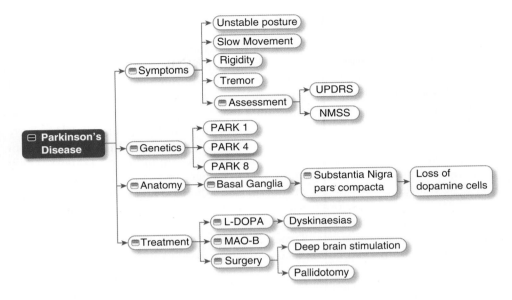

Figure 13.4   *Parkinson's disease*

SIGNS AND SYMPTOMS

It is estimated that by the time of diagnosis at least 60% of dopamine neurons in the sub-stantia nigra have already been lost. Although the main symptom of Parkinson's disease is disruption of the motor system, several studies have identified non-motor symptoms that occur prior to the development of motor symptoms in a large number of patients with PD (Table 13.1) (Tolosa, Gaig, Santamaria, & Compta, 2009).

Table 13.1   *Symptoms of Parkinson's disease*

Strong association with development of PD	Possible association with development of PD
Olfactory dysfunction	Anxiety
Constipation	Apathy
Depression	Excessive daytime sleepiness
REM sleep behaviour disorder	Fatigue
	Midlife obesity
	Orthostatic hypotension
	Pain
	Restless leg syndrome
	Sexual dysfunction
	Urinary dysfunction

ASSESSMENT OF PARKINSON'S DISEASE

There are four cardinal motor symptoms in Parkinson's disease: tremor, rigidity, slow movement and unstable posture. Tremor is the most observable and best-known symptom of PD. Typically it is a resting tremor which is at its most prominent when the limb is resting, and subsides when there is voluntary movement or sleep. Symptoms have a more significant effect on the distal part of the limb; the signs of PD usually begin in only one arm or leg, and symptoms become bilateral after a period. Bradykinaesia (slow movement) is the most significant clinical symptom of PD, and is related to problems of planning, initiating and producing movement (Yanagisawa, Fujimoto, & Tamaru, 1989). Postural instability usually occurs later, leading to balance problems and falls.

A large percentage of individuals with Parkinson's disease will experience some cognitive impairment as the disease progresses. The most commonly reported cognitive deficits in non-demented individuals are associated with executive function, sometimes in conjunction with visual hallucinations (Barnes & Boubert, 2008). Other cognitive problems include inconsistent attention and reduced cognitive speed as well as difficulty in visuospatial skills (Park & Stacy, 2009).

An individual who has Parkinson's disease has six times the risk of developing dementia, with approximately 30% of all individuals with PD developing the condition (Aarsland, Zaccai, & Brayne, 2005). Other symptoms are disorders of affect including depressed mood, apathy and anxiety; impulse control problems like cravings, binge eating, hypersexuality and compulsive gambling; with psychosis sometimes appearing in the later stages of the disease, the hallmark symptoms of which are hallucinations and delusions. PD can also harm additional body functions. Sleep disturbance is a main characteristic of PD, with symptoms such as sleeping during the day, REM sleep disturbances, or inability to sleep (Barnes, Connelly, Wiggs, Boubert, & Maravic, 2010).

Assessment scales

The most frequently used assessment of PD symptoms is the Unified Parkinson's Disease Rating Scale or UPDRS scale, which is usually completed by the patient or caregiver (Fahn & Elton, 1987). The original UPDRS is composed of four sections: (1) mentation, behaviour, and mood; (2) activities of daily living; (3) real-time assessment of motor features; and (4) complications of therapy. The UPDRS was updated in 2008 to include a more detailed assessment of non-motor symptoms. A more detailed evaluation of non-motor symptoms can be achieved by use of the 30-item Non-Motor Symptom Scale (NMSS) (Chaudhuri et al., 2007). The NMSS focuses on cardiovascular symptoms, sleep/fatigue, mood/cognition, perceptual problems, attention/memory, gastrointestinal, urinary and sexual function, weight, olfaction, unexplained pain, and sweating.

CAUSES OF PARKINSON'S DISEASE

As previously mentioned, most cases of Parkinson's disease are of unknown cause and commonly called idiopathic Parkinson's disease. However, there is increasing evidence that there are genetic risk factors associated with common forms of PD, with certain rare monogenic forms representing around 5–10% of PD patients (Belin & Westerlund, 2008).

Multiple genes related to the development of PD have been identified, including the genes related to the mutations or duplications of α-synuclein, PARK1 and PARK4 autosomal dominant genes (Gasser, 2007). These genes are particularly interesting, as Lewy bodies, one of the hallmark pathological features of PD, are largely composed of the α-synuclein protein (Gasser, 2009). The leucine-rich repeat kinase 2 (LRRK2) gene (PARK8) is also an autosomal dominant gene and to date accounts for the largest proportion of patients with PD, which includes both familial and sporadic cases. LRRK2 is the most commonly observed cause of familial and sporadic Parkinson's. We see mutations in this gene in as many as 10% of the individuals who have a genetic history of PD and 3% of sporadic cases (Gasser, 2009). Finally, the Parkin gene (PARK2) is autosomal recessive and the most common mutation related to young-onset PD (Lucking et al., 2000).

NEURAL STRUCTURES INVOLVED IN PARKINSON'S DISEASE

As already mentioned, the basal ganglia and the brain structures that the dopaminergic system innervates are the most profoundly affected parts of the brain in people with Parkinson's disease (Gibb, 1992). The main Parkinsonian symptoms are caused by a drastic reduction in the activity of the dopamine releasing cells because of cell death in the pars compacta area of the substantia nigra. In the region of 60–80% of dopaminergic neurons are destroyed before the motor signs of Parkinson disease present for the first time. Other neural pathology associated with PD is the progressive accumulation of Lewy bodies in the substantia nigra and a number of other brain areas such as the cortex, the nucleus basalis, the locus coeruleus, and the intermediolateral column of the spinal cord (Tsuboi, Uchikado, & Dickson, 2007).

MOTOR CIRCUIT IN PARKINSON'S DISEASE

The cortical output necessary for normal movement is modulated by the basal ganglia. It does this by processing the signals originating from cortex through the basal-ganglia/thalamocortical motor circuit and then returning them to the same area via a feedback pathway. Output signals from the motor circuit which are inhibitory are sent through the internal segment of the globus pallidus (GPi) and the substantia nigra pars reticulata (SNr) and on to the thalamocortical pathway where they suppress movement. These output signals constitute the direct pathway, while the indirect inhibitory pathway connections link the striatum and the external segment of the globus pallidus (GPe) and the subthalamic nucleus (STN). The excitatory influence on the GPi and SNr comes from the subthalamic nucleus, and the inhibitory input to the ventral lateral (VL) originates from the GPi and SNr.

The direct pathway with projections to the GPi/SNr consists of striatal neurons containing D1 receptors, whereas the indirect pathway that projects to the GPe contains striatal neurons containing D2 (Figure 13.5). When dopamine is released from nigrostriatal compacta (SNc) neurons it triggers the direct pathway and inhibits the indirect pathway. In Parkinson's disease, a decrease in striatal dopamine causes an increase in inhibitory

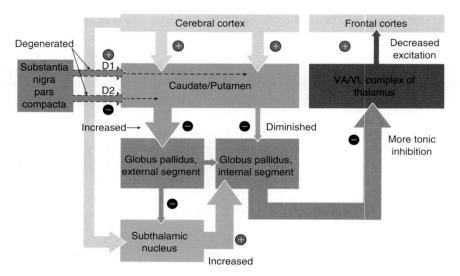

Figure 13.5   *Neural circuits in Parkinson's disease*

output from the GPi/SNr, which in turn leads to increased inhibition of the thalamocortical pathway that suppresses movement. The decrease of stimulation by striatal dopamine in the direct pathway leads to reduced inhibitory control of the GPi/SNr, and in the indirect pathway this decreased dopamine causes increased inhibition of the GPe. The inhibition of the GPe results in the disinhibition of the STN which in turn increases inhibitory output to the thalamus from the GPi/SNr.

MANAGEMENT OF PARKINSON'S DISEASE

Currently, Parkinson's disease is incurable, but drug therapies and surgery help to alleviate its symptoms. The classes of medications that most effectively treat motor symptoms are levodopa (L-DOPA), dopamine agonists, and MAOB (monoamine oxidase) inhibitors (Quinn, 1995). The type of treatment used is dependent on the stage of the disease. In the initial stage an individual has a disability that requires medication, and in the second stage the individual develops complications associated with using levodopa (Chase, Engber, & Mouradian, 1993). Dyskinaesias are involuntary movements similar to tics which are a complication of long-term L-DOPA treatment. To defer the onset of dyskinaesias L-DOPA may be postponed by prescribing other drugs like MAOB inhibitors and dopamine agonists. When drug therapies are not sufficient to regulate the symptoms, surgery and deep brain stimulation (DBS) may be prescribed (Hilker, Antonini, & Odin, 2010). DBS is currently the most widely utilised surgical treatment: a brain pacemaker is surgically implanted which emits electrical impulses to different parts of the brain. DBS or surgical lesions target the thalamus, the globus pallidus (a procedure is called a pallidotomy), or the subthalamic nucleus (Tsubokawa & Katatama, 1999).

SUMMARY

This chapter gave a brief insight into behavioural disorders. Affective disorders were discussed, particularly depression, a mood disorder with many classifications such as clinical depression, major depression, unipolar depression and unipolar disorder. The characteristic symptoms of major depressive disorder include depressed mood, poor self-esteem and anhedonia. Dysthymia is characterised by a chronic low-level depression. It was explained that individuals with bipolar disorder experience alternating episodes of mania and depression; cyclothymia is a condition similar to bipolar disorder, but the episodes of mania and depression are less intense. The genetics of affective disorders was explained, highlighting that the genetic contribution may be greater for bipolar disorder than for depression, as relatives of individuals with bipolar disorder are more likely to show symptoms of affective disorders than the relative of individuals with major depression. The two neurotransmitters which are major contributors in depression are noradrenaline and serotonin; it is believed that depression can result in structural modifications to the brain, and conversely that structural abnormalities in the brain can cause depression. The chapter then briefly explained the role of the hypothalamus, pituitary gland and adrenal gland in depression and abnormalities in the HPA regulatory system.

It was then explained that schizophrenia is a psychiatric disorder characterised by symptoms of delusions, hallucinations and disorganised thought (Keith & Matthews, 1991). Individuals diagnosed with schizophrenia usually experience a combination of positive, negative and cognitive problems. The dopamine hypothesis is the most established of the schizophrenia hypotheses, and proposes that hyperactivity of dopamine transmission is responsible for the disorder. This was based on the early observations that dopamine receptors are activated by psychostimulants. Other theories were discussed such as the NMDA and glutamate hypothesis of schizophrenia. Risk factors were discussed, and it was detailed that there is a genetic component that predisposes an individual to schizophrenia; although the general population has less than a 1% risk of developing the disorder, first-degree relatives of schizophrenics have around a 5% risk, and identical twins of affected individuals have a 40% risk. Anatomically, the lateral ventricles for many individuals with schizophrenia are enlarged, which suggests less brain matter and a loss of neurons around the areas of the amygdala and hippocampus.

The chapter then detailed Alzheimer's disease, which is the most common neurodegenerative disorder and is characterised by the presence of plaques and tangles in the brain. In order to diagnose Alzheimer's disease, these pathological inclusions must be present in the individual's CNS. AD can often be diagnosed through a history and physical exam, including a neurological examination, and administration of the mini mental state examination (MMSE). Alzheimer's disease is classified as either familial or sporadic in nature: the former includes familial Alzheimer's disease (FAD) and early-onset familial Alzheimer's disease (EOFAD). Sporadic Alzheimer's disease usually occurs later in life. Anatomically, there appears to be disruption of the cholinergic neurons originally in the basal forebrain in a structure called the nucleus basalis of Meynert. The amyloid-beta and tau hypotheses of Alzheimer's disease were then discussed. Genetically the best-known risk marker for

AD is inheriting the e4 allele of the ApoE on chromosome 19. In addition there is a great deal of evidence supporting the role of amyloid-beta and APP on chromosome 21.

The final disorder discussed in this chapter was Parkinson's disease, which is a degenerative disease affecting the central nervous system, resulting in impaired motor skills, cognitive processes and other functions The motor symptoms are the most apparent, including tremor, rigidity, slow movement and balance problems. The symptoms of PD develop when there is decreased formation and action of dopamine created in the dopaminergic neurons of the substantia nigra. The pathology of the disease is typified by the collection of Lewy bodies, alpha-synuclein protein forming inclusions. The most frequently used assessment of PD symptoms is the UPDRS. Genetically there are multiple genes related to the development of PD, including mutations or duplications of α-synuclein, PARK1 and PARK4 and the leucine-rich repeat kinase 2 (LRRK2) gene (PARK8). Areas that are affected in PD are the basal ganglia motor circuits which modulate the cortical output necessary for normal movement. Signals originating from the cortex are processed through the basal-ganglia/thalamocortical motor circuit and are returned to the same area via a feedback pathway. Finally, it was explained that Parkinson's disease is incurable, but drug therapies and surgery help to alleviate its symptoms. The classes of medications that most effectively treat motor symptoms are L-DOPA, dopamine agonists and MAOB inhibitors.

FURTHER READING

Isacson, O., Seo, H., Lin, L., Albeck, D., & Granholm, A.C. (2002). Alzheimer's disease and Down's syndrome: roles of APP, trophic factors and ACh. *Trends in Neuroscience*, 25(2), 79–84.

Lux, V., Aggen, S.H., & Kendler, K.S. (2010). The DSM-IV definition of severity of major depression: inter-relationship and validity. *Psychological Medicine*, 40(10), 1691–1701.

Schultz, S.H., North, S.W., & Shields, C.G. (2007). Schizophrenia: a review. *American Family Physician*, 75(12), 1821–1829.

KEY QUESTIONS

1   Describe the main symptoms of depression.

2   Detail the main theories as to the cause of Alzheimer's disease.

3   What do we know about the causes of Parkinson's disease?

GLOSSARY

Absolute refractory period   Time after an action potential during which the membrane cannot initiate another spike no matter how strong the stimulus.

Accommodation   Adjustment of the eye for near vision by contraction of ciliary muscle.

Acetylcholine   A neurotransmitter substance at many peripheral nervous system synapses and perhaps some central synapses.

Acetylcholinesterase   An enzyme present in nervous tissue and muscle that degrades (through its hydrolytic activity) the neurotransmitter acetylcholine into choline and acetic acid.

Actin   A protein of the thin myofilament localised to the I band of the sarcomere.

Action potential   The all-or-none conducted voltage response of a nerve or muscle membrane that is used to communicate information from one cell to another.

Adaptation   Decline in response of a sensory neuron to a maintained stimulus.

Adipsia   Absence of drinking or abnormal avoidance of drinking.

Afferent   Pathways leading to; in the case of peripheral nerves, those conducting to the central nervous system.

A fibre   A myelinated nerve fibre with conduction velocity in the range 1–120 m/s.

Agnosia   Loss of the power to recognise the import of sensory stimuli.

Agonist   Drugs that facilitate the effects of a particular neurotransmitter.

Akinaesia   Absence of movement.

Alexia   Inability to read.

All-or-nothing principle   Independence of action potential amplitude from stimulus strength.

Alpha motor neuron   A motor neuron whose axon is an A fibre

Alpha waves   EEG records characterised by high-voltage waves occurring at 8–14 per second.

Amino acids   The chemical elements from which proteins are synthesised.

Amnesia   Inability to remember past events; defect in formation of new long-term memories.

Annulospiral ending   The termination of a group Ia afferent fibre in the equatorial region of a muscle spindle.

Anorexia   Lack or loss of the appetite for food.

Antagonist   Drugs that inhibit the effects of a particular neurotransmitter.

Antagonist muscle   A muscle that acts in opposition to another at a joint.

Anterior   Towards the front of the head.

Antibodies   Proteins that bind specifically to antigens on invading a microorganism and promote its destruction.

Antigens   Proteins on the surface of cells that identify them as foreign or native.

Aphagia   Abstention from eating.

Aphasia   Impairment of communication by language in any form; expressive aphasia is an inability to speak or write; receptive aphasia is an inability to understand spoken or written language.

Apraxia   Inability to carry out motor acts on command in the absence of paralysis.

Ataxia   Loss of motor coordination.

Audition   The act of hearing or ability to hear.

Autonomic nervous system   The division of the nervous system that regulates the body's inner environment – the activity of cardiac muscle, smooth muscle and glands.

Axon   The straight, relatively unbranched process of a nerve cell or the efferent process of a nerve cell.

Axon hillock   The place where the axon arises from the soma of a neuron; thought to be the site of initiation of the spike.

Baroreceptors   Blood pressure receptors.

Beta waves   EEG records characterised by low-voltage waves occurring at 14–50 per second.

Bipolar   Having two poles; with respect to electrophysiology, stimulating or recording through two electrodes; cf. *Monopolar*.

Bradykinaesia   Slowness of movement.

Brain stem   The part of the brain which regulates reflex activities.

Broca's area   Areas 44 and 45 of the frontal cerebral cortex that plays a fundamental role in production of speech.

Cardiac muscle   Striated muscle found in the heart.

Cerebrum   The cerebral hemispheres.

C fibre   Unmyelinated primary afferent neurons.

Channel   A passage in the membrane through which ions can flow.

Cholinergic synapse   A junction between two cells that employs acetylcholine as its transmitter substance.

Chordates Animals with dorsal nerve cords.

Chromosomes Genetic structure in the cell nucleus, with each chromosome being a DNA molecule.

Circadian rhythms Diurnal (daily) cycles of the body functions.

Collateral sprouting The growth of axon branches to postsynaptic locations abandoned by adjacent axons that have degenerated.

Colour opponent cells Visual neurons in which one part of the receptive field is sensitive to light in one part of the visible spectrum (e.g. green light) while another part of the field (e.g. the surround) is sensitive to another part of the spectrum (e.g. red light).

Complex cells Neurons in visual cortex that are sensitive to bars of light moving in particular directions across the retina.

Conduction deafness Hearing loss due to impairment of movement of the tympanum, the ossicles, or the membrane of the oval window.

Cones Visual receptors in the retina specialised for colour vision in good lighting.

Consolidation The process by which a memory is transferred from short-term storage to long-term storage.

Contralateral On the opposite side.

Crossing over The exchange of sections between pairs of chromosomes during the first stage of meiosis.

Cyclic AMP Cyclic adenosine monophosphate, a second messenger system.

Decussate To cross over to the other side of the brain.

Delta waves EEG records characterised by high-voltage waves occurring at less than 4 Hz.

Dementia Loss of intellectual function.

Dendrite The branched projection of a neuron.

Denervation supersensitivity Elevated response of a nerve or muscle membrane receptor to a transmitter substance following disruption or removal of its afferent nerve supply.

Deoxyribonucleic acid (DNA) Double-stranded, coiled molecules of genetic material; chromosomes.

Depolarisation A change in a cell's membrane potential, making it more positive or less negative.

Dermatome The area of skin innervated by a dorsal root.

Diffusion The process of becoming widely distributed that occurs because of molecular concentration differences only.

Dominant hemisphere The cerebral hemisphere that contains the speech centres – generally the left hemisphere.

Dorsal   Toward the top of the head.

Dorsal horns   The two dorsal arms of the spinal grey matter.

Dream sleep   A stage of sleep characterised by desynchronised EEG patterns, REM and dreaming. Also known as paradoxical sleep or *REM sleep*.

Dysgraphia   Inability to write correctly.

Dyskinaesia   Impairment of the ability to move, resulting in fragmentary or incomplete movements.

Efferent   Pathways leading from; in the case of peripheral nerves, those conducting away from the central nervous system.

Electrical synapse   The junction between two nerve cells at which communication is by direct transfer of charge, not by release of a transmitter substance.

Electroencephalogram (EEG)   A recording from the scalp of the changes in electrical potential in the brain, primarily in the cerebral cortex.

Electromyogram (EMG)   A recording of the electrical activity of muscle during contraction.

Epilepsy   A neurological disorder characterised by spontaneously recurring seizures.

Evoked potential   An electrical response of a group of neurons produced by a stimulus to a sensory receptor or neural pathway.

Excitability   The ability to generate action potentials.

Excitatory postsynaptic potential (EPSP)   A hypopolarising change in the transmembrane potential of a neuron due to synaptic activity that tends to increase the probability of discharge of the neuron.

Extrafusal muscle fibre   The regular contractile fibres that produce the shortening of a muscle; they are located outside the muscle spindle.

Facial feedback hypothesis   The theory that our facial expressions can affect our feeling.

Fasciculation   The tendency of growing axons to follow the route of preceding axons.

Foetal alcohol syndrome (FAS)   A syndrome produced by alcohol consumption during pregnancy.

Fovea   The central region of the retina specialised for detail vision, i.e. for acuity.

Frequency theory   A theory that says the frequency of a sound wave is encoded by the auditory receptors in terms of their rate of discharge.

Frontal eye regions   Premotor areas of the cerebral cortex which controls eye movements.

Fusimotor neuron   A motor neuron whose activity results in contraction of intrafusal muscle fibres.

Gametes   Egg and sperm cells.

Gamma motor neuron   The efferent component of the fusimotor system, the system by which the central nervous system controls and modifies muscle spindle sensitivity.

Gate theory of pain   A theory that says the perception of pain depends not only upon activity in nociceptors, but also upon the balance between activity in nociceptors and large myelinated cutaneous afferent fibres.

Gene   The unit of inheritance and the section of a chromosome that controls the synthesis of one protein.

Genotype   The traits an organism can pass to its offspring in its genetic material.

Glucocorticoids   Steroid hormones that are released from the adrenal cortex in response to stressors.

Golgi tendon organ   A receptor located at the muscle–tendon junction that signals developed tension in the muscle.

Gonads   The testes or the ovaries.

Gustation   The sense of taste.

Hertz (Hz)   Cycles per second.

Heschl's gyrus   The temporal lobe gyrus that is the location of the primary auditory cortex.

Heterozygous   Possessing two different genes for a particular trait.

Homoeostasis   The stability of an organism's internal environment.

Homozygous   Possessing two identical genes for a particular trait.

Hormones   Chemicals released by the endocrine system.

Hypercomplex cells   Neurons in visual cortex that are sensitive to bars of light moving in particular directions across the retina.

Hyperphagia   Ingestion of a greater than optimal quantity of food.

Hyperpolarisation   A change in a cell's membrane potential that makes it more negative.

Hypovolemia   Decreased blood volume.

Inferior   Towards the bottom of the head.

Inhibitory postsynaptic potential (IPSP)   A hyperpolarising change in the membrane potential of a neuron due to synaptic activity that tends to decrease the probability of discharge in the neuron.

Insulin   A pancreatic hormone that facilitates the entry of glucose into cells.

Intrafusal muscle   A threadlike muscle that adjusts the tension on a muscle spindle.

Intrafusal muscle fibre   The skeletal muscle fibres that comprise the muscle spindle and are innervated by gamma motor neurons.

Ion   Positively or negatively charged particles.

Ion channels   Pores in membranes through which ions can pass.

Ionotropic transmission   Synaptic transmission in which the transmitter substance produces a change in ionic conductance of the postsynaptic membrane directly by interaction with a post-synaptic receptor.

Ipsilateral   On the same side.

K complexes   Large biphasic EEG waves that are a characteristic of stage 2 sleep.

Korsakoff's syndrome   A neurological condition that is common in alcoholics, the primary symptom of which is a disturbance in memory.

Latency   The time between application of a stimulus and appearance of a response.

Lateral   Away from the midline of the head.

Lateral inhibition   Refers to the inhibition of the discharge evoked by stimulation within a cell's excitatory receptive field that occurs when an area outside that receptive field is stimulated.

L-DOPA   The chemical precursor of dopamine; used in the treatment of Parkinson's disease.

Limbic system   A collection of interconnecting nuclei and tracts located around the thalamus which plays a role in emotion.

Long-term memory   Memory for responses or material having a duration of minutes to years.

Loudness   The 'perceived intensity' of a sound related to both the amplitude of the sound wave and its frequency.

Macrophage   A large phagocyte.

Medial   Towards the midline of the head.

Medial preoptic region   Area of the hypothalamus which plays a key role in sexual behaviour.

Meiosis   The process of cell division that produces cells with half the chromosomes of the parent cell.

Membrane potential   The electrical potential that exists across the cell membrane as a result of uneven ion distributions.

Mitosis   The process of cell division that produces cells with the same amount of chromosomes as the parent cell.

Monosynaptic reflex   Reflex involving only one synapse within the central nervous system.

Motor cortex   That area of cerebral cortex which controls movement.

Motor end-plate   The specialised terminal of a motor neuron that forms a synaptic contact with the muscle membrane.

Motor homunculus   The somatotopic map in the primary motor cortex.

Motor unit   An alpha motor neuron and the muscle fibres it innervates.

Müllerian system   The embryonic precursors of the female reproductive system.

Muscle spindle   A fusiform mechanoreceptor found mixed with extrafusal muscle fibres and in parallel with them.

Myelinated fibre   A nerve fibre wrapped by a series of glial cells, resulting in greater conduction velocity.

Myofilament   Any of the small filaments that comprise a myofibril; either a thick or myosin filament, or a thin or actin filament.

Nerve   A collection of axons or nerve fibres.

Nerve cell   Another name for a neuron which is specialised for excitability and conductivity.

Nerve fibre   The straight, relatively unbranched process of a nerve cell, sometimes called an axon.

Nerve growth factor   A small secreted protein that is important for the growth, maintenance and survival of certain target neurons.

Nervous system   The neurons and associated cells of the body.

Neural cell adhesion molecule (NCAM)   Molecule on the surface of cells that has the ability to recognise specific molecules and bind to them.

Neuroanatomy   The study of the structure of the nervous system.

Neuromuscular junction   The synaptic contact between a motor neuron and the muscle fibre it innervates.

Neuron   A cell specialised for excitability and conductivity; can be called a nerve cell.

Neurotrophins   Substances that promote the survival of neurons.

NMDA (N-methyl-D-aspartate) receptors   Glutamate receptors.

Nociceptor   A sensory receptor that responds to potentially damaging stimuli by sending nerve signals to the spinal cord and brain.

Nucleotide bases   A class of molecules that include adenine, thymine, guanine and cytosine which are constituents of the genetic code.

Oestradiol   The most common oestrogen.

Oestrogens   The class of steroid hormones that includes oestradiol.

Olfaction   The sense of smell.

Ontogeny   The development of individuals through their lifespan.

Osmoreceptors   Receptors sensitive to dehydration.

Ossicles   The three small bones of the middle ear: the malleus, the incus and the stapes.

Ovaries   The female gonads.

Papilla   A small nipple-shaped projection or elevation, as on the tongue.

Paradoxical sleep   A stage of deep sleep characterised by desynchronised EEG patterns, REM and dreaming.

Paralysis   Loss of function in a part of the body due to lesion of the neural or muscular mechanisms controlling it.

Parasympathetic nervous system   Responsible for stimulation of 'rest-and-digest' activities that occur when the body is at rest, made up of ocular, bulbar and sacral segments.

Parkinsonism   Basal ganglion disorder characterised by hypokinaesia, tremor at rest, and muscular rigidity.

Peptide hormones   Hormones that are short strings of amino acids.

Phagocytosis   In the immune system, the act of absorbing cellular debris or foreign cells.

Phantom limb pain   Pain referred to a limb that has been removed.

Phenotype   An organism's observable traits.

Phylogeny   The evolutionary development of species.

Pioneering cells   The first cells to travel along a particular route in the developing nervous system

Pitch   The quality of a sound determined by the frequency of its waves.

Place theory   A theory that says pitch is encoded in terms of the place on the basilar membrane that gives maximum vibration in response to a given frequency of sound.

Polysynaptic reflex   A reflex involving more than one synapse in the central nervous system.

Posterior   Towards the back of the head.

Prefrontal lobes   The areas left and right at the front of the brain.

Presynaptic inhibition   Decrease in the probability of firing of a neuron due to the decrease in transmission to it that results from hypopolarisation of afferent terminals on it.

Prosopagnosia   Visual agnosia for faces.

Protein   Long chain of amino acids.

Protein hormones   Hormones that are long strings of amino acids.

Receptive field   The area of the periphery whose stimulation influences the firing of a neuron.

Receptor   In sensory systems, a structure specialised to be sensitive to certain forms of energy; in synaptic transmission, the site of binding of transmitter substances with postsynaptic membranes.

Relative refractory period   The period after a spike when greater than normal stimuli are required to excite a nerve or muscle cell.

REM sleep   The stage of sleep in which dreaming is associated with mild muscle jerks and rapid eye movement (REM), also characterised by a desynchronised EEG.

Renshaw inhibition   A form of collateral inhibition of motor neurons involving a special inhibitory interneuron, the Renshaw cell.

Repolarisation phase   The return of the membrane potential from the peak overshoot of the spike back to the resting potential.

Resting membrane potential   The membrane potential of a cell that is at rest, i.e. not conducting an action potential.

Reticular activating system   Arousal system in the reticular formation; ascending RAS is a group of interconnected nuclei of the brain stem responsible for producing desynchronisation of the EEG.

Retinotopic   Laid out according to the map of the retina.

Rhodopsin   The photopigment of rods.

Ribonucleic acid (RNA)   A molecule that is similar to DNA except that it has a uracil nucleotide and a phosphate and ribose backbone.

Ribosome   A structure in the cytoplasm that reads the genetic code from strands of messenger RNA.

Rigidity   Stiffness of a limb due to increased tone in both flexors and extensors.

Rods   Visual photoreceptors in the retina specialised for low light conditions.

Saccade   An abrupt, rapid, small eye movement that usually occurs in a series during scanning.

Saltatory conduction   Conduction of the nerve spike where the spike jumps from node to node along the myelin sheath.

Sarcomere   The serially repeating unit of muscle that gives it its striated appearance.

Scotoma   An area of depressed or absent vision within the visual field, surrounded by an area of normal vision.

Second messenger   A substance activated by interaction of a synaptic transmitter substance with the postsynaptic receptor.

Semicircular canals   The receptive organs of the vestibular system.

Sex chromosomes   The pair of chromosomes that determine an individual's sex: XX for a female and XY for a male.

Sexual dimorphic nucleus   Nucleus in the medial preoptic area which is larger in male rats than female rats.

Sham rage   An eruption of behaviour resembling anger in an animal with a lesion located above the tectum.

Short-term memory   Recall of learnt responses or material having a duration of minutes to hours.

Simple cells   Neurons in visual cortex that are sensitive to narrow bars of light oriented in a particular direction across the retina.

Slow-wave sleep (SWS)   Sleep stages 2, 3 and 4.

Smooth muscle   Muscle of the linings of internal organs and blood vessels that lacks cross-striations.

Sodium/potassium pump   Mechanism for extrusion of sodium and uptake of potassium by cells against the concentration gradients for these ions.

Solitary nucleus   The medullary relay nucleus of the gustatory system.

Soma   Cell body.

Somatotopic organisation   The systematic mapping of parts of the body onto the cerebral cortex and other parts of the nervous system.

Spatial summation   Addition of generator potentials elicited by stimuli at two different points.

Split-brain patient   A patient who has had her or his corpus callosum sectioned.

Striated muscle   Any muscle whose fibres are divided by transverse bands into striations.

Superior   Towards the top of the head.

Suprachiasmatic nucleus (SCN)   Nucleus of the hypothalamus that controls the circadian cycles of the body.

Sympathetic nervous system   The division of the autonomic nervous system that mobilises the body's resources under stress, to induce the fight-or-flight response.

Synapse   The site at which neurons make functional contact.

Synaptic cleft   Space between presynaptic and postsynaptic cells at a chemical synapse across which the transmitter substance must diffuse.

Synaptic delay   The time required for release of a chemical transmitter substance, its diffusion across the synaptic cleft, its interaction with the postsynaptic receptor, and the beginning of a change in postsynaptic membrane potential.

Synaptic knob   A swelling of an axon near where it terminates; the presynaptic structure in most synapses.

Synaptic vesicles   Small membrane-bound sacs in the presynaptic terminals that contain the neurotransmitter.

Temporal lobe epilepsy   Seizures characterised by stereotyped behaviour, often with emotional outbursts and partial responsiveness.

Temporal summation   Addition of generator potentials elicited by two stimuli applied at the same point in rapid succession.

Testes   The male gonads.

Testosterone   The most common androgen.

Theta waves   EEG records characterised by high-voltage waves occurring at 4–8 Hz.

Threshold   Minimal stimulus required for a response or sensation.

Tonotopic representation   A distribution of sensitivity in auditory structures such that the range of audible tones is represented in sequence across the structure.

Transfer RNA   Molecules of RNA that carry amino acids to ribosomes during protein synthesis.

Tremor at rest   An involuntary trembling which is suppressed or reduced when a movement is attempted.

Trichromatic theory   Theory of colour vision that says there are three fundamental colour sensations and three different colour receptors; colour sensation is the result of activity in this ensemble   Also called *Young–Helmholtz theory.*

Tricyclic antidepressants   Drugs used to treat depression.

Unmyelinated fibre   A nerve fibre without myelin surrounding it.

Ventral   Towards the bottom of the head.

Ventral horns   The two ventral arms of the spinal grey matter.

Vertebrates   Chordates that possess spinal bones.

Vision   The act of seeing; sight; sensations induced through photoreceptors.

Visual agnosia   Failure to recognise visual stimuli not attributed to sensory or intellectual impairment.

Voltage-gated channel   A normally closed ionic channel that is opened by a change in trans-membrane voltage.

Wernicke's area   Area 22 of the temporal cerebral cortex that plays a fundamental role in reception and comprehension of speech.

Withdrawal reflex   Automatic contraction of the flexor muscles of a limb so as to remove the limb from a noxious stimulus.

Wolffian system   The embryonic precursors of the male reproductive system.

Young–Helmholtz theory   Theory of colour vision that says there are three fundamental colour sensations and three different colour receptors; colour sensations are the result of activity in this ensemble. Also called *Trichromatic theory.*

Zeitgebers   Environmental cues such as the light–dark cycle.

Zygote   A fertilised egg cell.

REFERENCES

Aardal-Eriksson, E., Eriksson, T.E., & Thorell, L.-H. (2001). Salivary cortisol, posttraumatic stress symptoms, and general health in the acute phase and during 9-month follow-up. *Biological Psychiatry, 50*(12), 986–993.

Aarsland, D., Zaccai, J., & Brayne, C. (2005). A systematic review of prevalence studies of dementia in Parkinson's disease. *Movement Disorders, 20*(10), 1255–1263.

Abercrombie, H.C., Kalin, N.H., Thurow, M.E., Rosenkranz, M.A., & Davidson, R.J. (2003). Cortisol variation in humans affects memory for emotionally laden and neutral information. *Behavioral Neuroscience, 117*(3), 505–516.

Abuelo, D. (2007). Microcephaly syndromes. *Seminars in Pediatric Neurology, 14*(3), 118–127.

Aggleton, J.P. (Ed.) (2000). *The amygdala: a functional analysis.* Oxford: Oxford University Press.

Aglioti, S., Beltramello, A., Girardi, F., & Fabbro, F. (1996). Neurolinguistic and follow-up study of an unusual pattern of recovery from bilingual subcortical aphasia. *Brain, 119*(Pt 5), 1551–1564.

Aldrich, M.S. (1992). *Narcolepsy. Neurology, 42* (Suppl. 6), 34–43.

Anand, B.K., & Brobeck, J.R. (1951). Hypothalamic control of food intake in rats and cats. *Yale Journal of Biological Medicine, 24*, 123–140.

Anglin, J.M. (1993). Vocabulary development: a morphological analysis. *Monographs of the Society for Research in Child Development, 58*(10), 1–165.

Antonijevic, I. (2008). HPA axis and sleep: identifying subtypes of major depression. *Stress, 11*(1), 15–27.

Anzaki, F., & Izumi, S. (2001). Differences between conduction aphasia and Wernicke's aphasia. *Tokai Journal of Experimental and Clinical Medicine, 26*(2), 45–61.

Arbib, M.A. (2009). Evolving the language-ready brain and the social mechanisms that support language. *Journal of Communication Disorders, 42*(4), 263–271.

Ardila, A. (1998). Clinical forum: bilingualism, a neglected and chaotic area. *Aphasiology, 12*, 131–134.

Arkin, A.M., Toth, M.F., Baker, J., & Hastey, J.M. (1970). The frequency of sleep talking in the laboratory among chronic sleep talkers and good dream recallers. *The Journal of Nervous and Mental Disease, 151*(6), 369–374.

Arranz, B., Eriksson, A., Mellerup, E., Plenge, P., & Marcusson, J. (1994). Brain 5-HT1A, 5-HT1D, and 5-HT2 receptors in suicide victims. *Biological Psychiatry, 35*(7), 457–463.

ASDA (2005). *The international classification of sleep disorders, second edition. Diagnostic and coding manual.* Westchester, IL: ASDA.

Aserinsky, E., & Kleitman, N. (1953). Regularly occurring periods of eye motility and concomitant phenomena during sleep. *Science, 118*, 273–274.

Atkinson, R.C., & Shiffrin, R.M. (1968). Human memory: a proposed system and its control processes. In K.W. Spence & J.T. Spence (Eds), *The psychology of learning and motivation* (Vol. 2, pp. 89–195). New York: Academic.

Aue, T., Lavelle, L.A., & Cacioppo, J.T. (2009). Great expectations: what can fMRI research tell us about psychological phenomena? *International Journal of Psychophysiology*, 73(1), 10–16.

Baddeley, A.D. (1999). *Essentials of human memory*. Hove: Psychology.

Baddeley, A.D. (2000). The episodic buffer: a new component of working memory? [review]. *Trends in Cognitive Sciences*, 4(11), 417–423.

Baddeley, A.D., & Hitch, G.J.L. (1974). Working memory. In G.A. Bower (Ed.), *The psychology of learning and motivation: advances in research and theory* (pp. 47–89). New York: Academic.

Bailey, C.H., Giustetto, M., Huang, Y.Y., Hawkins, R.D., & Kandel, E.R. (2000). Is heterosynaptic modulation essential for stabilizing Hebbian plasticity and memory? [review]. *Nature Reviews Neuroscience*, 1(1), 11–20.

Barbato, M., Bernard, M., Borrelli, L., & Fiorito, G. (2007). Body patterns in cephalopods. *Pattern Recognition Letters*, 28(14), 1854–1864.

Bard, P. (1929). The central representation of the sympathetic system. *Archives of Neurology and Psychiatry*, 22, 230–246.

Bardenstein, K.K., & McGlashan, T.H. (1990). Gender differences in affective, schizoaffective, and schizophrenic disorders: a review. *Schizophrenia Research*, 3(3), 159–172.

Barker, P. (2003). *Psychiatric and mental health nursing: the craft of caring*. London: Arnold.

Barnes, J., & Boubert, L. (2008). Executive functions are impaired in patients with Parkinson's disease with visual hallucinations. *Journal of Neurology Neurosurgery Psychiatry*, 79(2), 190–192.

Barnes, J., & David, A.S. (2001). Visual hallucinations in Parkinson's disease: a review and phenomenological survey. *Journal of Neurology Neurosurgery Psychiatry*, 70(6), 727–733.

Barnes, J., Connelly, V., Wiggs, L., Boubert, L., & Maravic, K. (2010). Sleep patterns in Parkinson's disease patients with visual hallucinations. *International Journal of Neuroscience*, 120(8), 564–569.

Barnes, J., Hinkley, L., Masters, S., & Boubert, L. (2007). Visual memory transformations in dyslexia. *Perception and Motor Skills*, 104(3 Pt 1), 881–891.

Bartolomeo, P., & Chokron, S. (2002). Orienting of attention in left unilateral neglect. *Neuroscience Biobehavioral Reviews*, 26(2), 217–234.

Bashir, A.S., & Hook, P.E. (2009). Fluency: a key link between word identification and comprehension. *Language Speech and Hearing Services in Schools*, 40(2), 196–200.

Basso, D., Ferrari, M., & Palladino, P. (2010). Prospective memory and working memory: asymmetrical effects during frontal lobe TMS stimulation. *Neuropsychologia*, 48(11), 3282–3290.

Baum, S., & Pell, M. (1999). The neural bases of prosody: insights from lesion studies and neuroimaging. *Aphasiology*, 13, 581–608.

Baylor, D.A. (1996). How photons start vision. *Proceedings of the National Academy of Sciences USA*, 93, 560–565.

Bearden, C.E., Hoffman, K.M., & Cannon, T.D. (2001). The neuropsychology and neuroanatomy of bipolar affective disorder: a critical review. *Bipolar Disorders*, 3(3), 106–150; discussion 151–163.

Beck, B. (2000). Neuropeptides and obesity. *Nutrition, 16*(10), 916–923.

Becker, A.E., Grinspoon, S.K., Klibanski, A., & Herzog, D.B. (1999). Eating disorders. *New England Journal of Medicine, 340*(14), 1092–1098.

Beland, R., & Mimouni, Z. (2001). Deep dyslexia in the two languages of an Arabic/French bilingual patient. *Cognition, 82*(2), 77–126.

Belin, A.C., & Westerlund, M. (2008). Parkinson's disease: a genetic perspective. *The FEBS Journal, 275*(7), 1377–1383.

Bench, C.J., Frackowiak, R.S., & Dolan, R.J. (1995). Changes in regional cerebral blood flow on recovery from depression. *Psychological Medicine, 25*(2), 247–261.

Bennett, M.R. (1994). Nitric oxide release and long term potentiation at synapses in autonomic ganglia. *General Pharmacology, 25*(8), 1541–1551.

Bennett, M.V., & Zukin, R.S. (2004). Electrical coupling and neuronal synchronization in the mammalian brain. *Neuron, 41*(4), 495–511.

Benschop, R.J., Godaert, G.L., Geenen, R., Brosschot, J.F., De Smet, M.B., Olff, M., et al. (1995). Relationships between cardiovascular and immunological changes in an experimental stress model. *Psychological Medicine, 25*(2), 323–327.

Benson, D.F., & Geschwind, N. (1985). Aphasia and related disorders: a clinical approach. In M.M. Mesulam (Ed.), *Principles of behavioral neurology* (pp. 193–238). Philadelphia: Davis.

Berlucchi, G., Maffei, L., Moruzzi, G., & Strata, P. (1964). EEG and behavioral effects elicited by cooling of medulla and pons. *Archives Italiennes de Biologie, 102*, 372–392.

Bermond, B., Mos, J., Meelis, W., van der Poel, A.M., & Kruk, M.R. (1982). Aggression induced by stimulation of the hypothalamus: effects of androgens. *Pharmacology Biochemistry and Behavior, 16*(1), 41–45.

Bernal, B., & Ardila, A. (2009). The role of the arcuate fasciculus in conduction aphasia. *Brain, 132*(Pt 9), 2309–2316.

Bernard, L.C., & Krupat, E. (1994). *Health psychology: biopsychosocial factors in health and illness.* New York: Harcourt Brace.

Bernhardt, P. (1997). Influences of serotonin and testosterone in aggression and dominance: convergence with social psychology. *Current Directions in Psychological Science, 6*, 44–48.

Berry, C., La Vecchia, C., & Nicotera, P. (2010). Paraquat and Parkinson's disease. *Cell Death and Differentiation, 17*(7), 1115–1125.

Bird, C.M., & Burgess, N. (2008). The hippocampus and memory: insights from spatial processing [review]. *Nature Reviews Neuroscience, 9*(3), 182–194.

Birmingham, C.L., & Gritzner, S. (2006). How does zinc supplementation benefit anorexia nervosa? *Eating and Weight Disorders, 11*(4), 109–111.

Bishop, K.M., & Wahlsten, D. (1997). Sex differences in the human corpus callosum: myth or reality? *Neuroscience & Biobehavioral Reviews, 21*(5), 581–601.

Bizley, J.K., & Walker, K.M. (2010). Sensitivity and selectivity of neurons in auditory cortex to the pitch, timbre, and location of sounds. *Neuroscientist, 16*(4), 453–469.

Blaha, C.D., Coury, A., Fibiger, H.C., & Phillips, A.G. (1990). Effects of neurotensin on dopamine release and metabolism in the rat striatum and nucleus accumbens: cross-validation using *in vivo* voltammetry and microdialysis. *Neuroscience, 34*, 699–705.

Blass, E.M., & Epstein, A.N. (1971). A lateral preoptic osmosensitive zone for thirst in the rat. *Journal of Comparative & Physiological Psychology, 76*(3), 378–394.

Blonder, L.X., Bowers, D., & Heilman, K. (1991). The role of the right hemisphere in emotional communication. *Brain, 114*, 1115–1127.

Bogerts, B., Lieberman, J.A., Bilder, R.M., Ashtari, M., Degreef, G., Lerner, G., et al. (1992). A volumetric MRI study of limbic structures in chronic schizophrenia: relationship to psychopathology. *Clinical Neuropharmacology, 15*(Suppl. 1 Pt A), 112A–113A.

Booth, A., & Mazur, A. (1998). Old issues and new perspectives on testosterone research. *Behavioral and Brain Sciences, 21*, 386–390.

Bowers, W.A. (2001). Basic principles for applying cognitive-behavioral therapy to anorexia nervosa. *Psychiatric Clinics of North America, 24*(2), 293–303.

Boyd, L.A., & Winstein, C.J. (2004). Providing explicit information disrupts implicit motor learning after basal ganglia stroke. *Learning and Memory, 11*(4), 388–396.

Boydell, J., van Os, J., McKenzie, K., Allardyce, J., Goel, R., McCreadie, R.G., et al. (2001). Incidence of schizophrenia in ethnic minorities in London: ecological study into interactions with environment. *British Medical Journal, 323*(7325), 1336–1338.

Braddick, O.J., O'Brien, J.M., Wattam-Bell, J., Atkinson, J., Hartley, T., & Turner, R. (2001). Brain areas sensitive to coherent visual motion. *Perception, 30*(1), 61–72.

Brain, P.F., & Benton, D. (Eds) (1981). *The biology of aggression*. Alphen aan den Rijn: Sijthoff Noordhoff.

Bremer, F. (1935). Cerveau 'isol' et physiologie du sommeil. *Comptes Rendus des Séances et Mémoires de la Société de Biologie, 118*, 1235–1241.

Brick, J.F., Frost, J.L., Schochet, S.S., Gutman, L., & Crosby, T.W. (1985). Pure word deafness: CT localization of the pathology. *Neurology, 35*(3), 441–442.

Bristol, A.S., Marinesco, S., & Carew, T.J. (2004). Neural circuit of tail-elicited siphon withdrawal in *Aplysia*. II. Role of gated inhibition in differential lateralisation of sensitisation and dishabituation. *Journal of Neurophysiology, 91*(2), 678–692.

Britt, M.D., & Wise, R.A. (1981). Opiate rewarding action: independence of the cells of the lateral hypothalamus. *Brain Research, 222*(1), 213–217.

Broca, P. (1861). Perte de la parole: ramollissement chronique et destruction partielle du lobe antérieur gauche du cerveau. *Bulletin de la Société d'Anthropologie, 2*, 235–238.

Brunello, N., Blier, P., Judd, L.L., Mendlewicz, J., Nelson, C.J., Souery, D., et al. (2003). Noradrenaline in mood and anxiety disorders: basic and clinical studies. *International Clinical Psychopharmacology, 18*(4), 191–202.

Brunner, H.G., Nelen, M., Breakefield, X.O., Ropers, H.H., & van Oost, B.A. (1993). Abnormal behavior associated with a point mutation in the structural gene for monoamine oxidase A. *Science, 262*(5133), 578–580.

Bruska, M., & Wozniak, W. (1999). Differentiation, maturation, and function of Schwann cells (lemmocytes). *Folia Morphological (Warsz), 58*(3), 101–107.

Buck, R. (1980). Nonverbal behavior and the theory of emotion: the facial feedback hypothesis. *Journal of Personality and Social Psychology, 38*(5), 811–824.

Carver, C.S., & White, T.L. (1994). Behavioral inhibition, behavioral activation, and affective responses to impending reward and punishment: the BIS/BAS scales. *Journal of Personality and Social Psychology, 67*, 319–333.

Caspi, A., McClay, J., Moffitt, T.E., Mill, J., Martin, J., Craig, I.W., et al. (2002). Role of genotype in the cycle of violence in maltreated children. *Science, 297*(5582), 851–854.

Castellucci, V.F., Blumenfeld, H., Goelet, P., & Kandel, E.R. (1989). Inhibitor of protein synthesis blocks long term behavioral sensitization in the isolated gill-withdrawal reflex of *Aplysia*. *Journal of Neurobiology*, 20(1), 1–9.

Chase, T.N., Engber, T.M., & Mouradian, M.M. (1993). Striatal dopaminoceptive system changes and motor response complications in L-dopa-treated patients with advanced Parkinson's disease. *Advances in Neurology*, 60, 181–185.

Chater, N., & Manning, C.D. (2006). Probabilistic models of language processing and acquisition. *Trends in Cognitive Sciences*, 10(7), 335–344.

Chatterjee, A. (1995). Cross-over, completion and confabulation in unilateral spatial neglect. *Brain*, 118(Pt 2), 455–465.

Chaudhuri, K.R., Martinez-Martin, P., Brown, R.G., Sethi, K., Stocchi, F., Odin, P., et al. (2007). The metric properties of a novel non-motor symptoms scale for Parkinson's disease: results from an international pilot study. *Movement Disorders*, 22(13), 1901–1911.

Chaytor, N., & Schmitter-Edgecombe, M. (2003). The ecological validity of neuropsychological tests: a review of the literature on everyday cognitive skills. *Neuropsychology Review*, 13(4), 181–197.

Chomsky, N. (1986). *Knowledge of language: its nature, origin and use*. New York: Praeger.

Chozick, B. (1987). The nucleus basalis of Meynert in neurological dementing disease: a review. *International Journal of Neuroscience*, 37(1–2), 31–48.

Chozick, B.S. (1985). The behavioral effects of lesions of the septum: a review. *International Journal of Neuroscience*, 26(3–4), 197–217.

Clark, R.E., Zola, S.M., & Squire, L.R. (2000). Impaired recognition memory in rats after damage to the hippocampus. *Journal of Neuroscience*, 20(23), 8853–8860.

Clarke, C.E. (2007). Parkinson's disease. *British Medical Journal*, 335(7617), 441–445.

Cohen, S., Tyrrell, D.A., & Smith, A.P. (1993). Negative life events, perceived stress, negative affect, and susceptibility to the common cold. *Journal of Personality and Social Psychology*, 64(1), 131–140.

Commins, D., & Yahr, P. (1984). Lesions of the sexually dimorphic area disrupt mating and marking in male gerbils. *Brain Research Bulletin*, 13(1), 185–193.

Considine, R.V., & Caro, J.F. (1996). Leptin in humans: current progress and future directions. *Clinical Chemistry*, 42(6 Pt 1), 843–844.

Copolov, D., & Crook, J. (2000). Biological markers and schizophrenia. *Australian and New Zealand Journal of Psychiatry*, 34(Suppl.), S108–112.

Corkin, S. (2002). What's new with the amnesic patient H.M.? *Nature Reviews Neuroscience*, 3(2): 153–160.

Coss, R.G., Brandon, J.G., & Globus, A. (1980). Changes in morphology of dendritic spines on honeybee calycal interneurons associated with cumulative nursing and foraging experiences. *Brain Research*, 192(1), 49–59.

Cousens, G., & Otto, T. (1998). Both pre- and posttraining excitotoxic lesions of the basolateral amygdala abolish the expression of olfactory and contextual fear conditioning. *Behavioral Neuroscience*, 112(5), 1092–1103.

Cowey, A. (2010). Visual system: how does blindsight arise? *Current Biology*, 20(17), R702–704.

Cowey, A., & Stoerig, P. (1995). Blindsight in monkeys. *Nature*, 373(6511), 247–249.

Crawley, J.N., & Kiss, J.Z. (1985). Tracing the sensory pathway from the gut to the brain: regions mediating the actions of cholecystokinin on feeding and exploration. *Annals of the New York Academy of Sciences, 448*(July), 586–588.

Crick, F., & Mitchison, G. (1983). The function of dream sleep. *Nature, 304*(5922), 111–114.

Crockett, M.J., Clark, L., Tabibnia, G., Lieberman, M.D., & Robbins, T.W. (2008). Serotonin modulates behavioral reactions to unfairness. *Science, 320*(5884), 1739.

Crone, S.A., & Lee, K.F. (2002). The bound leading the bound: target-derived receptors act as guidance cues. *Neuron, 36*(3), 333–335.

Cruts, M., & Van Broeckhoven, C. (1998). Presenilin mutations in Alzheimer's disease. *Human Mutation, 11*(3), 183–190.

Csibra, G., Davis, G., Spratling, M.W., & Johnson, M.H. (2000). Gamma oscillations and object processing in the infant brain. *Science, 290*(5496), 1582–1585.

Culebras, A. (1996). Sleep and neuromuscular disorders. *Neurologic Clinics, 14*(4), 791–805.

Cummings, J.L., & Back, C. (1998). The cholinergic hypothesis of neuropsychiatric symptoms in Alzheimer's disease. *American Journal of Geriatric Psychiatry, 6*(2 Suppl. 1), S64–78.

Dalzell, L., Connor, S., Penner, M., Saari, M.J., Leboutillier, J.C., & Weeks, A.C. (2010). Fear conditioning is associated with synaptogenesis in the lateral amygdala. *Synapse, 65*(6), 513–519.

Darwin, C.R. (1859). *On the origin of species by means of natural selection, or the preservation of favoured races in the struggle for life*. London: Murray.

David, A.S. (1999). Auditory hallucinations: phenomenology, neuropsychology and neuroimaging update. *Acta Psychiatrica Scandinavica, 395*(Suppl.), 95–104.

Davis, M. (1992). The role of the amygdala in fear and anxiety. *Annual Review of Neuroscience, 15*(1), 353–375.

De Bode, S., & Curtiss, S. (2000). Language after hemispherectomy. *Brain and Cognition, 43*(1–3), 135–138.

De Lacoste-Utamsing, C., & Holloway, R.L. (1982). Sexual dimorphism in the human corpus callosum. *Science, 216*, 1431–1432.

Deary, I.J., Johnson, W., & Houlihan, L.M. (2009). Genetic foundations of human intelligence. *Human Genetics, 126*(1), 215–232.

Dement, W. (1960). The effect of dream deprivation. *Science, 131*, 1705–1707.

Démonet, J.F., Thierry, G., & Cardebat, D. (2005). Renewal of the neurophysiology of language: functional neuroimaging. *Physiological Reviews, 85*, 49–95.

Desai, H.D., & Jann, M.W. (2000). Major depression in women: a review of the literature. *Journal of the American Pharmacists Association, 40*(4), 525–537.

Deutsch, J.A., & Ahn, S.J. (1986). The splanchnic nerve and food-intake regulation. *Behavioral and Neural Biology, 45*(1), 43–47.

Dheen, S.T., Kaur, C., & Ling, E.A. (2007). Microglia activation and its implications in brain diseases. *Current Medicinal Chemistry, 14*(11), 1189–1197.

Dott, N.M. (Ed.) (1938). *The hypothalamus: morphological, functional, clinical and surgical aspects*. Edinburgh: Oliver and Boyd.

Dow, B.M. (2002). Orientation and color columns in monkey visual cortex. *Cerebral Cortex, 12*(10), 1005–1015.

Drevets, W.C., Ongur, D., & Price, J.L. (1998). Neuroimaging abnormalities in the subgenual prefrontal cortex: implications for the pathophysiology of familial mood disorders. *Molecular Psychiatry, 3*(3), 220–226.

Dronkers, N.F., Wilkins, D.P., Van Valin, R.D. Jr, Redfern, B.B., & Jaeger, J.J. (2004). Lesion analysis of the brain areas involved in language comprehension. *Cognition, 92*(1–2), 145–177.

Duncan, J., & Owen, A. (2000). Consistent response of the human frontal lobe to diverse cognitive demands. *Trends in Neurosciences, 23*, 475–483.

Dursunoglu, N. (2009). Effects of menopause on obstructive sleep apnea. *Tuberk Toraks, 57*(1), 109–114.

Eckert, D.J., Jordan, A.S., Merchia, P., & Malhotra, A. (2007). Central sleep apnea: pathophysiology and treatment. *Chest, 131*(2), 595–607.

Eichenbaum, H. (1997). Declarative memory: insights from cognitive neurobiology [review]. *Annual Review of Psychology, 48*, 547–572.

Ekman, P. (1992). Facial expressions of emotion: an old controversy and new findings. *Philosophical Transactions of the Royal Society of London, 335*, 63–69.

Ekman, P., & Friesen, W.V. (1977). *Facial action coding system.* Palo Alto, CA: Consulting Psychologist Press.

Ekman, P., & Friesen, W.V. (1986). A new pan-cultural facial expression of emotion. *Motivation and Emotion, 10*(2), 159–168.

Ekman, P., Davidson, R.J., & Friesen, W.V. (1990). The Duchenne smile: emotional expression and brain physiology. II. *Journal of Personality and Social Psychology, 58*(2), 342–353.

Elder, G.A., Gama Sosa, M.A., De Gasperi, R., Dickstein, D.L., & Hof, P.R. (2010). Presenilin transgenic mice as models of Alzheimer's disease. *Brain Structure and Function, 214*(2–3), 127–143.

Empson, J.A., & Clarke, P.R. (1970). Rapid eye movements and remembering. *Nature, 227*(5255), 287–288.

Endo, T., Schwierin, B., Borbely, A.A., & Tobler, I. (1997). Selective and total sleep deprivation: effect on the sleep EEG in the rat. *Psychiatry Research, 66*(2–3), 97–110.

Enz, R. (2001). GABA(C) receptors: a molecular view. *Biological Chemistry, 382*(8), 1111–1122.

Erfle, V., Stoeckbauer, P., Kleinschmidt, A., Kohleisen, B., Mellert, W., Stavrou, D., et al. (1991). Target cells for HIV in the central nervous system: macrophages or glial cells? *Research in Virology, 142*(2–3), 139–144.

Fabbro, F. (2001). The bilingual brain: bilingual aphasia. *Brain and Language, 79*(2), 201–210.

Fahn, S., & Elton, R.L. (1987). *Members of the UPDRS Development Committee. Unified Parkinson's disease rating scale.* Florham Park, NJ: Macmillan Health Care Information.

Falleti, M.G., Maruff, P., Collie, A., Darby, D.G., & McStephen, M. (2003). Qualitative similarities in cognitive impairment associated with 24 h of sustained wakefulness and a blood alcohol concentration of 0.05%. *Journal of Sleep Research, 12*(4), 265–274.

Farah, M.J. (1996). Is face recognition 'special'? Evidence from neuropsychology. *Behavioural Brain Research, 76*(1–2), 181–189.

Farah, M.J., Levinson, K.L., & Klein, K.L. (1995). Face perception and within-category discrimination in prosopagnosia. *Neuropsychologia, 33*(6), 661–674.

Farah, M.J., Wilson, K.D., Drain, M., & Tanaka, J.N. (1998). What is 'special' about face perception? *Psychological Review, 105*(3), 482–498.

Farbman, A.I. (1994). The cellular basis of olfaction. *Endeavour*, *18*(1), 2–8.

Faw, B. (2003). Pre-frontal executive committee for perception, working memory, attention, long-term memory, motor control, and thinking: a tutorial review. *Consciousness and Cognition*, *12*(1), 83–139.

Fawcett, A.J., Nicolson, R.I., & Maclagan, F. (2001). Cerebellar tests differentiate between groups of poor readers with and without IQ discrepancy. *Journal of Learning Disabilities*, *34*(2), 119–135.

Fendrich, R., Wessinger, C.M., & Gazzaniga, M.S. (1992). Residual vision in a scotoma: implications for blindsight. *Science*, *258*(5087), 1489–1491.

Finch, C.E. (2002). Neurons, glia, and plasticity in normal brain aging. *Advances in Gerontology*, *10*, 35–39.

Flament-Durand, J. (1980). The hypothalamus: anatomy and functions. *Acta Psychiatrica Belgica*, *80*(4), 364–375.

Fletcher, P.C., & Henson, R.N.A. (2001). Frontal lobes and human memory: insights from functional neuroimaging [review]. *Brain*, *124*, 849–881.

Folk, G.E. Jr, & Long, J.P. (1988). Serotonin as a neurotransmitter: a review. *Comparative Biochemistry and Physiology Part C*, *91*(1), 251–257.

Forster, B.B., MacKay, A., Whittall, K.P., Kiehl, K.A., Smith, A.M., Hare, R.D., & Liddle, P.F. (1998). Functional MRI: The basics of the BOLD (blood oxygen level dependent) technique. *Canadian Journal of Radiology*, *47*, 320–329.

Francke, U. (1999). Williams–Beuren syndrome: genes and mechanisms. *Human Molecular Genetics*, *8*(10), 1947–1954.

Franken, R.E. (1994). *Human motivation* (3rd ed). Belmont, CA: Brooks/Cole Publishing Company.

Franken, R.E. (2001). *Human motivation* (4th edn). St Paul, MN: Brooks/Cole.

Freed, C.R., Greene, P.E., Breeze, R.E., Tsai, W.Y., DuMouchel, W., Kao, R., et al. (2001). Transplantation of embryonic dopamine neurons for severe Parkinson's disease. *New England Journal of Medicine*, *344*(10), 710–719.

Freudenreich, O., Holt, D.J., Cather, C., & Goff, D.C. (2007). The evaluation and management of patients with first-episode schizophrenia: a selective, clinical review of diagnosis, treatment, and prognosis. *Harvard Review of Psychiatry*, *15*(5), 189–211.

Friederici, A.D., von Cramon, D.Y., & Kotz, S.A. (2007). Role of the corpus callosum in speech comprehension: interfacing syntax and prosody. *Neuron*, *53*(1), 135–145.

Friedman, J.M. (2002). The function of leptin in nutrition, weight, and physiology. *Nutrition Reviews* (60), S1–S14.

Froestl, W. (2010). Novel GABA(B) receptor positive modulators: a patent survey. *Expert Opinion on Therapeutic Patients*, *20*(8), 1007–1017.

Fuster, J.M. (2004). Upper processing stages of the perception–action cycle. *Trends in Cognitive Science*, *8*(4), 143–145.

Gan, W.B. (2003). Glutamate-dependent stabilization of presynaptic terminals. *Neuron*, *38*(5), 677–678.

Gao, Y.J., Ren, W.H., Zhang, Y.Q., & Zhao, Z.Q. (2004). Contributions of the anterior cingulate cortex and amygdala to pain- and fear-conditioned place avoidance in rats. *Pain*, *110*(1–2), 343–353.

Gasser, T. (2007). Update on the genetics of Parkinson's disease. *Movement Disorders*, 22(Suppl. 17), S343–350.

Gasser, T. (2009). Genomic and proteomic biomarkers for Parkinson disease. *Neurology*, 72 (7 Suppl.), S27–31.

Gates, G.A., Cobb, J.L., Linn, R.T., Rees, T., Wolf, P.A., & D'Agostino, R.B. (1996). Central auditory dysfunction, cognitive dysfunction, and dementia in older people. *Archives of Otolaryngology Head & Neck Surgery*, 122(2), 161–167.

Gazzaniga, M.S., Glass, A.V., Sarno, M.T., & Posner, J.B. (1973). Pure word deafness and hemispheric dynamics: a case history. *Cortex*, 9(1), 136–143.

Gerlai, R. (2001). Alzheimer's disease: beta-amyloid hypothesis strengthened! *Trends in Neuroscience*, 24(4), 199.

Giannini, A.J., Underwood, N.A., & Condon, M. (2000). Acute ketamine intoxication treated by haloperidol: a preliminary study. *American Journal of Therapeutics*, 7(6), 389–391.

Gibb, W.R. (1992). Neuropathology of Parkinson's disease and related syndromes. *Neurologic Clinics*, 10(2), 361–376.

Glanzman, D.L., Kandel, E.R., & Schacher, S. (1990). Target-dependent structural changes accompanying long-term synaptic facilitation in *Aplysia* neurons. *Science*, 249(4970), 799–802.

Glaser, R., & Kiecolt-Glaser, J. (2005). How stress damages immune system and health. *Discovery Medicine*, 5(26), 165–169.

Goldberg, J.L., & Barres, B.A. (2000). Nogo in nerve regeneration. *Nature*, 403(6768), 369–370.

Goldstein, B., Little, J.W., & Harris, R.M. (1997). Axonal sprouting following incomplete spinal cord injury: an experimental model. *Journal of Spinal Cord Medicine*, 20(2), 200–206.

Goldstein, J.M., Seidman, L.J., Horton, N.J., Makris, N., Kennedy, D.N., Caviness, V.S. Jr, et al. (2001). Normal sexual dimorphism of the adult human brain assessed by *in vivo* magnetic resonance imaging. *Cerebral Cortex*, 11(6), 490–497.

Gorski, R.A. (2002). Hypothalamic imprinting by gonadal steroid hormones. *Advances in Experimental Medicine and Biology*, 511, 57–70; discussion 70–83.

Gottesmann, C. (2004). Brain inhibitory mechanisms involved in basic and higher integrated sleep processes. *Brain Research (Reviews)*, 45(3), 230–249.

Gozal, D., Daniel, J.M., & Dohanich, G.P. (2001). Behavioral and anatomical correlates of chronic episodic hypoxia during sleep in the rat. *Journal of Neuroscience*, 21(7), 2442–2450.

Greenberg, M.E., Xu, B., Lu, B., & Hempstead, B.L. (2009). New insights in the biology of BDNF synthesis and release: implications in CNS function. *Journal of Neuroscience*, 29(41), 12764–12767.

Grem, J.L., King, S.A., O'Dwyer, P.J., & Leyland-Jones, B. (1988). Biochemistry and clinical activity of N-(phosphonacetyl)-L-aspartate: a review. *Cancer Research*, 48(16), 4441–4454.

Grigorenko, E.L. (2001). Developmental dyslexia: an update on genes, brains, and environments. *Journal of Child Psychology and Psychiatry*, 42(1), 91–125.

Haaland, K.Y., Harrington, D.L., & Knight, R.T. (2000). Neural representations of skilled movement. *Brain*, 123, 2306–2313.

Haas, H., & Panula, P. (2003). The role of histamine and the tuberomamillary nucleus in the nervous system. *Nature Reviews Neuroscience*, 4(2), 121–130.

Hadjikhani, N., Liu, A.K., Dale, A.M., Cavanagh, P., & Tootell, R.B.H. (1998). Retinopy and color sensitivity in human visual cortical area V8. *Nature Neuroscience*, 1, 235–241.

Halaas, J.L., Gajiwala, K.S., Maffei, M., Cohen, S.L., Chait, B.T., Rabinowitz, D., et al. (1995). Weight-reducing effects of the plasma protein encoded by the obese gene. *Science*, *269*(5223), 543–546.

Haldane, M., & Frangou, S. (2004). New insights help define the pathophysiology of bipolar affective disorder: neuroimaging and neuropathology findings. *Progress in Neuro-Psychopharmacology & Biological Psychiatry*, *28*(6), 943–960.

Halligan, P.W., Marshall, J.C., & Wade, D.T. (1989). Visuospatial neglect: underlying factors and test sensitivity. *Lancet*, *2*(8668), 908–911.

Halpern, A.R., & Zatorre, R.J. (1999). When that tune runs through your head: a PET investigation of auditory imagery for familiar melodies. *Cerebral Cortex*, *9*, 697–704.

Haramati, S., Soroker, N., Dudai, Y., & Levy, D.A. (2008). The posterior parietal cortex in recognition memory: a neuropsychological study. *Neuropsychologia*, *46*(7), 1756–1766.

Hawkins, R.D., Cohen, T.E., Greene, W., & Kandel, E.R. (1998). Relationships between dishabituation, sensitisation, and inhibition of the gill- and siphon-withdrawal reflex in *Aplysia californica*: effects of response measure, test time, and training stimulus. *Behavioral Neuroscience*, *112*(1), 24–38.

Hawkins, R.D., Kandel, E.R., & Siegelbaum, S.A. (1993). Learning to modulate transmitter release: themes and variations in synaptic plasticity [review]. *Annual Review of Neuroscience*, *16*, 625–665.

Haxby, J.V., Grady, C.L., Horwitz, B., Ungerleider, L.G., Mishkin, M., Carson, R.E., et al. (1991). Dissociation of object and spatial visual processing pathways in human extrastriate cortex. *Proceedings of the National Academy of Sciences USA*, *88*(5), 1621–1625.

Hebb, D.O. (1949). *The organization of behavior*. New York: Wiley.

Heilman, K.M., Scholes, R., & Watson, R.T. (1975). Auditory affective agnosia: disturbed comprehension of affective speech. *Journal of Neurology Neurosurgery & Psychiatry*, *38*(1), 69–72.

Helmstaedter, C., & Kockelmann, E. (2006). Cognitive outcomes in patients with chronic temporal lobe epilepsy. *Epilepsia*, *47*(Suppl. 2), 96–98.

Helmstaedter, C., Kurthen, M., Linke, D.B., & Elger, C.E. (1994). Right hemisphere restitution of language and memory functions in right hemisphere language-dominant patients with left temporal lobe epilepsy. *Brain*, *117*(Pt 4), 729–737.

Hennenlotter, A., Dresel, C., Castrop, F., Ceballos-Baumann, A.O., Wohlschlager, A.M., & Haslinger, B. (2009). The link between facial feedback and neural activity within central circuitries of emotion: new insights from botulinum-toxin-induced denervation of frown muscles. *Cerebral Cortex*, *19*(3), 537–542.

Herbert, C., Ethofer, T., Anders, S., Junghofer, M., Wildgruber, D., Grodd, W., et al. (2009). Amygdala activation during reading of emotional adjectives: an advantage for pleasant content. *Cognitive and Affective Neuroscience*, *4*(1), 35–49.

Hernandes, M.S., & Troncone, L.R. (2009). Glycine as a neurotransmitter in the forebrain: a short review. *Journal of Neural Transmission*, *116*(12), 1551–1560.

Hernandez, A.E., Dapretto, M., Mazziotta, J., & Bookheimer, S. (2001). Language switching and language representation in Spanish–English bilinguals: an fMRI study. *Neuroimage*, *14*(2), 510–520.

Hetherington, A.W., & Ranson, S.W. (1940). Hypothalamic lesions and adiposity in the rat. *The Anatomical Record*, *78*, 149–172.

Heywood, C.A., Gadotti, A., & Cowey, A. (1992). Cortical area V4 and its role in the perception of color. *Journal of Neuroscience, 12*(10), 4056–4065.

Hidalgo, A. (2003). Neuron–glia interactions during axon guidance in *Drosophila. Biochemical Society Transactions, 31*(Pt 1), 50–55.

Hilker, R., Antonini, A., & Odin, P. (2010). What is the best treatment for fluctuating Parkinson's disease: continuous drug delivery or deep brain stimulation of the subthalamic nucleus? *Journal of Neural Transmission, 118*(6), 907–914.

Hobson, J.A., & McCarley, R.W. (1977). The brain as a dream-state generator: an activation-synthesis hypothesis of the dream process. *American Journal of Psychiatry, 134*, 1335–1368.

Holash, J.A., Noden, D.M., & Stewart, P.A. (1993). Re-evaluating the role of astrocytes in blood–brain barrier induction. *Developmental Dynamics, 197*(1), 14–25.

Hollins, M. (2010). Somesthetic senses. *The Annual Review of Psychology, 61*, 243–271.

Holmes, M.D. (2008). Dense array EEG: methodology and new hypothesis on epilepsy syndromes. *Epilepsia, 49*(Suppl. 3), 3–14.

Houldin, A.D., Lev, E., Prystowsky, M.B., Redei, E., & Lowery, B.J. (1991). Psychoneuroimmunology: a review of literature. *Holistic Nursing Practice, 5*(4), 10–21.

Howard, B.M., Zhicheng, M., Filipovic, R., Moore, A.R., Antic, S.D., & Zecevic, N. (2008). Radial glia cells in the developing human brain. *Neuroscientist, 14*(5), 459–473.

Howland, R.H. (2009). Somatic therapies for seasonal affective disorder. *Journal of Psychosocial Nursing and Mental Health Services, 47*(1), 17–20.

Huang, W., Sved, A.F., & Stricker, E.M. (2000). Water ingestion provides an early signal inhibiting osmotically stimulated vasopressin secretion in rats. *American Journal of Physiology Regulatory Integrative Comparative Physiology, 279*(3), R756–760.

Hubel, D.H., & Wiesel, T.N. (1977). Functional architecture of macaque monkey visual cortex. *Proceedings of the Royal Society of London Series B, 198*, 1–59.

Hubel, D.H., & Wiesel, T.N. (1979). Brain mechanisms of vision. *Scientific American, 241*(3), 150–162.

Hubel, D.H., Wiesel, T.N., & Stryker, M.P. (1977). Orientation columns in macaque monkey visual cortex demonstrated by the 2-deoxyglucose autoradiographic technique. *Nature, 269*(5626), 328–330.

Hugdahl, K., Loberg, E.M., Specht, K., Steen, V.M., van Wageningen, H., & Jorgensen, H.A. (2007). Auditory hallucinations in schizophrenia: the role of cognitive, brain structural and genetic disturbances in the left temporal lobe. *Frontiers in Human Neuroscience, 1*, 6.

Hughes, C., Happé, F., Taylor, A., Jaffee, S.R., Caspi, A., & Moffitt, T.E. (2005). Origins of individual differences in theory of mind: from nature to nurture? *Child Development, 76*, 356–370.

Imtiaz, K.E., Nirodi, G., & Khaleeli, A.A. (2001). Alexia without agraphia: a century later. *International Journal of Clinical Practices, 55*(3), 225–226.

Isacson, O., Seo, H., Lin, L., Albeck, D., & Granholm, A.C. (2002). Alzheimer's disease and Down's syndrome: roles of APP, trophic factors and ACh. *Trends in Neuroscience, 25*(2), 79–84.

Ito, M. (2002). Historical review of the significance of the cerebellum and the role of Purkinje cells in motor learning. *Annals of the New York Academy of Sciences, 978*, 273–288.

Iurescia, S., Fioretti, D., Mangialasche, F., & Rinaldi, M. (2010). The pathological cross talk between apolipoprotein E and amyloid-beta peptide in Alzheimer's disease: emerging gene-based therapeutic approaches. *Journal of Alzheimer's Disease*, 21(1), 35–48.

Izumikawa, M., Minoda, R., Kawamoto, K., Abrashkin, K.A., Swiderski, D.L., Dolan, D.F., et al. (2005). Auditory hair cell replacement and hearing improvement by Atoh1 gene therapy in deaf mammals. *Nature Medicine*, 11(3), 271–276.

Jablensky, A. (2000). Epidemiology of schizophrenia: the global burden of disease and disability. *European Archives of Psychiatry and Clinical Neuroscience*, 250(6), 274–285.

Jackson, T., & Ramaswami, M. (2003). Prospects of memory-modifying drugs that target the CREB pathway. *Current Opinion in Drug Discovery & Development*, 6(5), 712–719.

Jacobs, B., Schall, M., & Scheibel, A.B. (1993). A quantitative dendritic analysis of Wernicke's area in humans. II. Gender, hemispheric, and environmental factors. *Journal of Comparative Neurology*, 327(1), 97–111.

Janowitz, H.D., & Hollander, F. (1955). The time factor in the adjustment of food intake to varied caloric requirement in the dog: a study of the precision of appetite regulation. *Annals of New York Academy of Sciences*, 63(1), 56–67.

Jarrard, L.E. (2001). Retrograde amnesia and consolidation: anatomical and lesion considerations. *Hippocampus*, 11(1), 43–49.

Javitt, D.C., & Zukin, S.R. (1991). Recent advances in the phencyclidine model of schizophrenia. *American Journal of Psychiatry*, 148(10), 1301–1308.

Jellinger, K.A. (2009). Recent advances in our understanding of neurodegeneration. *Journal of Neural Transmission*, 116(9), 1111–1162.

Johansson, C., Smedh, C., Partonen, T., Pekkarinen, P., Paunio, T., Ekholm, J. et al (2001). Seasonal affective disorder and serotonin-related polymorphisms. *Neurobioloical Disorders*, 8, 351–357.

Jones, E.G. (1995). Cortical development and neuropathology in schizophrenia. *CIBA Foundation Symposium*, 193, 277–295.

Jurado, M.B., & Rosselli, M. (2007). The elusive nature of executive functions: a review of our current understanding. *Neuropsychology Review*, 17(3), 213–233.

Kahn, E. (1970). Age-related changes in sleep characteristics. *International Psychiatry Clinics*, 7(2), 25–29.

Kalin, N.H., Risch, S.C., Janowsky, D.S., & Murphy, D.L. (1981). Use of dexamethasone suppression test in clinical psychiatry. *Journal of Clinical Psychopharmacology*, 1(2), 64–69.

Kamdar, B.B., Needham, D.M., & Collop, N.A. (2011). Sleep deprivation in critical illness: its role in physical and psychological recovery. *Journal of Intensive Care Medicine*, 27(2), 97–111.

Kandel, E.R. (2009). The biology of memory: a forty-year perspective [review]. *Journal of Neuroscience*, 29(41), 12748–12756.

Kanwisher, N., McDermott, J., & Chun, M.M. (1997). The fusiform face area: a module in human extrastriate cortex specialized for face perception. *Journal of Neuroscience*, 17(11), 4302–4311.

Kapur, S. (2003). Psychosis as a state of aberrant salience: a framework linking biology, phenomenology, and pharmacology in schizophrenia. *American Journal of Psychiatry*, 160(1), 13–23.

Kapur, S., & Mamo, D. (2003). Half a century of antipsychotics and still a central role for dopamine D2 receptors. *Progress in Neuro-Psychopharmacology & Biological Psychiatry*, *27*(7), 1081–1090.

Karagogeos, D. (2003). Neural GPI-anchored cell adhesion molecules. *Frontiers in Bioscience*, *1*(8 Suppl.), 1304–1320.

Kathol, R.G., Jaeckle, R.S., Lopez, J.F., & Meller, W.H. (1989). Pathophysiology of HPA axis abnormalities in patients with major depression: an update. *American Journal of Psychiatry*, *146*(3), 311–317.

Keesey, R.E., & Powley, T.L. (1986). The regulation of body weight. *Annual Review of Psychology*, *37*, 109–133.

Keith, S.J., & Matthews, S.M. (1991). The diagnosis of schizophrenia: a review of onset and duration issues. *Schizophrenia Bulletin*, *17*(1), 51–67.

Keller, J., Schatzberg, A.F., & Maj, M. (2007). Current issues in the classification of psychotic major depression. *Schizophrenia Bulletin*, *33*(4), 877–885.

Kerkhof, G.A. (1998). The 24-hour variation of mood differs between morning- and evening-type individuals. *Perception and Motor Skills*, *86*(1), 264–266.

Kertesz, A. (1993). Clinical forms of aphasia. *Acta Neurochirurgica Supplement (Wien)*, *56*, 52–58.

Kesner, R.P., & Goodrich-Hunsaker, N.J. (2010). Developing an animal model of human amnesia: the role of the hippocampus. *Neuropsychologia*, *48*(8), 2290–2302.

Kiefer, R., Kieseier, B.C., Stoll, G., & Hartung, H.P. (2001). The role of macrophages in immune-mediated damage to the peripheral nervous system. *Progress in Neurobiology*, *64*(2), 109–127.

Kim, K.H.S., Relkin, N.R., Lee, K.M., & Hirsch, J. (1997). Distinct cortical area associated with native and second languages. *Nature*, *388*, 171–174.

King, D.P., & Takahashi, J.S. (2000). Molecular genetics of circadian rhythms in mammals. *Annual Review of Neuroscience*, *23*, 713–742.

Kirshner, H.S., Webb, W.G., & Duncan, G.W. (1981). Word deafness in Wernicke's aphasia. *Journal of Neurology Neurosurgery & Psychiatry*, *44*(3), 197–201.

Kirwan, C.B., Bayley, P.J., Galvan, V.V., & Squire, L.R. (2008). Detailed recollection of remote autobiographical memory after damage to the medial temporal lobe. *Proceeding of the National Academy of Sciences USA*, *105*(7), 2676–2680.

Kiyashchenko, L.I., Mileykovskiy, B.Y., Maidment, N., Lam, H.A., Wu, M.F., John, J., et al. (2002). Release of hypocretin (orexin) during waking and sleep states. *Journal of Neuroscience*, *22*(13), 5282–5286.

Knecht, S., Drager, B., Deppe, M., Bobe, L., Lohmann, H., Floel, A., et al. (2000). Handedness and hemispheric language dominance in healthy humans. *Brain*, *123*(Pt 12), 2512–2518.

Koelsch, S., Fritz, T., Schulze, K., Alsop, D., & Schlaug, G. (2005). Adults and children processing music: an fMRI study. *Neuroimage*, *25*(4), 1068–1076.

Koenigs, M., Huey, E.D., Raymont, V., Cheon, B., Solomon, J., Wassermann, E.M., et al. (2008). Focal brain damage protects against post-traumatic stress disorder in combat veterans. *Nature Neuroscience*, *11*(2), 232–237.

Kolb, B., Stewart, J., & Sutherland, R.J. (1997). Recovery of function is associated with increased spine density in cortical pyramidal cells after frontal lesions and/or noradrenaline depletion in neonatal rats. *Behavioural Brain Research*, *89*(1–2), 61–70.

Koob, G.F. (1992). Drugs of abuse: anatomy, pharmacology and function of reward pathways. *Trends in Pharmacological Science*, 13(5), 177–184.

Kozma, C. (1996). Autosomal dominant inheritance of Brachmann–de Lange syndrome. *American Journal of Medical Genetics*, 66(4), 445–448.

Krasne, F.B., & Glanzman, D.L. (1995). What can we learn from invertebrate learning? [review]. *Annual Review of Psychology*, 46, 585–624.

Kringlen, E. (1985). Depression research: a review with special emphasis on etiology. *Acta Psychiatrica Scandinavica: Suppl.*, 319, 117–130.

Kroeger, D., & de Lecea, L. (2009). The hypocretins and their role in narcolepsy. *CNS Neurological Disorders – Drug Targets*, 8(4), 271–280.

Kuffler, S.W. (1953). Discharge patterns and functional organization of mammalian retina. *Journal of Neurophysiology*, 16(1), 37–68.

Kushida, C.A., Bergmann, B.M., & Rechtschaffen, A. (1989). Sleep deprivation in the rat. IV. Paradoxical sleep deprivation. *Sleep*, 12(1), 22–30.

Kyobe, J., & Gitau, W. (1984). Turner's syndrome and its variants. *East African Medical Journal*, 61(2), 154–158.

Lambert, G.W. (2001). Paring down on Descartes: a review of brain noradrenaline and sympathetic nervous function. *Clinical and Experimental Pharmacology and Physiology*, 28(12), 979–982.

Land, E.H. (1977). The retinex theory of color vision. *Scientific American*, 237(6), 108–128.

Langner, G. (1997). Neural processing and representation of periodicity pitch. *Acta Otolaryngolica Supplement*, 532, 68–76.

Laurent, J.P., Guerrero, F.A., & Jouvet, M. (1974). Reversible suppression of the geniculate PGO waves and of the concomitant increase of excitability of the intrageniculate optic nerve terminals in cats. *Brain Research*, 81(3), 558–563.

Lawrence, D.G., & Kuypers, H.G. (1968a). The functional organization of the motor system in the monkey. I. The effects of bilateral pyramidal lesions. *Brain*, 91(1), 1–14.

Lawrence, D.G., & Kuypers, H.G. (1968b). The functional organization of the motor system in the monkey. II. The effects of lesions of the descending brain-stem pathways. *Brain*, 91(1), 15–36.

Lee, A.C., Bussey, T.J., Murray, E.A., Saksida, L.M., Epstein, R.A., Kapur, N., Hodges, J.R., & Graham, K.S. (2005). Perceptual deficits in amnesia: challenging the medial temporal lobe "mnemonic" view. *Neuropsychologia*, 43, 1–11.

Lee, A.C., Robbins, T.W., & Owen, A.M. (2000). Episodic memory meets working memory in the frontal lobe: functional neuroimaging studies of encoding and retrieval. *Critical Reviews of Neurobiology*, 14(3–4), 165–197.

Leibowitz, S.F. (1975). Catecholaminergic mechanisms of lateral hypothalamus: their role in mediation of amphetamine anorexia. *Brain Research*, 98(3), 529–545.

Leisman, G., & Koch, P. (2000). Continuum model of mnemonic and amnesic phenomena [article]. *Journal of the International Neuropsychological Society*, 6(5), 593–607.

Leonard, B.E. (1997). The role of noradrenaline in depression: a review. *Journal of Psychopharmacology*, 11(4 Suppl.), S39–47.

Levin, E.D. (1988). Psychopharmacological effects in the radial-arm maze. *Neuroscience & Biobehavioral Reviews*, 12(2), 169–175.

Levy, W.B., Hocking, A.B., & Wu, X. (2005). Interpreting hippocampal function as recoding and forecasting. *Neural Networks*, *18*(9), 1242–1264.

Levy, J., & Trevarthen, C. (1976). Metacontrol of hemispheric function in human split-brain patients. *Journal of Experimental Psychology: Human Perception and Performance*, *2*(3), 299–312.

Li, L.Y., Li, J.T., Wu, Q.Y., Li, J., Feng, Z.T., Liu, S., et al. (2008). Transplantation of NGF-gene-modified bone marrow stromal cells into a rat model of Alzheimer's disease. *Journal of Molecular Neuroscience*, *34*(2), 157–163.

Lin, S.C., & Bergles, D.E. (2004). Synaptic signaling between GABAergic interneurons and oligodendrocyte precursor cells in the hippocampus. *Nature Neuroscience*, *7*(1), 24–32.

Livingstone, M.S., Rosen, G.D., Drislane, F.W., & Galaburda, A.M. (1991). Physiological and anatomical evidence for a magnocellular defect in developmental dyslexia. *Proceeding of the National Academy of Sciences USA*, *88*(18), 7943–7947.

Lucking, C.B., Durr, A., Bonifati, V., Vaughan, J., De Michele, G., Gasser, T., et al. (2000). Association between early-onset Parkinson's disease and mutations in the parkin gene. *New England Journal of Medicine*, *342*(21), 1560–1567.

Lueck, C.J., Zeki, S., Friston, K.J., Deiber, M.P., Cope, P., Cunningham, V.J., et al. (1989). The colour centre in the cerebral cortex of man. *Nature*, *340*(6232), 386–389.

Lyman, C.P., O'Brien, R.C., Greene, G.C., & Papafrangos, E.D. (1981). Hibernation and longevity in the Turkish hamster *Mesocricetus brandti*. *Science*, *212*(4495), 668–670.

Lynch, M.A. (2004). Long-term potentiation and memory. *Physiological Review*, *84*, 87–136.

Maas, J.W., Dekirmenjian, H., & Fawcett, J.A. (1974). MHPG excretion by patients with affective disorders. *International Pharmacopsychiatry*, *9*(1), 14–26.

Macey, P.M., Henderson, L.A., Macey, K.E., Alger, J.R., Frysinger, R.C., Woo, M.A., et al. (2002). Brain morphology associated with obstructive sleep apnea. *American Journal of Respiratory and Critical Care Medicine*, *166*(10), 1382–1387.

Machado, S., Portella, C.E., Silva, J.G., Velasques, B., Bastos, V.H., Cunha, M., et al. (2008). Learning and implicit memory: mechanisms and neuroplasticity [review]. *Revista De Neurologia*, *46*(9), 543–549.

MacIntosh, C.G., Sheehan, J., Davani, N., Morley, J.E., Horowitz, M., & Chapman, I.M. (2001). Effects of aging on the opioid modulation of feeding in humans. *Journal of the American Geriatrics Society*, *49*(11), 1518–1524.

Maguire, E., Gadian, D.G., Johnsrude, I.S., Good, C.D., Ashburner, J., Frackowiak, R.S., et al. (2000). Navigation-related structural change in the hippocampi of taxi drivers. *Proceedings of the National Academy of Sciences USA*, *97*(8), 4398–4403.

Maier, S.F., & Watkins, L.R. (1998). Cytokines for psychologists:implications of bi-directional immune-to-brain communication for understanding behavior, mood, and cognition. *Psychological Review*, *105*, 83–107.

Malhotra, S.K., Shnitka, T.K., & Elbrink, J. (1990). Reactive astrocytes: a review. *Cytobios*, *61*(246–247), 133–160.

Mandoki, M.W., Sumner, G.S., Hoffman, R.P., & Riconda, D.L. (1991). A review of Klinefelter's syndrome in children and adolescents. *Journal of American Academy of Child and Adolescent Psychiatry*, *30*(2), 167–172.

Mann, J.J., Oquendo, M., Underwood, M.D., & Arango, V. (1999). The neurobiology of suicide risk: a review for the clinician. *Journal of Clinical Psychiatry*, 60(Suppl. 2), 7–11; discussion 18–20, 113–116.

Manni, R. (2005). Rapid eye movement sleep, non-rapid eye movement sleep, dreams, and hallucinations. *Current Psychiatry Reports*, 7(3), 196–200.

Marin, O., & Rubenstein, J.L. (2001). A long, remarkable journey: tangential migration in the telencephalon. *Nature Reviews Neuroscience*, 2(11), 780–790.

Marino, S., Hoogervoorst, D., Brandner, S., & Berns, A. (2003). Rb and p107 are required for normal cerebellar development and granule cell survival but not for Purkinje cell persistence. *Development*, 130(15), 3359–3368.

Martinez, A.D., Acuna, R., Figueroa, V., Maripillan, J., & Nicholson, B. (2009). Gap-junction channels dysfunction in deafness and hearing loss. *Antioxidants and Redox Signaling*, 11(2), 309–322.

Mascie-Taylor, C.G., & Boldsen, J.L. (1984). Assortative mating for IQ: a multivariate approach. *Journal of Biosocial Science*, 16(1), 109–117.

Matwiyoff, G., & Lee-Chiong, T. (2010). Parasomnias: an overview. *Indian Journal of Medical Research*, 131, 333–337.

Mayer, J. (1995). Regulation of energy intake and body weight: the glucostatic theory and the lipostatic hypothesis. *Annals of New York Academy of Sciences*, 411, 221–235.

McElliskem, J.E. (2004). Affective and predatory violence: a bimodal classification system of human aggression and violence. *Aggression & Violent Behavior*, 10, 1–30.

Meddis, R. (1975). On the function of sleep. *Animal Behaviour*, 23(3), 676–691.

Medina, L.S., Aguirre, E., Bernal, B., & Altman, N.R. (2004). Functional MR imaging versus Wada test for evaluation of language lateralization: cost analysis. *Radiology*, 230(1), 49–54.

Meewisse, M.L., Reitsma, J.B., de Vries, G.J., Gersons, B.P., & Olff, M. (2007). Cortisol and post-traumatic stress disorder in adults: systematic review and meta-analysis. *British Journal of Psychiatry*, 191, 387–392.

Melzack, R., & Wall, P.D. (1965). Pain mechanisms: a new theory. *Science*, 150(699), 971–979.

Menon, V., & Desmond, J.E. (2001). Left superior parietal cortex involvement in writing: integrating fMRI with lesion evidence. *Cognitive Brain Research*, 12(2), 337–340.

Mihov, K.M., Denzler, M., & Forster, J. (2010). Hemispheric specialization and creative thinking: a meta-analytic review of lateralization of creativity. *Brain and Cognition*, 72(3), 442–448.

Miller, G.A. (1956). The magical number 7, plus or minus 2: some limits on our capacity for processing information. *Psychological Review*, 63, 81.

Miller, R.H., & Raff, M.C. (1984). Fibrous and protoplasmic astrocytes are biochemically and developmentally distinct. *Journal of Neuroscience*, 4(2), 585–592.

Misra, K., & Pandey, S.C. (2003). Differences in basal levels of CREB and NPY in nucleus accumbens regions between C57BL/6 and DBA/2 mice differing in inborn alcohol drinking behavior. *Journal of Neuroscience Research*, 74, 967–975.

Monti, J.M. (2010). The structure of the dorsal raphe nucleus and its relevance to the regulation of sleep and wakefulness. *Sleep Medicine Reviews*, 14(5), 307–317.

Moore, R.Y. (2007). Suprachiasmatic nucleus in sleep–wake regulation. *Sleep Medicine*, 8(Suppl. 3), 27–33.

Moran, J., & Desimone, R. (1985). Selective attention gates visual processing in the extrastriate cortex. *Science, 229*(4715), 782–784.

Morin, C.M., Blais, F., & Savard, J. (2002). Are changes in beliefs and attitudes about sleep related to sleep improvements in the treatment of insomnia? *Behaviour Research and Therapy, 40*(7), 741–752.

Moruzzi, G., & Magoun, H.W. (1949). Brain stem reticular formation and activation of the EEG. *Electroencephalography and Clinical Neurophysiology, 1,* 455–473.

Moses-Kolko, E.L., Perlman, S.B., Wisner, K.L., James, J., Saul, A.T., & Phillips, M.L. (2010). Abnormally reduced dorsomedial prefrontal cortical activity and effective connectivity with amygdala in response to negative emotional faces in postpartum depression. *American Journal of Psychiatry, 167*(11), 1373–1380.

Movshon, J.A., Lisberger, S.G., & Krauzlis, R.J. (1990). Visual cortical signals supporting smooth pursuit eye movements. *Cold Spring Harbor Symposia on Quantitative Biology, 55,* 707–716.

Mungas, D. (1991). In-office mental status testing: a practical guide. *Geriatrics, 46*(7), 54–58.

Murphy, T.M., & Finkel, L.H. (2007). Shape representation by a network of V4-like cells. *Neural Networks, 20*(8), 851–867.

Murray, J.B. (1992). Posttraumatic stress disorder: a review. *Genetic, Social and General Psycholology Monographs, 118*(3), 313–338.

Musiek, F.E., & Reeves, A.G. (1990). Asymmetries of the auditory areas of the cerebrum. *Journal of the American Academy of Audiology, 1*(4), 240–245.

Nadarajah, B., & Parnavelas, J.G. (2002). Modes of neuronal migration in the developing cerebral cortex. *Nature Reviews Neuroscience, 3*(6), 423–432.

Nakahara, D., Ozaki, N., Miura, Y., Miura, H., & Nagatsu, T. (1989). Increased dopamine and serotonin metabolism in rat nucleus accumbens produced by intracranial self-stimulation of medial forebrain bundle as measured by *in vivo* microdialysis. *Brain Research, 495*(1), 178–181.

Nakamura, K., Honda, M., Okada, T., Hanakawa, T., Toma, K., Fukuyama, H., et al. (2000). Participation of the left posterior inferior temporal cortex in writing and mental recall of kanji orthography: a functional MRI study. *Brain, 123*(Pt 5), 954–967.

Namekawa, M., Takiyama, Y., Aoki, Y., Takayashiki, N., Sakoe, K., Shimazaki, H., et al. (2002). Identification of GFAP gene mutation in hereditary adult-onset Alexander's disease. *Annals of Neurology, 52*(6), 779–785.

Nelson, R.J., & Chiavegatto, S. (2001). Molecular basis of aggression. *Trends in Neuroscience, 24*(12), 713–719.

Nelson, R.J., Trainor, B.C., Chiavegatto, S., & Demas, G.E. (2006). Pleiotropic contributions of nitric oxide to aggressive behavior. *Neuroscience and Biobehavoral Reviews, 30*(3), 346–355.

Newsome, W.T., Britten, K.H., & Movshon, J.A. (1989). Neuronal correlates of a perceptual decision. *Nature, 341,* 52–54.

Nicolson, R.I., & Fawcett, A.J. (1990). Automaticity: a new framework for dyslexia research? *Cognition, 35*(2), 159–182.

Nicolson, R.I., Fawcett, A.J., & Dean, P. (2001). Dyslexia, development and the cerebellum. *Trends in Neuroscience, 24*(9), 515–516.

O'Brien, G., Holton, A.R., Hurren, K., Watt, L., & Hassanyeh, F. (1987). Deliberate self harm: correlates of suicidal intent and severity of depression. *Acta Psychiatrica Scandinavica*, 75(5), 474–477.

Ojeda, N., Sanchez, P., Elizagarate, E., Yoller, A.B., Ezcurra, J., Ramirez, I., et al. (2007). Course of cognitive symptoms in schizophrenia: a review of the literature. *Actas españolas de psiquiatría*, 35(4), 263–270.

O'Keefe, J., & Dostrovsky, J. (1971). The hippocampus as a spatial map: preliminary evidence from unit activity in the freely-moving rat. *Brain Research*, 34(1), 171–175.

O'Keefe, J., & Nadel, L. (1978). *The hippocampus as a cognitive map*. London: Oxford University Press.

Olds, M.E., & Forbes, J.L. (1981). The central basis of motivation: intracranial self stimulation studies. *Annual Review of Psychology*, 32, 523–576.

Olney, A.H. (2007). Macrocephaly syndromes. *Seminars in Pediatric Neurology*, 14(3), 128–135.

Olson, E.J., Boeve, B.F., & Silber, M.H. (2000). Rapid eye movement sleep behaviour disorder: demographic, clinical and laboratory findings in 93 cases. *Brain*, 123(Pt 2), 331–339.

Olson, I.R., & Berryhill, M. (2009). Some surprising findings on the involvement of the parietal lobe in human memory. *Neurobiology of Learning and Memory*, 91(2), 155–165.

Olson, J.M., Vernon, P.A., Harris, J.A., & Jang, K.L. (2001). The heritability of attitudes: a study of twins. *Journal of Personality and Social Psychology*, 80, 845–860.

Olweus, D., Mattsson, A., Schalling, D., & Low, H. (1988). Circulating testosterone levels and aggression in adolescent males: a causal analysis. *Psychosomatic Medicine*, 50(3), 261–272.

O'Neill, Michael, J., & Clemens, James, A. (2001). Rodent models of focal cerebral ischemia. *Current Protocols in Neuroscience*.

Oppenheim, R.W. (1991). Cell death during development of the nervous system. *Annual Review of Neuroscience*, 14, 453–501.

Oswald, I. (1966). *Sleep*. Harmondsworth: Penguin.

Ourednik, V., & Ourednik, J. (2005). Graft/host relationships in the developing and regenerating CNS of mammals. *Annals of the New York Academy of Sciences*, 1049, 172–184.

Ozeren, A., Koc, F., Demirkiran, M., Sonmezler, A., & Kibar, M. (2006). Global aphasia due to left thalamic hemorrhage. *Neurology India*, 54(4), 415–417.

Papez, J.W. (1937). A proposed mechanism of emotion. *Archives of Neurology and Psychiatry*, 38, 725–743.

Paradis, M. (2004). *A neurolinguistic theory of bilingualism*. Amsterdam: Benjamins.

Park, A., & Stacy, M. (2009). Non-motor symptoms in Parkinson's disease. *Journal of Neurology*, 256(Suppl. 3), 293–298.

Partonen, T. (1995). A mechanism of action underlying the antidepressant effect of light. *Medical Hypotheses*, 45(1), 33–34.

Paulesu, E., Frith, C.D., & Frackowiak, R.S.J. (1993). The neural correlates of the verbal component of working memory. *Nature*, 362(6418), 342–345.

Pavlov, I.P. (Ed.) (1927). *Conditioned reflexes: an investigation of the physiological activity of the cerebral cortex*. London: Oxford University Press.

Pearl, P.L. (2004). Clinical aspects of the disorders of GABA metabolism in children. *Current Opinion in Neurology*, 17(2), 107–113.

Pearlin, L.I. (1982). The social contexts of stress. In L. Goldberger & S. Breznitz (Eds), *Handbook of stress: theoretical and clinical aspects*. New York: Free.

Pearlson, G.D., Wong, D.F., Tune, L.E., Ross, C.A., Chase, G.A., Links, J.M., et al. (1995). *In vivo* D2 dopamine receptor density in psychotic and nonpsychotic patients with bipolar disorder. *Archives of General Psychiatry*, 52(6), 471–477.

Pedersen, C.B., & Mortensen, P.B. (2001). Evidence of a dose–response relationship between urbanicity during upbringing and schizophrenia risk. *Archives of General Psychiatry*, 58(11), 1039–1046.

Pell, M.D. (2006). Cerebral mechanisms for understanding emotional prosody in speech. *Brain and Language*, 96(2), 221–234.

Penfield, W., & Boldrey, E. (1937). Somatic motor and sensory representation in the cerebral cortex of man as studied by electrical stimulation. *Brain*, 60, 389–443.

Peng, X.D., Huang, C.Q., Chen, L.J., & Lu, Z.C. (2009). Cognitive behavioural therapy and reminiscence techniques for the treatment of depression in the elderly: a systematic review. *Journal of International Medical Research*, 37(4), 975–982.

Pennisi, E. (1997). The architecture of hearing. *Science*, 278(5341), 1223–1224.

Pernet, C.R., Poline, J.B., Demonet, J.F., & Rousselet, G.A. (2009). Brain classification reveals the right cerebellum as the best biomarker of dyslexia. *BMC Neuroscience*, 10, 67.

Perry, E. (1988). Acetylcholine and Alzheimer's disease. *British Journal of Psychiatry*, 152, 737–740.

Petrill, S.A., Lipton, P.A., Hewitt, J.K., Plomin, R., Cherny, S.S., Corley, R., et al. (2004). Genetic and environmental contributions to general cognitive ability through the first 16 years of life. *Developmental Psychology*, 40, 805–812.

Phelps, E.A. (2004). Human emotion and memory: interactions of the amygdala and hippocampal complex. *Current Opinions in Neurobiology*, 14(2), 198–202.

Phillips, M.L., Young, A.W., Senior, C., Brammer, M., Andrew, C., Calder, A.J., et al. (1997). A specific neural substrate for perceiving facial expressions of disgust. *Nature*, 389(6650), 495–498.

Plachez, C., & Richards, L.J. (2005). Mechanisms of axon guidance in the developing nervous system. *Current Topics in Developmental Biology*, 69, 267–346.

Plomin, R., DeFries, J.C., McClearn, G.E., & Rutter, M. (1997). *Behavioral genetics* (3rd edn). New York: Freeman.

Pons, S., & Marti, E. (2000). Sonic hedgehog synergizes with the extracellular matrix protein vitronectin to induce spinal motor neuron differentiation. *Development*, 127(2), 333–342.

Potash, J.B., & DePaulo, J.R. Jr (2000). Searching high and low: a review of the genetics of bipolar disorder. *Bipolar Disorders*, 2(1), 8–26.

Prang, P., Del Turco, D., & Kapfhammer, J.P. (2001). Regeneration of entorhinal fibers in mouse slice cultures is age dependent and can be stimulated by NT-4, GDNF, and modulators of G-proteins and protein kinase C. *Experimental Neurology*, 169(1), 135–147.

Purves, D. and Hadley, R.D. (1985). Changes in the dendritic branching of adult mammalian neurones *Nature*, 3 15: 404–406.

Qiu, F.T., & von der Heydt, R. (2005). Figure and ground in the visual cortex: V2 combines stereoscopic cues with Gestalt rules. *Neuron*, 47, 155–166.

Quinn, N. (1995). Drug treatment of Parkinson's disease. *British Medical Journal*, 310(6979), 575–579.

Ramachandran, V.S., & Rogers-Ramachandran, D. (2000). Phantom limbs and neural plasticity. *Archives of Neurology, 57*(3), 317–320.

Ramachandran, V.S., & Seckel, E.L. (2010). Using mirror visual feedback and virtual reality to treat fibromyalgia. *Medical Hypotheses, 75*(6), 495–496.

Rattenborg, N.C., Amlaner, C.J., & Lima, S.L. (2000). Behavioral, neurophysiological and evolutionary perspectives on unihemispheric sleep. *Neuroscience and Biobehavioral Reviews, 24*(8), 817–842.

Rauschecker, J.P. (2011). An expanded role for the dorsal auditory pathway in sensorimotor control and integration. *Hearing Research, 271*(1–2), 16–25.

Rayner, K. (1998). Eye movements in reading and information processing: 20 years of research. *Psychological Bulletin, 124*(3), 372–422.

Remick, R.A. (2002). Diagnosis and management of depression in primary care: a clinical update and review. *Canadian Medical Association Journal, 167*(11), 1253–1260.

Renshaw, B. (1946). Central effects of centripetal impulses in axons of spinal ventral roots. *Journal of Neurophysiology, 9*, 191–204.

Rescorla, L. (2009). Age 17 language and reading outcomes in late-talking toddlers: support for a dimensional perspective on language delay. *Journal of Speech Language and Hearing Research, 52*(1), 16–30.

Ribeiro, S., Mello, C.V., Velho, T., Gardner, T.J., Jarvis, E.D., & Pavlides, C. (2002). Induction of hippocampal long-term potentiation during waking leads to increased extrahippocampal zif-268 expression during ensuing rapid-eye-movement sleep. *Journal of Neuroscience, 22*(24), 10914–10923.

Richter, P., Werner, J., Heerlein, A., Kraus, A., & Sauer, H. (1998). On the validity of the Beck Depression Inventory: a review. *Psychopathology, 31*(3), 160–168.

Ridley, M. (2003). *Genes, experience, & what makes us human.* Harper Collins.

Rihmer, Z. (2001). Can better recognition and treatment of depression reduce suicide rates? A brief review. *European Psychiatry, 16*(7), 406–409.

Riso, L.P., Miyatake, R.K., & Thase, M.E. (2002). The search for determinants of chronic depression: a review of six factors. *Journal of Affective Disorders, 70*(2), 103–115.

Rizzolatti, G., & Craighero, L. (2004). The mirror-neuron system. *Annual Review of Neuroscience, 27*, 169–192.

Robinson, T.E., & Justice, J.B. (Eds) (1991). *Microdialysis in the Neurosciences.* Amsterdam: Elsevier.

Rodin, J. (1981). Understanding obesity: defining the samples. *Personality and Social Psychology Bulletin, 7*(1), 147–151.

Rodriguez, E., George, N., Lachaux, J.P., Martinerie, J., Renault, B., & Varela, F.J. (1999). Perception's shadow: long-distance synchronization of human brain activity. *Nature, 397*(6718), 430–433.

Roepke, S.K., & Ancoli-Israel, S. (2010). Sleep disorders in the elderly. *Indian Journal of Medical Research, 131*, 302–310.

Roffwarg, H.A., Muzio, J.N., & Dement, W.C. (1966). Ontogenetic development of the human sleep–dream cycle. *Science, 152*, 604–619.

Rolls, B.J., Rowe, E.A., & Rolls, E.T. (1982). How flavor and appearance affect human feeding. *Proceedings of the Nutrition Society, 41*(2), 109–117.

Rolls, E.T., & Xiang, J.Z. (2006). Spatial view cells in the primate hippocampus and memory recall. *Reviews in the Neurosciences, 17*(1–2), 175–200.

Rosenbaum, R.S., Moscovitch, M., Foster, J.K., Schnyer, D.M., Gao, F., Kovacevic, N., et al. (2008). Patterns of autobiographical memory loss in medial-temporal lobe amnesic patients. *Journal of Cognitive Neuroscience, 20*(8), 1490–1506.

Ross, E.D. (1981). The aprosodias: functional-anatomic organization of the affective components of language in the right hemisphere. *Archives of Neurology, 38*(9), 561–569.

Rubin, R.T., Phillips, J.J., Sadow, T.F., & McCracken, J.T. (1995). Adrenal gland volume in major depression: increase during the depressive episode and decrease with successful treatment. *Archives of General Psychiatry, 52*(3), 213–218.

Russek, M. (1976). Hepatic glucoreceptors in the short-term control of feeding. *Acta Physiologica Polonica, 27*(6), 147–156.

Rutishauser, U. (1993). Adhesion molecules of the nervous system. *Current Opinions in Neurobiology, 3*(5), 709–715.

Rymarczyk, K. and Grabowska, A. (2007). Sex differences in brain control of prosody. *Neuropsychologia, 45*, 921–930.

Sakata, I., Nakamura, K., Yamazaki, M., Matsubara, M., Hayashi, Y., Kangawa, K., et al. (2002). Ghrelin-producing cells exist as two types of cells, closed- and opened-type cells, in the rat gastrointestinal tract. *Peptides, 23*(3), 531–536.

Sakurai, Y., Asami, M., & Mannen, T. (2010). Alexia and agraphia with lesions of the angular and supramarginal gyri: evidence for the disruption of sequential processing. *Journal of Neurological Science, 288*(1–2), 25–33.

Sakurai, Y., Momose, T., Iwata, M., Ishikawa, T., Sato, T., & Kanazawa, I. (1996). Regional cerebral blood flow in the covert reading of kana words: a comparison with the study of reading aloud tasks. *European Neurology, 36*(4), 237–239.

Sakurai, Y., Momose, T., Iwata, M., Sudo, Y., Ohtomo, K., & Kanazawa, I. (2001). Cortical activity associated with vocalization and reading proper. *Cognitive Brain Research, 12*(1), 161–165.

Salehi, A., Delcroix, J.D., & Swaab, D.F. (2004). Alzheimer's disease and NGF signaling. *Journal of Neural Transmission, 111*(3), 323–345.

Sammler, D., Kotz, S.A., Eckstein, K., Ott, D.V., & Friederici, A.D. (2010). Prosody meets syntax: the role of the corpus callosum. *Brain, 133*(9), 2643–2655.

Santens, P., Boon, P., Van Roost, D., & Caemaert, J. (2003). The pathophysiology of motor symptoms in Parkinson's disease. *Acta Neurologica Belgica, 103*(3), 129–134.

Sastry, B.R., Maretic, H., Morishita, W., & Xie, Z. (1990). Modulation of the induction of long-term potentiation in the hippocampus. *Advances in Experimental Medicine and Biology, 268*, 377–386.

Schachter, S. (1971). *Emotion, obesity, and crime.* New York: Academic.

Schiff, N.B., & Ventry, I.M. (1976). Communication problems in hearing children of deaf parents. *Journal of Speech and Hearing Disorders, 41*(3), 348–358.

Schneider, K. (1957). Primare und sekundare Symptome bei der Schizophrenie. *Fortschritte der Neurologie, Psychiatrie, und ihrer Grenzgebiete, 25*, 487–490.

Scholten, M.R., van Honk, J., Aleman, A., & Kahn, R.S. (2006). Behavioral inhibition system (BIS), behavioral activation system (BAS) and schizophrenia: relationship with psychopathology and physiology. *Journal of Psychiatric Research, 40*(7), 638–645.

Schultz, S.H., North, S.W., & Shields, C.G. (2007). Schizophrenia: a review. *American Family Physician*, 75(12), 1821–1829.

Scoville, W.B., & Milner, B. (1957). Loss of recent memory after bilateral hippocampal lesions. *Journal of Neurology, Neurosurgery & Psychiatry*, 20(1), 11–21.

Seedat, S., & Stein, M.B. (2001). Post-traumatic stress disorder: a review of recent findings. *Current Psychiatry Reports*, 3(4), 288–294.

Selye, H. (1951). The general adaptation syndrome. *Annual Review of Medicine*, 2, 327–342.

Selye, H. (1982). History and present status of the stress concept. In G.A.S. Breznit (Ed.), *Handbook of stress: theoretical and clinical aspects*. New York: Free.

Seri, B., García-Verdugo, J.M., McEwen, B.S., & Alvarez-Buylla, A. (2001). Astrocytes give rise to new neurons in the adult mammalian hippocampus. *Journal of Neuroscience*, 21(18), 7153–7160.

Shahi, G.S., & Moochhala, S.M. (1991). Smoking and Parkinson's disease: a new perspective. *Reviews of Environmental Health*, 9(3), 123–136.

Shamma, S.A., & Micheyl, C. (2010). Behind the scenes of auditory perception. *Current Opinions in Neurobiology*, 20(3), 361–366.

Shastry, B.S. (2002). Schizophrenia: a genetic perspective (review). *International Journal of Molecular Medicine*, 9(3), 207–212.

Sher, L. (2002). Suicidal behaviour and seasonality. Journal of Psychiatry, 56(1), 67.

Shin, K., & Shapiro, C. (2003). Menopause, sex hormones, and sleep. *Bipolar Disorders*, 5(2), 106–109.

Shin, Y.W., Kim, D.J., Ha, T.H., Park, H.J., Moon, W.J., Chung, E.C., et al. (2005). Sex differences in the human corpus callosum: diffusion tensor imaging study. *Neuroreport*, 16(8), 795–798.

Shoumaker, R.D., Ajax, E.T., & Schenkenberg, T. (1977). Pure word deafness (auditory verbal agnosia). *Disorder of the Nervous System*, 38(4), 293–299.

Shrager, Y., Gold, J.J., Hopkins, R.O., & Squire, L.R. (2006). Intact visual perception in memory-impaired patients with medial temporal lobe lesions. *Journal of Neuroscience*, 26(8), 2235–2240.

Shriberg, L.D., Aram, D.M., & Kwiatkowski, J. (1997). Developmental apraxia of speech. I. Descriptive and theoretical perspectives. *Journal of Speech Language and Hearing Research*, 40(2), 273–285.

Shukla, G.D., Srivastava, O.N., & Katiyar, B.C. (1979). Sexual disturbances in temporal lobe epilepsy: a controlled study. *British Journal of Psychiatry*, 134, 288–292.

Siegel, J. (2004). Brain mechanisms that control sleep and waking. *Naturwissenschaften*, 91(8), 355–365.

Silberman, E.K., & Weingartner, H. (1986). Hemispheric lateralization of functions related to emotion. *Brain and Cognition*, 5(3), 322–353.

Simos, P.G., Castillo, E.M., Fletcher, J.M., Francis, D.J., Maestu, F., Breier, J.I., et al. (2001). Mapping of receptive language cortex in bilingual volunteers by using magnetic source imaging. *Journal of Neurosurgery*, 95(1), 76–81.

Singer, W., & Gray, C.M. (1995). Visual feature integration and the temporal correlation hypothesis. *Annual Review of Neuroscience*, 18, 555–586.

Skinner, B.F. (1953). *Science and human behavior*. Oxford: Macmillan.

Smith, D.M., & Mizumori, S.J. (2006). Learning-related development of context-specific neuronal responses to places and events: the hippocampal role in context processing. *Journal of Neuroscience, 26*(12), 3154–3163.

Snowling, M.J. (1981). Phonemic deficits in developmental dyslexia. *Psychological Research, 43*(2), 219–234.

Soares, J.C., & Mann, J.J. (1997). The functional neuroanatomy of mood disorders. *Journal of Psychiatric Research, 31*(4), 393–432.

Soma, K.K., Wissman, A.M., Brenowitz, E.A., & Wingfield, J.C. (2002). Dehydroepiandrosterone (DHEA) increases territorial song and the size of an associated brain region in a male songbird. *Hormones and Behavior, 41*(2), 203–212.

Sowell, E.R., Thompson, P.M., Holmes, C.J., Jernigan, T.L., & Toga, A.W. (1999). In vivo evidence for post-adolescent frontal and striatal maturation. *Nature Neuroscience, 2,* 859–861.

Sowell, E.R., Thompson, P.M., Tessner, K.D., & Toga, A.W. (2001). Mapping continued brain growth and gray matter density reduction in dorsal frontal cortex: Inverse relationships during post adolescent brain maturation. *Journal of Neuroscience.* Nov 15; 21(22), 8819–8829.

Sperling, G. (1979). Information available in brief visual presentations. *Current Contents/ Social & Behavioral Sciences, 21,* 18–18.

Sperry, R.W. (1943). Visuomotor coordination in the newt (*Triturus viridescens*) after regeneration of the optic nerve. *Journal of Comparative Neurology, 79,* 33–55.

Sperry, R.W. (1961). Cerebral organization and behavior. *Science, 133,* 1749–1757.

Sperry, R.W., Gazzaniga, M.S., & Bogen, J.E. (1969). Interhemispheric relationships: the neocortical commissures; syndromes of hemisphere disconnection. In P.J. Vinken & G.W. Bruyn (Eds), *Handbook of Clinical Neurology* (pp. 177–184). Amsterdam: North-Holland.

Spiers, H.J., Maguire, E.A., & Burgess, N. (2001). Hippocampal amnesia. *Neurocase, 7*(5), 357–382.

Squire, L.R. (1992). Memory and the hippocampus: a synthesis from findings with rats, monkeys, and humans. *Psychological Review, 99,* 195–231.

Squire, L.R., Ojemann, J.G., Miezin, F.M., Petersen, S.E., Videen, T.O., & Raichle, M.E. (1992). Activation of the hippocampus in normal humans: a functional anatomical study of memory. *Proceedings of the National Academy of Sciences USA, 89*(5), 1837–1841.

Squire, L.R., Wixted, J.T., & Clark, R.E. (2007). Recognition memory and the medial temporal lobe: a new perspective. *Nature Reviews Neuroscience, 8*(11), 872–883.

Squire, L.R., & Zola, S.M. (1997). Amnesia, memory, and brain systems. *Philosophical Transactions of the Royal Society of London, Series B, Biological Sciences, 352*(1362), 1663–1673.

Stanewsky, R. (2003). Genetic analysis of the circadian system in *Drosophila melanogaster* and mammals. *Journal of Neurobiology, 54*(1), 111–147.

Stanley, B.G., & Leibowitz, S.F. (1985). Neuropeptide-Y injected in the paraventricular hypothalamus: a powerful stimulant of feeding behavior. *Proceedings of the National Academy of Sciences USA, 82*(11), 3940–3943.

Starkstein, S.E., Federoff, J.P., Price R.C., Leiguarda, R.C., & Robinson, R.G. (1994). Neuropsychological and neuroradiological correlates of emotional prosody comprehension. *Neurology, 44,* 515–522.

Stein, J. (2001). The magnocellular theory of developmental dyslexia. *Dyslexia, 7*(1), 12–36.

Stein, J., & Walsh, V. (1997). To see but not to read; the magnocellular theory of dyslexia. *Trends in Neuroscience, 20*(4), 147–152.

Stein, J., Riddell, P.M., & Fowler, M.S. (1987). Fine binocular control in dyslexic children. *Eye (London), 1*(Pt 3), 433–438.

Steinhausen, H.C., Seidel, R., & Winkler Metzke, C. (2000). Evaluation of treatment and intermediate and long-term outcome of adolescent eating disorders. *Psychological Medicine, 30*(5), 1089–1098.

Stewart, L., Ellison, A., Walsh, V., & Cowey, A. (2001). The role of transcranial magnetic stimulation (TMS) in studies of vision, attention and cognition. *Acta psychologica, 107*(1–3), 275–291.

Stickgold, R. (2004). Dissecting sleep-dependent learning and memory consolidation. Comment on Schabus M. et al., Sleep spindles and their significance for declarative memory consolidation (*Sleep*, 27, 1479–1485). *Sleep, 27*(8), 1443–1445.

Stickgold, R., Whidbee, D., Schirmer, B., Patel, V., & Hobson, J.A. (2000). Visual discrimination task improvement: a multi-step process occurring during sleep. *Journal of Cognitive Neuroscience, 12*(2), 246–254.

Stone, J.M., Morrison, P.D., & Pilowsky, L.S. (2007). Glutamate and dopamine dysregulation in schizophrenia: a synthesis and selective review. *Journal of Psychopharmacology, 21*(4), 440–452.

Strotzer, M. (2009). One century of brain mapping using Brodmann areas. *Klinische Neuroradiologie, 19*(3), 179–186.

Sullivan, E.V., & Pfefferbaum, A. (2009). Neuroimaging of the Wernicke–Korsakoff syndrome. *Alcohol, 44*(2), 155–165.

Summers, C.H., Watt, M.J., Ling, T.L., Forster, G.L., Carpenter, R.E., Korzan, W.J., et al. (2005). Glucocorticoid interaction with aggression in non-mammalian vertebrates: reciprocal action. *European Journal of Pharmacology, 526*(1–3), 21–35.

Suvorov, N.F. (1998). Basal ganglia: structure and function. *Neuroscience and Behavioral Physiology, 28*(3), 219–223.

Syvalahti, E. (1987). Monoaminergic mechanisms in affective disorders. *Medical Biology, 65*(2–3), 89–96.

Tabba, M.K., & Johnson, J.C. (2006). Obstructive sleep apnea: a practical review. *Molecular Medicine, 103*(5), 509–513.

Takahashi, L.K., Chan, M.M., & Pilar, M.L. (2008). Predator odor fear conditioning: current perspectives and new directions. *Neuroscience and Biobehavioral Reviews, 32*(7), 1218–1227.

Takashima, A. (2009). Amyloid-beta, tau, and dementia. *Journal of Alzheimer's Disease, 17*(4), 729–736.

Taylor, I., & Martin, T.M. (1990). *Learning and using language.* Englewood Cliffs, NJ: Prentice Hall.

Tedroff, J.M. (1997). The neuroregulatory properties of L-DOPA: a review of the evidence and potential role in the treatment of Parkinson's disease. *Reviews in the Neurosciences, 8*(3–4), 195–204.

Teitelbaum, P., & Epstein, A.N. (1962). The lateral hypothalamic syndrome: recovery of feeding and drinking after lateral hypothalamic lesions. *Psychological Review, 69*, 74–90.

Tekin, S., & Cummings, J.L. (2002). Frontal-subcortical neuronal circuits and clinical neuropsychiatry: an update. *Journal of Psychosomatic Research, 53*(2), 647–654.

Thach, W.T. (1998). A role for the cerebellum in learning movement coordination. *Neurobiology of Learning and Memory*, 70(1–2), 177–188.

Tillmann, B., Janata, P., & Bharucha, J.J. (2003). Activation of the inferior frontal cortex in musical priming. *Cognitive Brain Research*, 16(2), 145–161.

Timmann, D., Drepper, J., Frings, M., Maschke, M., Richter, S., Gerwig, M., et al. (2010). The human cerebellum contributes to motor, emotional and cognitive associative learning: a review. *Cortex*, 46(7), 845–857.

Toh, K.L. (2008). Basic science review on circadian rhythm biology and circadian sleep disorders. *Annals Academy of Medicine Singapore*, 37(8), 662–668.

Tolosa, E., Gaig, C., Santamaria, J., & Compta, Y. (2009). Diagnosis and the premotor phase of Parkinson disease. *Neurology*, 72(7 Suppl.), S12–20.

Tootell, R.B., Reppas, J.B., Dale, A.M., Look, R.B., Sereno, M.I., Malach, R., et al. (1995). Visual motion aftereffect in human cortical area MT revealed by functional magnetic resonance imaging. *Nature*, 375(6527), 139–141.

Tree, J.J. (2008). Two types of phonological dyslexia: a contemporary review. *Cortex*, 44(6), 698–706.

Tremblay, R.E., Nagin, D.S., Seguin, J.R., Zoccolillo, M., Zelazo, P.D., Boivin, M., et al. (2005). Physical aggression during early childhood: trajectories and predictors. *Canadian Child and Adolescent Psychiatry Review*, 14(1), 3–9.

Trojanowski, J.Q., & Lee, V.M. (2002). The role of tau in Alzheimer's disease. *Medical Clinics of North America*, 86(3), 615–627.

Tsuang, M.T. (1998). Genetic epidemiology of schizophrenia: review and reassessment. *The Kaohsiung Journal of Medical Sciences*, 14(7), 405–412.

Tsuboi, Y., Uchikado, H., & Dickson, D.W. (2007). Neuropathology of Parkinson's disease dementia and dementia with Lewy bodies with reference to striatal pathology. *Parkinsonism Related Disorders*, 13(Suppl. 3), S221–224.

Tsubokawa, T., & Katatama, Y. (1999). Lesion-making surgery versus brain stimulation for treatment of Parkinson's disease. *Critical Reviews Neurosurgery*, 9(2), 96–106.

Tulving, E. (1983). *Elements of episodic memory*. Oxford: Clarendon.

Uneyama, H., Kawai, M., Sekine-Hayakawa, Y., & Torii, K. (2009). Contribution of umami taste substances in human salivation during meal. *Journal of Investigative Medicine*, 56(Suppl.), 197–204.

Ungerleider, L.G., & Pasternak, T. (2003). Ventral and Dorsal Cortical Processing Streams. *The Visual Neurosciences*, 1st Edition. MIT Press, vol. 1, pp. 541–562.

Van de Poll, N.E., Taminiau, M.S., Endert, E., & Louwerse, A.L. (1988). Gonadal steroid influence of sexual and aggressive behaviour of female rats. *International Journal of Neuroscience*, 41, 271–286.

Van Ooyen, A. (2001). Competition in the development of nerve connections: a review of models. *Network*, 12(1), R1–47.

Van Rossum, J.M. (1966). The significance of dopamine-receptor blockade for the mechanism of action of neuroleptic drugs. *Archives Internationales de Pharmacodynamie et de Therapie*, 160(2), 492–494.

Varon, S., & Conner, J.M. (1994). Nerve growth factor in CNS repair. *Journal of Neurotrauma*, 11(5), 473–486.

Vertes, R.P., & Eastman, K.E. (2000). The case against memory consolidation in REM sleep. *Behavioral and Brain Science*, 23(6), 867–876; discussion 904–1121.

Vogel, J.J., Bowers, C.A., & Vogel, D.S. (2003). Cerebral lateralization of spatial abilities: a meta-analysis. *Brain and Cognition*, 52(2), 197–204.

Vogt, B.A. (2005). Pain and emotion interactions in subregions of the cingulate gyrus. *Nature Reviews Neuroscience*, 6(7), 533–544.

Wada, J.A., Clarke, R., & Hamm, A. (1975). Cerebral hemispheric asymmetry in humans: cortical speech zones in 100 adults and 100 infant brains. *Archives of Neurology*, 32(4), 239–246.

Wagner, U., Gais, S., Haider, H., Verleger, R., & Born, J. (2004). Sleep inspires insight. *Nature*, 427(6972), 352–355.

Watson, J.D., Myers, R., Frackowiak, R.S., Hajnal, J.V., Woods, R.P., Mazziotta, J.C., et al. (1993). Area V5 of the human brain: evidence from a combined study using positron emission tomography and magnetic resonance imaging. *Cerebral Cortex*, 3(2), 79–94.

Wearing, D. (2005). *Forever today*. New York: Doubleday.

Webb, W.B. (1974). Sleep as an adaptive response. *Perception and Motor Skills*, 38(3), 1023–1027.

Weiskrantz, L. (1993). Sources of blindsight. *Science*, 261(5120), 494; author reply 494–495.

Weisz, N., Wienbruch, C., Hoffmeister, S., & Elbert, T. (2004). Tonotopic organization of the human auditory cortex probed with frequency-modulated tones. *Hearing Research, 191*, 49–58.

Werner, F.M., & Covenas, R. (2010). Classical neurotransmitters and neuropeptides involved in major depression: a review. *International Journal of Neuroscience*, 120(7), 455–470.

Wernicke, C. (1874). *Der Aphasische Symptomencomplex*. Breslau: Cohn and Weigert.

Whalley, H.C., Mowatt, L., Stanfield, A.C., Hall, J., Johnstone, E.C., Lawrie, S.M., et al. (2008). Hypofrontality in subjects at high genetic risk of schizophrenia with depressive symptoms. *Journal of Affective Disorders*, 109(1–2), 99–106.

Whitelaw, V., & Hollyday, M. (1983). Neural pathway constraints in the motor innervation of the chick hindlimb following dorsoventral rotations of distal limb segments. *Journal of Neuroscience*, 3(6), 1226–1233.

Wierup, N., Svensson, H., Mulder, H., & Sundler, F. (2002). The ghrelin cell: a novel developmentally regulated islet cell in the human pancreas. *Regulatory Peptides*, 107(63), 9.

Wilkinson, L., Khan, Z., & Jahanshahi, M. (2009). The role of the basal ganglia and its cortical connections in sequence learning: evidence from implicit and explicit sequence learning in Parkinson's disease. *Neuropsychologia*, 47(12), 2564–2573.

Williams, G., Cai, X.J., Elliott, J.C., & Harrold, J.A. (2004). Anabolic neuropeptides. *Physiology and Behavior*, 81(2), 211–222.

Wilson, P.H., & McKenzie, B.E. (1998). Information processing deficits associated with developmental coordination disorder: a meta-analysis of research findings. *Journal of Child Psychology and Psychiatry*, 39(6), 829–840.

Wilson, S.A. (2007). Review: SSRIs lead to improvement in depression by the end of the first week. *Evidence Based Medicine*, 12(3), 72.

Wolkin, A., Sanfilipo, M., Wolf, A.P., Angrist, B., Brodie, J.D., & Rotrosen, J. (1992). Negative symptoms and hypofrontality in chronic schizophrenia. *Archives of General Psychiatry*, 49(12), 959–965.

Wong-Riley, M. (1979). Columnar cortico-cortical interconnections within the visual system of the squirrel and macaque monkeys. *Brain Research*, 162(2), 201–217.

Woolf, N.J. (1997). A possible role for cholinergic neurons of the basal forebrain and ponto-mesencephalon in consciousness. *Consciousness and Cognition*, 6(4), 574–596.

Wu, L.G., & Saggau, P. (1997). Presynaptic inhibition of elicited neurotransmitter release. *Trends in Neurosciences*, 20(5), 204–212.

Wyllie, A.H. (2010). 'Where, O death, is thy sting?' A brief review of apoptosis biology. *Molecular Neurobiology*, 42(1), 4–9.

Xu, X., Aron, A., Brown, L., Cao, G., Feng, T., & Weng, X. (2011). Reward and motivation systems: a brain mapping study of early-stage intense romantic love in Chinese participants. *Human Brain Mapping*, 32(2), 249–257.

Yamaoka, Y., Shimohama, S., Kimura, J., Fukunaga, R., & Taniguchi, T. (1993). Neuronal damage in the rat hippocampus induced by in vivo hypoxia. *Experimental and Toxicologic Pathology*, 45, 205–209.

Yamazaki, Y., Hozumi, Y., Kaneko, K., Fujii, S., Goto, K., & Kato, H. (2010). Oligodendrocytes: facilitating axonal conduction by more than myelination. *Neuroscientist*, 16(1), 11–18.

Yanagisawa, N., Fujimoto, S., & Tamaru, F. (1989). Bradykinesia in Parkinson's disease: disorders of onset and execution of fast movement. *European Neurology*, 29(Suppl. 1), 19–28.

Yew, D.T., Chan, W.Y., Luo, C.B., Zheng, D.R., & Yu, M.C. (1999). Neurotransmitters and neuropeptides in the developing human central nervous system: a review. *Biological Signals and Receptors*, 8(3), 149–159.

York, D.A., & Bray, G.A. (1996). Animal models of hyperphagia. *Regulation of Body Weight*, 57, 15–31.

Zatorre, R.J., Evans, A.C., & Meyer, E. (1994). Neural mechanisms underlying melodic perception and memory for pitch. *Journal of Neuroscience*, 14, 1908–1919.

Zatorre, R.J., Perry, D.W., Beckett, C.A., Westbury, C.F., & Evans, A.C. (1998). Functional anatomy of musical processing in listeners with absolute pitch and relative pitch. *Proceedings of the National Academy of Sciences* (U.S.A.), 95, 3172–3317.

Zeis, T., & Schaeren-Wiemers, N. (2008). Lame ducks or fierce creatures? The role of oligodendrocytes in multiple sclerosis. *Journal of Molecular Neuroscience*, 35(1), 91–100.

Zeki, S.M. (1977). Colour coding in the superior temporal sulcus of rhesus monkey visual cortex. *Proceedings of the Royal Society of London B Biological Sciences*, 197(1127), 195–223.

Zeki, S. (1980). The representation of colours in the cerebral cortex. *Nature*, 284(5755), 412–418.

Zeki, S. (1991). Cerebral akinetopsia (visual motion blindness): a review. *Brain*, 114(Pt 2), 811–818.

Zeki, S., & Bartels, A. (1999). The clinical and functional measurement of cortical (in)activity in the visual brain, with special reference to the two subdivisions (V4 and V4 alpha) of the human colour centre. *Philosophical Transactions of the Royal Society of London B Biological Sciences*, 354(1387), 1371–1382.

Zeng, Y., Zhang, Y., Xin, G., & Zou, L. (2010). Cortical blindness: a rare complication of severe burns. A report of seven cases and review of the literature. *Burns*, 36(1), e1–3.

Zhang, Y.W., Thompson, R., Zhang, H., & Xu, H. (2011). APP processing in Alzheimer's disease. *Molecular Brain*, 4, 3.

Zihl, J., von Cramon, D., & Mai, N. (1983). Selective disturbance of movement vision after bilateral brain damage. *Brain*, 106(2), 313–340.

Zola-Morgan, S. (1995). Localization of Brain Function: The Legacy of Franz Joseph Gall (1758–1828). *Annual Review of Neuroscience*, 18: 359–383.

NAME INDEX

SUBJECT INDEX

Page references to Figures or Tables will be in *italics*

neutral stimulus, 267
newborn infants, 151–152, 218
nicotinin acetylcholine receptors (nAChR), 23
night terrors, 221, 231–232
nitric oxide (NO), 280
N-methyl-D-aspartate (NMDA), 19–20, 334, 335, 343
nociceptors, 343
nodes of Ranvier, 8, 12
non-declarative memory, 267
Non-Motor Symptom Scale (NMSS), 332
non-rapid eye movement (NREM) sleep, 219, 222, 227
non-verbal communication, 247
noradrenaline, 20–21, 37, 38, 224, 318, 320
nuclear layers, retina, 106
nucleolus, 5
nucleotide bases, 343
nucleus accumbens, 187
nucleus basalis of Meynert, 328, 335

obesity, 201, 202
object perception disorders, 124–125
object recognition
  lateral inhibition, 115–116
  receptive fields, 116–118, 344
obstructive sleep apnoea (OSA), 230, 231
occipital lobe, 33, 52, 284
occipito-frontal circumference (OFC), 91
ocular dominance
  columns, 95, 97, 118, 119
  effects of visual deprivation on, 94–95
oestrogens/oestradiol, 211, 343
Okazaki fragments, 59
olfaction, 158–159, 343
olfactory pathway, 159
oligodendrocyte precursor cell, 7
oligodendrocytes, 8, 9, 111
ontogenetic activities, 80
operant conditioning, 269, 288
opponent-process theory (Hering), 121–122, 128
optic disc, 107
optic nerve, 109, 111
optic nerve layer, retina, 106
orbicularis oculi muscle, 248, 259
orbitofrontal cortex (OFC), 202
orexin, 224, 225, 231
organ of Corti, 148
organelles, 59
organum vasculosum lamina terminalis (OVLT), 209
oscillatory neural circuits, 123

osmoreceptors, 207, 209, 343
osmotic thirst, 207–209
ossicles, 343
outer ear, 145–146
outer hair cells, 148
overweight and genetics, 205
oxygen-15, PET scanning, 44
oxytocin, 31

pain, gate theory, 142–143, 341
pancreas, 17
Papez circuit, 242, 243, 258
papilla, 343
paradoxical sleep, 222, 344
paralysis, 175, 344
paramedian pontine reticular assemblage, 180
parasomnias, 231–234, 235
parasympathetic nervous system, 3, 37, 39, 344
parathyroid glands, 17
paraventricular nucleus (PVN), 198, 200, 209
parietal lobe, 33, 34, 52, 283
Parkinson's disease, 21, 30, 97, 330–334
  assessment, 332
  causes, 332–333
  genetic factors, 330, 333
  management, 334
  motor circuit in, 333–334
  movement problems, 188, 191
  neural structures involved, 333
  signs and symptoms, 331
  tremor, 188, 332
partial report paradigm, 263
parvocellular (P) layers, 111, 113
passive sleep theory, 222–223
Pavlovian conditioning, 267–268, 288
peptide hormones, 344
perceptual span, 306
perceptual unification, 123
periaqueductal grey matter (PAG), 30
periodic limb movement disorder (PLMD), 232
peripheral nervous system (PNS), 2–3, 24, 27
  autonomic nervous system, 3, 37–39, 38, 239
  cranial nerves, 36, 37, 39
  glial cells in, 8
  parasympathetic nervous system, 3, 37, 39
  spinal nerves, 35–36
  sympathetic nervous system, 38–39
peristalsis, 194
personality disorders, 315

phagocytes/phagocytosis, 8, 257, 344
phantom limb syndrome, 99, 344
pharmacological manipulations, 41
phenotypes, 50, 69, 344
phenylalanine hydroxylase (PAH), 93
phenylketonuria (PKU), 93
phonological loop, working memory, 265, 266
phonological theory, dyslexia, 308–309
phonology, 295
phosphodiester bonds, DNA, 58
photopigments, 106, 126
photoreceptors, eye, 105, 106–107, 111, 115–116, 217
phylogenetic tree, 71, 78
pineal body, 17
pioneering growth, 89, 344
pitch, 344
pituitary gland, 17, 31, 52
'place' cells, 272–273
place theory, 344
planes of section, 28
plaques, in Alzheimer's disease, 329
plasma cells, 256
plasma membrane, 3
plasticity, neural
  cell transplantations, 99–100
  contralateral sprouting, 98, 339
  critical period, 95–98
  cross-modal plasticity in blind humans, critical period for, 95–96
  denervation supersensitivity, 99, 102, 339
  neuronal regeneration, 98
  ocular dominance, effects of visual deprivation on, 94–95
  regeneration of nervous system, 99–100
  reorganisation of sensory representations, 99
plexiform layers, retina, 106
polymerases, DNA, 58
polysynaptic reflex, 171, 172, 344
pons, 30
ponto-geniculo-occipital (PGO) waves, 222
pontomesencephalon, 224
positron emission tomography (PET), 21, 44–45, 52
posterior inferior temporal cortex (PITC), 307
posterior lobe, brain, 31
posterior parietal cortex, 176
postganglionic fibres, 37
postsynaptic potential (PSP), 14